Success Factor Modeling
Volume II

Generative Collaboration

Releasing the Creative Power of Collective Intelligence

by

Robert B. Dilts

Design and illustrations by
Antonio Meza

Published by:

Dilts Strategy Group

Dilts Strategy Group
P. O. Box 67448
Scotts Valley CA 95067
USA
Phone: (831) 438-8314
E-Mail: info@diltstrategygroup.com
Homepage: http://www.diltstrategygroup.com

Library of Congress Control Number: 2015904441

I.S.B.N. 978-0-9962004-2-4

Success Factor Modeling

Volume II

Generative Collaboration

Releasing the Creative Power of Collective Intelligence

by

Robert B. Dilts

Design and illustrations by
Antonio Meza

Table of Contents

Table of Contents

Table of Contents

Table of Contents

Dedication

This book is dedicated with deep love and appreciation to my wife

Deborah Bacon Dilts

She has been my most important partner and teacher in my exploration of the joys, the challenges and the power of generative collaboration.

Robert Dilts

With much love and gratitude I dedicate this book to my wife

Susanne Kischnick

She has being literally "by my side" through the creation of these pages. My hands drew the illustrations, but they were animated by the spirit of our generative collaboration.

Antonio Meza

Acknowledgements

A first and very special acknowledgment goes to Antonio Meza for his work on the design of the layout of the book and for his brilliant and masterful illustrations. Antonio's intuition, creativity and artistry have continued to increase as we have worked together to prepare these pages. Antonio has also continued to be a valued advisor and partner in many ways throughout the process of bringing this book to publication. It was Antonio's idea to break what would have originally been a very long book into three volumes

I would like to gratefully acknowledge Glenn Bacon, Michael Dilts and Benoit Sarazin for their time and efforts in reading over the initial draft of this book and offering their feedback and suggestions. Many thanks also go to Amanda Frost for her expert proofreading of this book and of Volume I.

Of course, a major contribution to this book has come from the individuals, groups and organizations that are featured in the Success Factor Case Examples. I would like to gratefully acknowledge CrossKnowledge founders Steve Fiehl, Michaël Ohana, Pascal El Grably and Hervé Goudchaux; Stefan Crisan of EDHEC; Randy Williams, founder of the Keiretsu Forum, Chuck Dudek, Dave Redys, John Vance and Mike Mercer of the Comau Pico Custom Products Team; Drew Dilts' and his work with the United States Peace Corps; and Julia Dilts and Alejandro Moxey of Expedia. And special thanks go to Dorothy Oger for her poem on Collective Intelligence at the end of the Conclusion.

I would also like to acknowledge the other individuals, leaders and entrepreneurs who serve as inspirations and examples and are referenced throughout these pages such as Steve Jobs, Barney Pell, Cindana Turkatte, Mark Fizpatrick, Samuel Palmisano and Walt Disney.

Adam Grant and his work on wisdom and task significance, and James Surowiecki's work on the "wisdom of crowds" have also been important influences in the development of several key ideas and principles in this book.

Grateful acknowledgments also go to a number of my colleagues whose collaborations with me have produced important contributions mentioned in this volume: Mitchell and Olga Stevko, co-founders with me of the Successful Genius and Conscious Leadership Mastermind groups; Miklos (Mickey) Feher and his work with me on the SFM Mindset Map; Robert McDonald and our study of Group Mind and Team Spirit; Stephen Gilligan and our developments on the principles and practices of Generative Change; Anne Deering and Julian Russell and our collaborative efforts with Alpha Leadership; Benoit Sarazin and our study of Disruptive Innovation; and Ian McDermott and our work on Intentional Fellowship.

Finally, I would like to deeply acknowledge my brother John Dilts whose love of generative collaboration and passion for creating a world of visionary entrepreneurs was the foundation and remains the spirit of Success Factor Modeling.

— Robert Dilts

Preface

As I mentioned in the preface to *Success Factor Modeling Volume I*, this book series is the fulfillment of a dream that began in 1999 when my late brother John (profiled in Chapter 4 of this book pp. 236-246) and I founded the Dilts Strategy Group and began our first explorations with the Success Factor Modeling process.

The questions we sought to answer were: "What is the difference that makes the difference between successful and average or poor ventures, teams and entrepreneurs?" "What are the critical success factors related to launching or growing a successful and sustainable business."

Many of our discoveries are described in the first volume of this work, *Next Generation Entrepreneurs: Live Your Dreams and Create a Better World Through Your Business*, and summarized in the Introduction to this book (pp. 2-37). These include defining your passion, vision, mission, ambition and role and building what we called a "Circle of Success." Volume I captured the spirit and exhilaration (as well as the commitment and skill) related to launching a venture based on your passion and vision.

One of the other major success factors that we discovered was what we called "generative collaboration." As we studied successful individuals, it soon became clear that the refrain "Nobody creates anything of significance on their own" is a very accurate description of success in the 21st Century. We found that highly successful people were able to work creatively and productively with others in order to achieve their dreams and visions.

This has certainly been very true of my own career. Every one of my major achievements has been a result of some type of generative collaboration. In fact, this book, as is the whole series of volumes, is itself a product of generative collaboration, starting with the obvious creative collaboration between myself and the illustrator Antonio Meza.

In the Acknowledgements, I mentioned a number of others as well: Mitchell and Olga Stevko, co-founders with me of the Successful Genius and Conscious Leadership Mastermind groups; Miklos (Mickey) Feher and his work with me on the SFM Mindset Map; Stephen Gilligan and our developments on the principles and practices of Generative Change; Anne Deering and Julian Russell and our collaborative efforts with Alpha Leadership; Benoit Sarazin and our study of Disruptive Innovation; and Ian McDermott and our work on Intentional Fellowship.

There have been many, many other collaborations over the years that have resulted in significant developments, projects and books. My own path of generative collaboration started with the founders of NeruoLinguistic Programming Richard Bandler and John Grinder. The development of what has become a body of work that is taught and studied all over the world was the result of an intense amount of collective intelligence and generative collaboration involving not only Bandler and Grinder, but a number of others in their early group of students, such as Stephen Gilligan, Judith DeLozier, Frank Pucelik, Leslie Lebeau and David Gordon.

My work with the late Todd Epstein, who was also involved with the early group of NLP developers, culminated in our work (and book) on Dynamic Learning and the founding of NLP University in Santa Cruz, California. Much of that work has continued and evolved through my years of collaboration with Todd's wife Teresa Epstein and Judith DeLozier. Judy and I co-authored a two volume *Encyclopedia of Systemic NLP* and the book *NLP II: The Next Generation*.

My collaboration with Tim Hallbom and Suzi Smith led to many important developments and applications of NLP to health, summarized in our book *Beliefs: Pathways to Health and Well-Being* and covered experientially in the Health Certification Trainings that we have done around the world.

I also collaborated with my colleague Robert McDonald studying the spiritual dimension of individuals and groups. This resulted in our book *Tools of the Spirit* and our seminars on Group Mind and Team Spirit.

Other collaborations have included those with Richard Moss and our developments on Depth Coaching; Mia Segal and out work integrating NLP with the Feldenkrais Method of body work; Gino Bonissone and our exploration of leadership and innovation in large organizations; and my wife Deborah Bacon Dilts and the processes we have developed on Identity Coaching and integrating the Hero's Journey and the 5Rhythms® movement practice.

Each of these generative collaborations has produced some significant contribution to the lives of others and has also stimulated those of us involved in the collaboration to grow and expand in some important way. It is this dual dynamic of personal expansion through the contribution to something larger than oneself that is one of the key explorations of this volume. In this book. I will present principles, models, tools and practices designed to bring out and contribute the best in yourself through your interactions with others.

I hope you find this world of Success Factor Modeling and generative collaboration as exciting and rewarding to explore as John and I have. May it bring you much success and satisfaction as you unleash the creative power of collective intelligence to make a better world.

Robert Dilts
May, 2016
Santa Cruz, California

Introduction
Overview of Success Factor Modeling™

There are two questions that we have to ask ourselves. The first is "Where am I going?" and the second is "Who will go with me?"
Howard Thurman

A clear purpose will unite you as you move forward, values will guide your behavior, and goals will focus your energy.
Kenneth H. Blanchard

There is no greater thing you can do with your life and your work than follow your passions – in a way that serves the world and you.
Richard Branson

SUNNY CAR
ANTONIO MEZA

Success Factor Modeling™ explores the question, "What is the difference that makes the difference?" in order to find the success factors that distinguish between poor, average and remarkable performance.

An effective model provides a description of the lock (strategic challenges and objectives) and the key which opens it (skills and actions).

Overview of Success Factor Modeling™

As I pointed out in *Volume 1* of this series, Success Factor Modeling™ (SFM) is a methodology developed by myself and my brother John Dilts in order to identify, understand and apply the critical success factors that drive and support successful people and organizations. Success Factor Modeling™ is founded upon a set of principles and distinctions which are uniquely suited to analyze and identify crucial patterns of *business practices* and *behavioral skills* used by successful individuals, teams and companies. The SFM™ process is used to identify key characteristics and capabilities shared by successful entrepreneurs, teams and business leaders and then to define specific models, tools and skills that can be used by others to greatly increase their chances of producing impact and achieving success.

The SFM™ process is used to identify key characteristics and capabilities shared by successful entrepreneurs, teams and business leaders and then to define specific models, tools and skills that can be used by others to greatly increase their chances of producing impact and achieving success.

By examining successful businesses, projects and ventures, and observing the behavior of high performing individuals and teams, SFM helps people and organizations to distinguish the factors that have created a particular pattern of success and to identify the trends necessary to extend that legacy into the future. These factors can then be "baked into" people's daily activities by providing the appropriate strategies, tools and support.

One of the strengths of the SFM process is its integration of effective business practices with key behavioral skills. *Modeling behavioral skills* involves observing and mapping the crucial personal and interpersonal processes that produce a successful or remarkable performance of some type. The goal of the behavior modeling process is to identify the essential elements of thought and action required by an individual or group to produce the desired response or outcome—i.e., discovering what is *"the difference that makes a difference."* It is the process of taking a complex performance or interaction and breaking it into small enough chunks so that it can be recapitulated in some way. The purpose of behavior modeling is to create a pragmatic map or "model" of that behavior which can be used to reproduce or simulate some aspect of that performance by anyone who is motivated to do so.

Success Factor Modeling can be likened to identifying the particular key needed to unlock the door to success for various life situations. The "key" to a particular "lock" is the appropriate combination of behaviors and the corresponding mindset required to effectively address the issues and constraints presented by a certain context.

Thus, the objective of the Success Factor Modeling process is to make an *instrumental map*—one supported by a variety of exercises, formats and tools that allows people to apply the factors that have been modeled in order to reach key outcomes within their chosen context. To accomplish this, SFM applies the following basic template:

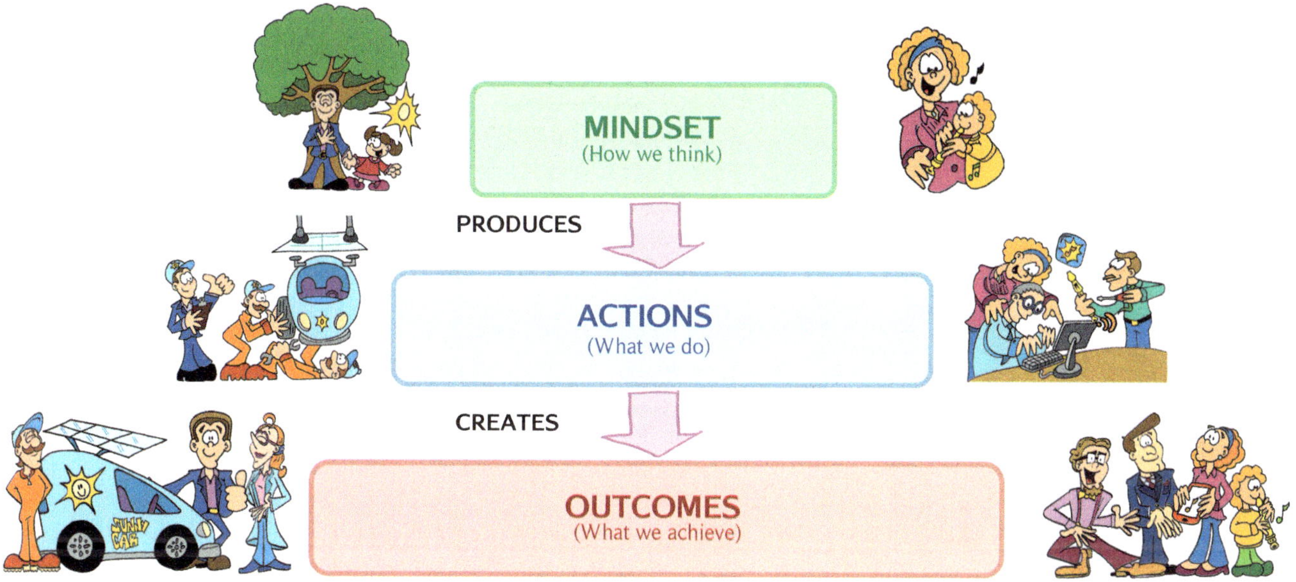

The Basic Success Factor Modeling Template

Our *mindset*—which is made up of our inner state, attitude and thinking processes—produces outer behavioral *actions*. It is our mindset that determines what we do and the type of actions we take in a particular situation. These actions, in turn, create *outcomes* in the external world around us. Achieving desired outcomes in our environment thus requires the proper mindset in order to produce the necessary and appropriate actions.

The steps leading to our desired outcomes are the "locks" we seek to open. Our mindset and actions form the "key" which will open a particular lock. The goal of Success Factor Modeling is to find the proper "keys" which open the "locks" necessary to achieve authentic and sustainable success.

Key Levels of Success Factors

When seeking to identify the characteristics of the mindsets and actions that form the "keys" associated with successful performance, the Success Factor Modeling process takes into account a number of different levels of factors:

- **Environmental factors** which determine the external opportunities or constraints which individuals and organizations must recognize and to which they must react. They involve considering *where* and *when* success occurs.
- **Behavioral factors** relating to the specific action steps taken in order to reach success. They involve *what*, specifically, must be done or accomplished in order to succeed.
- **Capabilities** which make up to the mental maps, plans or strategies that lead to success. They direct *how* actions are selected and monitored.
- **Beliefs and values** which provide the reinforcement that supports or inhibits particular capabilities and actions. They relate to *why* a particular path is taken and the deeper motivations which drive people to act or persevere.
- **Identity factors** relating to people's sense of their role and unique distinguishing characteristics. These factors are a function of *who* a person or group perceives themselves to be.
- **Vision and purpose** which relate to people's view of the larger system of which they are a part. These factors involve *for whom* or *for what* a particular action step or path has been taken.

These levels have been defined in depth in the first volume of this work and in other books that I have written (see *From Coach to Awakener*, 2003 and *NLP II: The Next Generation*, 2010).

Environment: *Our holistic orchard network focuses on sharing sustainable fruit growing techniques that emphasize orchard soil health which in turn makes for healthy trees and thus healthy apples and healthy people.*

Behavior: *Our activities cover everything needed to bring our juice from our farms to our customers, including juicing, packing and distribution.*

Capabilities: *We have developed an innovative system to organize our fleet of electrical trucks so that we can distribute our juice without preservatives in a fast and clean way.*

Values: *Have you guessed? Our values are quality, taste, health and ecology. They guide our decisions as an organization.*

Identity: *We see ourselves as being like a modern "Johnny Appleseed" who was known for his kind, generous ways and his leadership in conservation, and because of the symbolic significance of apples to health.*

Purpose: *And we want our community to benefit from our work by inspiring people with our values and providing the best apple juice!*

Ego and Soul

The part of our existence that we experience as an *individual whole* we typically call our *ego*. The part of our existence that we experience as a *holon* (part of a larger whole) can be referred to as our *soul*.

In examining the outcomes, actions and mindset associated with successful performance, Success Factor Modeling also takes into account the fact that each person, team or organization is what Arthur Koestler called a "holon." On the one hand, they are whole and independent systems in and of themselves. On the other hand, they are also part of successively bigger systems that include and transcend the individual, team or organization.

Thus, Success Factor Modeling views our lives and motivations as driven by these two complementary aspects of our identities: those emerging from (1) our existence as a separate, independent whole and those arising from (2) our existence as a part of a larger whole (e.g., family, profession, community, etc.). The part of our existence that we experience as an *individual whole* we typically call our *ego*. The part of our existence that we experience as a *holon* (part of a larger whole) can be referred to as our *soul*.

From the perspective of Success Factor Modeling, both of these aspects, ego and soul, are necessary for a healthy and successful existence. The primary questions relating to our *ego* are about what we want to achieve for ourselves in terms our *ambition* and *role*: "What type of life do I want to create for myself?" and "What type of person do I need to be in order to create the life I want?" These are about living out our dreams for ourselves. The primary questions with respect to the *soul* are those related to our *vision* and *mission* for the larger systems of which we are a part: "What do I want to create in the world through me that is beyond me?" and "What is my unique contribution to bringing that vision into expression?"

In the SFM approach, these distinctions of *ego* (one's self as an independent whole) and *soul* (ourselves as holons that are a part of a bigger system) are combined together with the various levels of success factors, as shown in the following diagram.

The complementary dimensions of ego and soul tend to bring out a different emphasis for each level of success factors. The ego side accentuates ambition, role, the importance of permission, strategy and appropriate reactions to constraints and potential dangers in the environment. The soul side puts priority on vision, mission, inner motivation and activating the energy and emotional intelligence needed to proactively take advantage of environmental opportunities.

Teil eines großen Ganzen

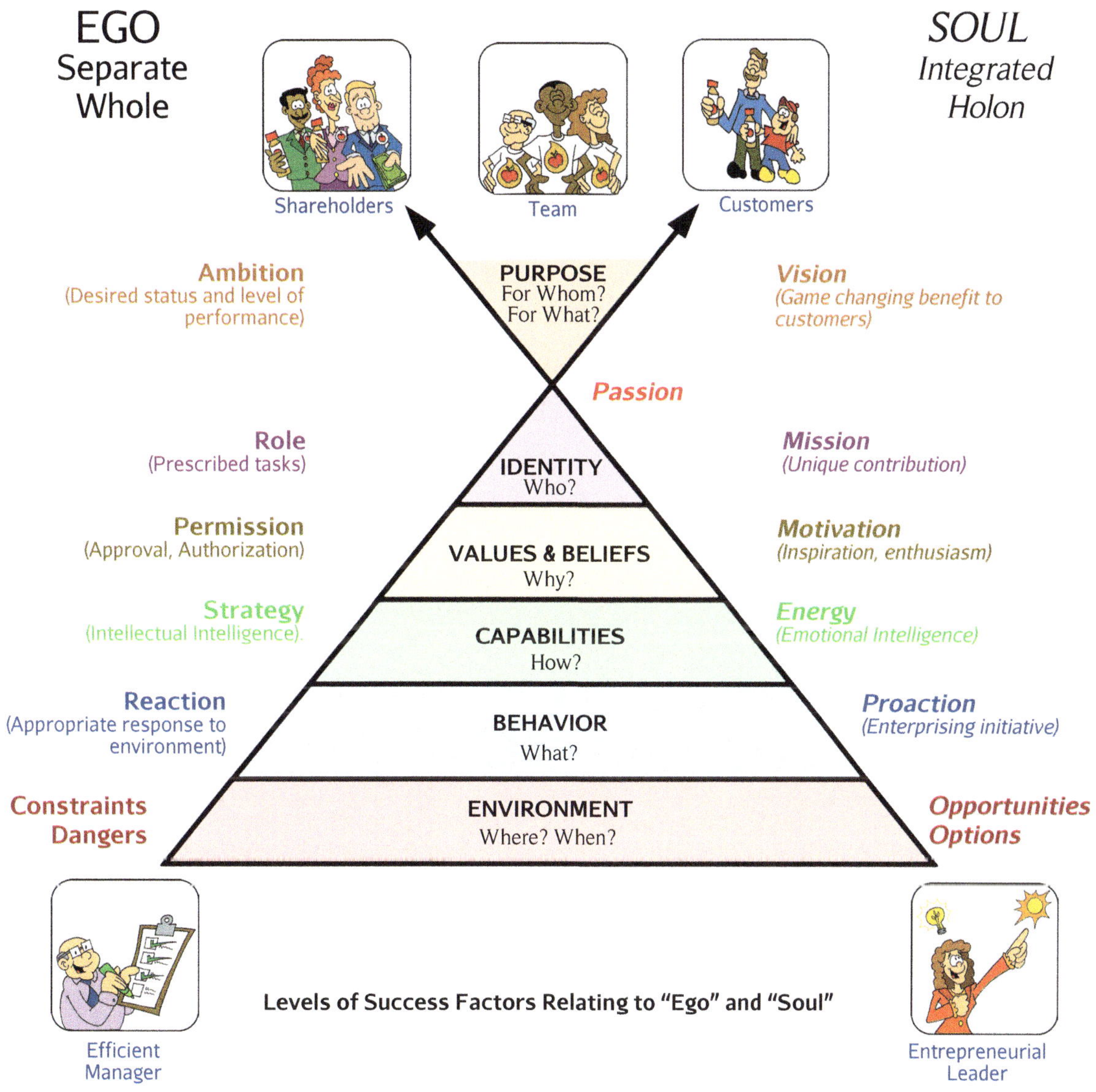

Levels of Success Factors Relating to "Ego" and "Soul"

The main purpose of Success Factor Modeing is to identify the key skills and other factors necessary to reach success in your projects, ventures or businesses and, in doing so, live your dreams and make a better world.

Research with Success Factor Modeling indicates that the highest levels of performance of an individual, team or organization occur when the levels of success factors related to both ego and soul are balanced, aligned and integrated. Clarifying and aligning one's vision, mission, ambition and role are an essential part of achieving this balance and integration. These four guideposts are the foundations of a successful entrepreneurial mindset and form the basis for the projects and ventures we undertake as entrepreneurs.

On a deeper level, however, our vision, mission, ambition and role are all expressions of the fundamental life force that we bring into the world through our bodies and minds. We know and connect to this fundamental life force through our personal sense of *passion*.

The Dynamic Between Passion, Vision, Mission, Ambition and Role

Passion

Personal *passion* is the foundation for an entrepreneurial mindset. Passion, in this sense, can be defined as *an intense desire or enthusiasm for something.* As Richard Branson claims, it is the expression of "wanting to live life to the full." **Passion** has to do with such questions as:

What do you really love to do?

What are you excited about?

What do you find to be interesting and compelling?

What brings you a deep sense of enthusiasm and energy?

The foundation of an entreprenerial mindset is your personal passion for what you are doing. Your passion gives you the enthusiasm, energy and determination needed to create a successful venture.

The most successful of the next generation of entrepreneurs have a passion and desire to create something new and different that is "revolutionary" and "game changing" in a positive way for the larger systems of which they are a part. This passion serves to unite their "ego" with their "soul" and becomes the vehicle through which they grow personally and spiritually. Some examples of the passions of next generation entrepreneurs that we have interviewed include:

- Creating global solutions to common problems
- Solving social challenges
- Changing things for the better – improving the world
- Creativity and thinking "outside the box"
- Promoting growth, in oneself and others
- Creating connection and developing rich relationships
- Making something that is both useful and beautiful

It is their deep personal passion for what they are doing and creating that drives entrepreneurs to take risks and stay focused in the face of the many challenges they confront. It is what pushes them beyond what they ever dreamed possible and causes them to grow their confidence and their skills to new heights. Without a high level of desire and enthusiasm it is practically impossible to create a successful venture. In the words of Apple co-founder Steve Jobs:

> *People say you have to have a lot of passion for what you are doing and its totally true. And the reason is because it is so hard that, if you don't, any rational person would give up. Its really hard and you have to do it over a sustained period of time. So if you don't really love it and you are not having fun doing it, you are going to give up.*

Steve Jobs lived his passion to create innovative technology products that would make a positive difference in the world.

Barney Pell from "Powerset" envisioned a world where people could communicate with computers using "natural language." (See *SFM Volume I,* p. 105.)

Vision

Vision can best be defined as *"a mental image of what the future will or could be like."* The creative vision of successful entrepreneurs has to do with this ability to imagine and focus on longer-term possibilities that improve our lives in some way. It involves the ability to see beyond the confines of the "here and now" and imagine future scenarios. It also involves the capacity to set and stay focused on longer-term goals, adopting long-term plans and a holistic view.

A key characteristic of the vision of successful next generation entrepreneurs and leaders is that it is always directed outward beyond themselves (i.e., it is a product of their "soul"). That is, it is about what they want to see more of or different in the world – it is about "creating a world to which people want to belong." Thus, entrepreneurial **vision** involves the answers to the questions:

What do you want to create in the world through you that is beyond you?

What do you want to see more of and less of in the world?

What is the world to which you want to belong?

Mark Fizpatrick (Tidal Wave Technologies) states his and his team's mission was to "create the best possible solutions" for their customers. (See *SFM Volume I,* p. 159.)

Mission

The *mission* of an individual or organization has to do with their contribution to manifesting a particular vision. The word comes from the Latin *missio*, which means "the act of sending." In fact, *mission* is defined in the dictionary as *"an important assignment carried out for political, religious, or commercial purposes."*

Like an entrepreneur's vision, then, his or her sense of mission comes from the perspective of being a "holon." A mission is the act of contributing something to a system greater than the individual or group who is carrying it out in order to achieve some purpose for that larger system. Thus, the mission of individual within an organization has to do with his or her contribution to that organization and its vision. Similarly, an organization's mission will be with respect to the larger system of its customers and their needs.

According to this perspective, **mission** has to do with the questions:

What is your service to the bigger system and vision?

What is your unique contribution to making the vision happen?

What are the special gifts, resources, capabilities and actions that you bring to the larger system in order to help reach the vision?

Your vision and mission provide a sense of direction and purpose for your venture.

Ambition

Ambition is a result of the desire and determination to achieve success and recognition for oneself. Ambition is defined as *"a strong desire to do or to achieve something, typically requiring determination and hard work"* that brings us personal benefit. Our ambitions, in the form of dreams and aspirations for our lives, arise from a healthy ego and come from the *drive for growth and mastery.*

Ambitions arise from our personal dreams, desires, drives and needs. In addition to making a reasonable or good living from our endeavors, for example, we may have a desire for growth, a drive for achievement or a need for recognition and approval.

Ambition has to with such questions as:

What type of life do you want to create for yourself?

What do you want to accomplish? What type of status and performance do you want to achieve with respect to yourself and others?

What would you like to be recognized and/or remembered for? What would like to be able to add to your resume or biography?

Your ambition fuels your desire to grow, accomplish and achieve.

Cindana Turkatte was recruited as President and CEO of Xindium Technologies because of her clear sense of ambition that motivates her to move into a viable market quickly and show a positive return on investment. **(See *SFM Volume I*, p. 165.)**

Your role defines the position and status, and the supporting skills and capabilities, necessary to reach your vision, mission and ambition.

When Samuel Palmisano was the CEO of IBM, he wanted the company to have a positive role in its local environment. One of the questions he used to make decisions was "why would a social group allow you to operate in their territory?" (See *SFM Volume I*, p. 117.)

Role

Role is defined as *"the function assumed or part played by a person in a particular situation."* Thus, roles are related to both "function"—which is based upon competency—and "the part played"—which is determined by one's position or status. So, on one hand, a role reflects personal skills, abilities, and effort. It is related to what a person *does* (or is expected to do). In fact, people are most successful in roles that are *"compatible with their personal characteristics and skills."* On the other hand, role reflects "status"; i.e., who we are *in relation to others.* In other words, role is an intersection of both the position a person occupies with respect to others, and the expected capabilities and behaviors attached to that position.

Similar to the notion of mission, it is not meaningful to think of a role in terms of one person alone. It has to do with being a "holon"; being both a unique individual and a part of a larger whole. In addition to service to the vision, however, role also focuses on the ways in which a person complements, co-operates and competes with others with respect to his or her personal ambitions.

Thus, **role** has to do with questions such as:

> *What type of person do you need to be in order to create the life you want as well as make your unique contribution to your vision?*
>
> *What type of position and status would support you to succeed in your ambition? Mission? Vision?*
>
> *What are the core competencies necessary to be the type of person you need to be or to achieve and remain in the necessary position or status?*

Vision, mission ambition and role all have to do with integrating our double reality of being both a unique and independent individual and simultaneously a part of something bigger than ourselves. They are all an expression of our personal passion expressed outward toward the larger systems of which we are a part.

The COACH State – Integrating Ego and Soul into a "Holon"

The ability to reconnect and stay connected to the experience of being both an individual whole and connected to something beyond ourselves gives us purpose and energy. Maintaining this dual perspective is an essential characteristic of a successful mindset and is at the foundation of any effective performance. The ability to do this on an individual level can be defined by an inner state characterized by the acronym COACH:

In a COACH state you are centered, open, aware, connected and holding your context with curiosity.

Center yourself, especially in the "gut" (your belly center)

Open your field of awareness

Attend to what is going on within you and around you with mindfulness

Connect to yourself and to the larger system(s) of which you are a part

Hold whatever is happening from a state of resourcefulness and curiosity (hospitality)

The opposite of this occurs when we collapse into an inner stuck state that can be summarized by the letters CRASH:

In a CRASH state you are contracted, reacting to the environment, analyzing, separated and feeling hurt or hostile.

Contraction

Reactivity

Analysis Paralysis

Separation

Hurting or hating (hostility)

When we "CRASH," we no longer perceive ourselves as a holon. We lose our connection to our soul, and everything becomes more difficult. When we confront an outer obstacle from the CRASH state, we experience it as an unsolvable problem.

Being able to achieve and maintain the COACH state, especially in difficult and challenging circumstances, is one of the most important individual success factors defined by SFM.

Next Generation Entrepreneurship

Through the application of Success Factor Modeling over many years, I have recognized that a new generation of entrepreneurs is emerging. This new generation of entrepreneurs, or *"zentrepreneurs,"* are focused on more than achieving financial gain. They are equally committed to living their dreams and making a better world through their business. The skills needed to become a successful next generation entrepreneur were the main focus of *Volume 1* of this series.

Next generation entrepreneurs want to create both a successful *and* purposeful business or career; combining ambition with contribution and mission and the desire for personal growth and fulfillment. They also desire to attract and collaborate with others who share the same vision, mission and ambition. In other words, next generation entrepreneurship involves *creating a world to which people want to belong.*

Our research with Success Factor Modeling has shown that successful next generation entrepreneurs accomplish this through the following five key commitments:

- Growing personally and spiritually
- Contributing to society and the environment
- Building a successful and sustainable venture and career
- Supporting the emotional and physical well-being of oneself and others
- Sharing visions and resources with a community of peers, igniting new possibilities

These five keys are summarized in the diagram on the right.

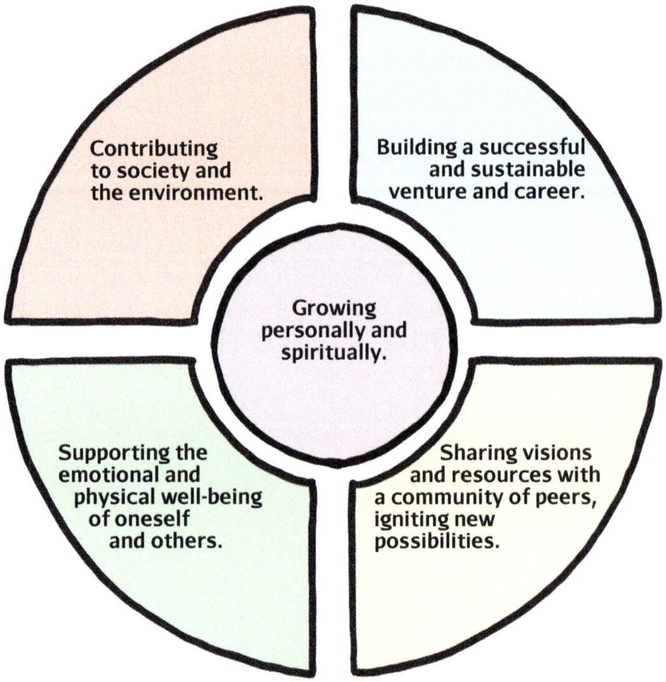

Key Factors Relating to Authentic Success and Creating a World to Which People Want to Belong

Example:

Growing personally and spiritually.

"I WANT TO GROW AS A BUSINESSMAN AND AS A FATHER, AND CONTRIBUTE TO CREATE A HEALTHIER WORLD"

Contributing to society and the environment.

"THROUGH MY VENTURE, PEOPLE WILL HAVE ACCESS TO CARS POWERED BY SUNLIGHT. THE ENERGY NEEDED WILL BE CLEAN AND CHEAP"

Building a successful and sustainable venture and career.

"AS WE ARE PIONEERS, THERE IS A BIG MARKET TO BUILD AND OPPORTUNITIES FOR LONG-TERM INNOVATION."

Supporting the emotional and physical wellbeing of oneself and others.

"AS A LEADER I WILL PROVIDE OPPORTUNITIES FOR GROWTH TO MY COLLABORATORS AND WILL ENCOURAGE THEIR CONTRIBUTIONS."

Sharing visions and resources with a community of peers, igniting new possibilities.

"BY SHARING KNOWLEDGE AND IDEAS WITH OTHERS, WE CAN MAKE A DIFFERENCE AND THRIVE TOGETHER."

The SFM Circle of Success™

The SFM Circle of Success™ identifies the outcomes, actions and mindset necessary to build a successful and sustainable venture.

Our research with Success Factor Modeling has shown that, in order to turn these five keys of authentic success into a project or venture, next generation entrepreneurs create what we call the *SFM Circle of Success™*. A "Circle of Success" is constructed by bringing together the outcomes, actions and mindset needed to build a successful and sustainable venture.

The Five Core Outcomes of Next Generation Entrepreneurs

Firstly, we have found that the five key factors of authentic success defined above translate naturally into *five core outcomes* to be achieved to make a truly next generation venture. Those five core outcomes are:

1. Personal Satisfaction
2. Meaningful Contribution
3. Innovation and Resilience
4. Scalable Growth
5. Financial Robustness

In order to build successful and sustainable ventures, next generation entrepreneurs must achieve five fundamental outcomes:

1. Personal Satisfaction
2. Meaningful Contribution
3. Innovation and Resilience
4. Scalable Growth
5. Financial Robustness

Personal satisfaction is a consequence of connecting with one's passion and growing personally and spiritually.

Making a *meaningful contribution* follows from our ability to both contribute to society and the environment and also support the emotional and physical wellbeing of ourselves and others.

Innovation and resilience result from sharing visions and resources with others to ignite new possibilities and applying them to support the emotional and physical wellbeing of ourselves and others in order to take advantage of opportunities and bounce back from adversity.

Scalable growth is a result of leveraging new possibilities and shared visions to build a successful and sustainable venture.

Financial robustness results when we are able to connect our contribution to society and the environment with building a successful and sustainable venture or career.

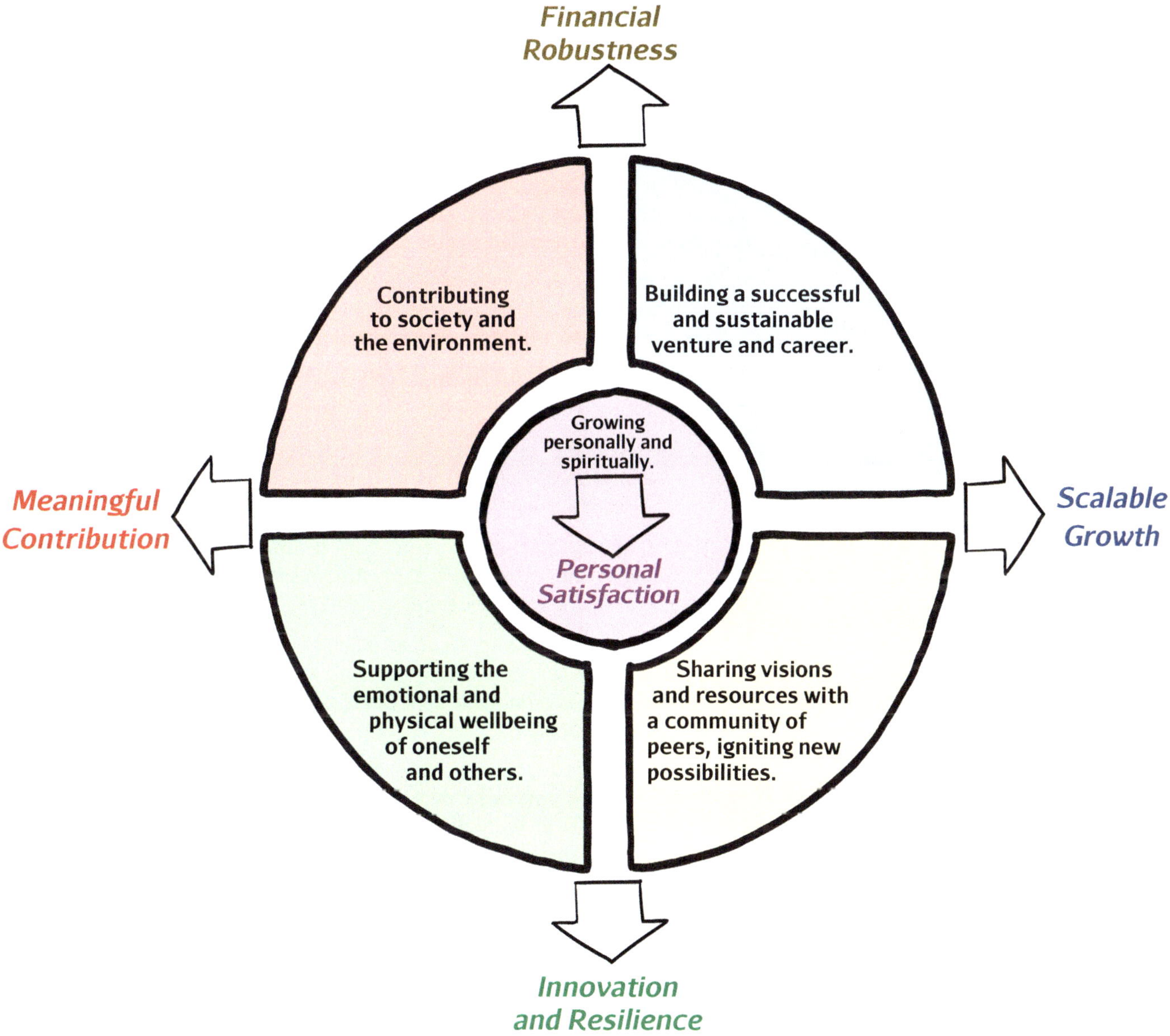

The Five Core Outcomes of Successful Next Generation Entrepreneurs

The SFM Circle of Success identifies five fundamental areas of focus necessary for entrepreneurs to build a successful and sustainable venture through which they can live their dreams and make a better world:

- *Self / Identity*
- *Customers / Market*
- *Team Members / Employees*
- *Stakeholders / Investors*
- *Partners / Alliances*

Critical Actions and Key Perspectives Necessary to Achieve the Five Core Outcomes of Next Generation Entrepreneurs

In order to achieve these outcomes, we have observed that the founders of successful ventures divide their focus of attention and their actions in a balanced way between five fundamental perspectives: 1) themselves and their sense of purpose and motivation for what they are doing, 2) their customers and their products or services, 3) their investors and stakeholders, 4) their team members or employees and 5) their strategic partners and allies.

In other words, in order to achieve the five core outcomes for a successful next generation venture, entrepreneurs need to engage in a number of critical actions directed toward key people and groups. These *critical actions* include:

1. *Connecting* with **themselves** and their *purpose and motivation* for the venture.
2. *Developing products and services* for their **customers** and *generating enough interest and revenue* to support their enterprise — establishing both sufficient "mind share" and market share.
3. Growing a team of competent **team members** by *creating alignment* with respect to the mission of the venture and continuing to *increase their competency* as the business matures.
4. *Raising funds and securing other essential resources* needed to support the venture to reach its ambition, then continuing to *expand the business and create value* for **stakeholders and investors.**
5. *Building win-win relationships* and establishing alliances with strategic **partners** that allow all parties to *enrich and leverage resources* in such a way that they can increase visibility and expand their roles in the marketplace.

As the name "circle of success" implies, we represent the relationship between these critical actions and the core outcomes they create as a circle, with oneself and one's purpose and motivation in the center surrounded by four quadrants of customers/market, team members/employees, stakeholders/investors and partners/alliances.

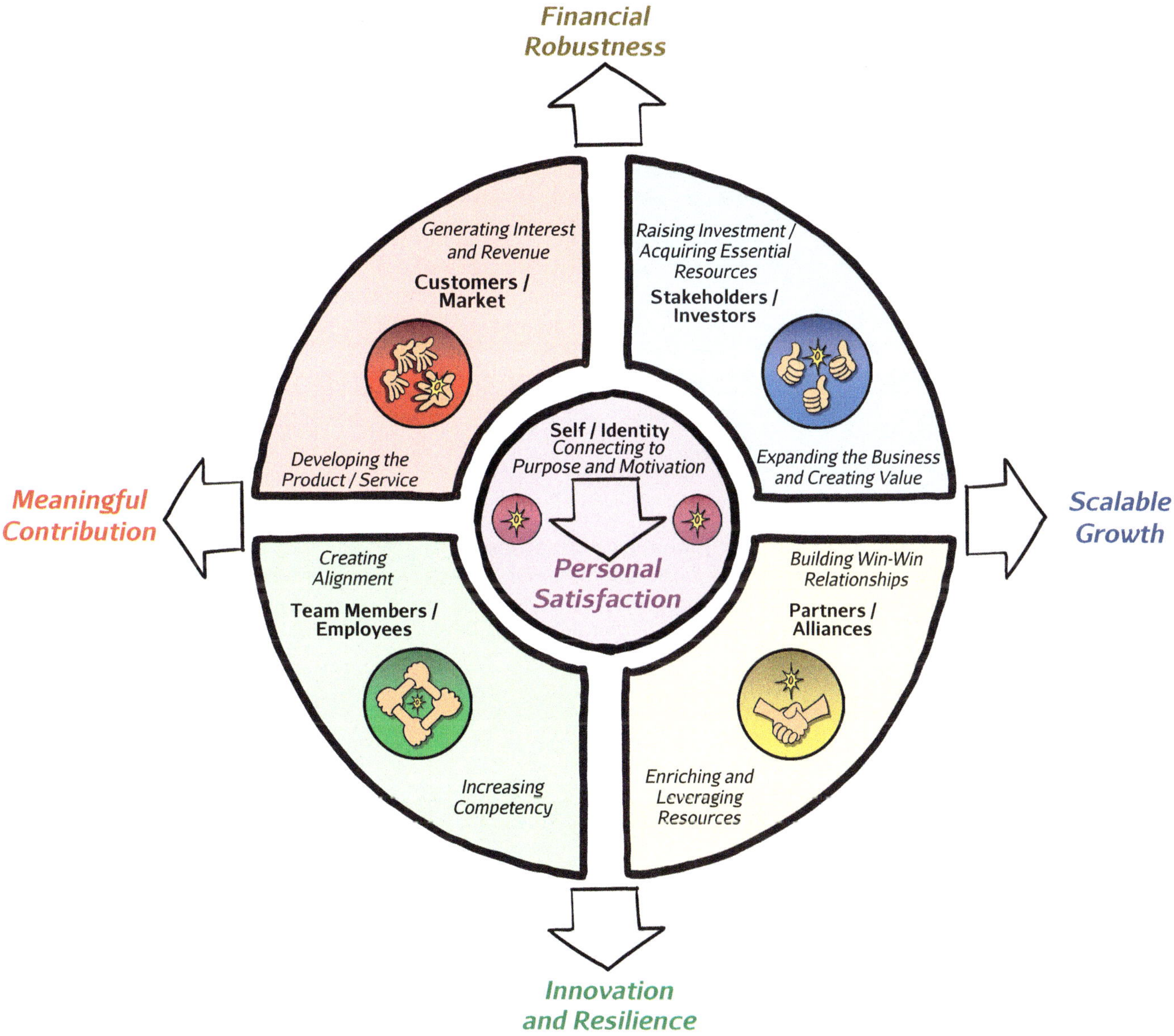

The SFM Circle of Success™

There are nine key actions that combine to create the five core outcomes of next generation entrepreneurs.

As the diagram of the Circle of Success on the previous page implies, attaining **personal satisfaction** comes from (1) *connecting to purpose and motivation.*

The outcome of **meaningful contribution** is primarily achieved through the actions of (2) *developing a product or service* that benefits customers and (3) *creating alignment* among team members. (See the CrossKnowledge Success Factor Case Example, pp. 103-115.)

Achieving the outcomes of **innovation and resilience** is fundamentally a consequence of the actions of (4) *increasing competency* of one's team members and (5) *enriching and leveraging resources* through partnerships and alliances. (See the Success Factor Case Example of Stefan Crisan's Masters in Management program, pp. 158-167.)

The outcome of **scalable growth** is predominantly achieved through the actions of (6) *building win-win relationships* with partners and allies and (7) *expanding the business and creating value* for stakeholders and investors. (See the Success Factor Case Example of Randy Williams and Keiretsu, pp. 198-209.)

Financial robustness is largely the result of the actions of (8) *raising investment and acquiring essential resource*s from stakeholders and investors and (9) *generating interest and revenue* from customers. (See the Comau Pico Success Factor Case Example, pp. 270-277.)

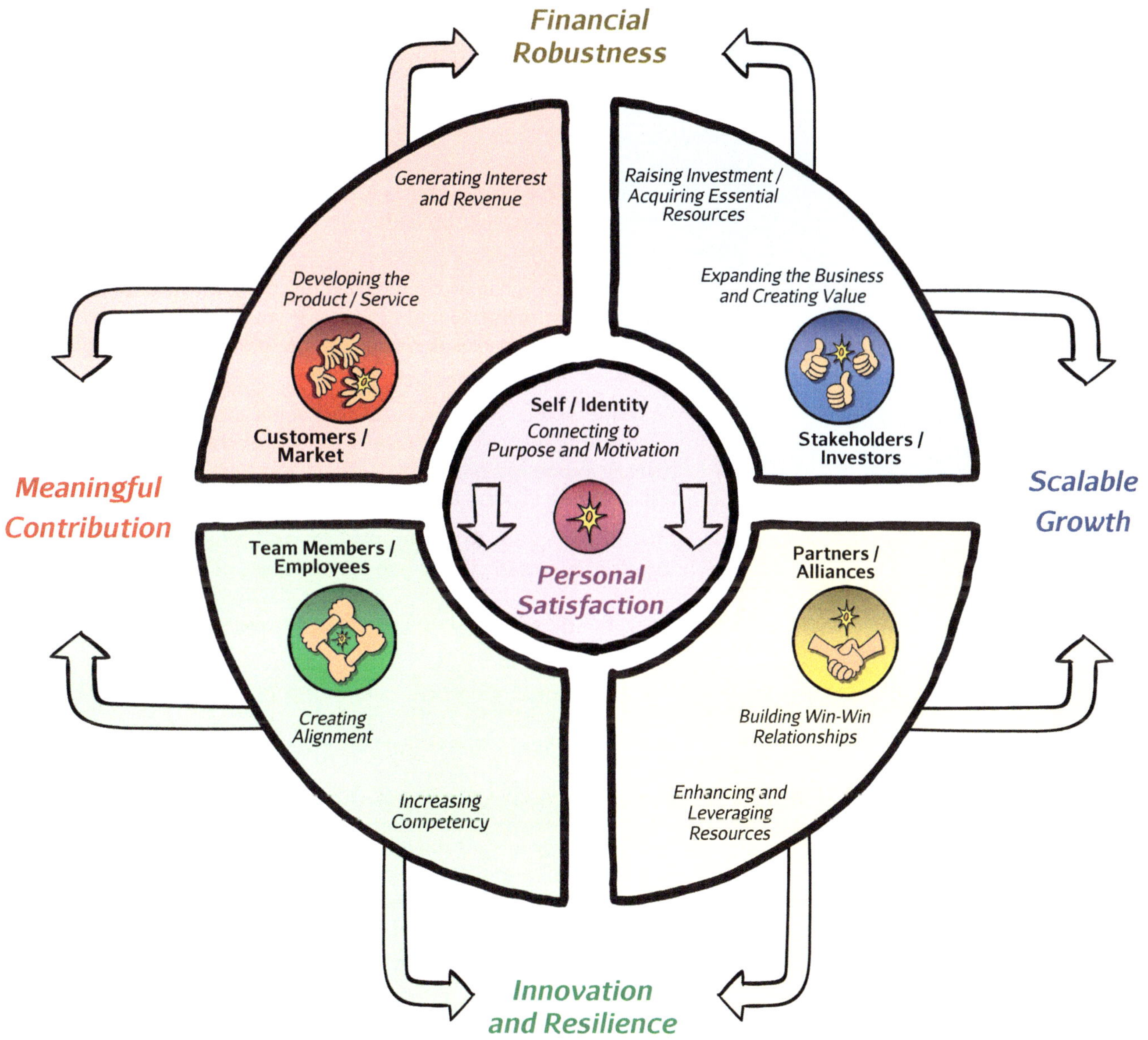

According to The SFM Circle of Success™ the Core Outcomes of Next Generation Entrepreneurs Are Reached through Critical Actions Directed Toward Customers, Stakeholders, Team Members and Partners.

The five fundamental aspects of an entreprenerуial mindset – passion, vision, mission, ambition and role – drive the nine key actions necessary to achieve the core outcomes required to establish a successful and sustainable venture.

Establishing an Entrepreneurial Mindset – Integrating Passion, Vision, Mission, Ambition and Role with The Circle of Success™

Our Success Factor Modeling studies have shown that creating a successful venture is ultimately founded upon an *entrepreneurial mindset* that produces and encourages the actions necessary to reach core outcomes. This mindset a function of an entrepreneur's capacity to share his or her *passion*, in the form of *vision, mission, ambition* and *role*, with respect to the key perspectives defined by the Circle of Success.

- Personal *passion* comes from connecting fully with one's **self** and one's deepest **identity** and discovering what brings us enthusiasm and energy. It involves exploring the question: *What do you really love to do?*
- The entrepreneur's *vision* is a function of his or her personal passion expressed outward toward **customers and the market** in order to make a contribution. It is the answer to the question: *What do you want to create in the world?*
- The alignment of **team members and employees** working together to reach the vision is a result of the entrepreneur communicating and sharing his or her passion in the form of the *mission* of the venture. It is a result of answering the question: *What is your unique contribution to the vision?*
- The entrepreneur's passion in the form of his or her *ambition* to build a successful and sustainable venture and create value is what motivates **stakeholders and investors** to offer the resources and take the risk to join the venture. It involves being clear about the answer to the question: *What do you want to accomplish for yourself?*
- The entrepreneur's passion for applying his or her area of excellence in the form of a *role* and building win-win relationships with peers that enrich and leverage resources is what forms the basis for effective **partnerships and alliances.** This requires clarifying: *Who do you need to be in order to fulfill your mission and ambition?*

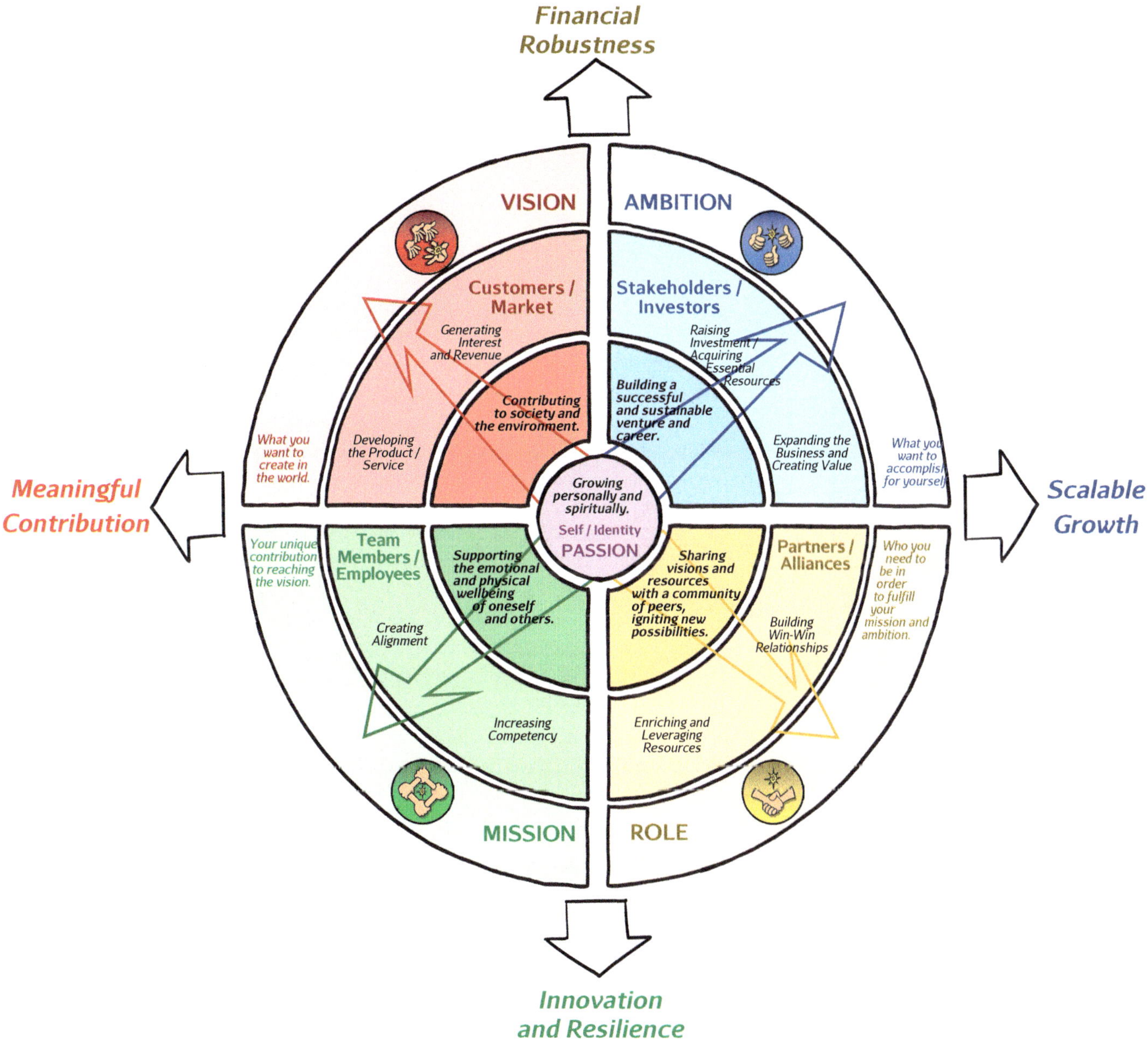

Passion, Vision, Mission, Ambition and Role, and the SFM Circle of Success™

Making an Elevator Pitch

Once you have defined your Circle of Success – getting a sense of your identity and passion; your vision and customers; your mission and team; your ambition and stakeholders; and your role and partners – you have the fundamental pillars from which to build a successful venture. It is then time to synthesize and summarize your Circle of Success into what is known as an "elevator pitch."

An elevator pitch is a brief and concise description of your project or venture

A well crafted elevator pitch should evoke positive emotion as much as cognitive understanding.

As I pointed out at the end of *SFM Volume I*, the notion of an elevator pitch evolved in the fast paced world of Silicon Valley. In such a dynamic context, an entrepreneur needs to be able to communicate the essence of his or her vision and venture to someone in the time it takes to ride up or down with that person several floors in an elevator. Sometimes that is the only chance you will get to interest a prospective investor, partner or team member in what you are planning. Thus, the term *elevator pitch* has come to mean a brief and concise description of your project, idea or venture.

An elevator pitch needs to be a succinct, carefully planned, and well-practiced description of you, your venture or your product/service that your intended listener can understand in the time it would take to ride several floors an elevator. Whether you are an entrepreneur with a start-up company trying to find investors, a recent graduate trying to find a job, a parent with ideas on how to improve the classroom, or a nonprofit looking for donations, a good elevator pitch can help you to generate interest in your project or venture.

An elevator pitch isn't about cramming as much information into as short a time as possible. A well-crafted elevator pitch should evoke emotion as much as cognitive understanding. There are three fundamental characteristics of a successful elevator pitch:

1) *Precision* – You should be able to give your pitch in just a couple of minutes.

2) *Passion* – Customers, investors, team members and potential partners expect energy and dedication from entrepreneurs.

3) *A request* – At the end of your pitch, you must ask for something. Do you want their business card, to schedule a full presentation, to ask for a referral, etc.?

Elevator Pitch Worksheet

In my Success Factor Modeling programs and coaching sessions, I have entrepreneurs use the following worksheet to integrate their work with their Circle of Success into a basic Elevator Pitch. By answering the questions and filling in the statements, you will have the essence of an effective and compelling Elevator Pitch.

My passion is ______________________________

What do you love to do? Why are you motivated to take on this project/venture?

My vision is of a world in which ______________________________

What are the positive benefits that your project/venture will produce?

My mission is to ______________________________

What actions/resources will you and your project/venture provide to help reach the vision?

____

For whom will you direct those actions and provide those resources and for what purpose?

The specific project/venture that is an expression of this mission is

____

What is the product or service that is a concrete expression of your mission?

My ambition is to achieve ______________________________

____

What do you want to become and to accomplish? By when? Use specific numbers if possible.

The basic steps I will take (storyboard) to achieve this ambition are:

1. ______________________________
2. ______________________________
3. ______________________________
4. ______________________________

What are the key steps of your critical path to success?

My role is that of a ______________________________

What is the part you will take, with respect to others, to reach your vision, mission and ambition?

My area of excellence is ______________________________

What are the unique talents and abilities that make it possible for you to take that role?

The resources/types of support I need are ______________________________

____

____

What types of resources and support (money, information, contacts, etc.) do you need in order to succeed?

My request is ______________________________

What would you like to receive from your listeners?

Example of an Elevator Pitch

The SFM Mindset Map™

In addition to the fundamental elements that make up your Circle of Success and Elevator Pitch, it is necessary to have the ability to take on a number of different and more specific complementary mindsets in order to turn your Circle of Success into a viable venture. My colleague Miklos (Mickey) Feher and I have identified eight fundamental mindsets used by successful entrepreneurs to implement their projects or ventures: MarketMaker, ProductCreator, TeamMaker, CompetenceBuilder, Resourcerer, MatchMaker, VentureBuilder and FinanSourcerer. Each of these mindsets corresponds to a particular part of the Circle of Success.

The SFM Mindset Map™ identifies eight specific mindsets that entrepreneurs need to be able to adopt in order to create a viable venture.

- The **ProductCreator** mindset aims to anticipate and fulfill customer needs and desires by developing innovative and empowering solutions (products and services).
- The emphasis of the **TeamMaker** mindset is to attract and give direction to people who support the mission of the venture (its products and services) by fostering synergy, complementarity and alignment.
- The primary attention of the **CompetenceBuilder** mindset is on providing opportunities and resources necessary for team members to grow and to increase competency.
- The primary concern of the **Resourcerer** mindset is to recognize, explore and implement significant synergies with the products, services, competences, etc., of other complementary ventures (Partners/Alliances) in order to enrich and leverage resources.
- The focus of the **MatchMaker** mindset is to seek other ventures (Partners/Alliances) that share common visions and values and complement one another's roles and strengths (through sharing, combining or exchanging) in order to build win-win relationships.
- The **VentureBuilder** mindset concentrates on establishing a sustainable infrastructure, and a path to growth and scalability for the venture, in order to create value for Stakeholders.
- The priority of the **FinanSourcerer** mindset is to identify sources of funds and other essential resources (Stakeholders and Investors) and creatively connect them to the ambitions and strengths of the venture.
- The focus of the **MarketMaker** mindset is to open and maintain dialog with multiple customers and customer representatives in order to generate interest and revenue.

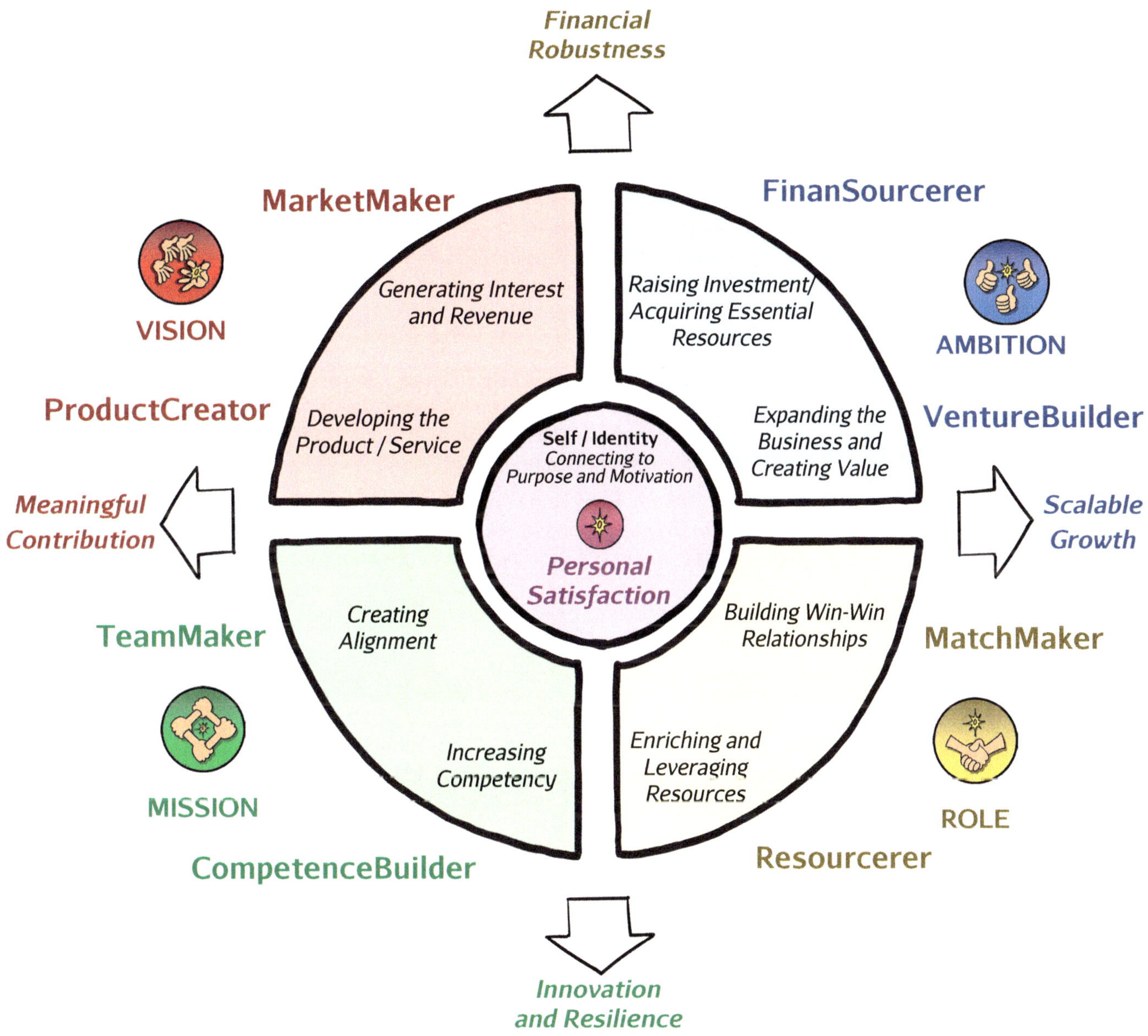

There are eight specific mindsets that entrepreneurs need to be able to take on in order to create a viable venture.

The eight SFM Mindsets are essential for achieving the core outcomes necessary to build a successful and sustainable venture.

The ProductCreator and TeamMaker mindsets are essential for making a *meaningful contribution*. The CompetenceBuilder and Resourcerer mindsets are necessary in order to produce *innovation and resilience*. The MatchMaker and VentureBuilder mindsets are what make it possible to achieve *scalable growth*. The MarketMaker and FinanSourcerer mindsets are required to attain *financial robustness*.

Frequently, we are more competent and comfortable with some of these mindsets than others. Thus, to build our Circle of Success, we need to either develop some of these mindsets more fully or partner with others who are more naturally inclined to the mindsets we lack in order to complement our areas of weaknesses.

In this volume we will be exploring both paths. I will be providing exercises and practices that will help you to develop and strengthen the various mindsets. I will also be showing you how to use the principles and practices of collective intelligence to augment the different mindsets by leveraging the competence of others in your team or network.

Mickey Feher and I have also created an SFM Mindset Map app that helps you to evaluate and develop these various aspects of mindset needed to build a successful venture. For more information, see *http://www.mindsetmaps.com*.

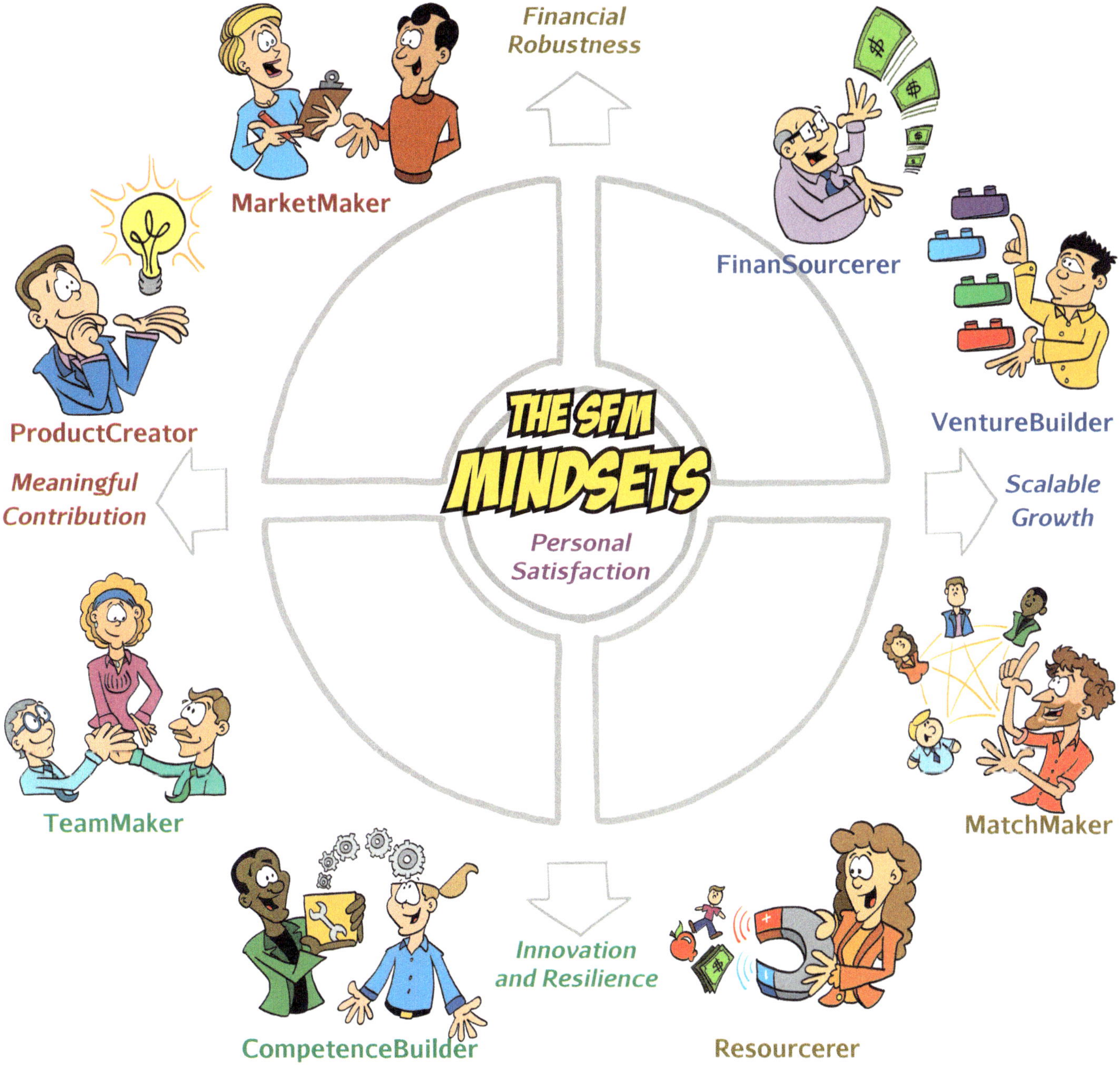
Financial Robustness
MarketMaker
FinanSourcerer
ProductCreator
VentureBuilder
THE SFM MINDSETS
Meaningful Contribution
Scalable Growth
Personal Satisfaction
TeamMaker
MatchMaker
Innovation and Resilience
CompetenceBuilder
Resourcerer

Integrating Multiple Mindsets into the Circle of Success

Practicing the different SFM Mindsets can help you to create a stronger Circle of Success and to refine and expand your elevator pitch into a more in-depth venture presentation.

The following exercise can help you apply the eight SFM Mindsets in order to enrich your Circle of Success and expand your Elevator Pitch into more complete venture presentation. In the exercise, the explorer/presenter stands in the center of the Circle of Success while four others act as representatives of each of the outer quadrants and their related mindsets. The exercise begins by the explorer/presenter giving his or her Elevator Pitch, being sure to answer the key questions relating to his or her self and identity: *What is my passion?* And *What is my purpose and motivation?*

The representatives then take the perspective their respective parts of the Circle of Success and ask questions of the explorer/presenter relating to mindsets connected with their quadrant.

Customers:

ProductCreator: *What is your product or service?*

MarketMaker: *How will you generate interest and revenue from your customers?*

Team:

TeamMaker: *Who are your team members? What are your core values?*

CompetenceBuilder: *What are your unique competencies?*

Stakeholders:

FinanSourcerer: *What essential resources to you need? How will you acquire them?*

VentureBuilder: *How will you expand your project/business and create value?*

Partners:

MatchMaker: *Who are your key partners?*

Resourcerer: *How will your partnerships enhance and leverage resources?*

This is a good way for the representatives to practice taking on the different mindsets as well as for the entrepreneur to rehearse fielding different types of questions about his or her presentation and venture.

Representatives from each part of the Circle of Success ask questions from their perspective about the presenter's project or venture.

The Influence of Context and the "Field of Innovation" on the Circle of Success

The success of new ventures is a consequence of how well they serve and are received into the larger socio-economic system within which they are launched.

Like everything else, the success of new ventures is largely determined by their fit into the larger systems of which they are a part. The evolving state of these bigger systems defines the context in which the entrepreneur's passion and intention takes shape with respect to the different parts of the Circle of Success. The state of these larger systems can be viewed as a type of field that is a function of the evolving socio-economic dynamics as well as technical developments. Such a field is composed of not just the existing needs, attitudes and opinions of the individuals making up the Circle of Success but also their latent or developing needs and attitudes.

Evolving technical developments and shifts in people's needs and attitudes make up a type of "field of innovation" that determines the feasibility, desirability and acceptability of new products and ideas.

It is the state of this larger field of possibilities that determines whether an entrepreneur's idea is perceived as feasible and desirable. Those ventures that are most successful are the ones that produce something that is truly a breakthrough and "game changing." This happens when they are able to catch the "crest of the wave" of an emerging trend in the surrounding field.

In order to be successful, entrepreneurs need to be able to sense and take advantage of emerging trends and opportunities within the dynamic "field of innovation."

The capacity to understand and track key developments in the larger field of interests and possibilities is a major success factor for both established business leaders and aspiring entrepreneurs. This has to do with understanding the forces that are shaping the field and applying what could be called "weak signal detection" to tune into upcoming trends. New possibilities and game changing potentials are constantly emerging. A key success factor for entrepreneurs is having a way to sense and predict where and when these game-changing developments will next arise. This is accomplished through the ability to promote and benefit from what is known as "*collective intelligence*" – which is the primary focus of this book.

In the first volume of this series we presented a series of models, principles and exercises to help readers develop and apply the skills necessary to build their own Circle of Success for a project or venture. In this volume, we will be exploring how to enrich, expand and bring more detail to your vision and venture through collective intelligence, generative collaboration and dynamic teaming.

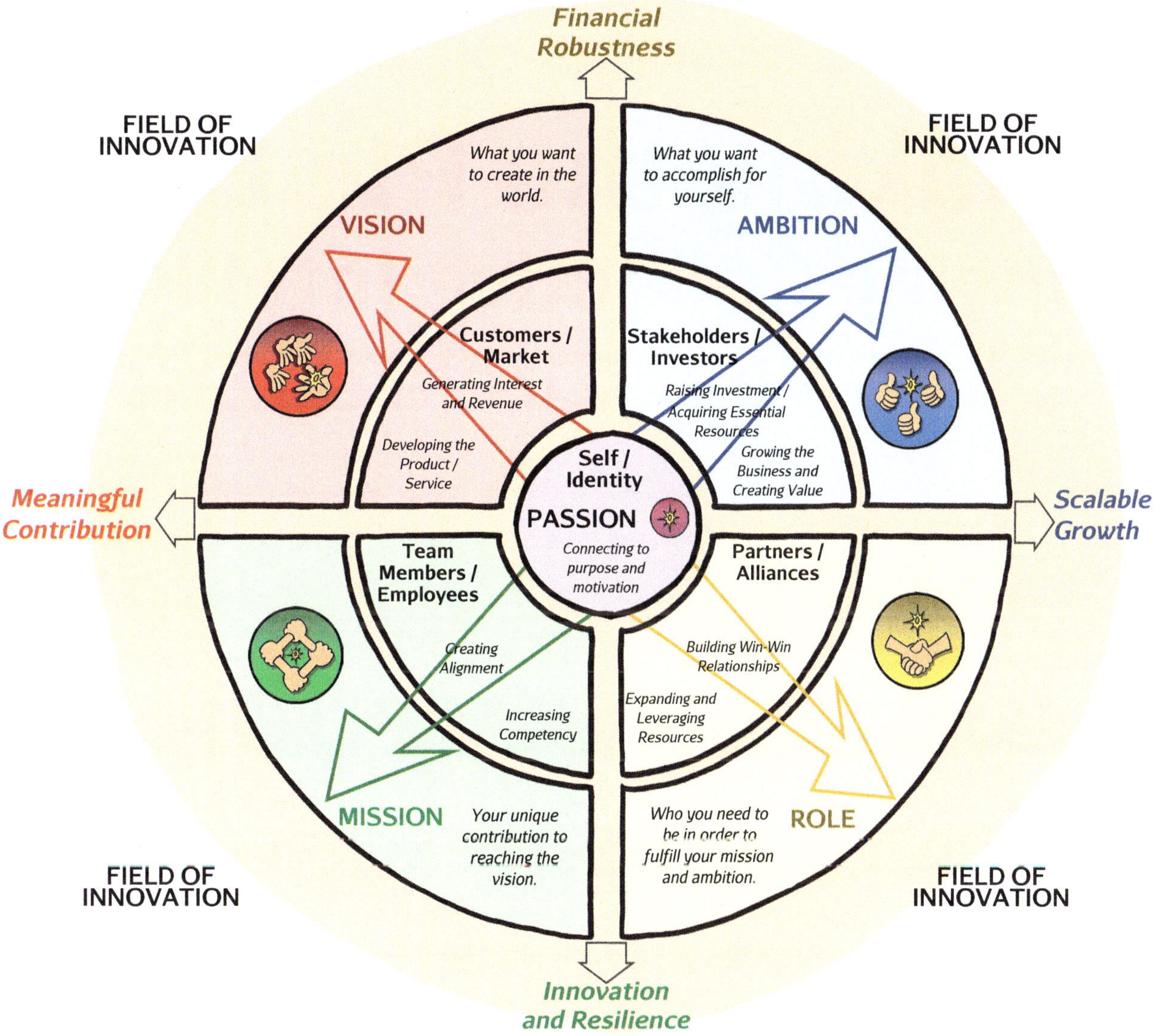

The Most Successful Entrepreneurial Ventures are those that Make a "Game Changing" Contribution to the Larger Socio-Economic Context or "Field of Innovation" in which they exist

01

Making the Pie Bigger

Bringing Collective Intelligence into Your Circle of Success

"The whole is greater than the sum of its parts."
Aristotle

"We shape our self to fit this world and by the world are shaped again. The visible and the invisible working together in common cause, to produce the miraculous."
David Whyte

"The greatest use of a life is to spend it on something that will outlast it."
William James

ANTONIO MEZA

Bringing Collective Intelligence into Your Circle of Success

Building an effective Circle of Success requires the ability to facilitate collective intelligence and generative collaboration with customers, team members, stakeholders and partners.

The first volume of this *Success Factor Modeling* series culminated in the process of creating an "elevator pitch" for your venture (pp. 286-290). As we pointed out in the previous section, an *elevator pitch* is a succinct description of you and your company, product or service that you can express to someone in the time it would take to ride several floors an elevator. The purpose of making an elevator pitch is to get the attention and hopefully the interest and ultimately cooperation of people who could potentially join and or contribute to your *Circle of Success* as a customer, stakeholder, team member or partner. This volume of *Success Factor Modeling* explores what happens next.

Truly successful entrepreneurs are able to work effectively and creatively with the members of their Circle of Success to enrich, expand and materialize their vision and achieve their ambition. This involves a practical understanding of and facility to promote "collective intelligence" and "generative collaboration." Like all successful entrepreneurial activities, this begins with a win-win mindset.

Creating a successful and sustainable venture requires us to invite others into our Circle of Success and promote collective intelligence and generative collaboration.

Making a "Bigger Pie"

It is not uncommon to hear people talk about fighting over who will get the "biggest slice of the pie." The implication is that individuals and organizations must constantly struggle and compete against one another in order to maximize their share of some limited market or resource.

This is inherently a win-lose or "zero sum" frame. As we have discussed in *Volume 1* of this work, a *zero sum* interaction is one in which in order for one person or party to win (+1) the other must lose (-1), the end result being zero (0). "Zero sum" interactions typically occur around situations in which there is a perceived or presupposed scarcity of resources, such that there is only enough for one party to succeed or survive.

Zero sum mentality: *Fighting about who gets a bigger piece of the pie.*

Win-win interactions, on the other hand, presuppose that there are potentially enough resources to go around, that everyone can benefit in some way and that, through cooperation, even more resources may be generated. Win-win interactions typically create a positively self-reinforcing feedback loop that produces evolution and growth—one that makes the "pie bigger" so that everyone gets more, regardless of their original portion.

The desire to make the pie bigger is at the heart of all true entrepreneurial activities. Entrepreneurs want to create greater wealth and new resources by making a contribution. As entrepreneur Cindana Turkatte (profiled in *Volume 1* of this series – pp. 163-171) pointed out, entrepreneurial satisfaction comes when others are able to achieve "something they did not know was possible" as a result of your success.

Win-win mentality: *Making the pie bigger*

Inventions such as the automobile, the telephone, air travel, the radio, the personal computer, the internet and the iPod, for example, are developments that have produced this type of generative, win-win capacity. They led to the creation of new markets and expanded existing capabilities in such a way as to produce newer and "bigger pies."

The driver behind such developments, and the engine of win-win interactions, is what is known in Success Factor Modeling™ as "generative collaboration." Generative collaboration involves people working creatively together to "make more of a good thing." Generative collaboration, in turn, is founded upon the phenomenon of collective intelligence.

***Collected intellgience* functions like a jigsaw puzzle: each member of the group contributes his or her skills or knowhow as a piece of a single static objective.**

***Collective intelligence* functions more like a fractal or neural network: the contribution of each member of the team or group influences, adds to and enhances the knowledge and competence of the other members creating a generative and frequently unpredictable result.**

Collective Versus Collected Intelligence

As I pointed out in the first volume of this work (pg. 87), *collective intelligence* is a shared intelligence that emerges from the collaboration and communication between individuals in groups. It relates to the ability of people in a team, group or organization to think and act in an aligned and coordinated fashion and transforms separate individuals into a cohesive group in which the whole is truly greater than the sum of its parts.

It is important to distinguish "*collective* intelligence" from "*collected* intelligence." As I said above, *collective intelligence* produces a result in which *the whole is greater than the sum of its parts.* The result of *collected intelligence*, on the other hand, is simply *the sum of the individual contributions.* A jigsaw puzzle would be a good analogy for collected intelligence. The various pieces fit together to produce a final, single static image. The pieces only fit together correctly one way and always produce the exact same image every time. This is the way that many tasks are organized in a company or business. Team members make an individual contribution of their skills or knowhow in order to achieve a clearly defined objective. When done correctly, each individual contribution provides a part or piece of the larger puzzle. A traditional assembly line is a good example of a type of collected intelligence.

While collected intelligence is important and sufficient for many situations, it does not have the creative or synergistic power of collective intelligence that is necessary to succeed as a next generation entrepreneur in a rapidly changing world. Collective intelligence functions more like a fractal or neural network. It is more dynamic than collected intelligence in that each individual contribution influences, adds to and enhances the knowledge and competence of the other individuals in the group or team.

In a *neural network*, for instance, "information" and "knowledge" are stored collectively by the whole network as patterns of activity in the interconnected neurons. The system's knowledge cannot be separated from the circuitry as a whole. The intelligence of the network is inherent in the system as a function of the number and quality of connections between the elements. Intelligent behavior emerges organically in the network through learning as the network is exposed to different circumstances. Different patterns of experience change the strength of connections between parts of the network according to the "Hebb" rule. This rule asserts that if two elements in a similar state "resonate" or respond simultaneously, their connection is strengthened; i.e., neurons that "fire" together "wire" together.

In a like fashion, in entrepreneurial ventures, collective intelligence emerges from the interconnections and quality of relationships between people. The intelligence of the group is a consequence of people working cooperatively to reach common visions and ambitions by constantly exchanging information and ideas, and by complementing and synergizing one another's skills, experience and imagination. Similar to a neural network, the intelligence of the system is facilitated by the strength of the connection or "resonance" between the individual members of the group or team around key values and issues. The resulting accumulation and integration of individual know-how, creativity and competence also serves as a platform from which to develop new insights, ideas and capabilities. As a result, a major benefit of promoting collective intelligence is that group members grow more quickly and the creativity and problem solving capacity of those involved in the venture are enhanced through increased access to knowledge, ideas and experience.

Collective intelligence results from exchanging information and ideas, and by complementing and synergizing one another's skills, experience and imagination.

Creating Collective Intelligence

Clearly, not all interactions create collective intelligence or generative collaboration. In fact, more often it is not the case. There are many examples of groups that do not display any increase of intelligence or creativity through the interactions of their individual members, but actually the opposite; a type of "degenerative collaboration." Mobs and dysfunctional teams and families are examples of this. What are the differences that make the difference?

Our research with Success Factor Modeling has shown that true collective intelligence is the product of three fundamental system dynamics: resonance, synergy and emergence.

Resonance is essentially the strengthening of vibration between two instruments (or people) that are attuned to one another.

Resonance

Resonance refers to the tendency of systems to vibrate more strongly at some frequencies than at others. At these frequencies, even small repeating forces can produce large changes. Derived from the Latin *resonantia*, meaning "echo" or literally "re-sound," "resonance" is also used to refer to a type of mutual influence between systems or objects that are specially attuned to one another. For example, if one has two guitars that are similarly tuned and plucks a string on one of the guitars, the corresponding string on the other guitar will begin to vibrate without being physically touched. The same kind of resonance can occur between corresponding notes on a piano, tuning fork, etc. It can even occur between different instruments. Playing a certain note on a flute, for instance, can cause a guitar string to vibrate at that frequency.

Psychologically, the term resonance is used to refer to "the complex of internal body processes that occur in emotional states such as rapport or empathy." In groups, resonance has to do with the degree to which members feel a sense of alignment or connection with other group members' ideas, values and goals. Intellectual and emotional resonance are key sources of motivation, synergy, generativity and collective intelligence in groups.

Resonance between people is the foundation for collective intelligence.

Practically speaking, in the context of creating an entrepreneurial venture, resonance has to do with the level of mutual interest and understanding you are able to generate with the various members of your Circle of Success. This is one of the reasons that presenting your elevator pitch with passion is so important.

Resonance in the form of mutual interest and understanding can occur between any of the levels of success factors that we have identified: environment, behavior, capabilities, beliefs and values, identity and purpose.

- Environmental resonance comes from simply sharing the same physical context.
- Resonance at the level of behavior comes when you engage in similar or parallel activities with others.
- A deeper level of resonance occurs when you share common strategies, skills and ways of thinking with others.
- Resonance created by shared valued and beliefs can be particularly powerful for strengthening motivation, loyalty and setting common priorities.
- Sharing common roles and missions produces a strong resonance at the identity level.
- Having a shared vision and ambition creates perhaps the most profound form of resonance of all and can bring unprecedented levels of energy into a group or team.

In the coming chapters, we will be exploring practical ways to create and assess resonance at all of these levels as a crucial part of building your Circle of Success.

Levels of Resonance

Synergy

Synergy occurs when two or more things function together to produce a result that is not independently obtainable by any of the things on their own. The word comes from the Greek *synergia*, which literally means to "work together." As a simple example, if two people are each too short to reach an object on a high shelf, one can sit on the shoulders of the other and thus achieve a result that neither can accomplish alone.

In the context of organizational behavior, synergy is the ability of a group to outperform even its best individual member; i.e., to produce an overall better result than if each person within the group were working toward the same goal individually. Synergy requires an exchange of energy in addition to an exchange of information in order to produce a result that includes and extends the capabilities of the contributing individuals.

Synergy between you and each of the members of each part of your Circle of Success is clearly essential to create a successful project or venture.

Synergy goes beyond resonance. It results from complementary qualities that create something beyond the individual contributions.

A synergic relationship produces a result that none of the individual participants can accomplish alone.

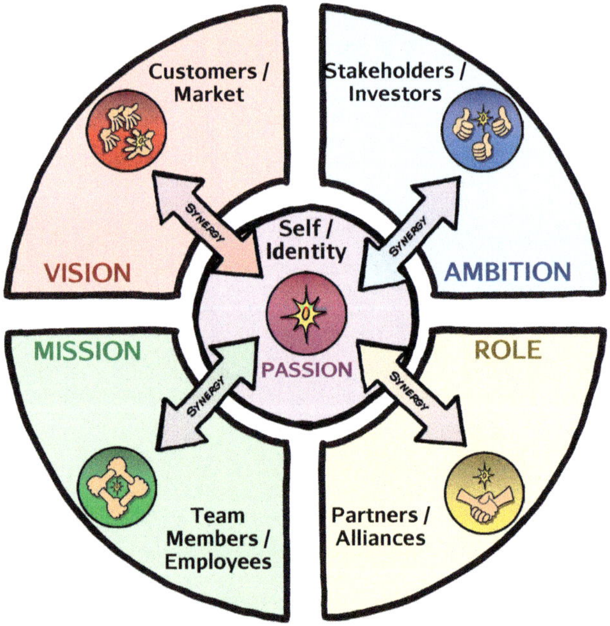

Creating synergy between yourself and the members of your Circle of Success is key to building a successful venture..

Likewise, some degree of synergy between the various members of your Circle of Success is also crucial to the success of your project or venture.

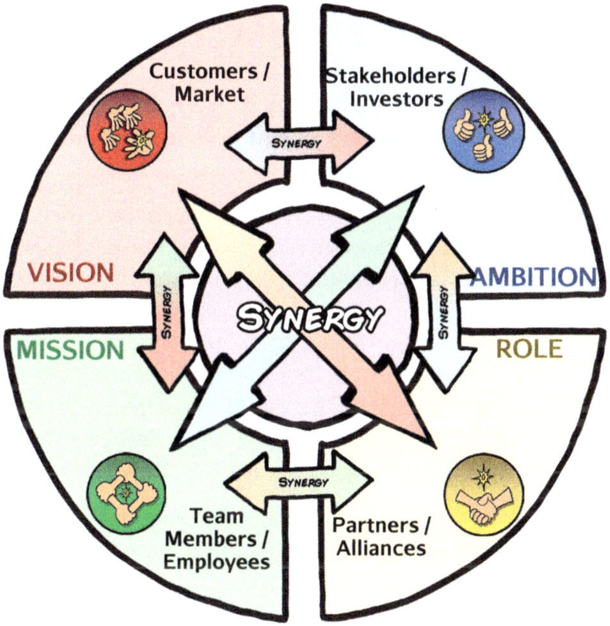

Promoting synergy between the various members of your Circle of Success is also a major success factor.

Forming synergies between yourself and the various members of your Circle of Success is an important part of building a successful venture.

Synergistic roles

Synergistic values

Synergistic actions

Levels of Synergy

As with resonance, synergy in the form of complementary qualities that dramatically boost performance can occur between any of the levels of success factors.

- Different individuals or companies can combine or swap environmental resources in order to collectively leverage or expand their markets.
- Like the example of sitting on the shoulders of another person to reach a high object, individuals, teams and organizations can collaborate, working together to combine and enhance core activities and behaviors.
- Synergizing different capabilities is clearly the foundation for forming strategic alliances and engaging in open innovation with respect to products or services.
- Complementary values and beliefs are absolutely essential in order to form strong and productive relationships for each part of the Circle of Success. Differing values such as "creativity" and "attention to detail" can combine to produce powerful results. This is frequently the case with values related to "soul" – such as "contribution" or "service" – and values related to "ego" – such as "recognition" or "return on investment." The degree to which you and the various members of your Circle of Success value and believe in one another will determine the ultimate degree of success of your venture.
- Complementary and synergistic roles and missions are the source of evolving and expanding identities in both individuals and organizations, and are clearly the primary reason for mergers and acquisitions.
- Synergizing and complementing one another at the level vision and ambition is undoubtedly the force behind the creation of whole new markets.

In the chapters ahead, I will be providing examples, tools, methods and strategies for finding and creating synergy with the members of your Circle of Success at multiple levels.

Emergence

Emergence occurs when something new arises out of interactions between different elements in a system. Complex patterns can arise out of a combination of relatively simple interactions. The moiré patterns that result from the overlap of two other visual patterns, as shown in the diagrams below, are one example of the property of emergence.

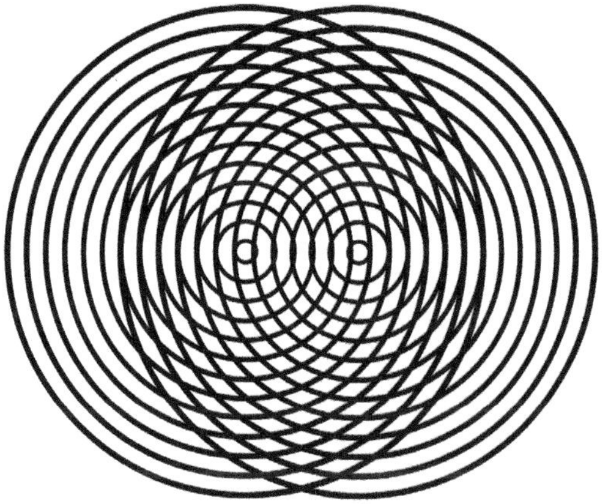

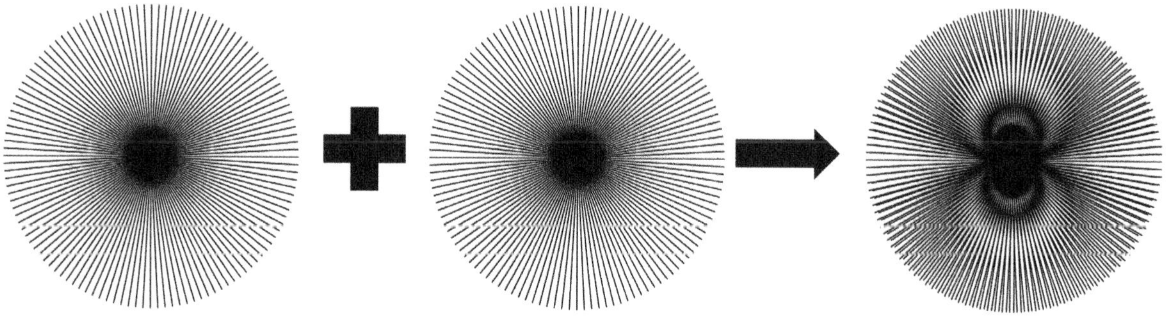

The moiré pattern itself becomes a third entity. Something similar happens when musical notes combine to make a chord. In general, as system theorist Gregory Bateson pointed out, "When two repetitive systems are combined, a third is necessarily generated." Thus, the fundamental principle of emergence is: 1 + 1 = 3.

Emergence: Unpredictable shapes arise from a vibrating speaker filled with a mixture of cornstarch and water.

Emergence occurs when complex and unpredictable patterns appear as a result of a combination of relatively simple interactions.

The term "emergence" comes from the Latin *emergere*, which literally means to "unsink"; indicating something that is "rising up" out of liquid or some other medium. It is the opposite of *sub*merging something by sinking it. A concrete and graphic illustration of this quality of emergence can be made by mixing cornstarch and water together and then pouring the mixture into a vibrating speaker. As the oscillating speaker gives energy to the mixture, different shapes and forms begin to emerge out of the liquid — as shown in the photo to the left.*

The results of this simple experiment create a scene similar to how one might imagine the first life forms looked as they emerged out of the "primordial soup" on our planet billions of years ago.

Emergent behaviors, or properties like this, begin to appear in any interconnected system as soon as several simple entities (agents) interact together with the proper level of energy in a shared environment. Elementary interactions between individual entities build upon one another and produce more complex behaviors as a collective.

What is known as *strong emergence* occurs when the patterns resulting from the collective behavior in a system are not directly traceable to the system's components, but rather to how those components interact. It is in this case that the whole is truly greater than the sum of its parts. A common example of this type of emergence is the formation of snowflakes and other natural "fractal" structures.

The set of images on the following page is a good illustration of strong emergence. The images come from an experiment done in an area of physics known as "cymantics." *Cymatics* is the study of the effects of sound and vibration on matter. These images graphically illustrate some of the key properties of emergence. The images are all of same collection of sand on a metal plate. The shifting patterns in the sand emerge as an escalating frequency of sound is played onto the plate. The sound vibrations create a complex interaction between the plate and the sand, and between the individual grains of sand. The images show what happens as the sound frequency gets progressively higher. Even though the sound frequency is increased at an incremental, linear rate, the pattern of sand on the plate becomes more and more complex in unpredictable ways. If you didn't already know what was going to happen, it would be practically impossible to predict what the next pattern would look like.

---

* A fascinating video of the phenomenon can be seen on Youtube under the title "Non-Newtonian Fluid on a Speaker Cone"

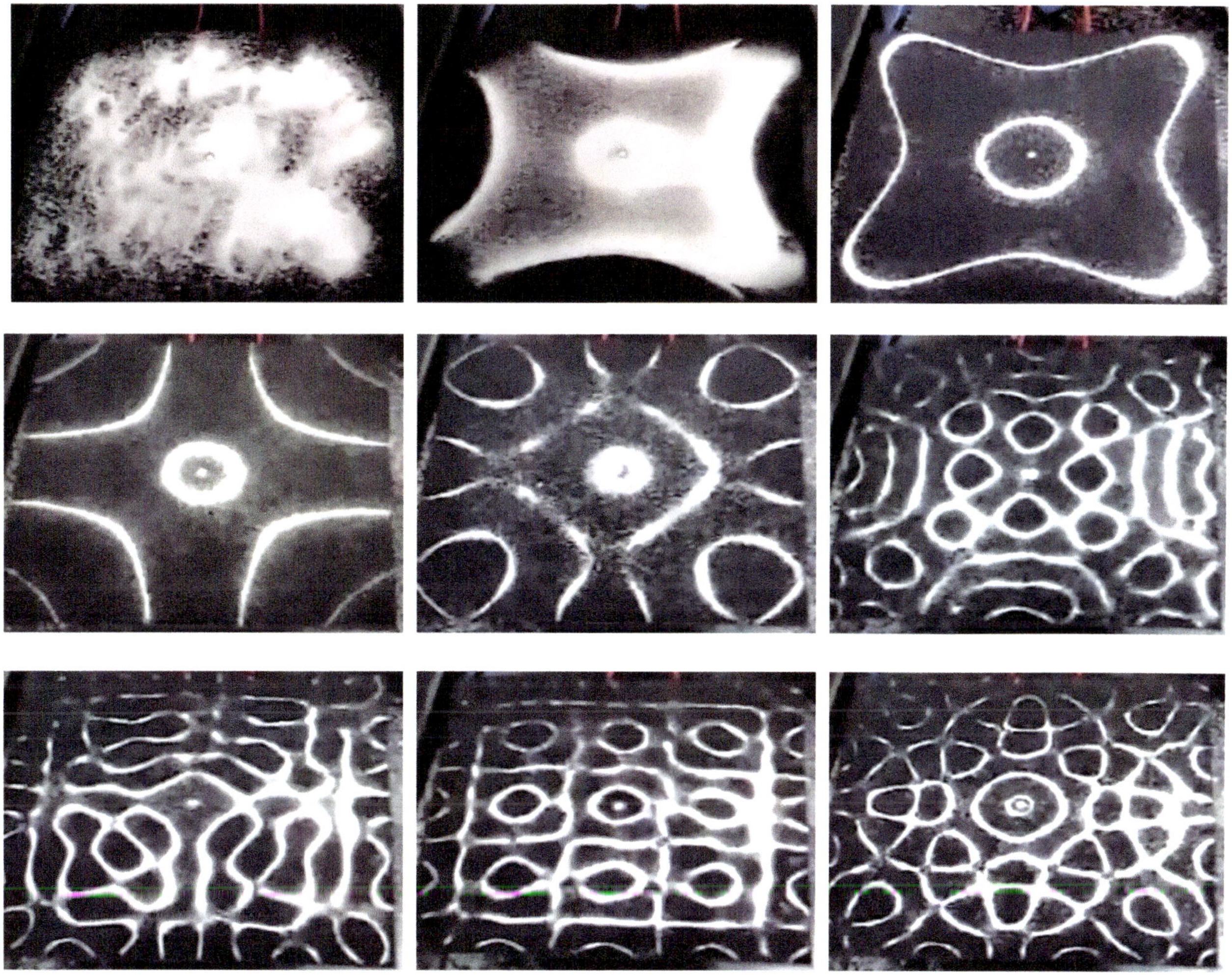

Complex patterns emerge as a result of a simple increase in sound vibration on sand on a metal plate.*

*You can watch the full video on Youtube under the title "Cymatics Experiment."

I frequently show this video to my clients and to participants at my Success Factor Modeling workshops as a metaphor to illustrate the effects of an energetic "field" and the significance that different levels of resonance have on the potential for emergence. We can consider the sand to be the individuals in an organization or the contents of a particular product or problem. The metal plate is the context within which the individuals or contents are brought together. The thing that ultimately determines what emerges is the quality of the energetic field (in this case literally vibration) that animates the interaction. In a human group or organization this energetic field is created by the degree and level of emotional and psychological resonance with respect to the various levels of success factors – especially vision, mission and ambition.

In entrepreneurial endeavors, emergence comes in the form of breakthrough innovations that appear unexpectedly as the consequence of combinations of seemingly unrelated or incompatible ideas, beliefs and technologies.

In entrepreneurial endeavors, where there is an appropriate degree of resonance between the various members within the Circle of Success, emergence comes in the form of breakthrough innovations that appear unexpectedly as the consequence of combinations of seemingly unrelated or incompatible ideas, beliefs and technologies.

Similar to the qualities of resonance and synergy, emergence can take place at a number of different levels in venture.

- The trend toward globalization and the increasing multinational presence of many companies and ventures is an example of emergence at the level of environment.
- At the level of behavior, musicians, dancers and performance artists have known for a long time that new forms of expression can spontaneously emerge as a result overlapping and integrating other actions and activities. Similarly, new products and services can emerge as existing products and services are integrated and applied together into more complex and sophisticated variations. Think of the combination printer, scanner, photocopier, fax machines that are commonplace today. Only a few years ago, they all used to be separate activities.
- New ideas and capabilities can also spontaneously and unexpectedly emerge from sharing and synthesizing other ideas and capabilities to produce surprising breakthroughs. Many innovations emerge as a result of interdisciplinary "think tanks" such as Xerox PARC.
- New organizational cultures emerge as existing older beliefs and values are synthesized and integrated with new ones. Samuel Palmisano's "values jam" described in *Volume I* (p. 118) is a powerful example of this. CEO of IBM in the early 2000's Palmisano recognized that IBM's

existing command-and-control culture was no longer working. He launched a massive, online, interactive "values jam" involving all 440,000 employees from 170 countries for 72 hours to determine what IBM's values should be. The three core values that emerged from the collective collaboration – *Dedication to every client's success*; *Innovation that matters, for our company and for the world* and *Trust and personal responsibility in all relationships* – have since served to guide decision-making throughout the organization and have supported the creation of a unique collaborative organizational structure, leveraging the potential for greater collective intelligence.

- Of course, emergence can also happen at the level of identity. Roles and missions can overlap, combine and evolve to produce completely new types of companies and ventures. Organizations like Amazon, Google and Facebook have emerged in the last decade that could never have existed 25 or 30 years ago.
- The emergence of new visions and ambitions create what are known as "disruptive innovations" which represent quantum leaps in our society and/or technologies. *Disruptive innovations* are those that create a new market whose boundaries do not fit within existing markets. Disruptive innovations are a classic example of "making the pie bigger." The mass-production of automobiles, digital photography, the Nespresso machine, the iPod, smart phones and social media are all examples of disruptive innovations. They each created entirely new markets that had not existed before.

A major focus of *Success Factor Modeling Volume II* is about how to create the conditions for emergence within your venture and between you and the various members of your Circle of Success. This capacity will be one of the most important factors in your success and that of your venture.

Levels of Emergence

Other Influences on Collective Intelligence and Generative Collaboration

In addition to the systemic dynamics of resonance, synergy and emergence, our research with Success Factor Modeling has revealed some other important influences on creating collective intelligence and generative collaboration.

Whole and holon: We are each unique, independent individuals and, at the same time, we are part of larger systems.

Holons and Holograms

A key theme in *Volume I* of *Success Factor Modeling™* was the notion that each of us is a "holon" (pp. 22-23). On the one hand, we are whole and independent individuals in and of ourselves. On the other hand, we are also part of successively bigger systems that include but also transcend us. Specifically, we are made up of whole atoms, which make up whole molecules, that combine to create whole cells, which join together to make whole organs and a whole interconnected nervous system from which our whole body is formed. We, in turn, are part of progressively larger wholes: a family, a professional community, the whole system of living creatures on this planet and ultimately the whole universe.

Our ongoing, concrete participation as holons is another key success factor in creating collective intelligence. Wholes combine to form even larger wholes that have new and different properties and capabilities from the parts of which they are made. The human brain as a whole has different properties from the individual nerve cells of which it is made. Water has different properties from the hydrogen and oxygen atoms that create it. Similarly, groups have different properties from the individuals that form them.

An additional critical factor in creating collective intelligence has to do with holograms and holographic systems. A *hologram* is a three-dimensional image in which the whole picture is contained in every part of the image. If you take the plate of glass or piece of film upon which the hologram is recorded and break it in half, you can still see the whole picture. If you break those halves in quarters, the whole image is still there, and so on. As a phenomenon, the hologram has become a metaphor for the notion that, in many systems, all of the information relevant to that system is distributed through every part of the system in some form.

Our own bodies clearly have this property. Every cell in our body shares the same DNA. So, even though each cell is unique, and a cell in our eye is quite different from a cell in our toenail, they all share a common code that allows them to function as a larger coordinated whole.

We can see the same process at work in a successful company or culture. A high level of resonance regarding various levels of success factors (especially the higher levels – vision, mission, values, etc.) functions as a type of DNA for the venture. If you divide the company into separate divisions, teams or even individuals, the vision, mission, ambition, role, values, etc., of the whole company should be present in each part. If it is not, there is more likely to be anarchy and chaos instead of coherency. If a manager in a company went to a meeting and simply acted upon his or her own goals, interests and values, that manger would be endangering the interests and, in some cases, potentially the survival of the larger organization.

A hologram is a three-dimensional image in which the whole picture is contained in every part of the image

We can thus conclude that a successful venture is a hologram created by interactions of holons, in which:

1. *Each part contains the whole*
2. *Each part can recreate the whole*

A business is a whole, holon and hologram.

You are not a drop of water in the ocean.
You are the entire ocean in a drop.
– **Rumi**

Task Significance and Performance

Adam Grant
Author of "Give and Take: Why Helping Others Drives Our Success"

Renowned Wharton professor Adam Grant, author of *Give and Take: Why Helping Others Drives Our Success* (2013), has done a compelling series of experiments demonstrating the importance of "task significance" on motivation and job performance. *Task significance* is defined as "the extent of the importance of an identifiable piece of work to others within and outside of the organization." Task significance is a result of a person's awareness and understanding of the extent to which the results of their activities affect other people within or outside their organization.

In a typical experiment, Grant will divide members of a team (such as fundraising callers) into several different groupings. One group is given information, through written, video or in-person testimonials, about how performing their job has made a positive difference in others people's lives. A second group is informed by others who have done the same job about the personal benefits that performing the job could make in their own lives; such as using the knowledge and skills that they gain in order to build successful careers. The third group receives no information regarding task significance, but instead may be given skill training or the promise of a bonus for good performance.

"Task significance" has to do with the perception that one's work and actions affect others in an important and meaningful way.

The results of Grant's experiments have significant implications for both managers and entrepreneurs. According to his studies, the first group that receives information about how performing their job makes a difference in the lives of others (typically their customers) frequently almost double their level of performance. One group of fundraising callers, for instance, spent 142 percent more time on the phone and brought in 171 percent more revenue in the months after they understood the benefits of their activities on others.

There are many things in life that catch your eye, but only a few will catch your heart . . . pursue those.
– **Michael Nolan**

In comparison, the group that is informed about the personal benefits that performing the job could make in their own lives generally makes only a small improvement in their performance. The third group that receives no information regarding task significance also makes little to no significant performance improvements.

In another experiment, Grant put up two signs over handwashing stations in a hospital. The first one read: "Hand hygiene prevents you from catching diseases"; while the other read, "Hand hygiene prevents patients from catching diseases." He assessed the effect of the signs simply by recording the amount of soap used. The sign pointing out the benefit to patients increased soap and gel usage by more than 45%, and handwashing behavior by more than 10% compared to the sign stating the benefit to oneself.

Grant's experiments clearly distinguish between motivations related to what I referred to as "ego" and "soul" in the previous volume of *Success Factor Modeling* (pp. 24-27), summarized in the Introduction to this volume on pages 8 and 9. The obvious implication of these experiments is that our sense of connection of our activities to a larger mission and purpose that serves others is a powerful motivator. Meaningful activity connects us to our sense of service and our "soul."

As with resonance, synergy and emergence, the perception of task significance can relate to different levels of success factors; ie., environment, behaviors, capabilities, beliefs and values, identity and purpose.

Knowing that their work has a positive impact on others increases people's level of energy an effort.

The perception of task significance has a marked influence on motivation and performance.

Allegory of the Stoneworkers

In *Success Factor Modeling Volume I* (pg. 20) I presented the analogy of the stoneworkers that I frequently use to illustrate our degree or connection with our projects and ventures on different levels:

The allegory focuses on six individuals whose work ranges from poor to excellent as does their level of satisfaction. As they work, the lowest performing and least satisfied worker is asked, "What are you doing?"

Looking at the clock, he grumbles, "I am waiting for my time here to be through so I can go home and do something I care about."

The next stone-worker, who performs a little better and is not so completely bored, is asked, "What are you doing?" He looks up from his task. "What does it look like I'm doing. I am hitting a rock," he answers, slightly annoyed.

The next stone-worker, who does average work and is somewhat more engaged in what he is doing, is asked, "What are you doing?" "I am using my skills to craft this block of stone," is his matter-of-fact reply.

The fourth stone-worker, who is quite motivated and doing decent work, is asked, "What are you doing?" He responds with determination, "I am earning a living to support my family and put my children through school. That's what I am doing."

The fifth stone-worker, who is not only doing excellent work but also looking over the others to be sure that their work is adequate, is asked, "What are you doing?" "I am a master stone mason and I am building a cathedral," he responds with enthusiasm.

The sixth and most accomplished stone-worker is completely involved and present in each movement he makes. He constantly surveys the work of the others and does his best to keep them focused and interested as well. When asked, "What are you doing?" he says with deep reverence, "I am creating a sacred space to help people to connect with their souls."

Clearly, the sixth stoneworker expresses the greatest sense of task significance and larger purpose.

The allegory of the stoneworkers illustrates the impact of the the perception of successively greater degrees of task significance.

A society grows great when old men plant trees in whose shade they know they shall never sit.
— **Greek Proverb**

THE ALLEGORY OF
THE SIX STONE-WORKERS
SIX STONE-WORKERS
WITH DIFFERENT MOTIVATIONS
ARE ASKED THE SAME QUESTION:
"WHAT ARE YOU DOING?"
I AM WAITING TO BE THROUGH SO I CAN GO HOME AND DO SOMETHING I CARE ABOUT
WHAT DOES IT LOOK LIKE I'M DOING? I AM HITTING A ROCK!
I AM USING MY SKILLS TO CRAFT THIS BLOCK OF STONE.
I AM EARNING A LIVING TO SUPPORT MY FAMILY AND PUT MY CHILDREN THROUGH SCHOOL.
I AM A MASTER STONE MASON AND I AM BUILDING A CATHEDRAL.
I AM CREATING A SACRED SPACE TO HELP PEOPLE TO CONNECT WITH THEIR SOULS.
ANTONIO MEZA
ENVIRONMENT
BEHAVIOR
CAPABILITIES
VALUES & BELIEFS
IDENTITY
PURPOSE

Benefits and Applications of Collective Intelligence

There are a number of significant benefits of nurturing collective intelligence in groups including: enhanced performance, wiser decisions, new ideas and more creative solutions.

Collective intelligence arises out of groups who share a strong sense of task significance and purpose. The people within these groups possess a perception of a mutual mission in service of a common vision of benefitting others. The conditions for creating collective intelligence are open communication, mutual trust and respect, curiosity and the commitment to something larger than oneself. To become generative, collective intelligence also requires a certain amount of time for people to dream together as well as work on existing projects. This underscores the importance of the *creative unconscious* in synergy and emergence. All of these factors together produce a greatly increased level of motivation, performance and sense of satisfaction.

Some of the other benefits of collective intelligence include:

- Supporting the healthy functioning of groups and communities
- Sustaining and revitalizing teams and organizations
- Increasing innovation, productivity and profit for companies
- Resolving conflicts and social and environmental problems
- Bringing breakthroughs, insights and inspiration to individuals and groups
- Evoking significant transpersonal experiences such as cohesion, trust and team spirit
- Sensing emerging futures and predicting events better than individual experts
- Facilitating the emergence of new social forms, functions and capabilities

We can summarize these benefits as four fundamental *outcomes* to which collective intelligence may be directed:

1. Enhanced Performance
2. Wiser Decisions
3. New Ideas
4. Creative Solutions

Collective intelligence requires individuals to engage in open and meaningful dialogue and discussion; therefore group members must develop the capacity to engage in clear and transparent communication in order to develop shared meaning and common understanding. In organizational interactions, collective intelligence manifests itself in several different fundamental forms including:

- *Sharing* – exchanging information and ideas and finding resonance
- *Swarming* – directing and synergizing knowledge and action toward a particular problem or outcome
- *Flocking* – joining together to provide mutual support and generate solutions

In organizational interactions, collective intelligence manifests itself in several different fundamental forms including: sharing, swarming and flocking.

Success Factor Modeling Volume I provided some practical examples of these different forms of collective intelligence. Steve Jobs' description of "moving ideas around" his group of 100 people at Apple, "seeing what different people think" and "getting people talking about it" (p. 266) is a classic expression of the process of *sharing*. Former IBM CEO Samuel Palmisano's "values jam", involving all employees for 72 hours to determine what IBM's values should be in order to reach its new vision and mission (p. 118), is a demonstration of *swarming*. The example of the pilot, crew and passengers cooperating together and supporting each other to deal with their dangerous situation when their airliner lost both engines in the "Miracle on the Hudson" incident (pp. 30-31) is a good illustration of *flocking*.

Sharing encourages and promotes the discovery and development of *resonance* between group members. *Swarming* synergizes complementary skills and actions towards a common goal or intention. *Flocking* produces the possibility of the *emergence* of unique and unpredictable behaviors and ideas.

In entrepreneurial ventures, these processes for fostering collective intelligence are frequently applied toward the actions of:

- *Benchmarking* – setting standards
- *Best Practices* – sharing successful strategies for reaching key objectives
- *Brainstorming* – imagining innovative options
- *Generative Collaboration* – co-creating something unique

Collective intelligence is fostered in entrepreneurial ventures through benchmarking, sharing best practices, brainstorming and generative collaboration.

The SFM Collective Intelligence Model™

Benchmarking

Best Practices

Brainstorming

Generative Collaboration

The SFM Collective Intelligence Model summarizes the relationships between the fundamental processes, actions and outcomes associated with applying collective intelligence in an entrepreneurial venture.

We can summarize these fundamental elements of promoting collective intelligence in the following SFM Collective Intelligence Model.

According to the model:

- The actions of *benchmarking* and exchanging *best practices* produce the outcome of *enhanced group performance.*
- *Brainstorming* and *generative collaboration* spark *new ideas.*
- *Benchmarking* and *brainstorming* create the conditions for making *wise decisions.*
- The exchange of *best practices* combined with *generative collaboration* gives rise to *creative solutions.*

All of these actions and outcomes are supported by the fundamental processes of:

1. *sharing* information and ideas, and finding *resonance.*
2. *swarming*, by directing multiple complementary perspectives and knowhow toward a common goal or problem, creating *synergy.*
3. *flocking*, through gathering and aligning diverse skills and resources in the service of a common purpose, fostering cohesion and creating the possibility for the *emergence of something new*

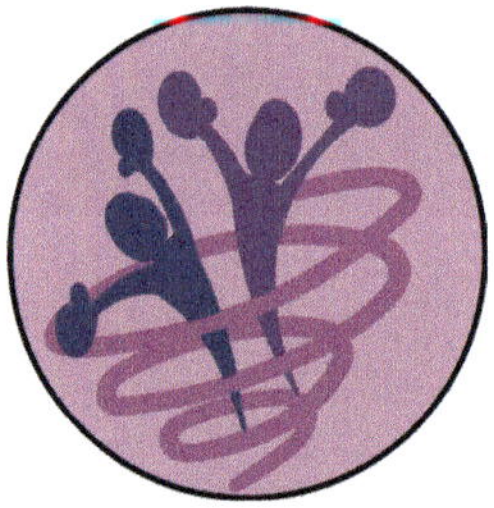

Resonance, Synergy and Emergence

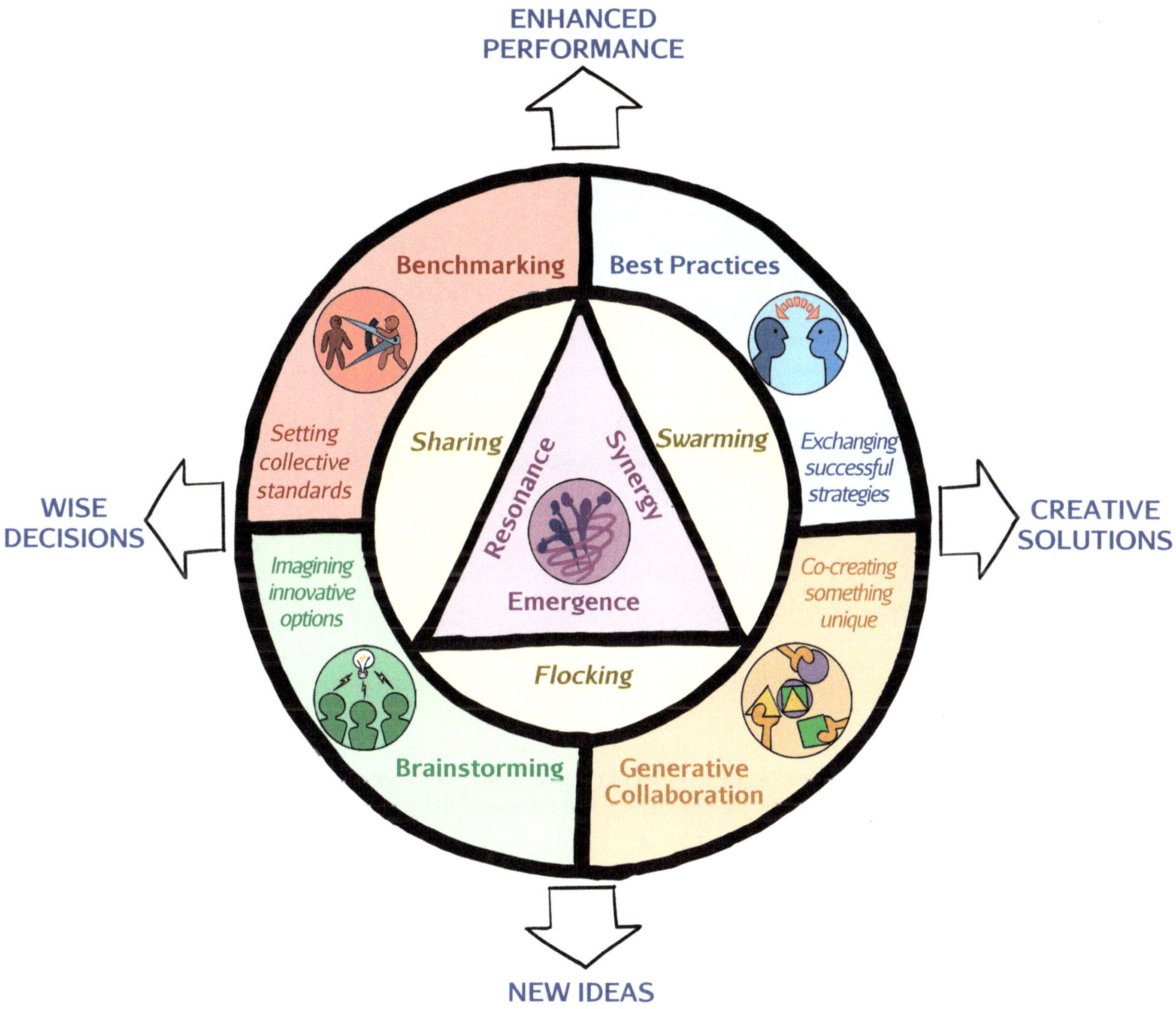

SFM Collective Intelligence Model™

The processes, actions and outcomes defined by the SFM Collective Intelligence Model can be applied to amplify the effectiveness of your Circle of Success.

Integrating the SFM Collective Model and the Circle of Success

The processes described by the SFM Collective Intelligence Model can greatly augment your Circle of Success. While the entire SFM Collective Intelligence Model can be applied to any part of the Circle of Success, there are some particularly important links. For instance:

- *Enhanced performance* contributes substantially to *financial robustness.*
- *Creative solutions* greatly support *scalable growth.*
- *New ideas* are necessary for *innovation and resilience.*
- *Wiser decisions* foster more *meaningful contributions.*

Similarly the actions associated with promoting collective intelligence significantly strengthen those associated with the Circle of Success. Exchanging successful strategies through best practices, for instance, helps to expand the venture and create value. Setting collective standards through benchmarking is important for accelerating the development of a high quality product or service. Imagining possible options by brainstorming is necessary for increasing competency. Co-creating something unique through generative collaboration is the foundation for enhancing and leveraging resources.

In the coming chapters we will be exploring how to put these processes and applications of collective intelligence into ongoing practice in order to increase the chance of success for your project or venture.

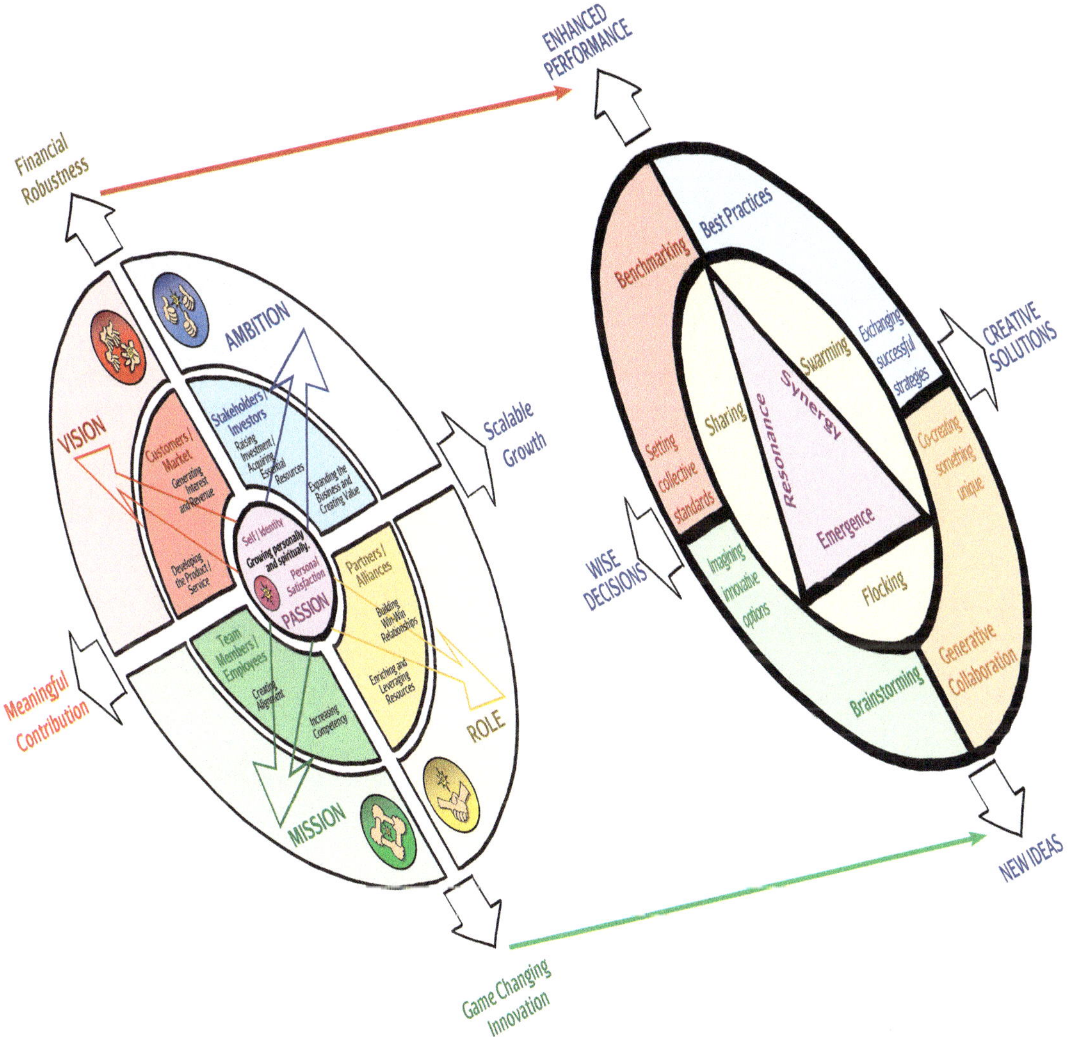

The SFM Collective Intelligence Model can be used to enhance your Circle of Success.

Mastermind Groups — An Example of Applied Collective Intelligence

A Mastermind group is a good example of applying the pinciples of collective intelligence to entrepreneurial activities.

Mastermind groups offer a combination of brainstorming, education, peer accountability and support in a group setting in order to sharpen each member's business and personal skills.

The "Mastermind" is the collective intelligence of the whole group

A good illustration of how collective intelligence can be applied to entrepreneurial endeavors are Mastermind Groups. The concept of a *Mastermind Group* was initially formulated by author Napoleon Hill in his bestselling book *Think And Grow Rich* (1937). In the book, Hill defined the *Mastermind principle* as, "The coordination of knowledge and effort of two or more people, who work toward a definite purpose, in the spirit of harmony."

According to Hill's principle, the so-called "mastermind" is not any particular individual (such as a cult leader, guru or criminal genius), but rather the collective intelligence of the whole group. Intuitively applying the notion of "holon" and the principle of "emergence" that we have introduced in this chapter, Hill points out in his book that "No two minds ever come together without thereby creating a third, invisible intangible force, which may be likened to a third mind." This "third mind" is the "Mastermind." As I have stated, when people work creatively together toward a larger common cause, 1 + 1 = 3.

In a Mastermind Group, the agenda belongs to the group, and each person's participation is essential. Group members give each other feedback, help each other to brainstorm new possibilities, and set up accountability structures that keep one another focused and on track. The Mastermind process creates a community of supportive colleagues who collaborate to move each member of the group to new levels of success in both their personal and professional lives.

In order to create the proper degree of collective intelligence, there is combination of passion, commitment, and accountability that participants must bring to a Mastermind Group. One of the key benefits of Mastermind Groups is that participants raise the bar for one another by challenging each other to set and implement new goals, brainstorm bigger ideas, and then supporting each other with total honesty, respect and compassion. Mastermind participants act as catalysts for growth, constructive critics and supportive colleagues. Thus, Mastermind groups offer a combination of brainstorming, education, peer accountability and support in a group setting in order to sharpen each member's business and personal skills. In other words, it is a practical application of *sharing* (exchanging ideas and brainstorming), *swarming* (directing the combined knowledge of the group toward reaching goals or solving problems) and *flocking* (joining together to provide mutual support).

Mastermind groups are a great example of building powerful partnerships – one of the essential elements of creating an effective Circle of Success.

How does a Mastermind Group work?

A Mastermind Group is not a class, a coaching group or a networking group. It is more like a peer advisory board. The typical term for a Mastermind Group is a year. During that period, a group of ambitious and intelligent people meet monthly, weekly and even daily if it makes sense, in order to tackle challenges and problems together. They support each other, give advice, share connections and may do business with each other when appropriate. It is essentially a powerful form of peer-to-peer mentoring. The goal is for each member to see a marked change in themselves, their lives and their businesses.

Mastermind groups are a powerful form of peer-to-peer mentoring.

Mastermind Groups can meet in person, on the telephone, through webconferencing or via online social media tools such as Google Hangout, Facebook groups, etc. Frequently, Mastermind Groups use some combination of these modalities. Participants support each other to set challenging and meaningful goals, and more importantly, to accomplish them. To be successful, the group requires commitment, confidentiality and the willingness to both give and receive advice and ideas. It works best with highly-motivated people who are willing to ask for – and give – help and support, and who are prepared to show up and fully participate in Mastermind meetings. Thus, Mastermind Groups work best with people who:

Mastermind group participants support each other to set challenging and meaningful goals and to accomplish them.

- Have a similar interest (such as a group for entrepreneurs, first-time authors, CEOs, real estate investors, Internet businesses or a group for people in a certain corporation or industry).
- Have comparable levels of skill and/or success; although it is better when participants have different backgrounds and skillsets in order to create enough diversity and complementarity of ideas and resources.
- Have the desire and motivation to move to a new level of achievement in their professional and personal lives, and are willing to work on themselves in order to accomplish it.
- Want a supportive team of partners.
- Are committed to reach or exceed their goals.

To be successful, the group requires commitment, confidentiality and the willingness to both give and receive advice and ideas.

Key to the effective functioning of a Mastermind Group is a facilitator or facilitator team. The role of a Mastermind Group Facilitator is distinct from an instructor, coach or team leader. Mastermind group facilitation has its own set of skills and methods, different from teaching adults or working with a corporate team to implement a single, common objective. The job of a Mastermind Facilitator is to create trust and rapport in the group, help the members coach and advise each other, assist participants in creating powerful goals, and hold members accountable to their commitments. During Mastermind Group meetings, facilitators provide focus, guide the group to deeper levels of discussion, monitor the group's energy level and manage any problems that arise among participants that threaten the harmony of the group.

When organized properly, Mastermind Groups can produce many benefits for their members including:

1. New answers and ideas, which emerge from brainstorming with the group
2. Access to the experience and skills of successful people
3. Increased confidence in decision making
4. Greater accountability to make progress in important professional and personal goals
5. An instant and valuable support network
6. Enhanced motivation coming from a sense of shared purpose
7. A more focused, enriched and positive mental attitude

Mastermind Benefits

The Successful Genius and Conscious Leadership Mastermind Grroups

In the summer of 2013, I established the Successful Genius Mastermind with my colleagues Mitchell Stevko (a Silicon Valley growth expert who has helped over 150 entrepreneurs achieve their dreams, raising over $5 billion in capital) and Dr. Olga Stevko (a Russian MD and Belief Medicine expert who specializes working with high level professionals). The *Successful Genius Mastermind* is organized around my applications of Success Factor Modeling; in particular my studies of successful next generation entrepreneurs and of well known geniuses, such as Mozart, Einstein, Walt Disney, Leonardo da Vinci and others. Based in the San Francisco Bay Area, it is a year-long program that includes three live mastermind meetings, monthly live webinars, monthly live small groups, and both in person and virtual support from our facilitator team.

The Successful Genius Mastermind group is organized around the application of Success Factor Modeling.

A product of the generative collaboration between myself and my two partners, the Successful Genius Mastermind is an exclusive, accelerated growth program for accomplished entrepreneurs and business owners. Current members include influential leaders from a variety of fields who have positively impacted the lives of hundreds of millions of people. The group is composed of highly successful people from different backgrounds including technology, psychology, medicine, education, nutrition, finance and management. For example, Barney Pell, one of the fathers of "conversational computing" and founder of Powerset, who was profiled in the first volume of this series (pp. 102-115), is one of the group members; as is John Gray, author of the international bestselling book *Men are from Mars, Women are from Venus.*

The group is composed of highly successful people from different backgrounds who have already succeeded in some area of their lives and careers and want to move to another level or build a new carreer platform.

All of the people in the Successful Genius Mastermind are individuals who have already succeeded in some area of their lives and careers and want to move to another level or build a new carreer platform. They are also interested in growing personally. Another common characteristic of all the Successful Genius Mastermind members is that they are "heart-based," conscious leaders who possess emotional and relational intelligence. They are all excellent examples of what I defined as "next generation entrepreneurs" in *Success Factor Modeling Volume I.* They are committed to living their dreams more fully and making a better world through their business ventures.

Group members support each other to apply the principles and distinctions of Success Factor Modeling and build a robust Circle of Success that will accellerate their growth and increase their impact.

A unique feature of the Successful Genius Mastermind is the introduction of specific thinking processes and practices that I have modeled from some of the world's most successful people. In addition to the typical Mastermind methods, Successful Genius Mastermind group members are coached to apply these processes in order to build a powerful Circle of Success that will accelerate their growth and increase their impact. This provides participants with a clear roadmap and a tremendous competitive advantage for achieving enhanced efficiency and greater potential for achievement.

The Successful Genius Mastermind explores fundamental strategies for success.

My Successful Genius Mastermind co-founders and I have found that there are seven fundamental strategies that creative and successful people use to create a potent Circle of Success. These seven strategies can be summarized as:

1. Master an Optimal Mindset
2. Create a Clear and Compelling Future
3. Establish a Critical Path to that Future
4. Achieve Internal Alignment
5. Build Powerful Partnerships
6. Effectively Transform Obstacles
7. Make Dynamic Course Corrections

We have found that the majority of individuals, including people who have already reached some degree of success, are only using one or two of the Seven Strategies of Successful Genius on a regular basis. In order to move to a next level of success and a higher degree of satisfaction, people need to consistently and effectively apply all of these strategies.

The goal of the Successful Genius Mastermind is to support participants to develop these strategies fully and thoroughly by exploring and practicing them as a group. Working together, members share best practices relating to these strategies and help one another to creatively and concretely implement them. As a result, many group members have been able to make 10 to 100 times return on their investment. Author John Gray, for example, reported, "After the first weekend group meeting, I got such clarity and energy and even inspiration. I finished the book I'd been working on for two years in just 30 days."

According to Barney Pell, "I'm a visionary and the Mastermind gave me some new frameworks to think about my vision, build some of the abilities I already have, and develp a new language and tools to be able to teach and lead others."

Many of the powerful processes that we apply to develop these strategies in the Successful Genius Mastermind will be touched upon to some degree in the course of this book.

At the time of the writing of this book, my colleagues and I decided to expand and evolve the Successful Genius Mastermind to a Conscious Leaders Mastermind. We define a *Conscious Leader* as "someone who aspires to exist in a state of centered presence, accessing multiple intelligences and living their highest values in service to a larger purpose to the benefit of all stakeholders." Conscious leadership involves being:

- Authentic
- Emotionally intelligent
- Purposive
- Responsible

The Conscious Leaders Mastermind builds upon the seven strategies of successful genius to include the practices of conscious leadership.

The Conscious Leaders Mastermind* builds on the Seven Strategies of Successful Genius and adds other important practices such as:

1. Formulating and and communicating a clear and meaningful vision for the future.
2. Maintining a focus on higher purpose.
3. Influencing through inspiration.
4. Balancing self-interest and the common good, in themselves and others.
5. Respecting and integrating multiple perspectives.
6. Practicing congruence – leading by example (walking your talk).
7. Exercising mindful self-leadership and reflecting thoughtfully on the lessons gained from experience.

Conscious leadership involves building your venture from a state of centered presence, accessing multiple intelligences and living your highest values in service to a larger purpose to the benefit of all stakeholders.

Conscious leadership is also a primary topic of the next volume of Success Factor Modeling which is titled *Conscious Leadership and Resilience*.

Conscious leadership is a primary topic of Success Factor Modeling Volume III.

* For more information on the Conscious Leaders Mastermind, see: http://www.consciousleadersmm.com.

SFM Collaboration Catalysts

Collaboration catalysts are processes that stimulate and reinforce effective collaboration and collective intelligence by producing some degree of resonance, synergy and/or emergence between members of a group.

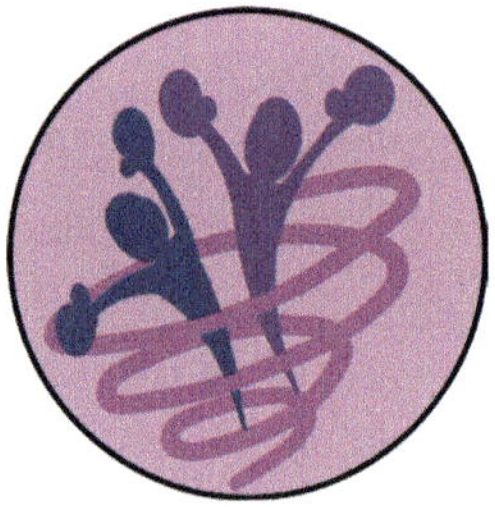

One of the primary processes I use to facilitate groups such as the Successful Genius and Conscious Leaders Masterminds is what my brother John and I have termed "collaboration catalysts." *Collaboration catalysts* are processes that have the purpose of stimulating and reinforcing effective collaboration and collective intelligence. The goal of collaboration catalysts is to produce some degree of resonance, synergy and/or emergence between members of a group who are working together in some way.

The collaboration catalysts described in this book can also help to increase your "luck factor" (see Chapter 3 of *Success Factor Modeling Volume 1* – pp. 150-155) with respect to a project or venture by supporting you to:

- Create a *network of luck* – i.e., people who can support you and let you know about new opportunities.
- Pick up subtle clues or *weak signals* that provide information about *future trends* (i.e., "where the puck is going to be").
- Encourage positive outcomes from those with whom you interact.
- Maintain a positive outlook and deal with challenges and adversity by expecting and working toward a positive outcome and finding something positive in any situation as opposed to dwelling on the negative.

Some collaboration catalysts are more relevant for certain parts of the Circle of Success, while others can be applied effectively to any of the quadrants. Certain collaboration catalysts are also more suited for particular phases of a collaborative endeavor. I encourage you to experiment with them and find the ones that work best for you and your venture.

Let's begin with a couple of collaboration catalysts that can help to build and reinforce a profound quality of resonance in a group or team.

SFM Collaboration Catalyst: Creating a "COACH Container"

My work with Success Factor Modeling demonstrates that the first and most significant factor in achieving success is mastering an optimal mindset. In *Success Factor Modeling Volume I* we began to put into practice what I called the COACH state (p.34). I have also summarized this state in the Introduction to this volume (p. 15). The COACH state is the basis of a successful mindset. The *COACH state* is essentially an internal state of presence, resourcefulness, curiosity and receptivity. The letters COACH stand for being centered, open, alert and aware, connected (to oneself and others) and holding whatever is happening from a state of resourceful curiosity.

The reason for putting ourselves into the COACH state is to "open our channel," as it were, and connect to the experience of being both an individual whole and part of something bigger than ourselves that gives us purpose and energy. Achieving and maintaining this state is the foundation for any successful performance. Making the COACH state one's baseline performance state is the first goal for participants of my Successful Genius Mastermind group.

A good analogy for entering the COACH state is putting an iPad or smartphone "online" and connected to a wireless network of some sort. This gives the device access to the "cloud" which makes it a type of "holon" in that it is connected to a larger field of "collective intelligence." When online and connected to the cloud, a tablet or smartphone can receive information about real time events from other parts of the world. It can even download new apps that expand its versatility and performance. It can also transmit information to other devices and the cloud through the wireless network. Once in the cloud, that information and knowledge can be accessed and utilized by many other devices.

Entering the COACH state is like putting an iPad or smartphone "online" and connecting it to the "cloud" and a larger field of "collective intelligence."

If our tablet or smartphone is "offline," however, it is limited only to previously existing data and applications that are currently in its memory.

Our nervous systems are in some ways like these devices. Our nerve cells form a type of circuitry that runs various programs or applications. In the COACH state we have full access to all of our applications and data, and we are online and have the potential to connect to the "cloud" of knowledge in the field of collective intelligence around us. In other states, we have more limited access to our own resources and to the knowledge and ideas coming from others. In the CRASH state, for instance, where we are contracted, reactive, stuck in our own analysis paralysis, separated and hurting, we have access to only a small portion of out own intelligence and resources.

Going "Online" Together

Thus, one simple and potentially very powerful collaboration catalyst is to create what can be called a "COACH Container." A *COACH Container* is a type of relational field or group rapport that emerges when all members of a group are simultaneously in the COACH state. When all of the members of a group are "online" together, it greatly enhances the potential for resonance between them at all of the various levels of success factors.

A "COACH Container" is a type of relational field or group rapport that emerges when all members of a group are simultaneously in the COACH state.

The following practice is a way to bring the qualities of the COACH state into an interaction or conversation between collaborators. It is a powerful way to begin a meeting or interactive session of practically any type. The purpose of this practice is to ensure that all participants begin their interaction from the best version of themselves, in order to get the most from the interaction. Just as athletes have warm-up practices that allow them to be the best of themselves – both as individuals and members of a team – during competition or practice, the COACH Container prepares participants in a group to get the best from one another.

1. Sit or stand facing each other in an aligned and balanced posture with both feet flat on the floor and your spine erect but relaxed (i.e., "in your vertical axis").
2. Take a minute or two to intentionally enter the COACH state together. This can be done by silently going through the following steps:

    a) Bring your attention to your belly center (just below the naval and in the physical center of your body) and breathe into it.

    b) Breathe into your chest and open your attention to include your whole body and your surroundings.

    c) Become aware of the three-dimensional volume of your body; then continue to expand your awareness to include the space below your feet, above your head, behind you, in front of you, to your left and to your right.

    d) Experience a sense of connection inwardly (being sure to include your head, heart, belly and feet) and outwardly (to the Earth through your feet, to the cosmos through the top of your head, and to the environment around you) so that you feel both being whole and part of something larger than you.

    e) Imagine projecting a sense of calm, confidence and curiosity into the space (holding environment) you sense around you.

3. As each group member senses that he or she is fully present and in his or her COACH state he or she says aloud to the others, "I am here" (as in a roll call) or "I am ready."
4. A nice additional step is for group members to look around the group and, as they make eye contact with one another, say aloud to each other, "I see you."

Collectively entering the COACH state can create a strong and rich sense of interconnection and resourcefulness.

When done with authenticity and presence, this simple process can create a strong and rich sense of mutual rapport and resourcefulness. This is what we call the relational field or "container."

I myself, routinely start all my seminars, Mastermind Groups, coaching sessions and meetings – both in person and virtual – with some version of this practice. I have done this all over the world with people of many different types and backgrounds. It creates a much smoother, more focused and higher quality interaction. Obviously, in webinars and teleconferences where people do not have visual contact with one another, the 4th step needs to be modified. For instance, people can instead say something like, "It is good to be here."

Of course, it also helps if people already know what the COACH state is and have experienced or practiced it before. If not, however, it does not take much time to simply explain the state and the reasons for doing the practice and then verbally walking through the various steps of getting into the state.

Beginning a meeting or interaction in a resourceful state and positive mindset saves a lot of wasted time, unnecessary inefficiency and potential conflict. It also greatly enhances the potential for synergy and emergence. Returning to this collaboration catalyst regularly during an extended interaction (such as workshop or coaching session) can also be very helpful. In fact, I encourage groups to collectively create a movement, verbalization, symbol, or some other type of signal or "anchor" that they can use to return to the experience of the COACH Container more quickly. Sports teams, for example, will often go through a brief ritual or cheer before starting a game to bring all of the players into a collective "zone of excellence."

A collective movement or gesture can be used by a group as an "anchor" to quickly return to a resourceful state.

SFM Collaboration Catalyst: Multi-Level Introductions

Multi-Level Introductions give group members an opportunity to share something about their background and their goals on several different levels before engaging in a collaborative interaction.

Another simple example of a collaboration catalyst is what I call "multi-level introductions." It is most useful for people who are meeting in a group for the first time. The purpose of this activity is to give group members an opportunity to share a little about their background and their goals on several different levels before engaging in a collaborative interaction. The process encourages the possibility of quickly finding resonance at deeper levels of success factors beyond the surface layers of environment, behavior and capabilities.

The process essentially involves each group member answering five questions related to the various levels of success factors: environment, behavior, capabilities, beliefs and values, identity and purpose. The multi-level introduction process involves each person giving his or her answer to the following questions:

1. *Where are you from?* (Environment)
2. *What do you do?* (Behavior)
3. *How would you like to improve or enrich your skills or capabilities as a result of the collaboration?* (Capabilities)
4. *Why would you like to improve or enrich those skills or capabilities? What are the personal values and beliefs they represent?* (Values and Beliefs)
5. *What is your mission and your role? What is a metaphor or symbol for who you are?* (Identity and Purpose)

While some of the information may initially feel a little risky for some people to provide, I have found that this process helps people to reach a level of mutual trust and intimacy more quickly. It also helps people to identify commonalities on levels that they might normally address in a typical interaction.

Multi-level introductions are something that would generally be done with people who do not know each other as a form of building rapport. It can, however, still be quite useful for groups where people already know one another as a means of clarifying their intentions for a particular interaction. In this case, questions 3-5 would be the most important.

Multi-Level Introductions help group members to discover resonance at several levels of success factors.

SFM Collaboration Catalyst: Setting Intention

Intentions are what we want or hope to accomplish through a particular activity.

The word "intention" is derived from the Latin *intendre*, which literally means "to stretch out" or "extend." *Intention* is typically defined as "the purpose, end or aim toward which thoughts are directed"; or "an anticipated outcome that guides your planned actions." It is also used to mean "a determination to act in a certain way." Thus, intentions are what we want or hope to accomplish through some activity.

A person with the intention "to help," for instance, may not know exactly what he or she is going to do or will need to do, but is ready and willing to engage in any number of specific actions which may satisfy that general intention. The intention to "bring positive energy" or to "stay centered" can have many different specific expressions. From this perspective, an intention is a type of filter that directs our attention and brings certain skills and actions into the foreground.

Setting intention at the beginning of a meeting or group interaction can be another powerful form of collaboration catalyst.

Having group members set their intention at the beginning of a meeting or interaction can be another effective collaboration catalyst.

Similar to one's passion, vision, mission, ambition and rol, intentions can be expressed in multiple ways (see *Success Factor Modeling Volume I*, pp. 178-179):

- *Verbal* (positive, succinct: 5 words or less, resonant)
- *Visual* (color images, either literal or symbolic)
- *Somatic* expression (show posture and movement that represents goal/ intention)

Expressing Intentions

In my MasterMind groups and Success Factor Modeling seminars, we begin each session or meeting with the same ritual. Each group member takes a few minutes and shares their answers to the following questions:

1. What has been your average COACH state (on a scale of 0 – 10) since our last meeting?
2. What have been your most important accomplishments or "wins" since out last meeting?
3. What have been your biggest challenges?
4. What is your intention for this meeting and for the time until the next meeting?

In some of my MasterMind meetings and Success Factor Modeling seminars, I will then ask people to get into a group of four and help each other define their longer-term intention more explicitly. Each person takes the role of being the speaker. The others take the position of A, B or C.

- Person A helps the speaker to explore the question: "What 5-7 key words would you use to express your intention?"
- Person B helps the speaker to explore: "What image, either literal or symbolic, represents your intention?"
- Person C helps the speaker to exlpore: "How could you express your intention in a gesture or movement with your body?"

Defining one's own intention and helping other group members to define theirs prepares everyone in the group to give and receive the most they can from the interaction.

It is important to represent one's goal or intention in a variety of ways

SFM Collaboration Catalyst: Fostering a "Field" of Co-Sponsorship

Essential to collective intelligence is the creation of a relational "field" built on trust, mutual respect and the recognition of each group member's unique resources and contributions. This is what we referred to as "sponsorship" in *Success Factor Modeling Volume I* (pp. 144-145).

Transformational teacher Richard Moss claims that "the greatest gift we can give to ourselves or another person is the quality of our attention." Sponsorship involves seeing, sensing and affirming positive qualities potential in others. Truly generative collaboration requires mutual sponsorship between all group members. One way to encourage mutual sponsorship among a group of people is to have them practice looking for and acknowledging what they perceive and appreciate about one another. When group members are able to give this quality of attention to one another, it can create a very deep and powerful form of resonance between them.

The following process, initially developed by my colleague, NLP trainer Robert McDonald, encourages people to sponsor each other by having them focus on what they perceive and authentically like about one another.

Group members take turns being Person A – the person to be focused on by the rest of the group. It is important that each person volunteers only when they feel ready to be the focus.

Person A states his or her intention to the group. Starting to Person A's left and going clockwise around the group, each member of the group is to comment on one thing that he or she physically observes and likes about Person A, and something he or she intuitively senses and likes about person A. "Observing" is based on our literal sensory-based perceptions of another person's behavior. "Sensing" is a somatic, intuitive impression about the deeper essence of the other person.

Each group member is to use the following format:

"I observe that you ______________________________.
And I like it."

"I sense that you _________________________________.
And I like it."

This process is repeated until everyone in the group has the opportunity to be Person A and receive these comments from all of the other group members.

Whether I am working with a group of entrepreneurs exploring partnership opportunities, the executive committee of a large organization or a simple team meeting, I often like to begin with this exercise. I don't always ask people to take the time to speak out loud. Often simply looking at one another from a sponsoring perspective is enough to catalyze the beginning of a felt sense of rapport and positive resonance.

Fostering a "field" of sponsorship involves having group members focus on what they perceive and authentically like about one another.

SFM Collaboration Catalyst: Exploring and Sharing Best Practices through Success Factor Modeling

The process of Success Factor Modeling can be used as a collaboration catalyst for both Benchmarking and exchanging Best Practices.

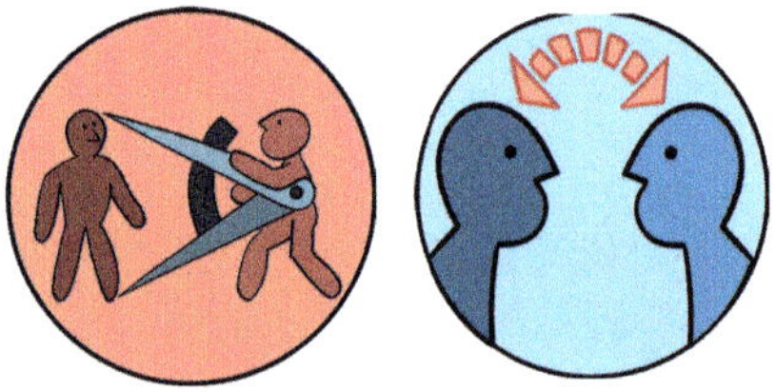

Group members share examples of past successes relating to a particular topic and then make a "Success Storyboard," defining the critical path of common key steps, involving both mindset and actions, that successfully created the desired outcomes.

As I mentioned earlier, some of the primary manifestations of collective intelligence in organizations occur in the form of *sharing* – exchanging information and ideas and finding resonance – and *swarming* – directing and synergizing knowledge and action toward a particular problem or outcome. These two processes may be combined to achieve both effective *Benchmarking* – setting standards – and *Best Practices* – sharing effective strategies for reaching key objectives.

In my MasterMind group and Success Factor Modeling coaching and training sessions, we apply the process of Success Factor Modeling as a collaboration catalyst for both Benchmarking and Best Practices. The group will choose a topic, such as "effective decision making" or "hiring new team members," and then share successful examples relating to the common topic from their own experiences.

The sharing is best done in groups of 4-6 people, who compare their answers to the following questions:

1. What are the *outcomes* you were attempting to achieve?
2. What were the main *actions* necessary to achieve or create those outcomes?
3. What was the *mindset* that guided your actions in terms of your:
   - inner state
   - thinking process
   - values and beliefs

As group members share their own successful examples, they are asked to record common answers on a flipchart or large piece of paper.

When all members of the group have finished sharing their answers, the group is asked to make a "Success Storyboard," defining the critical path of key steps, involving both mindset and actions, that successfully creates the desired outcomes. To promote finding the most important common success factors, the group is limited to defining six key steps.

Here is an example on effective decision making from my Successful Genius MasterMind group:

SFM Example: MasterMinding Effective Decision Making

Outcomes:

- Ecological
- Win-Win
- Avoid Disaster

Actions:

- Project Scenarios – Act "As If"
- Consider Consequences –
  - *What is really important?*
  - *How and at what level does this affect my mission?*
- Take Multiple Perspectives
- Use Intuition Plus Reason

Mindset:

- Connection, Compassion, Clarity, Calm, Congruence
- Belief: *I am the recipient of the consequences.*

Steps:

1. Enter Optimal Decision Mindset
2. Take an "Observer" Position
3. Ask, "What is important?" and "At which level?"
4. Project Scenarios – Act "As If"
5. Questions – Multiple Perspectives
6. Evaluation – Rational and Intuitive

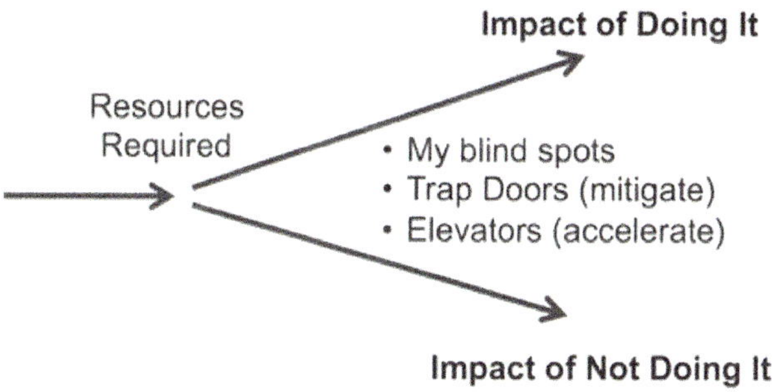

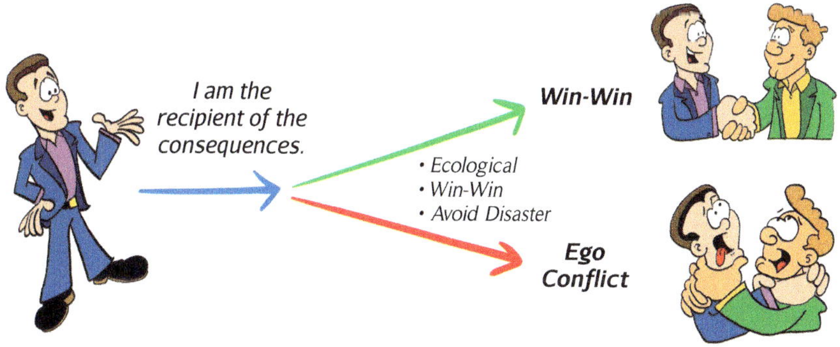

A preliminary "Success Storyboard" serves as a high-level summary that can form the basis for a more in-depth discussion that leads to more detailed practical applications.

This is clearly a very high-level summary of a much more rich and detailed discussion that may or may not be valuable to someone who was not in the modeling session. However, it leaves enough "tracks" for those involved in the exploration to reaccess and benefit from their shared learnings. It can also form the basis for a more in-depth shared model and some practical applications, such as the following process that came out of the MasterMinding session:

Think of a major decision you need to make for the coming year.

- What can you do to ensure that your *mindset* is connected, compassionate, clear, calm and congruent?
- What *beliefs* and *values* will support you to make the most ecological and beneficial decision?
- As you reflect on your vision and ambition for the year, what is most important to achieve and at which level?
- What possible *actions* can you take to accomplish what is most important?
- What *feedback* (both explicit and intuitive) will you use to know that the actions are taking you in the right direction?

In the coming chapters, we will revisit this type of SFM collaboration catalyst and show how it can be used to both enhance and harvest the collective intelligence of groups and teams.

As a support tool, I frequently use the following worksheets to help guide groups in their modeling of best practices.

Success Factor Modeling Worksheet

Outcomes

Which outcomes were the primary focus of your successful performance, project or venture?

List five or fewer outcomes.

1. ______________________________
2. ______________________________
3. ______________________________
4. ______________________________
5. ______________________________

Actions

What were the main actions you engaged in order to achieve those outcomes? List five or fewer actions.

1. ______________________________
2. ______________________________
3. ______________________________
4. ______________________________
5. ______________________________

Mindset

What were the key characteristics of mindset (i.e., inner state, attitude and thinking processes, values and beliefs, etc.) that supported taking the actions necessary to reach the outcomes.

List five or fewer key characteristics.

1. ______________________________

2. ______________________________

3. ______________________________

4. ______________________________

Which actions are most associated with creating or achieving which outcomes?

Which key characteristics of mindset are most associated with producing which actions?

Use the table on the following page to help organize what you have discovered.

Success Factor Modeling Table

Name:____________________________ Topic:____________________________

Outcomes	Actions	Mindset - Key Characteristics

Success Storyboard

Reflecting on the information you have gathered, define the critical path of key steps, involving both mindset and actions, that successfully creates the desired outcomes.

1. ______________________________

2. ______________________________

3. ______________________________

4. ______________________________

5. ______________________________

6. ______________________________

Chapter Summary

Successful entrepreneurs and business leaders are able to promote and leverage collective intelligence in order to share and leverage resources and to expand the business opportunities that are available to them—i.e., to make a "bigger pie" to share.

Collective intelligence is different than "collected" intelligence in that it creates a result that is greater than the sum of its parts. Not all interactions create collective intelligence. There are many examples of groups that do not display any increase of intelligence through the interactions of their individual members, but actually the opposite. Mobs and dysfunctional teams and families are examples of this. Collective intelligence requires open communication, mutual trust and respect, curiosity and the commitment to something larger than oneself.

Three processes that create the possibility of collective intelligence are resonance, synergy and emergence:

- *Resonance* refers to a type of mutual influence between systems or objects that are specially attuned to one another. Resonance has to do with the degree to which members of a group feel a sense of alignment or connection with other group members' ideas, values and qualities.
- *Synergy* occurs when two or more things function together to produce a result not independently obtainable. It is the ability of a group to produce a better result than if each person within the group were working toward the same goal individually; i.e., *1 + 1 = 3*. Synergy requires an exchange of energy in addition to an exchange of infomation in order to produce a result that includes and extends the capabilities of the contributing individuals.
- *Emergence* occurs when complex patterns arise out of a group of relatively simple interactions. Emergent qualities are those that are not directly traceable to the system's components, but rather to how those components interact; i.e., where the whole is greater than the sum of its parts. Breakthrough innovations, for instance, emerge as the consequence of combinations of seemingly unrelated or incompatible ideas or technologies.

A major part of this book is about how to create the conditions that produce these qualities in a group in order to produce collective intelligence.

The phenomena of holons and holograms are also important factors in creating collective intelligence. The term *holon* refers to the fact that each of us is a unique and separate whole, made up of other wholes (organs, cells, molecules, etc.) and simultaneously part of larger wholes (family, profession, community, culture, etc.). Collective intelligence is a result of our capacity to functions as a larger integrated holon.

Another key factor in creating collective intelligence has to do with holograms and holographic systems. A *hologram* is a three-dimensional image in which the whole picture is contained in every part of the image. As a phenomenon, the hologram has become a metaphor for the notion that, in many systems, all of the information relevant to that system is distributed through every part of the system in some form. Some level of holographic functioning is necessary for groups to produce collective intelligence. Key information, such as purpose, priorities and process must be shared by each individual in the group.

A certain degree of "task significance" is also important for creating collective intelligence. *Task significance* is defined as "the extent of the importance of an identifiable piece of work to others within and outside of the organization." Task significance is a result of a person's awareness and understanding of the extent to which the results of their activities affect other people within or outside their organization. Researchers such as Wharton's Adam Grant have demonstrated that a shared sense of task significance produce dramatic increases in performance of both individuals and groups.

In organizational interactions, collective intelligence manifests itself in several different fundamental forms including:

- *Sharing* – exchanging information and ideas and finding resonance
- *Swarming* – directing and synergizing knowledge and action toward a particular problem or outcome
- *Flocking* – joining together to provide mutual support and generate solutions

In entrepreneurial ventures, collective intelligence is frequently applied for the purposes of:

- Bench Marking – setting standards
- Best Practices – sharing effective strategies for reaching key objectives
- Brainstorming – generating ideas
- Generative Collaboration – creating something new

Mastermind groups are a good illustration of how these various aspects of collective intelligence can be applied to entrepreneurial endeavors. The term "Mastermind" refers to the collective intelligence of "two or more people, who work toward a definite purpose, in the spirit of harmony." A *Mastermind group* functions like a type of peer advisory board, offering a combination of brainstorming, education, peer accountability and support in a group setting in order to sharpen each member's business and personal skills. Mastermind groups meet monthly, weekly and even daily if it makes sense, in order to tackle challenges and problems together. They support each other, give advice, share connections and may do business with each other when appropriate with the goal to see a marked change in themselves, their lives and their businesses.

Rather than rely on an instructor, coach or team leader, Mastermind groups typically have a facilitator that helps the group engage in various types of collaboration catalysts. *Collaboration catalysts* are processes that stimulate and reinforce effective collaboration and collective intelligence. The goal of collaboration catalysts is to produce some degree of resonance, synergy and/or emergence between members of a group who are working together in some way.

Creating a *COACH Container* in which the members of a group collectively enter and optimal mindset is an example of a collaboration catalyst. When done on a regular bases, such a process can create a strong and rich sense of mutual rapport and resourcefulness.

Multi-Level Introductions is a collaboration catalyst, most valuable when a group is first forming, that gives group members an opportunity to share something about their background and their goals on several different levels before engaging in a collaborative interaction. The process encourages the possibility of quickly finding resonance at deeper levels of success factors beyond the surface layers of environment, behavior and capabilities.

Expressing Intentions creates a type of filter that directs the attention of group members and brings certain skills and actions into the foreground. By helping one another express personal intentions through words, images and a somatic model, group members become more prepared to give and receive the most they can from their interaction.

Fostering a "Field" of Co-Sponsorship is another example of a collaboration catalyst in which group members actively practice looking for and verbally acknowledging what they perceive and appreciate about one another. This can help to create a powerful relational "field" built on trust, mutual respect and the recognition of each group member's unique resources and contributions.

Exploring and Sharing Best Practices through Success Factor Modeling is a collaboration catalyst that helps to both enhance and harvest the collective intelligence in a group through the processes of sharing and swarming. By choosing an important topic of common interest and then exploring and breaking down examples of successful performances or projects, group members are able to find key success factors that they can put into practice in the future.

References and Further Readings

- *Give and Take: Why Helping Others Drives Our Success,*
  Adam Grant
  The Penguin Group, New York, NY, 2013.

- *Think and Grow Rich,*
  Napoleon Hill,
  Combined Registry Company, Chicago, Illinois, 1937, ISBN 1-60506-930.

- *From Coach to Awakener,*
  Robert Dilts
  Meta Publications, Capitola, CA, 2003.

02
Collective Intelligence
and Generative Collaboration

Synergy is what happens when one plus one equals ten or a hundred or even a thousand! It's the profound result when two or more respectful human beings determine to go beyond their preconceived ideas to meet a great challenge
Stephen Covey

Many ideas grow better when transplanted into another mind than the one where they sprang up.
Oliver Wendell Holmes

In everybody's life, at some time, our inner fire goes out.
It is then burst into flame by an encounter with another human being.
We should all be thankful for those people who rekindle the inner fire.
Albert Schweitzer

ANTONIO MEZA

Collaboration is Essential for a Successful Venture

Working together with others in groups and teams is an increasingly common and important part of modern business and contemporary life – and doing it effectively is an essential success factor for entrepreneurs and leaders. In a recent interview on *Forbes.com*, Journalist Dan Schawbel asked Adam Grant (the Wharton professor cited earlier) to explain why interacting with others is the new means to a successful career, and why it is even more important now than in years past. Grant made the following response:

> *The world of work has become much more interdependent, making relationships and reputations increasingly important in shaping the innovative ideas, business opportunities, client referrals, and promotions that come our way. There are at least three major trends behind the rise in interdependence.*
>
> *First is the growth of project-based work: organizations are bringing people together to collaborate on temporary teams, making interaction skills particularly important in shaping the results these short-term groups achieve.*
>
> *Second is the shift from a manufacturing economy to a service and knowledge economy: four out of every five Americans work in service roles, where meeting the needs of clients and customers is a defining feature of success.*
>
> *Third is the advent of online social networks: we can now track the reputations of job applicants, potential business partners, and service providers by identifying common connections on LinkedIn and tracking their behavior on social media.*

Effective collaboration is more important than ever before in order to create a successful and sustainable venture.

Grant's answer reveals a lot about how the world has changed in recent years and why collaboration is an essential success factor. Each of the trends he defines clearly point to the importance of perceiving ourselves and interacting with others from the perspective of being an integrated holon as opposed to merely a separate individual. Clearly, the capacity to work collaboratively together with others as a holon is crucial for success.

Levels of Collaboration

Collaboration literally means to "work together." There are many ways in which people work together and collaborate. Some are more effective than others. In fact, group performance could be categorized into three types:

1. In an *under performing* group or team, the performance or output of the group as a whole is actually *less* than it would be if the individuals were working separately; i.e., 1+1<2.
2. In an *average* group or team, the performance or output of the group as a whole is about the same as it would be if the individuals were working independently; 1+1=2.
3. In a *high performing* group or team, the performance or output of the group as a whole is much *greater* than it would be if the individuals were working by themselves; 1+1=3. This is what we are calling *generative* collaboration.

The capacity of groups or teams to collaborate effectively can vary widely.

In an underperforming group, the result is less than if the individuals were working separately.

In an average group, the performance is the sum of the individual contributions.

In a high performing group, the output is much greater than if the members were working alone.

We can say that an under performing group or team is essentially lacking the capacity to genuinely collaborate. Not only are the individuals failing to work together, their interactions are actually impeding their ability to accomplish even their individual tasks effectively (a type of "degenerative collaboration" or "negative sum" interaction – 1+1=0 or even -1).

An average group can be said to have reached a basic level of collaboration. *Basic collaboration* involves a group of individuals working together to reach a specific objective. It is a type of "collected" intelligence in which 1+1=2. Basic collaboration requires that people have a certain degree of rapport with one another, communicate effectively and each performs the task required of him or her in coordination with other partners or group members. The goal of basic collaboration is for people to perform according to what is expected of them in order to produce a result equaling the sum of the individual contributions.

As we mentioned before, the fruit of effective collective intelligence is what is known as generative collaboration. *Generative collaboration* involves people working together to create or generate something new, surprising and beyond the capacities of any of the group members individually; 1+1=3 or more. Through generative collaboration, individuals are able to utilize their abilities to the fullest and discover and apply resources that they did not yet realize they had. They draw new ideas and resources out of each other. Thus, the performance or output of the group as a whole is much *greater* than it would be if the individuals were working by themselves.

Consider the example of a large well-known multinational telecommunications company. The company was struggling to stay competitive and knew it needed to develop a product for a very important segment of its market. The situation was so critical that the company assembled a team of 1,000 people to develop the new product as quickly as possible. It turned out, to their surprise and embarrassment however, that one of their competitors was able to create a better product in a shorter time that cost much less—completely outperforming them in every key performance indicator and in the marketplace. The most astonishing thing was that the competitor accomplished this with a team of just 20 people!

Of course, the burning question for the large telecommunications company was, "How is it possible that 20 people can so completely outperform 1,000?!" The difference that made the difference is what we are referring to as the capacity for "generative collaboration." The group members in the team of 1,000 people had had operated in "silos," largely isolated from one another. The various team members simply worked to carry out the task that they had been assigned by the project leader, who viewed people as essentially parts of a machine or computer software program – what we call "brain and pencil" leadership in Success Factor Modeling.

The group of 20 people, on the other hand, were led by a person who was passionate about the vision for the project, and spread that passion to his team. This leader operated much more as an "orchestrator of innovation" and encouraged the team to be in constant communication and interaction; challenging, stimulating and supporting each other to be and give the best of themselves, think "outside of the box" and reach for excellence in everything they did.

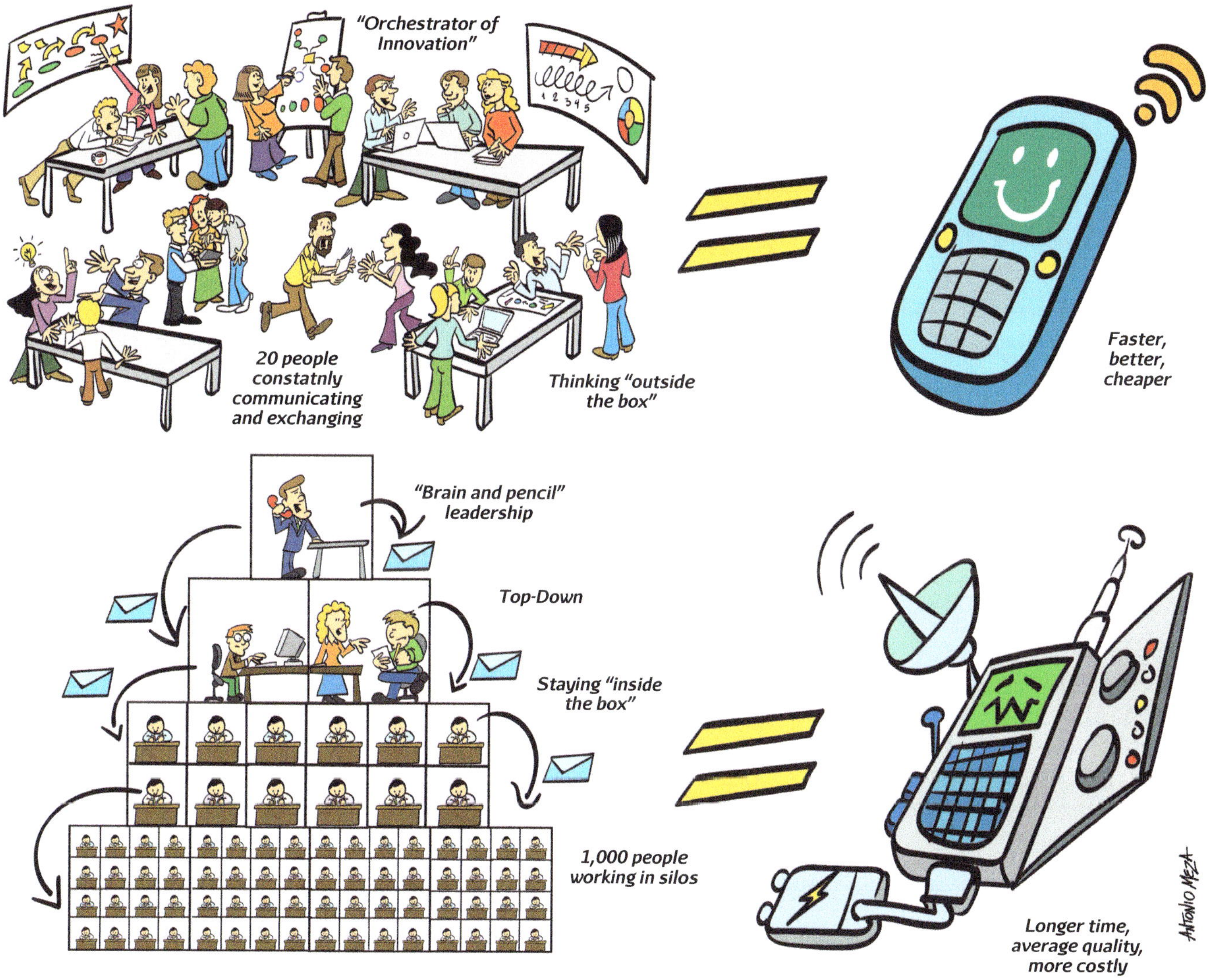

With the appropriate leadership style, the proper mindset and the fostering of generative collaboration, twenty people can outperform one thousand

Generative collaboration results from the development of a "group mind" or "relational field" in which the knowledge and know-how of individuals combine to produce a larger collective creativity that is impossible without the presence of the other group members.

They were able to achieve a high level of generative collaboration, stimulating and supporting one another to move forward in new ways and create something unprecedented. This required that the group members share vision, incorporate multiple perspectives and create a strong "relational field" based on trust mutual respect. As Steve Jobs said, "It's about the people you have, how you're led, and how much you get it."

As we have pointed out, generative collaboration of this type results from the development of a "group mind" or "relational field" in which the knowledge and know-how of individuals combine to produce a larger collective creativity that is impossible without the presence of the other partners or group members. This process is similar to what happens when two hydrogen atoms combine with an oxygen atom to create the third and new entity of water.

Yet, in order to create water, oxygen must remain fully oxygen and hydrogen must remain hydrogen. In the words of the philosopher Ken Wilbur, the new relationship expressed by the creation of water "includes and transcends" the individual entities which make it up, producing something which contains both, but is at the same time completely new.

To produce generative collaboration, people must be firmly rooted in themselves, centered in their personal resources and passionate about reaching their ambitions as well as seeing their common vision become a reality.

An important principle at work here is that individuality and people's personal interest and passion are necessary for generative collaboration. It has been said that "there is no 'I' in team," and perhaps this is true of basic collaboration, but not of generative collaboration (there is literally an "i" in both the words "generative" and "collaboration"). To produce generative collaboration, people must be firmly rooted in themselves, centered in their unique energy and personal resources and personally passionate about reaching their ambitions as well as seeing their common vision become a reality. When people "sacrifice their own interests for the good of the team," the team is losing their full passion, creativity and energy.

As an illustration, in "basic" collaboration, a group of six or seven people would get together, arrive at a consensus regarding a particular idea or approach and work together to achieve it, thus producing one result of the sum of their interaction. Applying the principles of "generative" collaboration, the group of six or seven would produce at least six or seven ideas or approaches, plus several possible synergies between some of those ideas or approaches.

As American founding father Thomas Jefferson said, "If two people get together and exchange a dollar, they both walk away with one dollar. But if two people get together and exchange an idea, they both walk away with at least two ideas" (and probably more resulting from the combinations and synergies between the ideas they have shared). Generative collaboration is a good example of this type of economics of ideas.

If two people get together and exchange a dollar, they both walk away with one dollar. But if two people get together and exchange an idea, they both walk away with at least two ideas.

– Thomas Jefferson

A good metaphor for understanding the synergic dynamic of generative collaboration is the interplay of bubbles. In this analogy, a bubble would represent a particular vision or idea. In basic collaboration, all of the partners or team members work together to create one bubble. Generative collaboration would involve each of the group members creating his or her own bubble and then noticing how that bubble joined together with the bubbles formed by the other group members.

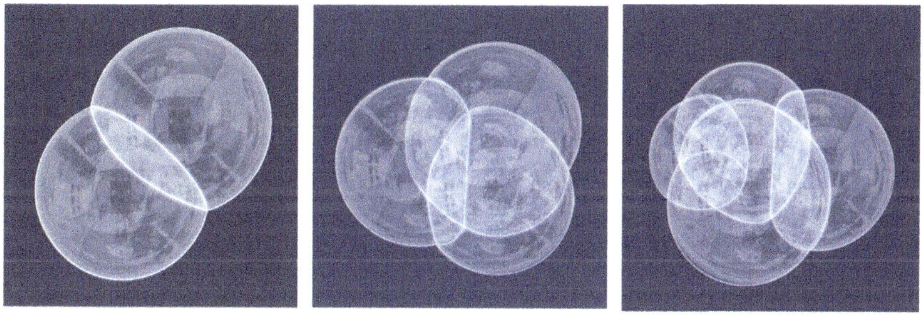

Similar to bubbles joining together to make a larger whole, generative collaboration involves the integration of complementary visions and ideas.

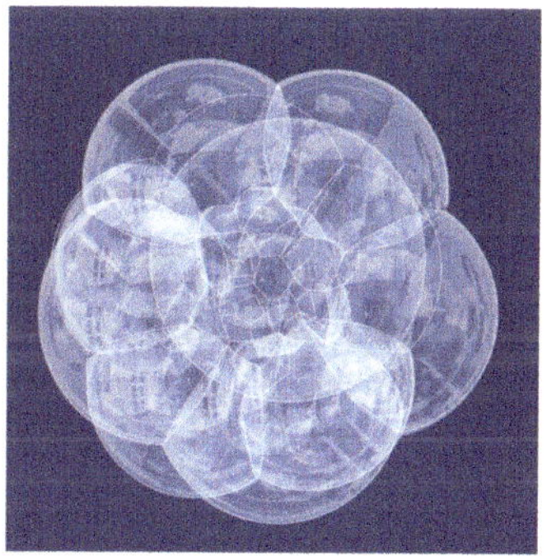

The result of generative collaboration is a unique collective vision

Many successful developments and accomplishments in our modern world have not been the result of the vision of a single person, but are rather the consequence of combining multiple visions and ideas. The creation of Success Factor Modeling itself is a good example of this. SFM emerged as a result of the integration of my own vision and ideas relating to behavioral skills development and my brother John's vision and ideas regarding the coaching and support of new ventures.

The development of the Internet is a good example of how collective visioning produces something unpredictable.

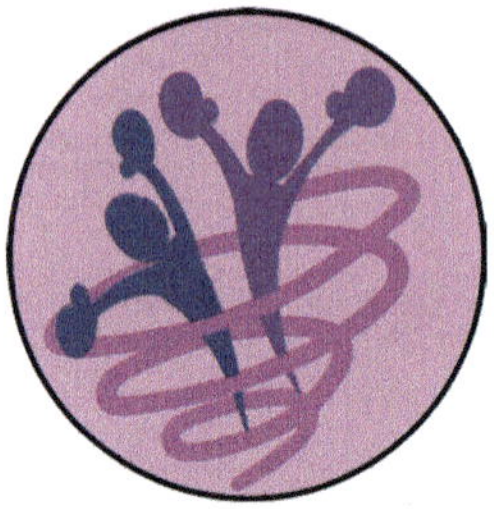

The creation of the Internet is another good example. The seeds of the Internet began in 1969 as the ARPANET, a U.S. Department of Defense research project to develop a network architecture for military use, and as a way to get the most economical use out of scarce large-computer resources. Universities, research labs and defense contractors soon discovered the Internet's potential as a medium of communication between "humans" and linked up in steadily increasing numbers. In the 1980s and the early 1990s, more and more pieces of the original government network were sold to major telecommunications companies until the Internet backbone had become completely commercialized. In 1994 mainstream computer users discovered the Internet, attracted by the hypertext and multimedia features of the World Wide Web. Today, the globally-extended Internet has become the key unifying communications technology for people across the planet.

However, as one of the original developers of the Arpanet pointed out, "Nobody back then had the vision of the Internet. What has developed today was not envisioned by anyone at that time."

Entrepreneur Don Pickens (quoted on page 137 in Volume I of this work) echoes this perspective when he claims, "Visionary leadership is not just having a vision, it is weaving that vision with other visions." Our first Success Factor Case Example provides a good illustration of the generative power of weaving visions together.

Success Factor Case Example:

CrossKnowledge

"Learning together and changing the world."

CrossKnowledge founders Steve Fiehl, Michaël Ohana, Pascal El Grably and Hervé Goudchaux

In June of 2009, CrossKnowledge founders Steve Fiehl, Michaël Ohana, Pascal El Grably and Hervé Goudchaux found themselves at a crossroads with the e-learning company they had launched eight years earlier. They had joined together to form the company out of a shared passion for *management and self-development.* As Steve Fiehl recalls, "I had the desire to bring these [skills] to a lot of people and knew I would do it with other people." The partners chose e-learning because, as Steve points out, "It gives access to a lot of people." The four also shared a desire to "do something revolutionary" by "changing the rules; taking a market and, without knowing anything, do it differently than anyone else." Like any other attempt to bring change into the world, and especially to organizations, the journey was not always an easy one. As Steve recalls with a smile, "I have persisted even though in the beginning I was told, 'You have chosen the wrong field.'"

The four had launched the company in the early days of online education. At that time, e-learning was little known or used in training; especially in the organizational context. In their first years, the company was essentially in the role of being a pioneer and the founders' challenge was to convince organizations that e-learning was a viable training method. Passionate and committed to their dream, they began to build a niche in the growing industry, attracting a top tier faculty and producing high quality interactive programs.

Transforming Crisis into Opportunity

After some years of enjoying a reasonable level of growth and success, however, the company encountered a challenging time of transition. In 2009, organizations were in the grips of a global financial crisis. Furthermore, as the e-learning industry matured and the marketplace evolved, more and more larger players had begun to create their own e-learning products; including big training

The founders of the e-learning company CrossKnowledge found themselves in a challenging situation during a global economic crisis which required that they reinvent their venture.

organizations who had major marketing budgets. The CrossKnowledge founders realized that in order to stay competitive, they had to reinvent the company in many ways and move to a whole new level. This would require clarifying their vision and their mission (specifying their unique contribution) and adjusting their ambition and role to fit the changing marketplace. Such a change meant that they had to anticipate the direction the e-learning industry was heading, readjust their business focus, shift their priorities, and then align their whole team to the new path. Furthermore, they needed to do this quickly or be left behind.

The CrossKnowledge founders shared a passion for shared passion for management and self-development.

As one of Crossknowledge's faculty members, it was a natural fit that I participate in helping them make this transition. Our work began with several sessions involving the four founders. Each meeting began with one or more of the collaboration catalysts described so far in this volume. We would invariably begin by establishing a *COACH Container* and *Fostering a Field of Co-Sponsorship.* We systematically went through a series of steps to define the company's current state, the obstacles it faced and both the success factors and "failure" factors that had brought the company to where it was. At each step, the founders shared and contrasted their views; finding resonance, acknowledging and integrating their differing but complementarity perspectives, and allowing new ideas and shared conclusions to emerge.

Preparing to Take the Venture to a New Level

The vision of the CrossKnowledge founders was "learning for a better life" in which learning would be "like water, turn on the faucet and it is there." This would enable organizations to evolve by developing individuals.

Then we focused on the future, defining the steps that would take the company to a new level.* The cornerstone of the process was to articulate the common **vision** that was the expression of their shared passion for management and self-development. The founders' simple but powerful expression of this was *Learning for a better life*. The essence of their vision was to *enable organizations to evolve by developing individuals* – leveraging self-development as a way to improve management and leadership, and ultimately the organization. Their mutual metaphor for what this meant to them was that that "learning should be like water" – "turn on the faucet and it is there"; available for "everyone at every level in a company or organization."**

---

* Definitions and processes for identifying vision, mission, ambition and role are summarized in the introduction to this book (pp. 11-14) and described in depth in *Success Factor Modeling Volume I* – pp. 193-245.

**Interestingly, one of the major obstacles has been training managers (who want to control the "faucet"). "Sometimes it takes a lot of time and determination to come back to the initial vision that 'we have to bring it to everyone,'" points out Steve Fiehl.

The founders viewed their **mission** and unique contribution to the vision as bringing *massive improvement of people's lives all over the world through e-learning and on-line education in leadership and management skills.* One of their primary ways of fulfilling that mission was through fostering collective intelligence with their customers. As they saw it, the mission involved "creating a community of clients; a learning community in which we are constantly sharing what we were learning." Their metaphor for this was a "cascading waterfall."

The CrossKnowledge founders' mission was to "bring massive improvement of people's lives all over the world through e-learning and on-line education in leadership and management skills;" like a "cascading waterfall".

As they clarified their vision and mission, the founders realized that they would have to strengthen their shared **ambition** in order to drive the company's progress and truly achieve the vision and mission. All of the founders agreed that they wanted to achieve a *premium position and brand.* They aspired to be the market reference for high quality online leadership and management training and to become the *preferred solution* for General Managers, Human Resource directors and end users.

Scalability was another important part of their ambition. Based in France and primarily operating in a European market at the time, they wanted to grow to become truly *international* and expand their user base from 400,000 to 2 million. This meant that they would need to be "robust," "fluid" and *growing twice as fast as the market.* Another key performance indicator for their reaching their ambition would be achieving *15% profitability.*

The ambition of Crossknowledge's founders was to achieve "a premium position and brand"; to become truly international and expand their user base from 400,000 to 2 million in two years.

To accomplish their vision, mission and ambition, the founders viewed the **role** of the company as being a *training innovator and integrator.* They were neither providers of customized solutions nor sellers of "off the shelf" commoditized products. Their focus was on comprehensive solutions and results versus products and offers. They saw their strength as offering *integrated solutions that used exclusive learning formats and a range of accompanying services, according to a client company's needs.*

The CrossKnowledge founders viewed their venture's role as being being a training innovator and integrator. Their metaphor was a "composer" using a piano keyboard to create music. Other musical instruments represented partner companies

One of their metaphors for their role was a "composer" using a piano keyboard to create music. The keys on the keyboard represented the different e-learning products in their catalog. The notes produced by the keys represented the learning outcome resulting from a particular product or lesson. Just like a piano, there are a fixed number of "keys" that do not change. Any one of them may be necessary to produce a particular song. The "music" does not come from the individual keys or notes, but rather from the way they are put together; in what order and in what relationship to one another. Other musical instruments represented partner companies who could provide other types of learning and training products. It is the composer's job to find the instruments that create the best music for a particular client.

A key to fully embracing this role was enhancing CrossKnowledge's network of partners. From the beginning, the CrossKnowledge founders had successfully partnered with other training providers on a local, regional and global level; *complementing the training domains not covered in their own catalog*, such as desktop IT, technical skills, languages, etc. They had also established important partnerships with business schools. To achieve their ambitions, they would have to expand such partnering activities even more.

Creating Alignment and Promoting Collective Intelligence

This new direction would require that all of the CrossKnowledge team members be aligned, capable and active contributors. It would also necessitate fostering genuine collective intelligence and generative collaboration.t

Once the CrossKnowledge founders had mapped out their new Circle of Success, they needed to engage the collective intelligence and generative collaboration of their team members to bring it to life.

Once the four founders were clear and congruent amongst themselves, we organized an event for all 160 members of the company at a large conference center. As preparation, the four founders had discussed and worked on how to communicate the updated vision and mission of the venture (see *Success Factor Modeling Volume I*, pp. 208-216).

As one of the facilitators of the event, I guided all of the participating company members into a simple version of the COACH state and invited them to reflect on why they had chosen to work for the company and what was important to them about it. Michaël, the company's official CEO, then presented the newly clarified vision and mission in a sincere and succinct address to the group. Group members were encouraged to find where they experienced their deepest resonance with the company's vision and mission.

The participants were organized into interfunctional groups of approximately 10-12 people and seated around round tables, each facilitated by a member of the company's Executive Committee. All 160 people were provided with papers and drawing supplies, and were invited to draw his or her image of what that vision meant for him or her as an individual within his or her role in the company. The group members at the various tables then shared and compared their drawings, looking for resonance and synergy with respect to their perception of the company's vision and mission. (This is a form of Masterminding process that I call "intervision" which we will explore in more detail later in this section).

All 160 pictures were then placed on folding screens set up around the conference room so that the team was surrounded by the images the presentation of the company's vision had generated. It was quite an inspiring "field" and the collective energy and motivation in the group was very high.

I then introduced the notion of the various levels of success factors – vision, mission, ambition, role, values, beliefs, capabilities and behaviors – and the steps of bringing vision into action. Each individual was asked to choose 5 key words to define his or her own sense of mission or contribution to the vision, and then to do the same for his or her personal ambition. These were shared within their group, again looking for areas of resonance and synergy. Each table was then asked to summarize the common elements of their missions and ambitions into 5 key words each. The facilitators from each table shared these results with the larger group.

A next step was to collectively assess the group's belief that the vision, missions and ambitions could be achieved. People were asked to be honest with themselves about their degree of belief that this evolving future was possible. If someone did experience doubts, they were not put on the spot to admit it or explain why they were unsure. Rather, those who had given a high rating to one or more of the statements were invited, as mentors and role models, to share why they had so much confidence. Each time an individual shared his or her reasons for believing in the future of the venture, the confidence level of the whole room seemed to palpably increase creating a field of energy and excitement.

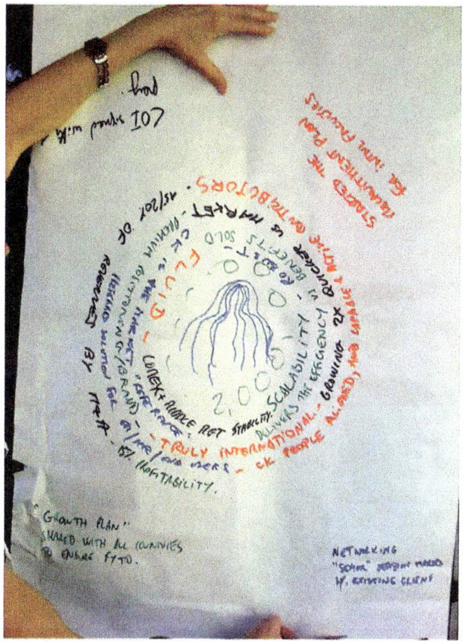

A photograph of a flip chart page from one of CrossKnowledge's working sessions showing the metaphorical image of a cascading waterfall in the center of the page and contributions from the four founders in different colors regarding the ambitions for the company. Specific commitments to action are in the four corners of the page.

The CrossKnowledge founders involved their team members in a powerful collective visioning process.

The final part of the event involved each of the 160 people making commitments to the team members at their table regarding specific actions they would take in the coming days, weeks and months to support creating the future of the company.

The event marked the beginning of a new chapter for CrossKnowledge. Several years later, the people who were at the event would still refer to it; and new employees would hear about the event as a key reference point in their introduction to the company and its culture.

Entrepreneurship

Passion for Excellence

People First

CrossKnowledge core values aligned the team and guided them during the next period of expansion for the company.

Fostering and Guiding a New Period of Expansion

With renewed clarity and alignment the company moved on into new period of expansion and growth, with each person contributing the larger vision and mission by acting from his or her own sense of mission and ambition. "We are a company of *entrepreneurs*," Steve Fiehl says about their clarified identity. "We organize ourselves and act on the basis of *three core values* shared by everyone in the company: *1) People First, 2) Passion for Excellence and 3) Entrepreneurship.*

"*People First* involves values about *communication – interpersonal values*," explains Steve. "It is important to respect everybody. That is what drives communication between people and creates an open environment." The CrossKnowledge founders also encouraged team members to "have a positive attitude and acknowledge the best in others' contributions" and to "build assertive and win-win relationships."

Passion for excellence requires "striving for premium quality." "Good is not enough," says Steve. "Our constant intention is to develop and propose solutions generating measurable and sustainable value for our customers," he explains, "and ask for feedback to improve our performance. We learn from our successes and failures by analyzing them."

"We encourage *entrepreneurship* by giving power to people," continues Steve. "We say, 'Don't expect us to tell you what to do because we don't know.'" According to Steve, "A key belief is that *people are allowed to do it*." A good example of the impact of this on the team was the integration of the new social network platform Yammer into CrossKnowledge's blended solutions. "There was a recognition in the team that 'We need this,'" he explains. "Management didn't organize it; it just popped up."

Steve and the other founders also realized that collective intelligence and entrepreneurship can be hard to sustain. According to Steve:

> *We take steps to make sure people remain entrepreneurs. A key question is "How to keep the 'magic touch' while you are growing and not lose the initial energy?" Too many "processes" drive people out of vision. People have to remain authorized to think for themselves, act as a rebel and retain ownership.*
>
> *Rather than implement a lot of processes, we have split operation into business units and then trust in the "DNA" of CrossKnowledge. We also try to create a "mythology"; i.e., stories in which team members are true heroes. For instance, people inventing things they have not been asked to do such as launching a mobile app.*

CrossKnowledge team members were empowered and encouraged to "think for themselves, act as a rebel and retain ownership."

One good example was a 23 year-old new employee's idea for a "failure bank." It involved going around to clients and team members and saying, "I want to talk to you about . . . (something that didn't go as expected)." By identifying and acknowledging things that "failed" or did not work as well as successes, it becomes more possible to identify the "differences that make a difference."

The CrossKnowledge founders also fostered collective intelligence and generative collaboration with their customers and clients.

Nurturing collective intelligence and generative collaboration with customers and clients has always been part of the success of CrossKnowledge, and that has continued to increase and expand in new ways since 2009. As Steve Fiehl explains:

> *We are against the traditional way of e-learning: i.e., that we know everything and have all the solutions. It is important for us to be humble in telling [clients] "we don't know."*
>
> *The first foundation for collective intelligence is building a feeling of trust with your clients that "we are trying to go somewhere together." They never see us as trying to sell them something.*

With respect to our marketing people, we emphasize that the way we select clients is a question of their alignment with our vision. If people are excited and part of the dream, we recreate the beginning. Salespeople who just want to reach sales targets get clients who are less loyal.

In *Volume I* of this series (p. 196) I pointed out that our research with successful next generation entrepreneurs has shown that they are highly *customer oriented* and that they:

1. Maintain a strong ongoing feedback loop with customers
2. Establish structures and infrastructures that create exchange and mutual feedback with customers
3. Base their products and services on customer-oriented values
4. Co-create products and services with customers instead of "selling"
5. Ensure that the economic growth of the venture comes from increasing the quality of products or services versus marketing and hype
6. Include customer needs and desires in their business decisions and management policies

CrossKnowledge is clearly an excellent example of what it means to be highly customer oriented. According to Steve Fiehl:

> *We take steps to promote social learning or collective learning with our customers; i.e., that "We will find a way together"; "We will invent it together"; "We are learning together and we are changing the world." We feel proud and excited to create something new together.*
>
> *We do this in a number of ways. For example, every three months there is a session initiated by clients exploring: "What are we learning about e-learning from CrossKnowledge?"*
>
> *We have also established the CrossKnowledge Academy, in which we give training for free to our clients. It is a free seminar to change things together. When we give something back, they will invent new things with us.*

Like all successful next generation ventures, CrossKnowledge has been highly customer oriented.

CrossKnowledge includes their clients in the process of improving their services. This way they promote collective intelligence. "We will find a way together, we will invent it together, we are learning together and changing the world."

The steps taken by the four founders of CrossKnowledge led to an ongoing path of success. By 2014 the company had grown to more than 200 employees, was bringing $37 million in revenue and had expanded to 5 million end-users (and has grown to 8 million at the time of this writing) in over 80 countries. They were acquired by publishing giant publishing giant Wiley in April of 2014 for $175 million in cash, making each of the four founders a multimillionaire.

Reflections on CrossKnowledge's Circle of Success

CrossKnowledge's story of success provides a clear illustration of the importance of collective intelligence and generative collaboration to create an effective Circle of Success; beginning with the interactions between the founders themselves. The four CrossKnowledge founders were a diverse group of people, ranging in age from 23 to 52 at the time that they first started the company. They were united, however, by a shared and unwavering passion for management and personal development which expressed itself in the fundamental vision of "learning for a better life" and the mission "to bring the massive improvement of people's lives all over the world through e-learning and on-line education in leadership and management skills."

The success of CrossKnowledge provides a clear illustration of the importance of collective intelligence and generative collaboration to create an effective Circle of Success.

It is interesting that, even though they did not consciously know about the SFM Circle of Success, the CrossKnowledge founders intuitively organized themselves to a focus on each of the essential quadrants. Michaël, the youngest of the four, began his career in a large, well-known consulting firm. As CEO and chief operating officer, Michaël focused his attention on growing the business and creating value for stakeholders through strategic alliances and international development. Steve, whose background was in custom publishing, took charge of innovation, running the training and technology research and development teams. Pascal, formerly sales director at Proctor & Gamble France, focused on generating interest and revenue with customers, managing the sales and services teams. Hervé, the oldest of the founders, had been a human resources director for several large companies. His focus was on leveraging his extensive network of connections to build partnerships and other win-win relationships.

The interaction between CrossKnowledge's founders shows an intuitive understanding of how to bring together and synergize the complementary mindsets needed to build a successful venture.

CrossKnowledge's Circle of Success

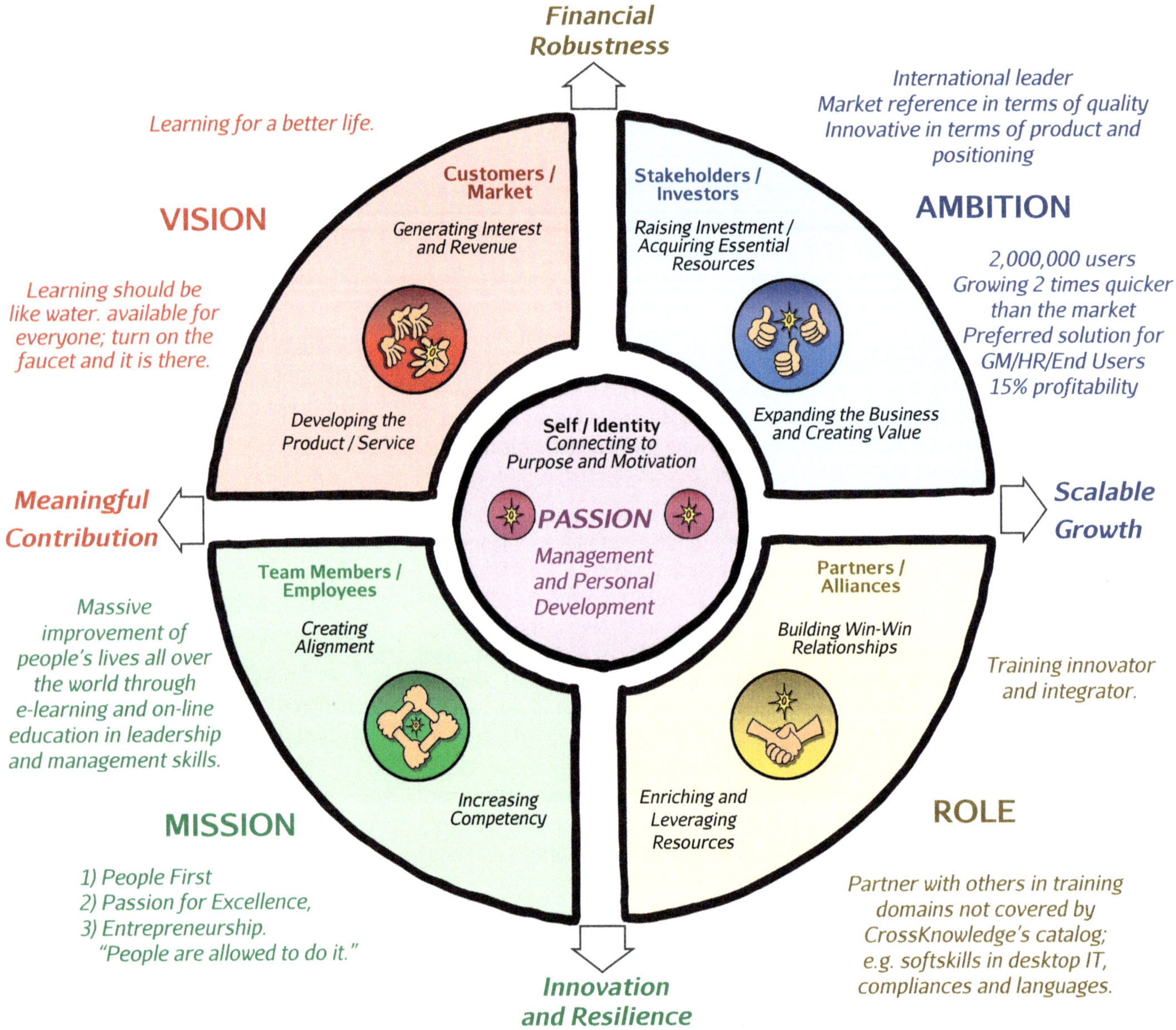

CROSSKNOWLEDGE'S CIRCLE OF SUCCESS

AMBITION
Stakeholders / Investors

* INTERNATIONAL LEADER
* MARKET REFERENCE IN TERMS OF QUALITY.
* INNOVATIVE IN TERMS OF PRODUCT AND POSITIONING

* 2,000,000 USERS
* GROWING 2 TIMES QUICKER THAN THE MARKET
* PREFERRED SOLUTION FOR GM/ HR/END USERS
* 15% PROFITABILITY

VISION
Customers / Market

* LEARNING FOR A BETTER LIFE

* LEARNING SHOULD BE LIKE WATER. AVAILABLE FOR EVERYONE; TURN ON THE FAUCET AND IT IS THERE.

MISSION
Team Members / Employees

* MASSIVE IMPROVEMENT OF PEOPLE'S LIVES ALL OVER THE WORLD THROUGH E-LEARNING AND ON-LINE EDUCATION IN LEADERSHIP AND MANAGEMENT SKILLS.

1) PEOPLE FIRST
2) PASSION FOR EXCELLENCE
3) ENTREPRENEURSHIP: "PEOPLE ARE ALLOWED TO DO IT".

ROLE
Partners / Alliances

* TRAINING INNOVATIOR AND INTEGRATOR

* PARTNER WITH OTHERS IN TRAINING DOMAINS NOT COVERED BY CROSSKNOWLEDGE, E.G. SOFTSKILLS IN DESKTOP IT, COMPLIANCES AND LANGUAGES.

PASSION:
MANAGEMENT AND PERSONAL DEVELOPMENT.

The four founders' willingness to utilize the principles of collective intelligence and Success Factor Modeling with respect to their own interactions is a powerful example of applying their own passion for management and personal development and their vision of learning for a better life to themselves as a team. Each step of their path to success, though not always easy, was a true generative collaboration.

A major factor in CrossKnowledge's success had to do with the founders' ability to create synergies between their team members and their customers, and between themselves and their partners.

The founders also intentionally and actively sought to foster collective intelligence and generative collaboration (i.e., resonance, synergy and emergence) with their team members and customers; and between their team members and customers. They clearly viewed both their team members and customers as "holons" – i.e., creative, independently thinking and acting individuals who simultaneously contribute to a larger whole when there is a shared vision. In this spirit, the CrossKnowledge founders worked to create their own particular collaboration catalysts with their team members and customers (such as the CrossKnowledge Academy). The CrossKnowledge core values of People First, Passion for Excellence and Entrepreneurship created alignment, stimulated an entrepreneurial spirit and supported the development of collective intelligence and generative collaboration amongst team members. The constant contact with clients and customers created a strong sense of "task significance" for their team members. The ongoing processes of benchmarking collective standards and brainstorming of imaginative options with their customers helped to align the team and co-develop products relevant to their customer's needs, leading to new ideas and wiser decisions.

The constant exchange of best practices and generative collaboration — fostered by events such as the "kick-off event" described earlier and the ongoing implementation of the values of people first, passion for excellence and entrepreneurship — led to creative solutions and enhanced performance.

By all measures, CrossKnowledge's success is a testament to the power of collective intelligence and generative collaboration.

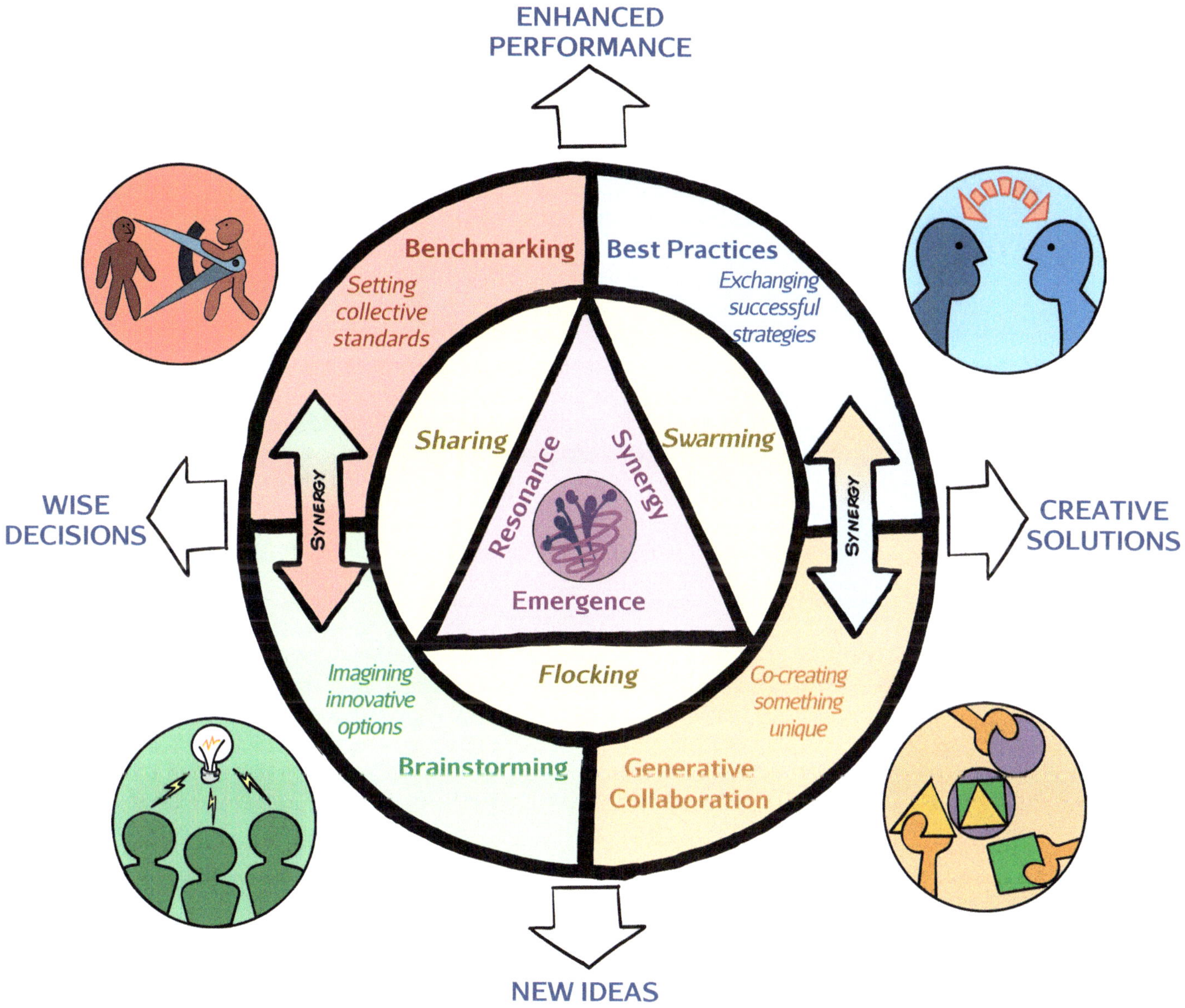

CrossKnowledge's ongoing collaboration catalysts created synergies between benchmarking and brainstorming and between best practices and generative collaboration.

Dynamics of Generative Change

Generative collaboration is an expression of the principles of generative change.

Times of crisis, growth and transformation in our ventures and our lives are usually accompanied by the need for "generative" change as opposed to incremental change. To achieve *generative change* our mental maps of who we are and what is possible in the world must become broader, and we must perceive old limitations in a completely new way. This requires that we break through our old mind set and "get outside of the box," creating something "completely new." Such a generative change must both "include and transcend" our previous knowledge and awareness.

Generative change involves shifts in "deep structure" as opposed to merely modifications in "surface structure." True generativity requires a breakdown of the current structure that is already in place and has become outdated or overly rigid. This breakdown naturally creates a state of a certain degree of chaos and uncertainty. If, however, we are able to stay centered in ourselves, connected to our resources and focused on our larger vision of what is possible, we can achieve a generative state of expansion and reorganization; as we saw in the case of CrossKnowledge.

My colleague Stephen Gilligan and I have been studying the dynamics of generative change in individuals and organizations for the past two decades. This exploration has led us to the development of programs on generative change, including Generative Coaching, Generative Leadership and, of course, Generative Collaboration as well as others. Our mutual passion for generative change has resulted in our establishment of the International Association for Generative Change (IAGC – http://www.generative-change.com).

IAGC Logo

Stephen and I summarize the basic process of facilitating generative change in the following five steps:

1. Set an intention (i.e., a vision or direction)
2. Develop a generative performance state
3. Apply multiple perspectives for defining goals and actions
4. Engage multiple perspectives to creatively transform obstacles
5. Establish ongoing practices for continued creativity

The CrossKnowledge case example provides a good illustration of how these steps work to create generative change. (1) The founders set an intention in the form of a clear, shared vision, providing direction for themselves and their company. (2) They then took steps to foster creative thinking in themselves, their team members and their customers. (3) They constructed events and infrastructures that allowed them to bring together multiple perspectives – i.e., their own as founders, their team, their customers and their partners – to define the goals and actions that would achieve their vision. (4) They also engaged multiple perspectives to actively and creatively transform obstacles, looking at their "failures" as important learning opportunities. The implementation of the "failure bank" is a good example this. (5) They proactively established ongoing practices for continued creativity, such as the CrossKnowledge Academy and their quarterly collective learning sessions with their clients.

Each of the steps of the generative change process can be supported by a variety of collaboration catalysts. We will be continuing to explore a number of these collaboration catalysts throughout the remainder of this book.

Steps of Generative Change.

Building the Foundations of Generative Collaboration

The lightning spark of thought generated in the solitary mind awakens its likeness in another mind.

—Thomas Carlyle

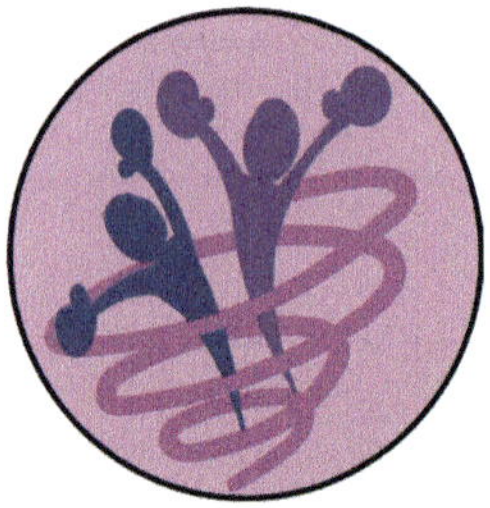

Generative collaboration results from a sense of connection, and the capacity to identify and engage complementary skills and resources, and to explore new possibilities that can emerge from your interaction with your collaborators.

As I pointed out in the previous chapter, collective intelligence and generative collaboration are a function of resonance, synergy and emergence. In the context of a group interaction, these qualities can be fostered by exploring a few simple, practical questions:

- **Resonance**
  What is the same? Where do we connect?
- **Synergy**
  Where are we different? How can those differences complement one another?
- **Emergence**
  What else becomes possible? What new can come through our interaction?

Taking the time to reflect upon these questions can serve to reveal and/or strengthen areas for both basic and generative collaboration. It can help to increase a sense of connection, identify and engage complementary skills and resources, and to explore new possibilities that your interaction can bring you and your collaborators.

There is a very instructive and inspiring music video segment that I often like to show in my coaching sessions, workshops and seminars as both an analogy and example that illustrates the phenomenon of synergy, generative collaboration and a generative "field" quite beautifully. The video is an excerpt from the recording of a concert put on by the New Age musician Yanni at the Acropolis in Athens, Greece. The segment is of a brief improvisational performance by two violinists: Karen Briggs – an African American woman with a background in jazz music – and Shardad Rohanian, a man of Iranian descent who has been classically trained.

While the two are overtly different in many respects – gender, training, style, cultural heritage, etc. – they are able to transform these differences into generative complementarities that produce an innovative and entertaining performance. Throughout their interaction, they maintain their uniqueness and creativity as individuals, and simultaneously perform as an integrated holon. Held and guided by the larger musical field created by the orchestra, the two violinists take turns playing during their improvisational duet. As they play, it is obvious that there is a positive and creative rapport between them that shows up in the somatic enthusiasm and playfulness that they demonstrate through their bodies as they both play and listen to one another. As part of their exchange, they incorporate musical ideas and melodies that they have just heard from each other and take those ideas new and creative directions.

The improvisational duet between the two violinists in the DVD *Yanni Live at the Acropolis* (1994) is an inspiring example of generative collaboration.

The end result is an inspired performance in which each musician has clearly given the best of themselves and elevated each other, playing things that would never had entered into either tone of their minds had they played by themselves. It is also clear that the result was not simply a consequence of their obvious high level of skill with their instruments. It is a function of the generative field formed between them and the orchestra through the principles resonance, synergy and emergence.

In the coming sections, we will explore some of the collaboration catalysts necessary for creating and applying this type of "generative field" within a group or team. In the previous chapter, I presented key collaboration catalysts such as *Creating a COACH Container* and *Setting Intention*. These two catalysts are the foundation for the first step in the process of generative change. A next collaboration catalyst has to do with developing a "generative performance state."

Developing a generative performance state is an important condition for producing generative collaboration.

A generative performance state emerges when each member of a group is focused on a common intention, centered in themselves and has a sense of connection to larger "field" of positive resources surrounding them.

SFM Collaboration Catalyst: Developing a Generative Performance State

A *generative state* comes from being in the COACH state and including what my colleague Stephen Gilligan and I refer to as the "three positive connections" in our work with generative change. These involve an ongoing, subjectively felt connection to:

1. An intention (or vision)
2. A state of personal "flow" that comes from the felt connection to yourself (your somatic center) and your individual excellence
3. The sense of potential and possibility that emerges from your connection to a surrounding "field" of positive resources

In a group, the connection to a shared *intention* produces *resonance* between group members. Each group member's connection to his or her *state of flow* and to him/herself as a unique, creative individual produces the possibility of *synergy* with the others in the group. The connection to the *field of positive resources* creates the potential for the *emergence* of something new and unpredictable.

In my previous example of the two musicians, their shared intention is to produce an innovative and entertaining performance for their audience as they enjoy themselves and support one another. The two also clearly are able to connect to their own state of personal flow and their unique, individual excellence. The support of the orchestra provides them with a larger field in which to perform that creates the potential and possibility for something new to emerge. The combination of these three things together produces a generative performance state.

To practice entering a generative performance state as a group, go through the following steps:

1. Begin by creating a COACH Container as described in Chapter 1 (pp. 74-75). As each group member senses that he or she is fully present and in his or her COACH state he or she says aloud to the others, "I am here" or "I am ready."
2. Group members bring their attention to a shared intention for generative collaboration. Group members can share any simple, succinct verbal statements, images or somatic expressions or gestures that represent that intention until each feels a strong sense of connection to that future reference point. This should bring a sense of focus and resonance to the group.

3. Group members then each bring their attention to their experience of their unique somatic center (the "C" of the COACH state) and their own individual excellence. It is often useful for group members to recall experiences of situations in which they felt a sense of personal "flow" – a state in which they were able to express themselves and their excellence in a congruent and unimpeded fashion. Again, group members may share any simple, succinct verbal statements, images or somatic expressions or gestures that represent their sense of their individual excellence. This creates the possibility for group members to complement and synergize their unique ideas and excellences with one another.

4. The members of the group then open their attention to include the other group members and the "field" between them. If the group has gone through the collaboration catalyst of Fostering a Field of Co-Sponsorship, it can be helpful to remember what they have seen and sensed about one another that they like. It can also be useful for group members to internally recall individuals (teachers, sponsors, friends), objects, places or other presences that bring them a feeling of self-confidence and resourcefulness; and the sense of being part of a larger holon.

5. Maintaining the COACH state, group members then open their focus of attention to simultaneously include all three positive connection

   – their shared intention
   – their state of personal flow and connection to their individual excellence
   – the larger field or holon of which they are a part

6. Each group member should begin to feel a sense of generative energy and resourcefulness flowing to them and through them from each of these connections individually and together. It can be useful for group members to "anchor" this state by each finding a symbol and a somatic gesture or movement.

Similar to the vibration on the metal plate of sand that shapes the sand into progressively more complex forms, a generative performance state stimulates greater imaginative potential among group members.

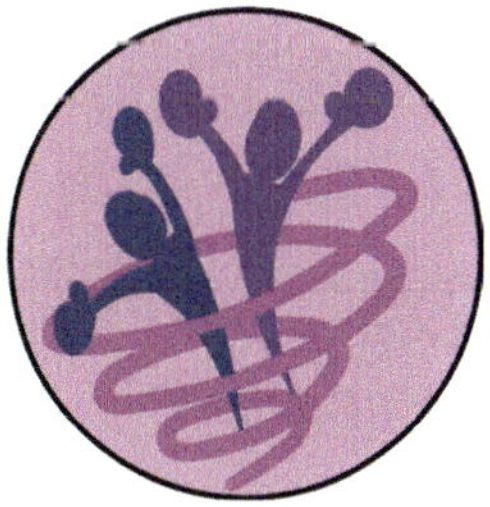

Similar to the vibration on the metal plate of sand that shapes the sand into progressively more complex forms, a generative performance state stimulates greater imaginative potential among group members.

Once a group has set an intention and entered a generative performance state, it can begin to utilize that state by applying the multiple perspectives of the group members to define goals and actions. One way to that is through a collaboration catalyst – that is also a fundamental Masterminding process – that I call "intervision."

SFM Collaboration Catalyst: Applying Multiple Perspectives to Promote Synergy through "Intervision"

One important source of collective intelligence and generative collaboration arises out of the fact that people have different maps or models of the world, different backgrounds and different skill sets.

The process of intervision assumes that group members are peers and that there is no single correct map of a situation. Rather, each person's perspective is valuable and contributes something to the overall venture.

The way that one individual represents a particular vision or idea can automatically help to stimulate and enrich the perception of others.

As I have already asserted, the mindset of generative collaboration is not about fighting over who will get the "bigger slice of the pie," but rather how to make the whole pie bigger through synergistic relationships and cooperation. The key to success is *connectivity*. Successful entrepreneurs are able to say, *"This my future. Can you contribute?"* and then ask, *"What is your vision so I can contribute?"*

One very powerful source of collective intelligence and generative collaboration arises out of the fact that people have different maps or models of the world, different backgrounds and different skill sets. When these differences are complementary, they form the basis for generative interactions through which something new can emerge. *Intervision* is a process that I developed in the early 1990s as a way to discover possible synergies and constructive overlaps between different people's visions, missions, ambitions, projects and ventures, and to promote the emergence of potential collaborations. Various forms of intervision are also the foundation for the Masterminding process.

Intervision can be contrasted with supervision. In "supervision" there is an implied hierarchical relationship between people; the supervisor provides the "right map" to the other person. In "inter-vision" it is assumed that people are peers and that there is no single correct map of a situation. Rather, each person's perspective is valuable and contributes something to the overall venture.

In addition to the assumption that people are peers, there is also an important implication in the term "vision." In fact, one of the goals of the intervision process is to encourage visual and symbolic thinking strategies in a group context so that new perspectives can emerge.

Thus, the key benefit of intervision has to do with the influence of the way we represent and conceptualize our ideas and visions. The way that one individual represents a particular vision or idea can automatically help to stimulate and enrich the perception of others. For this reason, the intervision process is best done in a group of at least four people in order to get enough of a range of diversity.

Another important goal of intervision is for each group member to become inspired by the visions and ideas of the others. This requires listening from one's whole being and engaging the creative unconscious as opposed to just using one's cognitive mind. Again, as my friend and colleague Richard Moss points out, "the greatest gift you can give to yourself or another person is the quality of your attention." Therefore, intervision sessions always begin by first applying collaboration catalysts such as *Creating a COACH Container*, *Fostering a Field of Co- Sponsorship and Developing a Generative Performance State.* This establishes a strong sense of resonance and connection between the individuals involved in the intervision process and enhances the possibility for synergy and emergence.

An important goal of intervision is for each group member to become inspired by the visions and ideas of the others.

In the CrossKnowledge Success Factor Case Example, for instance, I described an application of the intervision process during a key event whose purpose was to create alignment and enthusiasm and to promote collective intelligence regarding the company's new direction. The employees of the company were organized into interfunctional groups of approximately 10- 12 people and seated around round tables, each facilitated by a member of the company's Executive Committee. All 160 people were provided with papers and drawing supplies, and were invited to draw his or her image of what that company vision presented by the CEO meant for him or her as an individual within his or her role in the company. The group members at the various tables then shared and compared their drawings, looking for resonance and synergy with respect to their perception of the company's vision and mission. Then, all 160 pictures were then placed on folding screens set up around the conference room so that the team was surrounded by the images the presentation of the company's vision had generated.

The natural result of utilizing different perspectives is that people are more engaged because they feel their opinions are important.
— **Eunice Parisi-Carew**

When I work with groups of entrepreneurs, a typical intervision format involves each of the group members taking turns presenting his or her "elevator pitch." As group members listen, they are invited to let the words and ideas of the presenter touch and inspire them and look for possible synergies with their own visions, projects and ventures.

One at a time, each group member describes his or her vision or project; i.e., gives his or her "elevator pitch."

The other group members individually draw a picture or symbolic map of the vision project or venture, reflecting their own personal understanding of the vision or project.

As each person finishes describing his or her vision or venture, the rest of the group members individually draw a symbolic or metaphoric picture of their personal understanding of the presenter's vision or project. When drawing, each person makes his or her own representational map without looking at the other drawings. Each group member, including the presenter, is to draw his or her own individual picture of what the presenter's vision or project has inspired in him or her.

It can be any kind of a diagram or a sketch. For example, somebody might draw a tree or landscape; another person may just draw a group of symbols like rectangles, circles and stars and connect them with lines and arrows.

Each of the group members is then to consider where there may be areas of complementarity or synergy between the presenter's vision project or venture and their own. Group members can symbolically illustrate the relationship by adding a link to their own vision or venture as part of their drawing.

Group members are then to consider what resources they can freely offer to the presenter. A "resource" in this case would be something that the group member can contribute to help the presenter better manifest his or her vision, project or venture. Resources, for example, could be a book, article, website, contact information for a person or organization that could be helpful, etc. A resource could also be in the form of a suggestion, advice or guidance drawn from one's own experience or area of expertise.

It is important the resource be something that the group member can offer to the presenter without asking for anything in return.

Once group members have completed their pictures and thought of the resources they can offer, each person takes turns explaining what they have drawn and making their contribution using the following format:

1. "This is my picture of your idea or vision . . ." (Briefly explain the drawing as is necessary.)
2. "What your vision inspires in me is . . ." (Share any feelings, ideas, new perspectives, etc., the presenter's words or ideas have triggered in you.)
3. "A resource I can freely offer that can help you to implement your idea or vision is . . ."
4. "Some possible areas of synergy or collaboration are . . ."

When all the group members have finished sharing their pictures and offering their resources, the presenter gives feedback to the group in terms of how his or her own map of the vision or venture has been enriched.

After all of the group members have made their elevator pitches, the group can discuss where there may be areas of genuine collaboration and cooperation between their various visions and ventures. If there is time, the group can also explore creating a drawing or picture that represents overlaps or common areas of their visions.

To summarize the basic steps of this "intervision" format:

1. One at a time, each group member describes his or her vision or project; i.e., gives his or her "elevator pitch." As the other group members listen, they pay attention to what inspires them about the presentation and look for possible synergies with their visions, projects and ventures.
2. Following each presentation, the other group members individually draw a picture or symbolic map of the vision project or venture, reflecting their own personal understanding of the vision or project. Group members also reflect upon possible areas of complementarity or synergy with their own projects or visions and upon possible resources that they can freely offer to the presenter.
3. Group members then share their pictures, offer their resources to the presenter and mention possible areas of cooperation or synergy with the presenter.
4. When all group members have finished presenting their visions, the group reflects upon and solidifies key areas of collaboration between various members of the group.

Group members then share their pictures, offer their resources to the presenter and mention possible areas of cooperation or synergy with the presenter.

The group reflects upon and solidifies key areas of collaboration between various members of the group.

Perceiving a problem situation from multiple perspectives is an important part of problem solving.

Shifting or enriching our perception of a situation can open up whole new areas of possibilities.

Applying Intervision to Promote Generative Collaboration for Problem Solving

The process of intervision can also be applied to encourage collective intelligence and generative collaboration for problem solving and conflict resolution. In fact, the term "intervision" has been used for several decades by European psychotherapists as a way to describe group sessions in which they discuss how to handle challenging situations or clients within their practices. I originally introduced the notion of its use in a business context in 1990 at a Leadership Conference I was holding at the University of California at Santa Cruz. I brought it up as a process to be used for "meta leadership"—leading other leaders. The process essentially involved a group member bringing up a situation of difficulty to a group of peers. Rather than tell that individual what he or she *should* do, or what was the "correct" solution, fellow group members simply asked questions, clarified the "problem space" surrounding the situation, and related personal experiences. The clarification and multiple perspectives generated from the process assisted the individuals confronting difficult situations to arrive at their own solutions to address the problems or challenges.

When applying intervision for problem solving, I emphasize the important implications of "vision" and the use of symbolic visualization in the intervision process as a means to stimulate innovation and creativity. Much of the benefit of intervision has to do with the influence of the way in which we represent and conceptualize our problems, ideas and outcomes. Shifting our perception of a situation can open up whole new areas of possibilities. One of the goals of intervision, when used as a collaboration catalyst, is to apply visual and symbolic thinking strategies in a group context. A powerful form of co-creativity arises out of the fact that people have different mental maps of the world. Someone else's perspective of your problem or outcome can in and of itself help you to shift or enrich your perception of the situation.

The following is a description of how to apply intervision process to problem solving. It is one of the primary Masterminding formats I use with the Successful Genius Mastermind group. Again, it is best done in a group of at least four in order to get a big enough range of diversity. (And since "intervisible" literally means to be "mutually visible," intervision generally takes place with group members sitting in a circle so everyone can see each other.) Before beginning, the presenter should make sure that the group has created a COACH Container, set intention, developed a generative performance state and is ready to listen deeply.

In this form of intervision, each of the group members answers the question: "What is something I would like *this* group's support for that could also be of common interest to the group?"

One of the group members, the "explorer," describes his or her problem or challenge to the other group members. The explorer should keep his or her description to 5 minutes or less. Part of the purpose of limiting the time available for the description is to keep it from getting too long for people to be able to listen attentively. The explorer can also include an image and somatic model (gesture) for the challenge.

When listening, group members should maintain a generative performance state and keep in mind that *the greatest gift you can give to yourself or others is the quality of your attention.*

During the intervision process, rather than cognitively "thinking," group members should let their ideas come "to" them, emerging from the collective intelligence and creative unconscious (field) generated by the group.

When the explorer is finished describing his or her situation or challenge, each group member is to let a resource for the presenter to come "to" him or her in the form of words, images and somatic expressions. Rather than cognitively "thinking," group members should let their contribution to the presenter come from the collective intelligence and creative unconscious (field) generated by the group.

Group members are to explain their images and impressions without giving specific suggestions to the explorer. Rather than give suggestions, they are to help widen the explorer's mental map of the situation surrounding the problem or challenge. To do this, group members simply show and explain the way they represented their own perception of the situation. The simple fact that they've represented the explorer's situation differently will naturally start to expand or enrich his or her perception of it.

At the end of the process, the explorer is to share with the group members what he or she has received that is most valuable. Other group members may also want to comment on what they have received as a result of the process as well.

The explorer describes (in 5 minutes or less) his or her problem or challenge.

Each group member is to let the presenter's description of the challenge prompt a resource in the form of words, images and somatic expressions.

To summarize:

1. The explorer describes (in 5 minutes or less) his or her problem or challenge.
2. Drawing on the collective intelligence and creative unconscious (field) generated by the group, each group member is to let the presenter's description of the challenge prompt a resource in the form of words, images and somatic expressions.
3. Group members share their contributions and discuss the enrichments and synergies.
4. Presenter and group share what has been received.

The presupposition of the exercise is that making external maps in the form of drawings and other types of representations is an effective method to (1) acknowledge the diversity of maps between people and (2) develop multiple perspectives of a particular situation.

One variation of the intervision process is to have all group members select a similar context and explore their problems, goals or visions for that area, in order to find common issues and areas of overlap.

Example of Applying Intervision to Problem Solving with the Italian State Railway

As an example of this, in the mid 1990s I was involved in an intervention with State Railway of Italy. It was during the early days of the European Union and the company was transitioning from being a state run organization to becoming privatized. The company was also struggling to meet European transportation standards. The changeover was causing a lot of turmoil within various divisions of the organization. Instead of generative collaboration, the interactions between the managers of the various divisions invariably degenerated into conflict and "finger pointing."

As a component of my part of the intervention, I assembled a group of top managers from various functions within the organization. Instead of discussing their opinions verbally, I had the members of the group each create their own symbolic image of the problem situation their company was facing.

One person pictured their situation as being like a group of sailors on a sailing ship. Each had many tasks to do on board the ship. Under normal circumstances the sailors could both do their jobs and communicate with one another. But in a stormy sea, the sailors had to focus so much on their own tasks that they did not have the opportunity to observe or interact with one another, making it more difficult to coordinate their activities.

Another individual viewed their situation as being like astronauts whose capsule had crash-landed on a planet that had no natural resources to sustain them. So the astronauts were trying to salvage as many supplies and pieces of equipment as they could from the damaged spaceship in order to survive on the planet.

Still another manager saw the situation as if the company were a dysfunctional family. Another perceived it as also being like a family, but a normal one. She saw their situation as being similar to that of adolescents hesitantly preparing to leave home and live on their own for the first time.

By comparing their different symbolic images, the group members were able to hear and understand their different perspectives without having to feel like they needed to defend their map of the situation. Rather than arguing about whose perception was the right map, they were more easily able to perceive and explore the deeper assumptions presupposed by the various symbolic images, and to discover hidden strengths as well.

For instance, both the metaphor of the ship and the astronauts' capsule assumed a challenging environment, but one presupposed the problem as being a communication issue between a group of crew members, whereas the astronauts were contending with a hostile environment. And it was significant that the problem on board the ship was one of communication between the crew as opposed to poor leadership on the part of the captain.

By going back and forth between the different metaphors, the group began to become aware of what was the same between the various perspectives and which assumptions could be validated or reexamined. As a result of this process, the group was able to communicate about their differences in perception with much less tension, anxiety and defensiveness. They also had several new perspectives and metaphors from which to view their situation. This allowed them to explore innovative solutions because they were approaching the problem with a different type of thinking than they had done previously.

Group members share their contributions and discuss the enrichments and synergies.

Presenter and group share what has been received.

The Importance of "Second Position" for Generative Collaboration

Effective collaboration of any type involves some degree of understanding of and empathy for your collaborators.

It is difficult if not impossible to have an effective collaboration of any type without some degree of understanding of and empathy for your collaborators. As the examples of CrossKnowledge, the two musicians and the Italian State Railway illustrate, in order to have generative collaboration, it is even more important to know what is important for your collaborators and how they think and feel. This is true for every part of your Circle of Success.

We have found, for instance, that entrepreneurs frequently do not understand the mindset and values of investors. They don't understand why investors don't see the obvious value of their ideas and innovations and don't want to give them money. Likewise, investors frequently can't follow the priorities and level of risk entrepreneurs are willing to take (especially with the investors money!). This is most likely why Steve Jobs was forced out of Apple in the mid 1980s; a mutual misunderstanding between himself as an entrepreneur and the company's stakeholders.

Taking "second position" is a term used in Success Factor Modeling to describe the ability to step into another person's point of view or perspective.

According to Success Factor Modeling, our understanding of others comes from the ability to go to "second position" with them. Taking *second position* is the term used in NLP to describe the ability to step into another person's point of view or perspective with respect to a particular situation. It involves shifting from our own *first position* or "self" perspective and viewing the situation as though you were the other individual; to "be in his or her skin," "walk a mile in his or her shoes," "sit on the other side of the desk," etc.

This is a crucial ability in order to be able to create a successful product, company or team. As entrepreneur Cindana Turkatte pointed out, "Unless you put on a second position you cannot accomplish anything."

Making a Second Position Analysis

When I am coaching entrepreneurs, I encourage them to make a specific analysis of each of the positions making up SFM Circle of Success: customers, investors (stakeholders), employees and partners.

To develop a product or marketing plan, for instance, an entrepreneur must put him/herself into the shoes of potential customers. To establish a financial plan and raise capital, an entrepreneur must be able to take on the perspective of stakeholders and investors. To build and motivate an effective team, the entrepreneur must be able to view the situation through the eyes of his or her team members or employees. To establish strong alliances and relationships, the entrepreneur needs to take the point of view of possible partners.

The robustness of the second position perspective the entrepreneur has with each potential collaborator will determine the ease and effectiveness with which each of these core relationships are established.

There are different levels and degrees of taking second position. Being in someone's home or workplace is a way to get a second position on an environmental level. Imitating or acting like another person is a way of taking second position on a behavioral level. Learning about a person's thinking strategies and mental maps is a way to develop second position on a capability level. Taking on a person's values and beliefs is way of getting a second position at an even deeper level. Identifying with another person and taking on his or her personality would involve second position at a very deep identity level. Experiencing another person's passion for his or her vision and sense of purpose would provide the most profound second position.

Making a Second Position Analysis involves considering another person's point of view from a number of different levels.

Making a Collaborator Attribute Analysis of one of the members of your Circle of Success involves taking a second position with that person on each of these different levels and considering the ways you or your project or business can provide synergies, opportunities or benefits for that person at each level.

The following is a process that you can use in order to make a Collaborator Attribute Analysis for key members of your own Circle of Success in order to identify potential areas of fit or support.

Select a collaborator or potential collaborator who you would like to understand better and work with more effectively.

Imagine being "in the shoes" or "in the skin" of that person.

SFM Collaboration Catalyst: Collaborator Attribute Analysis

Applying second position to identify the essential attributes of key collaborators and find win- win scenarios is an important part of effective entrepreneurial collaboration. Investing the time to make a Collaborator Attribute Analysis, for instance, supports the so-called "law of attraction." According to this principle, being clear about what you want and need makes it easier for you to attract it. Putting out what you want into the "field" will make it more likely that you will perceive good chances when they emerge and makes it easier for others in your network to recognize and let you know about potential opportunities.

Defining key attributes can help you to widen and enrich each of the parts of your Circle of Success:

- Knowing the key attributes of *customers* helps you to develop and target products and marketing efforts to better fit your customers needs and motivations. You may also find that you can appeal to a wider range of potential customers than you originally thought.
- Knowing the key attributes of *team members* helps you to more easily select and align with those with whom you will be working.
- Knowing the key attributes of *stakeholders* helps you to identify and appeal to potential investors and others who have essential resources.
- Knowing the key attributes of *partners* helps you to define and recognize areas of potential synergy and complementarity.

In the following exercise you will be stepping into the shoes of a collaborator from any part of your Circle of Success, assuming the role of that collaborator and taking on various levels of attributes.

1. Imagine being in the environment of your collaborator.

   Ask yourself: *What are the attributes of my collaborator's environment? What environmental needs does my collaborator have that I can help to address? What constraints can I help him or her overcome? What opportunities can I provide?*

2. Imagine being "in the shoes" of your collaborator.

   Ask yourself: *What are the attributes of my collaborator's behavior? What behaviors and actions does my collaborator need to engage in that I can help support or facilitate? What tactics can I provide? What reactions can I help him or her avoid?*

3. Imagine being in the mind of your collaborator.

   Ask yourself: *What are the attributes of my collaborator's skills and abilities? What skills and capabilities does my collaborator need that I can help him or her to develop or acquire? What strategies or knowledge can I share?*

4. Imagine being in the belief system and value system of your collaborator.

   Ask yourself: *What are the attributes of my collaborator's beliefs and value systems? What values and beliefs does my collaborator have or need that I can help to promote, strengthen or fulfill? How can I help him or her to become or stay motivated? How can I help him or her feel that he or she has the permission that s/he needs to take a risk?*

5. Imagine being in the identity or role of your collaborator.

   Ask yourself: *What are the attributes of my collaborator's identity? What sense of mission or identity can I sponsor? How can I contribute to his or her sense of self-esteem? How can I help him or her see or feel his or her role more clearly?*

6. Imagine being in the larger system of your collaborator.

   Ask yourself: *What are the attributes of my collaborator's vision and purpose? What sense of vision and purpose can I help to awaken more fully? How can I help him or her to achieve a greater entrepreneurial spirit?*

Which level(s) seem(s) most significant? At which level should you focus your efforts to attract collaborators of the type you have identified?

For example, maybe it is more important that they be "warm-hearted and open" than that they have a particular technical background.

e.g., Steve Jobs' criterion that is team members "fall in love" with Apple.

Can you add synergies or complements on other levels than you are currently?

In the coming chapters, we will continue to apply the skill of taking second position as part of other collaboration catalysts that help to create an even more powerful and robust Circle of Success.

Consider your collaborator's perspective from each of the various levels of success factors.

Identify at which levels you can best support or synergize with your collaborator and how you can incoroprate that into your interactions.

Chapter Summary

Successful entrepreneurs encourage collective intelligence and apply principles of generative collaboration in order to share and leverage resources and to expand the business opportunities that are available to them—i.e., to make a "bigger pie" to share.

Generative collaboration differs from basic collaboration in that its purpose is to create something new and beyond expectations. In basic collaboration, people work together, following the actions prescribed by their roles, in order to accomplish a set objective or get a particular job done. For generative collaboration, people must stimulate each other to think "outside of the box" and support one another to do things that have not previously been accomplished.

Generative collaboration emerges as a result of collective visioning, in which people share and synergize their individual passions and visions; similar to bubbles joining together to create a larger whole, or two hydrogen atoms and an oxygen atom combining to form water. This helps to draw out the full participation of those involved in the collaboration.

The case example of CrossKnowledge illustrates the importance and effectiveness of using collective intelligence and generative collaboration in order to transform crisis into opportunity and move a venture to a new level by creating a potent Circle of Success. The CrossKnowledge co-founders applied various types of collaboration catalysts to foster generative collaboration among themselves as stakeholders, and with their customers, team members and partners.

CrossKnowledge's transformation is an example of *generative change*, which requires breaking through old mindsets in order to create something "completely new." The fundamental steps of generative change involve:

1. Setting an intention (i.e., a vision or direction)
2. Developing a generative performance state
3. Applying multiple perspectives for defining goals and actions
4. Engaging multiple perspectives to creatively transform obstacles
5. Establishing ongoing practices for continued creativity

These steps are designed to create the resonance, synergy and potential for emergence necessary for effective generative collaboration. Their purpose is to help individuals in a group maintain their uniqueness and creativity as individuals while simultaneously performing as an integrated holon. The steps of generative change can be supported by several important and powerful collaboration catalysts.

Creating a Generative Performance State is a collaboration catalyst that helps to produce *resonance* and the possibility of *synergy* between members of a group in order to create the potential for the emergence of something new and unpredictable. A generative performance state comes from each group member connecting to:

1. An intention (or vision)
2. A state of personal "flow" that comes from the felt connection to oneself (one's somatic center) and your individual excellence
3. The sense of potential and possibility that emerges from the connection to a surrounding "field" of positive resources

The process of *Intervision* applies the generative performance state of a group to help collaborators actively support and participate in the achievement of each others' visions and ventures. Intervision is a method of bringing together multiple perspectives in order to enrich the vision of what is possible and to creatively transform obstacles. Intervision is based on the fact that one very powerful source of collective intelligence and generative collaboration arises out of the fact that people have different maps or models of the world, different backgrounds and different skill sets. When these differences are complementary, they form the basis for generative interactions through which something new can emerge. The process of Intervision involves shifting from linear, logical and verbal thinking to symbolic visualization to stimulate more visionary and synthetic ways of thinking and communicating.

Second Position Analysis—understanding the worldview and mindset of another person—is another important collaboration catalyst. It is difficult to have any form of effective collaboration, basic or generative, without the ability to step into the shoes of one's collaborators and understand their thinking process and motivations. Second Position Analysis is one of the key capabilities of effective entrepreneurs. Making a *Collaborator Attributes Analysis*, for instance, involves taking Second Position with representatives of your Circle of Success at different levels in order to identify ways in which you can support them or contribute to their success.

References and Further Readings

- *Adam Grant: Be a Giver Not a Taker to Succeed at Work*, Dan Schawbel, Forbes.com, April 9, 2013
- *Yanni Live at the Acropolis*, Private Music, 1994.

03 Generative Collaboration and Disruptive Innovation

If you want to be incrementally better: Be competitive.
If you want to be exponentially better: Be cooperative.
Anonymous

These waves of technology, you can see them way before they happen, and you just have to choose wisely which ones you're going to surf.
Steve Jobs

SUNNY CAR
ANTONIO MEZA

Generative Collaboration and Disruptive Innovation

Disruptive innovations create a new market whose boundaries do not fit within existing markets.

Leveraging the process of generative collaboration to create a successful venture involves finding synergies between the different parts of your Circle of Success – between team members and customers; between customers and investors; between investors and partners; between partners and team members; and so on. The most profoundly generative changes occur when a number of synergies align with shifts in what I have called "the field of innovation." When this happens it produces what is known as a "disruptive innovation."

Disruptive innovations are those that create a new market whose boundaries do not fit within existing markets. Disruptive innovations are a classic example of "making the pie bigger." The mass-production of automobiles, digital photography, the Nespresso machine, the Internet, mobile phones and the iPod are all examples of disruptive innovations. They each created new markets that had not existed before.

Most innovations are "incremental innovations" which follow existing and well-identified trends

Most innovations are not disruptive. They do not create major changes for customers, or for ventures or their suppliers or partners. They are called "incremental innovations". They follow existing and well-identified trends. When our conscious cognitive minds and egos look into the future they can generally only project through the filters of what we already know. Extrapolating from our existing knowledge gives us only a very limited view of future possibilities.

The Future Isn't What it Used to Be

Extrapolating from our existing knowledge gives us only a very limited view of future possibilities.

As the famous comment by science fiction author Arthur C. Clarke above indicates, what we perceive as a possible or likely future is constantly evolving. Consider the images on the following page of what people from the year 1900 imiganed that the technology of the year 2000 would look like.

Even though there is much creativity in these visions for their time, and they anticipate technologies like television, radio, X-rays, manned flight and armored vehicles, these images clearly look much more like the year 1900 than they do like the year 2000. Many technologies that characterize our millennium are not even suggested in these images—such as commercial airliners, personal computers, smart phones, microwave ovens, the Internet, Global Positioning Systems (GPS), nuclear weapons, satellites, space stations, etc. Nor is their notion of how fashion would evolve over the coming century even close to today's clothing designs.

Communication

Air Travel

Entertainment

Surveillance

Military Combat

Imagination is More Important than Knowledge

Disruptive innovations emerge from synergies of vision and imagination more than from the extension of current knowledge.

Disruptive innovations emerge from synergies of vision and imagination more than from the simple extension of existing knowledge. In the words of Albert Einstein:

> *Imagination is more important than knowledge. Knowledge of what is does not open the door directly to what should be [or could be]. One can have the most complete knowledge of what is and yet not be able to deduce from that what should [or could] be the goal of our human aspirations.*

The dynamic between incremental innovation and disruptive innovation is another expression of the interaction between what I have referred to as the "ego" and the "soul" in businesses and organizations. Incremental innovations are more driven by our ego needs and ambitions. As I pointed out in *Success Factor Modeling Volume I*, the ego dimension of an individual or organization comes from the perception of ourselves as a separate entity and tends to:

"Ego" driven competition tends to favor incremental innovation because it is less risky and uncertain and the rules are well established.

- Orient toward survival, recognition and personal ambition.
- Relate to social roles and who we feel we should be or need to be to get approval or acknowledgement.
- Focus on permission, safety, security, approval, control, achievement and self-benefit.
- Emphasize the careful application of analysis and strategy.
- Respond reactively to external conditions.
- Sort for dangers and constraints

These characteristics foster a more competitive approach to business and innovation. The competitive race consists of matching or overtaking competitors in a game where rules are well established.

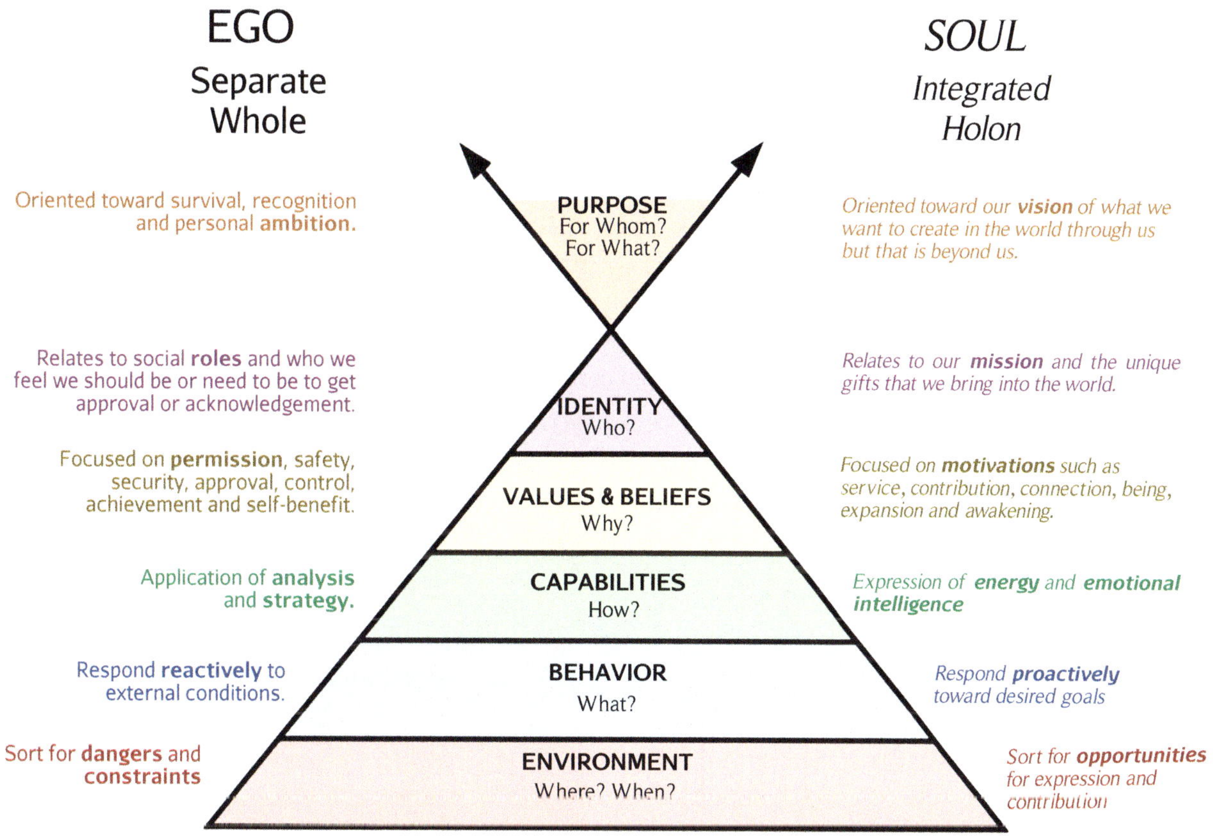

Incremental innovations result from an orientation toward ourselves as a separate entity, while disruptive innovations emerge from an orientation toward ourselves as part of a larger whole.

Disruptive innovations emerge from collective visions of groundbreaking possibilities, which create new markets. Because they diverge from past market evolutions, disruptive innovations are difficult to anticipate or predict using existing knowledge.

Disruptive innovation, on the other hand, involves major changes for customers, suppliers, team members, stakeholders and partners. Disruptive innovations tend to emerge from the collective visions of new possibilities (like the analogy of the bubbles joining together in the previous chapter) and diverge from past market evolutions. They result more from the "soul" dimension of individuals and organizations, which comes from our perception of being part of something larger than ourselves. This point of view tends to:

- Orient toward a vision of what is possible in order to create a better world.
- Relate to our mission and the unique gifts that we bring into the world.
- Focus on motivations such as service, contribution, connection, being, expansion and awakening.
- Emphasize the application of intuition and emotional intelligence.
- Respond proactively toward desired goals.
- Sort for opportunities for expression and contribution.

Thus, disruptive innovations emerge from synergies of vision and imagination, creating entirely new markets. They are notoriously difficult to predict from existing knowledge alone.

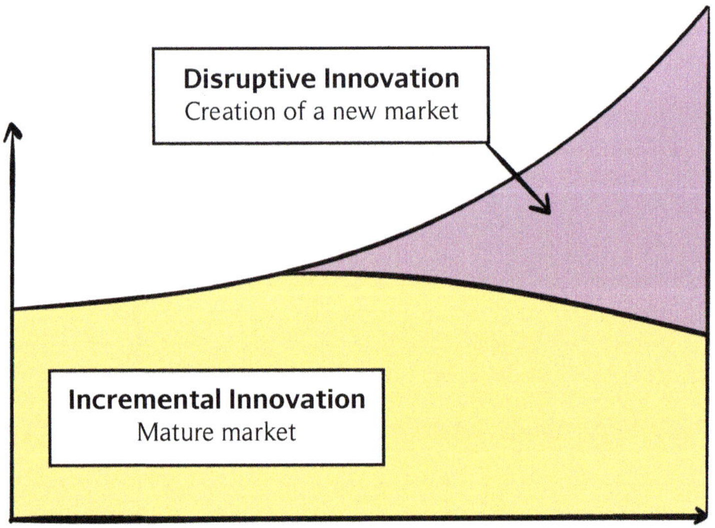

Disruptive innovations emerge from synergies of vision and imagination, creating entirely new markets.

Dynamics of Disruptive Innovation

Disruptive innovations initially take place in a market niche, but address a potentially much larger latent market.

Disruptive innovations arise from a "virtual community" composed of "early adopters" among customers and "pioneers" with the team who share a vision that transcends the current identity and capabilities of either group.

In his book *Misez sur les ruptures de marché* ("Betting on Disruptive Innovations"), my colleague Benoit Sarazin explains that a disruptive innovation initially takes place in a market niche. However, as a result of shifts in the "field of innovation," the market potential is much larger than this initial niche and is likely to reach market segments that the company could not attract before. Thus, even though the disruptive idea first appeared in a niche within an existing market, it is not limited to that market.

Synchronization of Early Adopters and Pioneers

In our study of the success factors that lead to "disruptive" innovation, Benoit and I discovered that this type of innovation emerges as a result of synergies between several different parts of the Circle of Success. They begin with a virtual community of "early adopters" from among *customers* and "pioneers" within the venture's *team members*. A disruptive innovation begins to emerge when these two groups have some way of joining and synergizing to form a new vision for a product or service. This vision transcends the current identity and capabilities of either group. In addition to the visions of the two groups being resonant and synchronized, early adopters among consumers and pioneers within the venture's team need to belong to the same "virtual" community. This virtual community emerges from developments in the larger "field of innovation."

We call this community virtual because it only materializes for the purpose of creating the innovation. Early adopting customers and pioneering team members within an organization may not initially know one another. They come together to undertake a common and exciting project. After completion, they do not feel the need to keep in touch. Early adopters and pioneers are united by the fact that they are passionate, excited by a vision and are committed to give life to what had not previously been imagined.

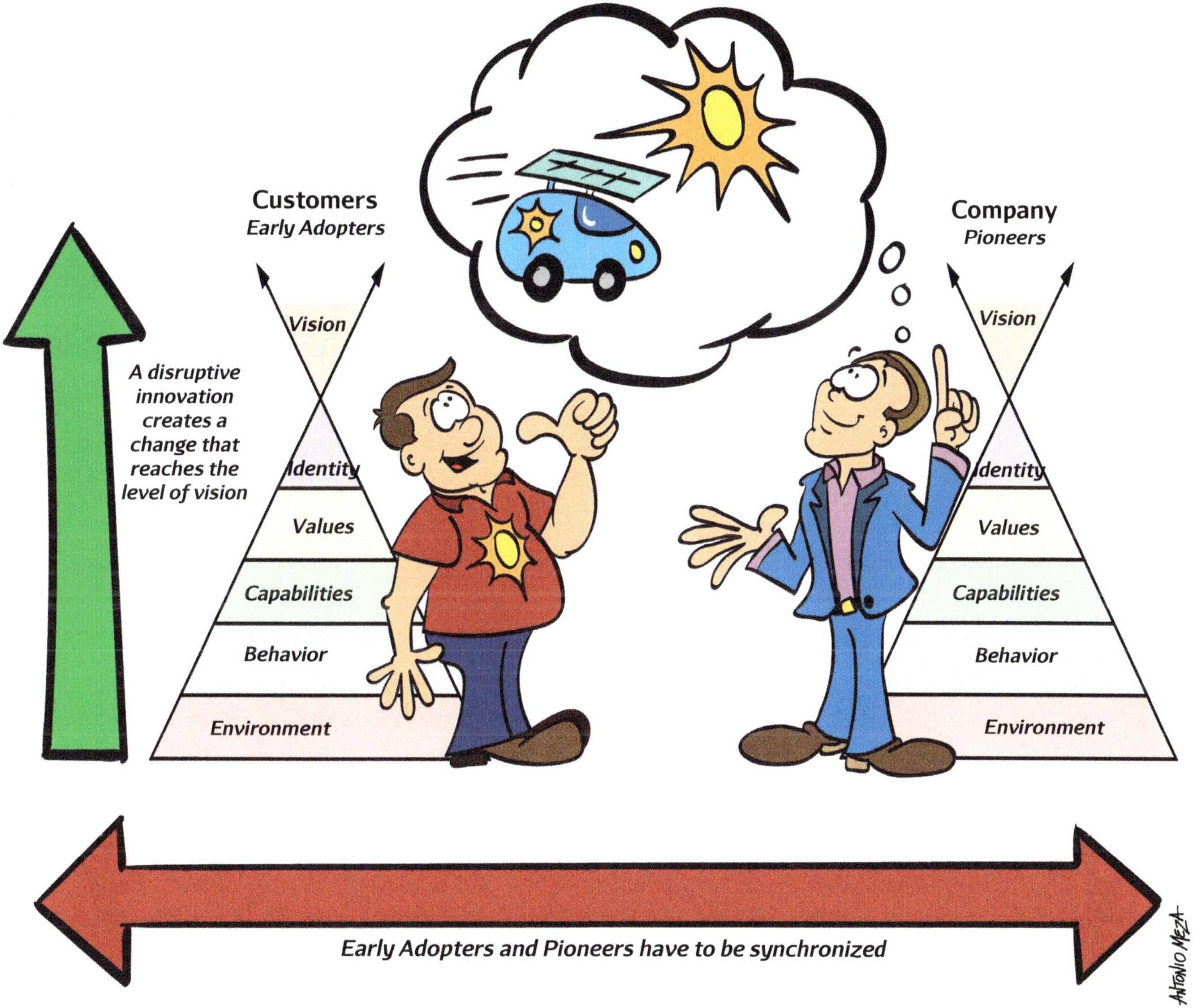

A disruptive innovation begins to emerge when early adopters among consumers and pioneers within the venture's team have some way of interacting and synergizing to form a new vision for a product or service.

Riding the Wave of Chaos and Uncertainty

A disruptive innovation generates a dramatic change for both customers and companies. Dramatic changes are also usually accompanied by a necessary period of chaos and uncertainty.

Consider the Cymatics experiment I presented in Chapter 1. As the vibration on the plate increases, the pattern of the sand becomes more complex and sophisticated. As the images on the following page show, however, in order for this to happen, the old pattern of sand must become be disrupted and go through a phase where the pattern is less clear. It is no longer the old pattern, but not yet the new pattern. The intermediate patterns (B, D, F and H) have less obvious structure than A, C, E, G and I.

This is a good analogy to what happens with disruptive innovation. The shift in the frequency of vibration on the plate is a metaphor for what I have called the "field of innovation." A shift in this field opens the possibility for a new structure to emerge. In order for that to happen, however, markets, customers and companies will go through a period of lack of clarity and uncertainty as the previous structure is disrupted and the new one not yet clear.

Disruptive innovations necessarily produce a period of chaos and uncertainty that can be threatening to existing status quo. Thus, they are frequently not initially embraced and may even be opposed at first.

This is one of the reasons companies and individuals find it difficult initially to embrace disruptive innovations. Disruptions are understandably considered threatening and unsafe by the "egos" of organizations and individuals. During these periods of chaos and uncertainty, it is important that individuals and teams work to remain in what I have called the COACH state versus CRASHing, and to maintain a generative state – by staying connected to themselves, the bigger vision and the field of resources within their virtual community.

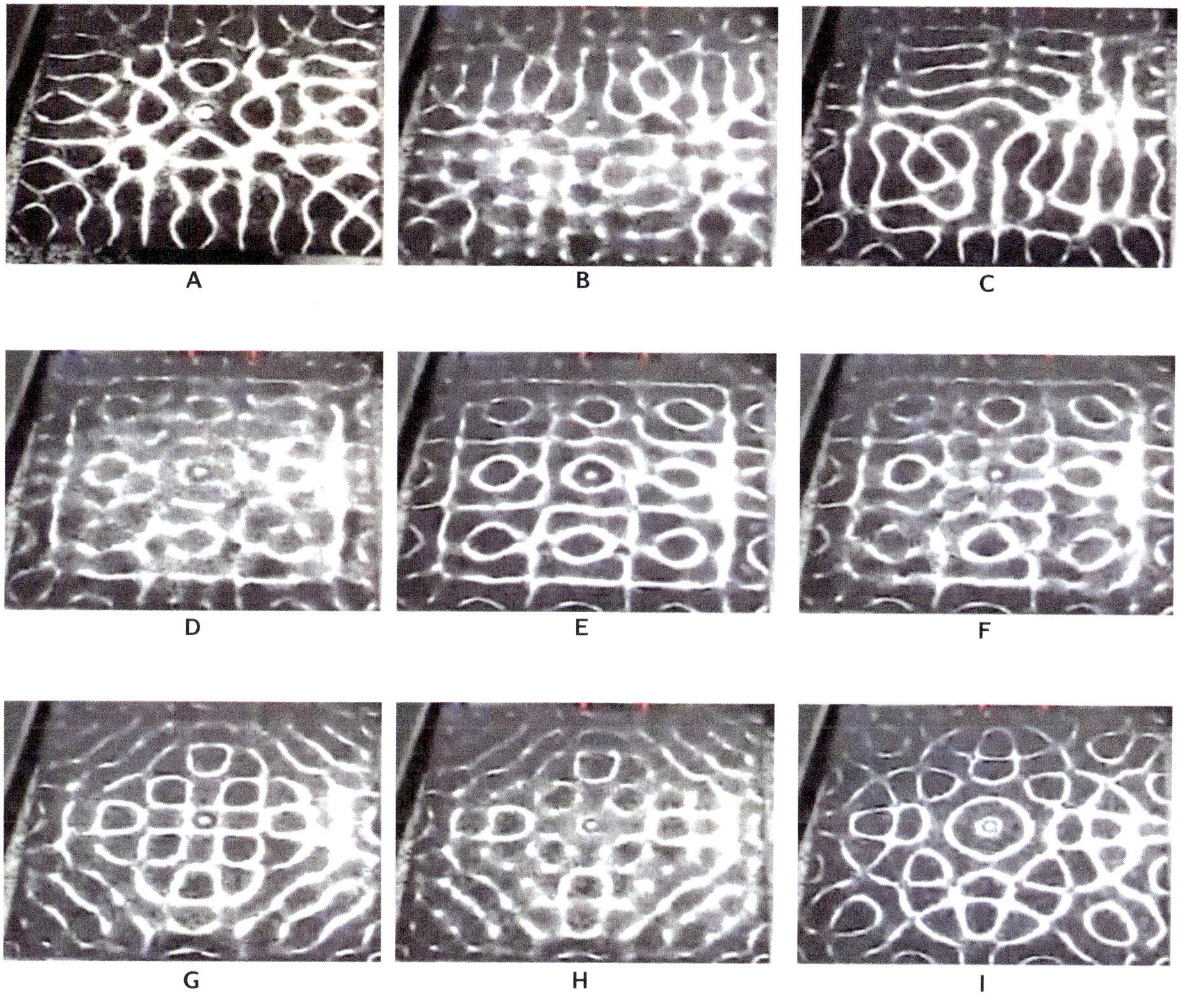

In order to move from one level of structure to another, a system must go through a period of chaos and uncertainty.

In this sense, disruptive innovations raise obstacles that only the adventurers' spirit of early adopters and pioneers can overcome. Disruptive innovations can succeed if two conditions are met:

1. The level of change experienced by early adopters and pioneers needs to reach the levels of values, identity and vision. If this is the case, it will generate the necessary amount of enthusiasm and commitment to prevail against uncertainty and doubt. If the change is limited to environment, behavior and capabilities, it will not create sufficient energy and commitment to support a disruptive innovation.
2. Early adopters and pioneers have to share an overwhelming passion based on the alignment of values, identity and vision. Their values, identity and vision are not necessarily identical because their backgrounds and situations may differ. But these key factors need to be resonant for the virtual community to bring a challenging project to completion.

To produce a disruptive innovation, the level of change experienced by early adopters and pioneers needs to reach the levels of values, identity and vision

Disruptive Innovation and Open Innovation

Disruptive innovation also generally requires a certain degree of "open innovation." That is, it requires that companies be open to the participation of external partners outside of the company, but who share common values, vision, etc. Thus, open innovation also includes the generative collaboration between "groundbreakers" within the company and partners who are "trailblazers."

Open innovation is essentially defined as "innovating with partners by sharing risk and sharing reward." According to Henry Chesbrough, "Open innovation is a paradigm that assumes that firms can and should use external ideas as well as internal ideas, and internal and external paths to market, as the firms look to advance their technology." The central idea behind open innovation is that in a world of widely distributed knowledge, companies cannot succeed by relying entirely on their own research. The knowledge and resources necessary for innovation resides in employees, suppliers, customers, competitors and universities. Thus, in order to accelerate innovation and leverage resources, companies to need to create win-win partnerships and alliances with other organizations and entities.

Example of the Apple iPod

As I pointed out in *SFM Volume I*, (pp. 270-271) the concept of Open Innovation is well illustrated by Apple's development of the iPod. The iPod was a very successful disruptive innovation. It transformed the portable media players market and altered the online music sales market. When the iPod was designed, Apple's management knew that it lacked the capabilities necessary to make an attractive music device. Instead, "groundbreakers" within the company acquired software from companies who were "trailblazers" to build iTunes and hired music software experts and hardware engineers from outside the company, integrating them with a team of Apple veterans. These new individuals helped make the connection between Apple and the virtual community of music lovers.

Disruptive innovations also frequently require "open innovation" and generative collaboration between "groundbreakers" within the company and partners who are "trailblazers."

In 2000, Steve Jobs' candy-colored iMac was leading the charge for Apple's comeback. As a way to further spur sales, groundbreakers within the company started asking: "What can we do to motivate more people to buy iMacs". The virtual community of dorm rooms, a big source of iMac sales, was made up of music lovers that traded tunes like crazy on the online site Napster. They were attaching speakers to their computers and stealing music from CDs. But unlike Windows computers, the iMac did not have music software.

To catch up with the music revolution, Apple licensed software from 3rd party "trailblazer" PortalPlayer and released iTunes on the iMac in January 2001. Then, Apple started to look for gadget opportunities to increase the iMac attractiveness. They found that there was no convenient portable device to play the music that was stored on a computer. Digital music players were either big and clunky or small and useless. They decided to generatively collaborate to create their own music player, partnering with another trailblazer, Pixo, to help design and implement the user interface, and the first iPod was released in October 2001.

Apple's development of the iPod in the early 2000's is a good example of a disruptive product produced by open innovation.

Initially, the iPod was just an accessory to the iMac. Its sales volumes were limited, as should be for an accessory. But pioneers and groundbreakers within Apple realized that the real market opportunity was much larger. The iPod could be sold as a portable device for all kinds of computers, including Windows based computers. iTunes was adapted for Windows XP in October 2003. This move triggered the major sales growth that we know of today.

Open innovation is an important modality of generative collaboration for companies, like Apple, that cannot rely on incremental innovation to survive and thrive.

Beginning in 2004, iPod sales rose dramatically eventually taking the largest market share of the portable media player market. By 2008, iTunes was the number one music vendor in the United States.

Apple has continued this practice of open innovation until today. The Apple Watch developed in part due to "its ecosystem of partners that make accessories that connect to the iPhone." This included trailblazers who have produced glass that can curve around the human body. Before he died, Steve Jobs envisioned the possibility of an Apple car that, at the time of this writing, is undergoing an intense period of open innovation.

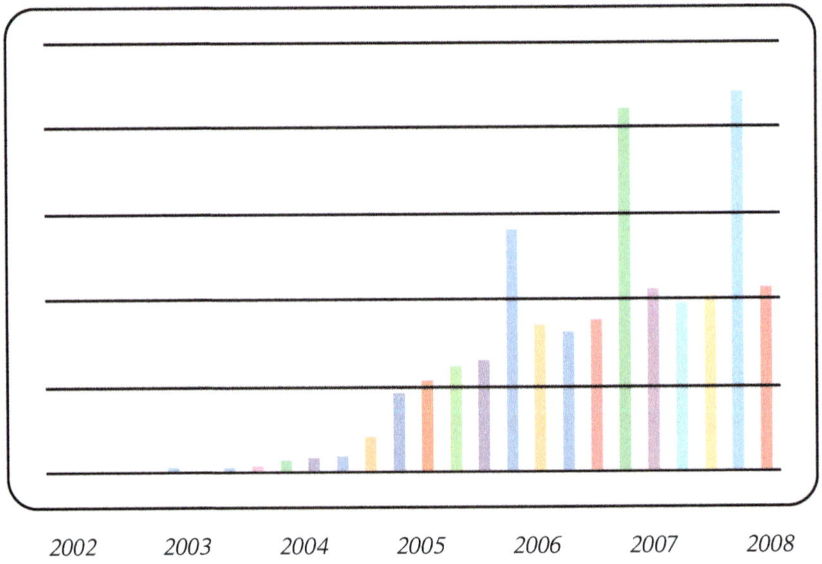

History of iPod unit sales per quarter from 2002 to 2008

iPod story
2008 – iTunes becomes the number one music vendor
portalplayer
pixo
I ♥ ♫!
2001 – Apple engages in Open Innovation with Pixo and portal player to produce the iPod and iTunes; releases iTunes for Windows in 2003
2000 – Steve Jobs' own love of music resonates with the virtual community of college students, but the iMac has no music software
ANTONIO MEZA

Open Innovation and the Circle of Success

In summary, successful disruptive innovations emerge from generative collaboration occurring within a "virtual community" consisting of *early adopters* among customers and *pioneers* within the company. Disruptive innovations do not usually arise from theory. They emerge from a collective change at the level of shared vision, identity and values.

Disruptive innovations emerge from a collective change at the level of shared vision, identity and values between customers who are early adopters and team members who are pioneers. This creates a meaningful contribution.

Disruptive innovations also typically require that companies and ventures do not hesitate to mix existing teams with outside partners. This produces the phenomenon of Open Innovation, in which *groundbreakers* within the company generatively collaborate with external partners who are *trailblazers* as passionate innovators who strive to go beyond what is possible today.

Disruptive innovations also require open innovation and generative collaboration between groundbreakers within the company and partners who are trailblazers. This is necessary to produce innovation and resilience.

Open Innovation and the Circle of Success

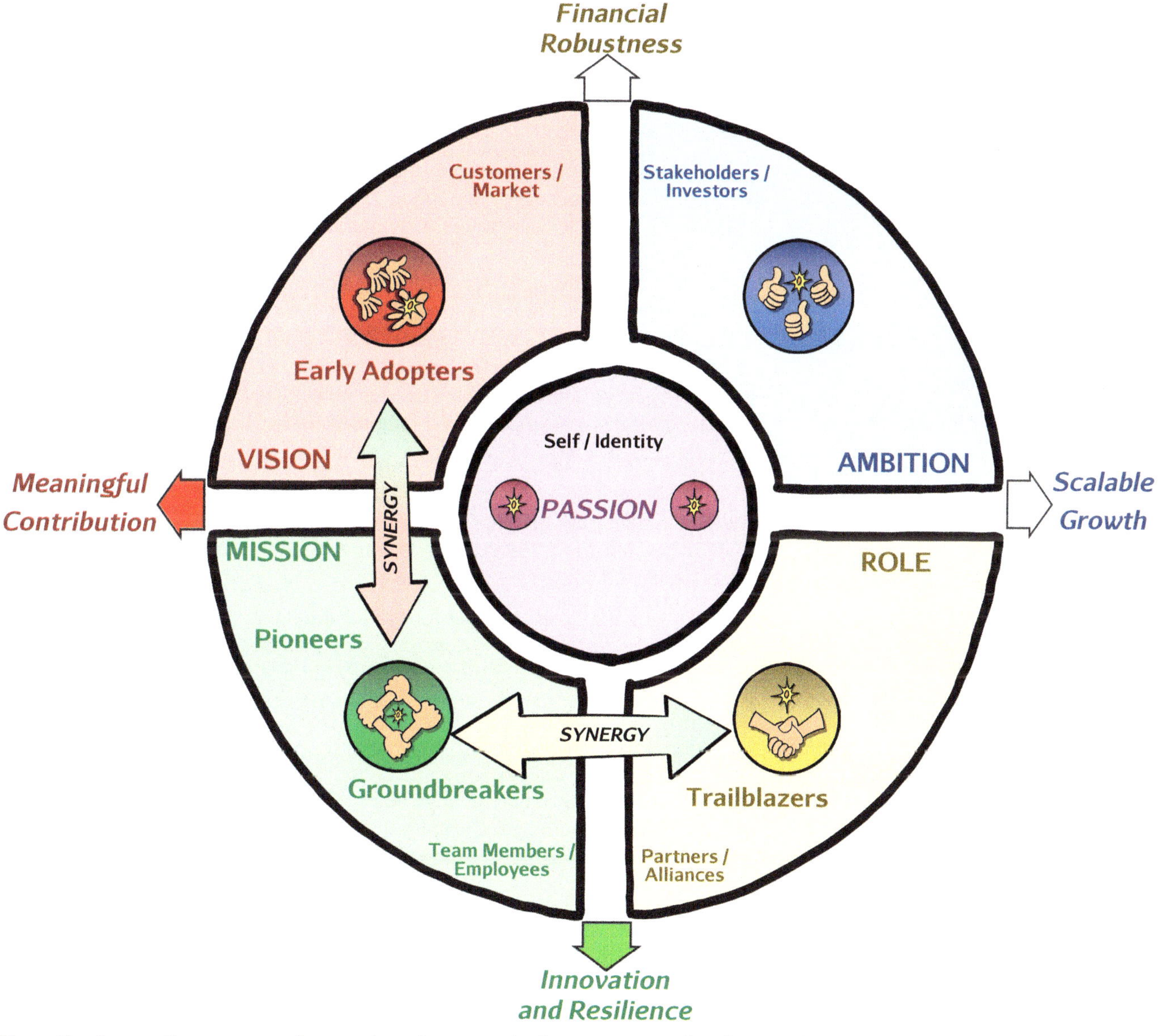

Disruptive Innovations emerge from a virtual community integrating Early Adopters from among customers with Pioneers in the company, and Groundbreakers within the company with external partners who are Trailblazers.

A significant factor in successful disruptive innovation is the ability to detect "weak signals" that herald new and previously unmet needs and interests within the field of innovation.

The analogy of frogs versus bats illustrates the significance of the ability to detect weak signals.

Frogs see only the most obvious trends.

Disruptive innovations create new markets whose reach is difficult to foresee in advance. In these new markets, leadership is up for grabs and leaders in previously existing markets do not have an edge over their competitors.

In order to succeed, companies need to "be ahead of the curve" and, in the words of Steve Jobs' hockey metaphor, "skate to where the puck is going to be" rather than where it currently is. Companies and ventures must identify new trends in the field innovation early enough to take advantage of opportunities. If they fail to do this, they fall under the domination of others who are more perceptive and agile. Thus, a significant factor in successful disruptive innovation is the ability to detect "weak signals" that herald new and previously unmet needs and interests. Disruptive innovations are not created by marketing nor customer surveys. They appeal to latent customer needs rather than to those that are already known. As Henry Ford famously put it, "If I had asked people what they wanted, they would have said faster horses."

In my book *Alpha Leadership*, my co-authors and I use the analogy of frogs and bats to illustrate the importance of detecting weak signals. Frogs and bats share the same food source— flying insects—but have completely different strategies for catching their prey.

Frogs sit on lily pads waiting for the food to come to them. (To use another metaphor, they subsist on the "low hanging fruit".) Frogs are notoriously poor at detecting weak signals. Consider the somewhat disturbing experiment in which a frog is placed in a pan of water that is then put over a flame. If the water is heated slowly enough, the frog fails to detect the change in temperature and never jumps out. It winds up boiling along with the water.

Similarly, frogs are only able to detect the most obvious features of flying insects. Unless something is a certain size and shape and moves in a certain way, a frog will fail to recognize it as food. A frog can starve to death in a box of flies if they do not move.

In contrast, bats use sophisticated sonar systems, capable of detecting extremely minute signals, to go out and track down their prey with impressive facility. A single brown bat, for example, can catch around 1,200 mosquito-size insects in one hour. (In Bracken Cave, Texas, it's estimated that the 20 million bats that live there eat about 200 tons of insects each night!)

Frogs can only see the most obvious trends. Bats listen for subtle signals. To put it another way, frogs are a metaphor for a more "ego" driven mindset. Bats represent a more "soul" driven mindset.

Perhaps the most important part of the comparison, though, has to do with the widely differing life spans of these two creatures. Most frogs live an average of about two to five years. Bats, on the other hand, have an average life span of twenty-five to forty years! Thus, the bat has clearly evolved a much longer-term survival strategy. The fact that bats make up a quarter of all mammals (there are more than 1,100 species of bats in the world) is another testimony to the effectiveness of their capacity for weak signal detection.

I often ask the companies, executives and entrepreneurs that I coach, whether they are more "frog-like" or "bat-like."

A key lesson here is that to succeed with disruptive innovations, a venture must create as large a network as possible of early adopters, pioneers, groundbreakers and trailblazers; i.e., "bats" who will be able to identify weak signals related to new opportunities. It is essential to have people ready to alert the company to potential innovative ideas and support their realization. Because they are on the lookout for opportunities, innovative teams and ventures often find opportunities that others fail to see. Because customers, team members and potential partners are a diverse population, they represent a large number of virtual communities. Therefore, each one is in contact with a network that can potentially bring about the seeds for a disruptive innovation.

New pathways open up when you stay in action and your "luck factor" increases. Opportunities arise when you are in communication with other people. The more connections you have, the more links you have to the "field" of possibilities and the "weak signals" indicating areas for potential disruptive innovations.

Bats listen for subtle signals.

The average life span of a bat is 10 times longer than that of a frog. The bat's capacity to detect weak signals is clearly a longer-term survival strategy.

To be successful, a venture needs to attract and encourage "bats" who will be able to identify weak signals related to new opportunities.

Success Factor Case Example:

Stefan Crisan: EDHEC Master in Management (Cycle Supérieur en Management)

"Discovering the Magic of Life with People"

Stefan Crisan

Stefan Crisan's development of the Master in Management (Cycle Supérieur en Management) degree program for the EDHEC Business School is an example of a type of disruptive innovation.

The idea behind the program is to give managers access to a new way of being a leader, by working on their personal development and self-awareness."

Stefan Crisan's development of the *Master in Management* (Cycle Supérieur en Management) degree program for the EDHEC Business School is an example of a type of disruptive innovation. Stefan launched the program in 2003 as a part of EDHEC's continuing education curriculum. Unlike a traditional classroom-based business degree program, however, the purpose of Stefan's Master in Management was something more revolutionary – to provide participants with the "experiences, skills and support to become more competent to succeed in a world that is difficult – filled with complexity, suffering and paradoxical situations."

The participants in the program (aged between 35-50) would not be college students, but middle managers who wanted to improve themselves. "They are very experienced self-made managers," explains Stefan, "who lack managerial knowledge since they built their career from scratch, but they all have high potential and the desire to grow professionally and personally. They mostly have arrived at a point where they understand: 'To succeed I have to do more.'" Unlike young people who are just beginning their careers, the participants in the Master in Management program have to "manage a personal and professional life that is overloaded and undergoing a change of paradigm."

The Necessity of Vision

Creating an innovative new program in an established international business school can be quite challenging and requires a strong *vision*. As Stefan points out, "The focus of the program is on developing a *leadership identity* in each participant and inviting them to a transformational experience over a one year cycle. The idea behind the program is to give them access to a new way of being a leader, by working on their personal development and self-awareness."

Stefan goes on to explain:

> *The vision is: Transform oneself to succeed – to see people become masters of transformation. The promise is not to transform the world, but rather to allow people to better understand in order to increase their ability to navigate the world with honesty and clarity versus fear and manipulation.*

To accomplish this, Stefan had to work out a completely new educational structure. Key to this structure was creating *collective events* where "participants can meet and experience leadership moments and gain personal insights." "We immerse people in a special context to experience something intense together," says Stefan, "and after to manage together some course of change experience pertinent and adapted to their professional situation."

Some examples are:

- Spending three days in an Air Force School, exploring how to develop self-control, responsiveness and leadership in the face of difficult situations. Participants wear different clothes, participate in military exercises, manage tension, etc.
- Going into a hospital emergency room and observing how doctors and staff manage clients and each other, and deal with the tension of the situation.
- Observing a philharmonic orchestra rehearsing for a performance.

"In a new context, such as these, participants are able to observe themselves in more easy way," says Stefan. The other parts of the program are composed of an innovative combination of e-learning and individual coaching.

Clearly the emphasis of Stefan's program is on being a true integrated *holon* – both a creatively thinking and acting individual and a contributing part of a larger whole – and developing the skills necessary for generative collaboration. As Stefan points out, "Collective intelligence is essential for the participants. The special course events are specifically designed to promote sharing among them." According to Stefan, the events also help participants "to live and practice situations where inner resources can be useful. To develop the capacity to link inside resources to difficult outside contexts."

Stefan Crisan's vision for the Master in Management at EDHEC was "Transform oneself to succeed".

To accomplish his vision, Stefan had to work out a completely new educational structure incorporating collective events, e-learning and individual coaching.

Stefan Crisan is passionate about innovation and problem solving, especially in situations where he gets to enjoy "the magic of life with people."

The Foundation of Passion

Such a profound reinventing of a business school education has been the culmination of a lifelong passion for Stefan for innovation and teamwork. As he maintains:

> *Innovation is the story of my life. I have met a lot of obstacles and difficulties and overcame them. I am also passionate about people. Since I was born, I have discovered the magic of life with people. I have lived magical moments with people in a context in which we have to attain something. I am motivated by challenging situations where a group has to achieve something.*

"In my student and professional life, I knew a lot of dynamic team situations," continues Stefan. "I had a dynamic, generous and clever education. I had five sisters and brothers and a very lively mother who was a social worker that cared for abandoned children. I learned that it is good to try to give a hand and live together. It creates the feeling to be useful and take participation in a dynamic team context and succeed. That is the story of my life."

In order to transform his passion and vision into a reality for his customers, Stefan had to concretely utilize collective intelligence and generative collaboration in order to build an effective Circle of Success – bringing together the right stakeholders, team members and partners.

Stefan's project had to be aligned with the ambitions of the business school EDHEC, helping their brand to shine internationally.

Fulfilling Ambitions

The primary stakeholder in the venture is clearly EDHEC. The business school supplies many of the essential resources for the program, provides credibility and also shares the risks and rewards of its success. A major success factor for Stefan has been aligning with the school's *ambitions*. "The ambition of EDHEC is very high and in an international context," says Stefan. "There is also an ambition for innovation." The success of a Business School, however, is based on its brand image. This presents a big challenge and potential resistance to projects such as Stefan's. As Stefan points out, "In this context, the risk of failure, which is a feature of innovation, is not good."

Stefan's capacity to create synergies, find key partnerships and facilitate generative collaboration allowed him to overcome many of the risks by building his program rapidly and for a low cost. Launched at the EDHEC campus in Nice, the program has expanded throughout all of France, and Stefan is now looking to expand it internationally. "As an innovator I am OK," says Stefan. "I led an e-learning Master Program to a successful state quickly. I was able to experiment and accomplish a lot without much means."

Stefan's ability to achieve such rapid success with the program was a result of establishing a *role* that allowed him to support the vision and mission of the project in a way that aligned with the ambition of EDHEC, his major stakeholder. As he explains:

> *The reason I could do this is because I am not a teacher, rather a developer. As a developer, I have an advantage to innovate. Also, I am not in the heart of the system, which is the education of youth (and involves thousands of people). I work in periphery in a small part of continuing education with 40-50 people. Within this satellite position I can experiment. My program is handmade, not "industrial." I am considered an "artisan." I provide a window of possibilities. My colleagues decide if they want to incorporate one of them into their way of teaching.*

Stefan's role as a "developer" alowed him to have the flexibility to "think out of the box" and to create interesting partnerships.

Establishing Powerful Partnerships

One of the key factors in Stefan's success has been establishing effective *partnerships*. "Partners give me means to be able to do key activities," he points out. "For example, the course in the Airforce is with a partner. The City Hall of Nice is my partner for the Philharmonic experience."

Stefan Crisan's ability to establish effective partnerships has been a key factor in his success.

Establishing powerful partnerships involves building trust. As Stefan explains:

> *Our primary partners are HR Directors of client companies. Clients become partners because they see the impact on their managers.*
>
> *When you sell courses, you sell "wind." So trust is very important. You have to develop trust with people. Behind the trust is the belief that I can be effective in the managerial development process.*

For example, I may have a number of managers from the same firm in my Masters Level program. The top management in the firm sees the impact on their managers; i.e., the difference in them between the beginning and the end. That is the reason they trust me. Their managers develop trust in themselves and smart behavior in difficult situations. When they see that, they say, "OK. It works." And we continue together .

To build lasting win-win partnerships, Stefan has learned to take on the role of advisor and to listen deeply for what his potential partners really want and need.

To develop a deep level of trust with his partners, Stefan has to create a clear "win" for them in return for their cooperation and participation. To accomplish this, he realized that he had take on the *role* of *advisor* with respect to them in addition to his role as *developer*. "My primary role is to be an advisor with partners," he maintains. "When I don't succeed to have this role, the partnership is cut. The role of advisor is essential for long-term partnerships. They trust me and I trust them."

To be an effective advisor and build lasting win-win relationships that expand and leverage resources for both himself (and EDHEC) and his partners, Stefan has had to learn to listen for what they really want and need. "The resource I have to develop is to listen very deeply and for a long time in order to understand their vision," he claims. "It is not always so evident."

Building an Aligned Team

Of course, central to the success of Stefan's vision and venture has been to attract, align and develop an effective *team*. "My team is my administrative staff, who help to coordinate actions, and also the teachers and coaches inside and outside of EDHEC," says Stefan. In line with the vision of the project, the mission of the team is to "help people in organizations to develop capabilities, heart and vision and to overcome obstacles." The impact of the teachers and coaches is particularly essential to the program's success. According to Stefan:

The mission of teachers and coaches is to be inspiring, to work with people over an extended time and facilitate their transformation. Since they are not in a traditional position of power, as they would be in a classroom, they can observe their impact on people and see the differences in their knowledge and behavior. This is very inspiring, especially for teachers.

To build a successful program, Stefan needed to align his team, including his administrative staff and the teachers and coaches both internal and external to the business school.

While this new way of interacting with students can be inspiring, it can also be quite challenging to implement. "The difficulty is that a classical academic master level program doesn't work like our program and people are used to it working in the classical structure," says Stefan. "For teachers, it is an identity change. They are used to lecturing to a large group. In the context of our program, they have to become a coach in an e-learning context. They have to touch the identity level of the participants."

In fact, one of Stefan's major investments of his time has been in developing and increasing the competency of his team. "I need 2-3 years to coach a teacher to become comfortable in this new posture," he explains. "My primary way is to go first and be an example. I have to demonstrate it is possible. Secondly, I coach people in the team. I practice with them what I practice with the clients. I also manage a collective session, but every teacher is coached. This takes a lot of my time (it is the water under the iceberg)."

One of Stefan's major investments of his time has been in increasing the competency of his team, through his own example, his personal coaching of team members and through collective sessions with team members.

Stefan also takes specific steps to promote *collective intelligence and generative collaboration* with his team. "I try to create situations where we think together collectively," he says. "Every year and quarter we have a meeting of teachers, coaches and staff. Sometimes there are a lot of good ideas to increase the quality of interactions and communication."

Summary: Creating a Circle of Success for a Disruptive Innovation

In summary, Stefan transformed his *passion* for innovation and personal development into a *vision* for middle managers to transform themselves to succeed through self-awareness and collective intelligence. The vision required the development of a unique program combining coaching, e-learning and specially designed experiences to help managers develop a "leadership identity" and acquire the skills to become more competent to navigate a changing and challenging world.

The steps Stefan Crisan took to build his Masters in Management program is a good example of how to create an effective Circle of Success.

Stefan was able to align his vision with the *ambition* for innovation and brand image of his major stakeholder EDHEC. Through his Masters in Management project, he was able to create a type of satellite that provided a window of possibilities for the business school. Stefan's capacity to generatively collaborate and create trust with partners allowed him to put an innovative program in place rapidly and with little cost, greatly reducing the amount of risk for his main stakeholder.

Stefan Crisan's Circle of Success

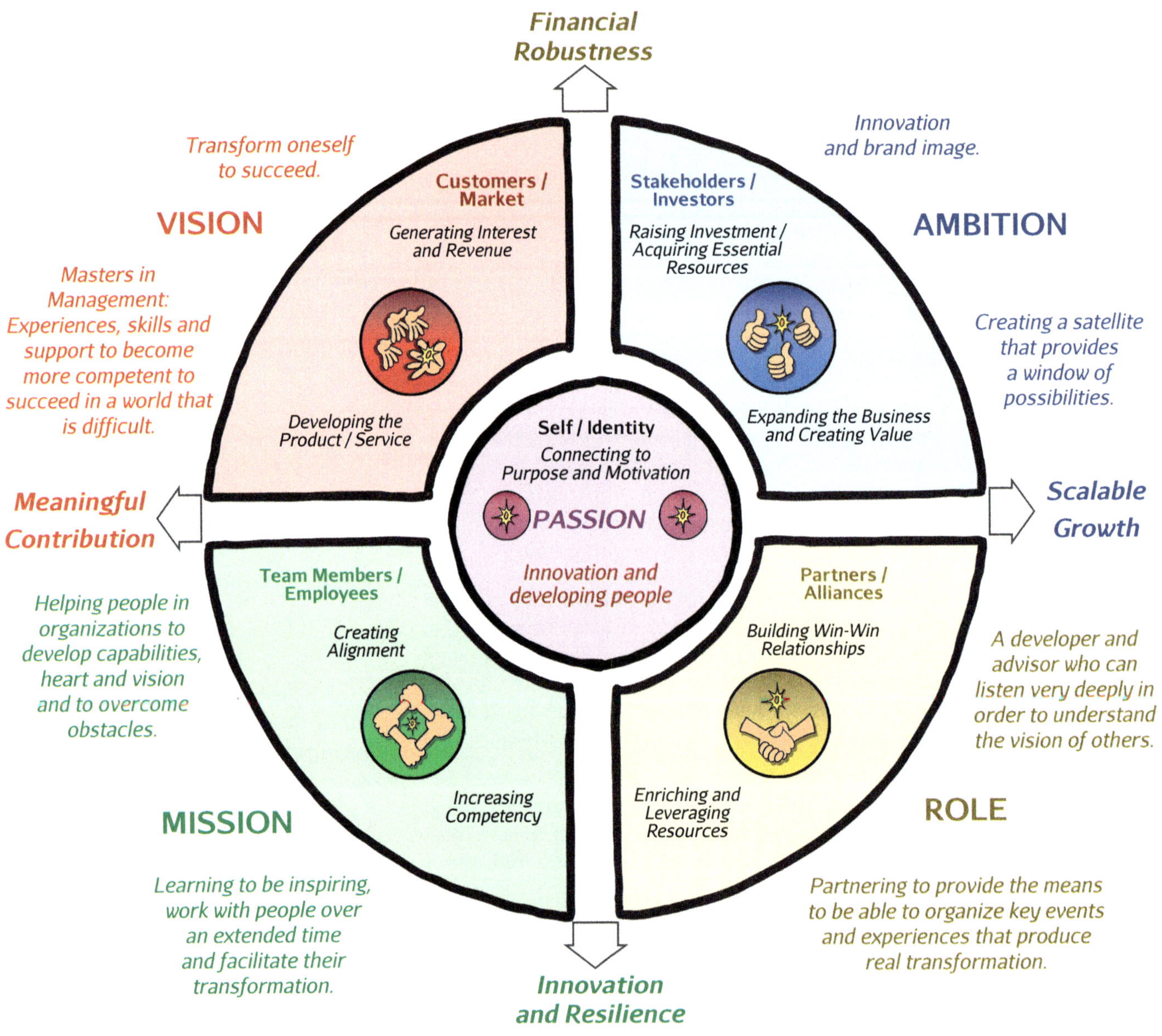

STEFAN CRISAN'S CIRCLE OF SUCCESS

VISION
Customers / Market

* TRANSFORM ONESELF TO SUCCEED.

* MASTERS IN MANAGEMENT: EXPERIENCES, SKILLS AND SUPPORT TO BECOME MORE COMPETENT TO SUCCEED IN A WORLD THAT IS DIFFICULT.

AMBITION
Stakeholders / Investors

* INNOVATION AND BRAND IMAGE

* CREATING A SATELLITE THAT PROVIDES A WINDOW OF POSSIBILITIES

MISSION
Team Members / Employees

* HELPING PEOPLE IN ORGANIZATIONS TO DEVELOP CAPABILITIES, HEART AND VISION AND TO OVERCOME OBSTACLES.

* LEARNING TO BE INSPIRING, WORK WITH PEOPLE OVER AN EXTENDED TIME AND FACILITATE THEIR TRANSFORMATION.

ROLE
Partners / Alliances

* A DEVELOPER AND ADVISOR WHO CAN LISTEN VERY DEEPLY IN ORDER TO UNDERSTAND THE VISION OF OTHERS.

* PARTNERING TO PROVIDE THE MEANS TO BE ABLE TO ORGANIZE KEY EVENTS AND EXPERIENCES THAT PRODUCE REAL TRANSFORMATION.

PASSION:
INNOVATION AND DEVELOPING PEOPLE

A major part of Stefan Crisan's success was his ability to create and encourage synergies through benchmarking, brainstorming and generative collaboration, allowing him, his team and his partners to generate new ideas, find creative solutions and make wiser decisions.

Stefan's success came largely as a result of making game changing innovations by increasing competency of his team members and enriching and leveraging resources through partnerships and alliances.

Assuming the *role* of both a developer and advisor who can listen very deeply in order to understand the vision of others, Stefan was able to establish trust and build long-term relationships with partners. This gave him the means to be able to organize key events and experiences that produce real transformation for his program's participants. Trust and motivation are strengthened through the partners' perception of the "task significance" of their contribution; i.e., its potential to produce positive impact on the lives of others.

A major success factor in creating life-changing transformation for his customers was aligning his team around the *mission* to help people in organizations to "develop capabilities, heart and vision and to overcome obstacles." This meant that the teachers had to switch from their traditional way of interacting with students and learn to be inspiring, to work with people over an extended time and facilitate their transformation.

As with all disruptive innovations, Stefan was able to successfully create and encourage synergies through benchmarking, brainstorming and generative collaboration. This has allowed him, his team and his partners to generate new ideas, find creative solutions and make wiser decisions.

Like many breakthrough innovations, Stefan Crisan's Masters in Management program has brought about a fundamental shift the level of identity; not only for his customers, but also his team members. And essential to this transformation is the ongoing, practical application of collective intelligence and generative collaboration, where each individual grows as a separate whole and simultaneously contributes more to their organizations, communities and society. To put it another way, Stefan has been able to attract a virtual community of "bats" in the form of early adopters, pioneers, groundbreakers and trailblazers who share a common vision and values for transforming themselves and their communities and for "discovering the magic of life with people."

A powerful expression of this is the symbolic image Stefan has of the ultimate purpose of his efforts in which "everyone is in a circle, holding in their hands an elastic carpet, and in the center of the carpet is the world."

In Stefan's symbol for his bigger vision, "everyone is in a circle, holding in their hands an elastic carpet, and in the center of the carpet is the world."

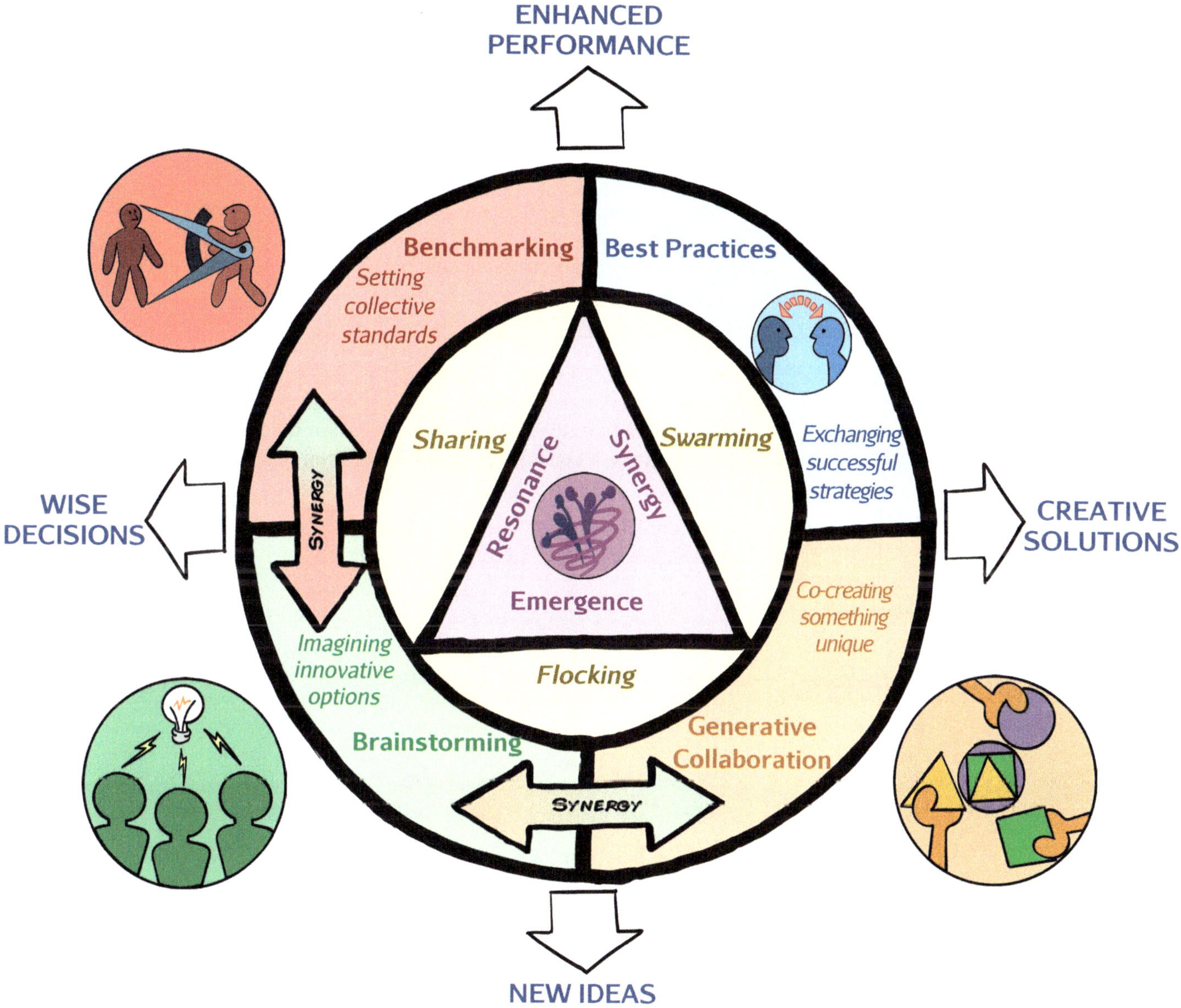

Stefan Crisan was able to synergize benchmarking, brainstorming and generative collaboration to create his ground breaking Masters in Management program for EDHEC.

The Power of Integrating Multiple Perceptual Positions

In the previous chapter, I emphasized the importance of mastering "second position" as an essential skill for the capacity to create generative collaboration. Disruptive innovation requires the ability to take on and incorporate two other important perspectives.

To foster collective intelligence and generative collaboration, next generation entrepreneurs need to master several key "perceptual positions."

Second Position is one of several key "perceptual positions" that are crucial for next generation entrepreneurs to develop proficiency in. A *perceptual position* is essentially a particular perspective or point of view from which one is perceiving a situation or relationship. *First position* involves experiencing something through our own eyes, associated in a "first person" point of view. Second position involves experiencing something as if we were in "another person's shoes." Third position involves standing back and perceiving the relationship between ourselves and others from an "observer" perspective. The notion of fourth position relates to the sense of the whole system or "relational field" (sense of a collective "we") derived from a synthesis of the other three positions.

A perceptual position is essentially a particular perspective or point of view from which one is perceiving a situation or relationship, characterized by specific physical, cognitive and linguistic patterns.

Perceptual positions are characterized by specific physical, cognitive and linguistic patterns. These patterns are summarized in the following descriptions:

First position is you, standing in your own physical space, in your own habitual body posture. When fully associated in first position, you will use words like "me," "I," and "myself" when referring to your own feelings, perceptions and ideas. In first position, you are experiencing the relationship from your own perspective: seeing, hearing, and feeling everything that is going on around you and inside of you in that experience from an associated perspective. If you are truly in first position, you will not see yourself, but will be yourself, looking out at the world through your own eyes, ears, etc. You will be fully associated in your own body and map of the world.

As we have already established, *second position* is being able to assume another person's perspective. In second position, you experience the world through another person's eyes, thoughts, feelings, beliefs, etc. In this position, you are outside of yourself and associated into the other person. You will address your "first position" self as "you" (as opposed to "I" or "me"), using "second person" language. Temporarily assuming another person's position is a wonderful way of evaluating how effective you are on your side of the relationship. (After you have stepped into another person's perspective, it is important to make sure you return to yourself fully, cleanly, and with the information that will aid you in your interactions with that person.)

Third position, or "observer" position, puts you temporarily outside of the relationship in order to gather information, as though you were a witness to, and not a participant in, the interaction. Your posture will be symmetrical and relaxed. In this position, you will see, hear, and sense what the relationship is like from the position of an interested but neutral observer. You will use "third person" language, such as "she" and "he," when referring to the persons you are observing (including the one that looks, sounds and acts like you). You will be disassociated from the interaction, and in a type of "meta" or reflecting position. This position gives you valuable information about the balance and fit of behaviors in the interaction. The information gathered from this perspective can be taken back to your own first position and used, along with the information gathered in second position, to assist in enhancing the quality and effectiveness of the interaction or relationship.

In addition to being able to be clear about our own perspective and understand the point of view others, it is important to be able to take on the perspective of a neutral witness and to develop a sense for the system as a whole.

Fourth position involves a synthesis of the other three perspectives, creating the sense of "being the whole system." It involves an identification with the system or relationship itself, producing the experience of being part of a collective, characterized by language such as "we" (first person plural). Fourth position is essential for producing a "group mind" or "team spirit." It is the essence of what I have referred to as a "virtual community" in this chapter.

An entrepreneur's ability to take all four key perceptual positions helps to create and enhance stronger generative collaborations and increase the potential for game-changing disruptive innovations.

In summary, perceptual positions refer to the fundamental points of view you can take concerning a relationship between yourself and another person or group of people:

- **1st Position:** Associated in your own point of view, beliefs and assumptions, seeing the external world through your own eyes—an "*I*" position or *self* position.
- **2nd Position:** Associated in another person's point of view, beliefs and assumptions, seeing the external world through his or her eyes—a "*you*" position or *other* position.
- **3rd Position:** Associated in a point of view outside of the relationship between yourself and the other person as a witness to the interaction—a "*they*" position or *observer* position.
- **4th Position:** Associated in the perspective of the whole relationship or system—a "*we*" position or *field* position.

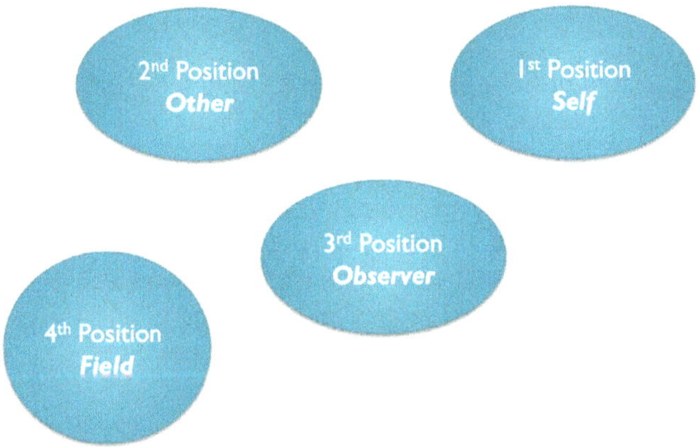

Your own "first position" is clarified and enriched by the process of defining your personal passion, vision, mission, ambition and role. "Second position" with your collaborators can be accomplished by going through the *Collaborator Attribute Analysis* presented at the conclusion of the previous chapter.

The following are tools that I use to coach entrepreneurs to apply the third and fourth position perspectives in order to create and enhance stronger generative collaborations and the potential for game-changing disruptive innovations.

There are four fundamental perceptual positions from which we can perceive any interaction.

SFM Collaboration Catalyst:
Creating Win-Win Collaborations through Third Position

The ability to skillfully take a 3rd (observer) position helps ensure win-win collaborations by exploring the ways that the various key players involved in your Circle of Success will benefit from potential collaborations.

Generative collaboration creates an expansion of ideas, resources and wealth by building strong and viable win-win frameworks. The more people that win and benefit from a personal or collective vision, the greater will be the positively reinforcing feedback loop that sustains it. The same will be true of strong partnerships.

Consider the example of Ed Hogan and the development of the holiday "vacation package" cited in *Success Factor Modeling Volume I* (p. 94). Ed created a structure in which multiple members of his Circle of Success would benefit through their collaboration. Ed's creative vision helped make the pie bigger for everyone involved.

A key question that entrepreneurs should be constantly asking is, "In what way can a collaboration create a 'bigger pie' for my project or venture?"

The following worksheet provides a "road map" to help ensure win-win collaborations by helping to define the ways that the various key players involved in your Circle of Success will benefit from potential collaborations. It also helps to clarify the positive consequences those benefits for others will produce for you and your project or venture. The best perspective from which to answer these questions is from a third position as an observer of yourself and your prospective collaborator.

My Vision/Venture: ____

Potential Collaborator: ____________________________

Customers

The win/benefit of the collaboration for the customers is ______________________________

The positive consequence of that for myself and my venture will be ______________________

Investors/Stakeholders

The win/benefit of the collaboration for investors/stakeholders is ______________________

The positive consequence of that for myself and my venture will be______________________

Partners/Allies

The win/benefit of the collaboration for partners/allies is _____________________________

The positive consequence of that for myself and my venture will be______________________

Team Members

The win/benefit of the collaboration for team members is _____________________________

The positive consequence of that for myself and my venture will be ______________________

SFM Collaboration Catalyst: Collaborator Audit

The SFM Collaborator Audit is a tool that can help to assess and identify areas of strength and weakness in collaborations with others.

Establishing a true win-win relationship is crucial for effective generative collaboration. When a relationship is not mutually beneficial, it is not wise to collaborate with another person, even if the other party is eager to do so.

Thus, it is equally important to know who not to collaborate with. Inappropriate relationships can be a drain of time, effort and energy.

It is important to keep in mind that collaborations that are not win-win are not necessarily win-lose either. A relationship could produce win-neutral results or neutral-neutral results in which parties are not necessarily losing, but are also not strongly benefiting either. Such collaborations at best produce only a level of basic collaboration and can take away as much time and energy as win-lose collaborations.

Sometimes a relationship starts out as win-win but then shifts or changes such that it is no longer equal and balanced in terms of benefits. Collaborations need to be periodically reassessed and evaluated.

The SFM Collaborator Audit is a simple tool that allows entrepreneurs to quickly assess the state of their relationship with a particular collaborator.

Win-lose, lose-lose and neutral-lose collaborations are ones that people generally recognize as needing to be dropped or seriously restructured.

It is the win-neutral and neutral-neutral collaborations that people frequently either miss or put up with because they do not see them as obvious problems, but which can pull time and attention away from other important issues.

If a collaboration is found to be imbalanced it should be set aside or the collaborators may want to use some of the other SFM Collaboration Catalysts described so far in this book to rejuvenate or rebalance the relationship.

Collaborator A

Collaborator B	WIN	NEUTRAL	LOSE
WIN			
NEUTRAL			
LOSE			

The SFM Collaborator Audit is a tool for entrepreneurs to quickly assess the potential of a collaboration.

SFM Collaborator Catalyst: Moving to Fourth Position
Forming a Relational Field or "Virtual Community"

Forming a solid and lasting win-win collaboration requires the ability to synthesize and align capabilities and resources within the framework of a common vision. This builds a type of joint identity or relational "field" (i.e., a "virtual community") characterized by a feeling of "we-ness."

We use the following worksheet to help prospective collaborators find areas of overlap and synergy at different levels. It is a powerful way for collaborators to solidify their understanding of the "big picture" of the collaboration and provide a road map for working together as a team.

1. "What themes are shared by your visions?"

"What is your common vision as collaborators?"

Our common vision is ______________________________

2. Given this common vision, what is your common purpose and identity as collaborators?

"Who are you together?" "What is your joint identity?" (This often is best expressed as a metaphor.)

We are ______________________________

"What is your common mission?"

Our common mission is to ______________________________

3. "What are your shared beliefs and values?"

Our shared values and motivations are ______________________________

We believe / assume ______________________________

4. "What capabilities do you have as collaborators that are beyond your individual capabilities?"

As collaborators, we have the additional capabilities to ______________________________

5. "What will be your joint actions together?"

We can use those capabilities in order to carry out the joint actions of

____

6. "What is the common environment or external context in which you will be operating?"

We will carry out those actions in the common context of______________________________

Another way of creating the conditions for 4th position is a collaboration catalyst that I call *Identifying Resonance for Task Significance.*

SFM Collaboration Catalyst: Identifying Resonance for Task Significance

Identifying Resonance for Task Significance has to do with exploring the level to which the perceived importance of an activity is shared between members of a group.

The phenomenon of "fellowship" emerges when there is a high level of resonance for task significance.

Fellowship is the process of helping one another reach a purposeful goal through joining with and supporting each other through a number of often unpredictable life situations and challenges.

As I mentioned in Chapter 1, resonance between members of a group regarding "task significance" is a major success factor in increasing performance and creating collective intelligence. *Task significance* has to do with the perceived importance of an activity with regard to its positive impact on the lives of others both within and beyond the group of which one is a member. There is a very high correlation between the degree of perceived task significance and people's level of motivation and performance.

Clearly, the more people within your Circle of Success who perceive your project or venture to have a high degree of task significance, the more time, focus and effort they will devote to it. The following collaboration catalyst provides a way of identifying people's degree of perceived task significance with respect to your venture.

It incorporates a tool I developed with my colleague Ian McDermott for our online *Fellowship Program* (http://www.thefellowshipprogramme.com). Our concept of "fellowship" is that it is a type of generative collaboration that comes from sharing a higher "soul" purpose. In J. R. R. Tolkien's epic novel *The Fellowship of the Ring* (transformed into the highly acclaimed 2001 film by Peter Jackson), for instance, an unlikely group of quite diverse individuals undertake a complex and dangerous journey together in order to save the "free races of Middle Earth." Though they are in many ways natural adversaries, their common higher purpose unites them and inspires them to remarkable actions and achievements beyond their previous capabilities. Working together in fellowship, they are able to accomplish things that would have been impossible for any of them to do as individuals.

From this perspective, *fellowship* is about helping each other reach our soul's purpose through joining with and supporting each other through a number of (generally unpredictable) life situations and challenges. Creating a successful venture in many ways requires the development of a certain degree of fellowship between ourselves and the various members of our Circle of Success.

In this particular collaboration catalyst, each group member is invited to present a summary or overview (elevator pitch) of his or her project or venture; and to do so with as much passion and authenticity as possible. As participants listen to each other's projects or ventures, they are to notice the level of "resonance" regarding task significance that they experience using a scale from 1 to 5 – in which "1" represents the minimum level of resonance around task significance and "5" represents the highest degree of resonance. The level of alignment regarding task significance is what Ian and I call the Resonance Index. We can represent these levels of resonance in the following statements:

1. *"I'm glad someone in the world is thinking about this. I wish you well. If I can think of something that might be useful for you I will let you know."*
2. *"This interests me. Let me know what I can do to help and I will do what I can."*
3. *"What you are doing inspires me too. Let's be in touch about what we can do to work together to further this.*
4. *"This is very important to me too right now. We are on parallel paths. I want to stay in touch. Let's share resources and ideas and keep each other updated regularly on our progress."*
5. *"I want to work with you. We are on the same path. Let's travel together for a while. I pledge to put my resources, time and effort in service of this calling."*

The Resonance Index is a tool that helps potential collaborators find others with whom they share common purposes and interests in order to identify opportunities for future partnerships and synergies.

When engaging in this process it is important to be honest with your assessment. None of the ratings are a rejection. They all imply support of some type and are simply authentic indicators of the level of task significance people perceive the projects or ventures of others.

After everyone has presented his or her vision, project or elevator pitch, group members discuss with one another how they will be in touch and offer support to one another. People are invited to exchange contact information and, if possible, specify the dates, times or time frames and modalities (i.e., telephone, email, text, face-to-face meeting, Skype, etc.) in which they will be in contact in the future. It also helps to establish what I call "collective creativity catalysts."

Collective Creativity Catalysts

Environments that provide comfortable spaces which promote opportunities for team members, partners and customers to congregate and share ideas in a pleasant and relaxed setting are a type of collective creativity catalyst.

Once a 4th position or "virtual community" has been established, it can be enhanced by providing various types of "collective" creativity catalysts to help stimulate collective intelligence and generative collaboration in order to increase the potential for disruptive innovation. *Collective creativity catalysts* are environments, activities and/or processes that promote generative interactions between pioneers and groundbreakers, stimulate a greater "fourth position" awareness, increase the chance of identifying "weak signals" and create access to the "creative unconscious" on a group or organizational level.t

At Google, for example, employees get 20% of their time (whatever part of their 70 hour piecework week that is) to work on projects or ideas that they are personally interested in or passionate about. In effect, this turns the whole company into a giant Research and Development laboratory for Google's new products.

Other Silicon Valley companies routinely provide what are called "Free Fridays." As the name implies, people are given paid free time on Friday afternoons to work on or explore whatever they feel drawn to.

Another example of a collective creativity catalyst was the policy of the winter sports company that I mentioned in *SFM Volume I* (pp. 38-39) that it was "the right and the duty of all employees to find interesting new market opportunities and share them with the right decision makers inside the company."

Collective creativity catalysts can also show up in the structuring of the environment. Pixar, for instance, provides comfortable creative rooms for employees to congregate and share ideas in a pleasant and relaxed setting.

Apple has similar innovation spaces; airy rooms and other stimulating environments. At times, Apple has also promoted activities, from massages to drumming circles, to help people move beyond the confines of their cognitive, rational minds. For example, they used to have a "beer bust" on Friday afternoons that migrated from one Apple building to another in order to encourage inter-departmental contact and congregation.v

George Lucas' designed the buildings at his Skywalker Ranch facility to represent the farm of a fictional family from the early days of California. In fact, he wrote a whole story about the make-believe family in order to develop the complex; which contains a barn with animals, vineyards, a garden with fruits and vegetables used in the on-site restaurant, an outdoor swimming pool and fitness center with racquetball courts, the man-made "Lake Ewok," a hilltop observatory, a 300-seat theater called "The Stag" as well as multiple theater screening rooms, and a parking facility that is mostly concealed underground to preserve the natural landscape. When you enter the property through the locked gate, you feel immediately feel transported into a world where normal reality is temporarily "on hold."

Of course, it is not necessary for an environment to be so elaborate to be a collective creativity catalyst. Walt Disney, for example, established a "dreaming room" at his company offices. The *dreaming room* had pictures and inspirational drawings all over the walls relating to the current project the team was working on. Everything was chaotic and colorful in this room, and criticisms were not allowed.

It was not uncommon for team members, and especially Disney himself, to take "second position" with the characters involved in the project while in this room. As one of Disney's co-workers claimed, "Walt felt the lines and the situation so completely that he could not keep from acting out the gestures and even the body attitudes as he said the dialogue."

Disney's Dreaming Room is another example of a collective creativity catalyst.

Walt Disney would frequently take "second position" with the characters in his animation project while in the Dreaming Room.

Disney instituted other forms of collective creativity catalysts as well. As an "orchestrator of innovation" similar to Steve Jobs, Disney strove to involve everyone that worked for him in the creative process, claiming that "Everyone has to contribute, or they become laborers." As far as Disney was concerned, the more ideas the better. According to members of his team, "Walt felt that every idea had been thought of, every gag and even every story – the key was how you used the material to express your own work. So he was never concerned about where ideas came from."

In fact, Disney was one of the first to institute and administrate an incentive system purely to cultivate and reinforce creativity throughout his whole company. As early as the mid 1930s, he introduced a bonus system whereby "anyone suggesting a gag that was used in a picture received five dollars and anyone providing an idea that formed the basis for an entire cartoon received a hundred dollars." Considering that these are depression era dollars, this represents a considerable incentive. Incidentally, this bonus system was not limited to his writers and animators. It extended to everyone at his studio, including the gardening and maintenance crews.

It is significant that Disney's bonus system was based on creative contribution and not on commercial results. As a contrast, in the early 1980s I was involved in a project for Activision, a well-known and successful video game company of that era. I had been called in to help restimulate creativity and innovation among the game designers. The company was originally started by five software engineers who, through their generative collaboration, produced a number of innovative games and achieved astonishing revenues in its initial years. As the company had grown, however, it had added a number of layers between management, marketing and the designers and was beginning to lag behind other video game companies in innovation (which ultimately led to a significant drop in income).

When I interviewed the top management, I discovered they had set up a bonus system that rewarded the software designers based on the sales of their games. While on the one hand, this seemed reasonable, the consequence was that it created a situation in which designers looked around for the games that were selling the best at that time and tried to copy those games. The result was a flood of imitations of the current best selling games. To use Steve Jobs' metaphor, everyone was "skating to where the puck was" rather than where it was going to be.

I suggested that, in order to catalyze true innovation, they needed to add a parallel bonus system to reward designers for their "degree of innovation." The receiver of this bonus would be determined by fellow designers rather than people in the marketing department. This would help to create a focus on tomorrow's business and an orientation on where the "puck was going to be" rather than simply chasing where it had recently been. Needless to say, this prompted a significant increase in innovation within the team of designers.

Reflect on the types of collective creativity catalysts you could put into place with respect to your own project or venture. What types of collective creativity catalysts can you implement in your environment, especially when and where you collaborate with others?

I frequently ask the business executives that I coach or consult for if they have a "dreaming room" for themselves and others at their workplace. Not surprisingly most do not, although there is usually plenty of boring, empty "work" space. How could you set up a "dreaming room" or an "innovation space" where you work and collaborate?

What types of activities or processes (e.g., dance, sports activities, presentations, field trips, etc.) could you set up with your team members or other collaborators to help think outside of the box and stimulate more connection to the creative unconscious and open innovation?

Walt Disney had a bonus system in place to encourage the contribution of ideas from all his employees, from screenwriters to maintenance people.

Chapter Summary

When generative collaboration is leveraged properly it can lead to disruptive innovations. *Disruptive innovations* are those that create a new market whose boundaries do not fit within existing markets. Disruptive innovations emerge from synergies of vision and imagination between different parts of the circle of success in alignment with evolutions within what I have called the field of innovation. They are notoriously difficult to predict from existing knowledge alone and create necessary periods of uncertainty and chaos.

Disruptive innovations frequently begin with a virtual community of *early adopters* from among *customers* and *pioneers* within the venture's *team members*. These virtual communities are united at the level of identity and vision. Their vision transcends the current identity and capabilities of either group and is aligned with evolutionary developments in the larger "field of innovation." This larger vision generates the necessary amount of enthusiasm and commitment to overcome the inescapable periods of uncertainty and doubt. Thus, early adopters and pioneers have to share an overwhelming passion based on the alignment of values, identity and vision.

Disruptive innovation also generally requires a certain degree of open innovation, which involves the generative collaboration between "groundbreakers" within the company and external partners who are "trailblazers." The central idea behind open innovation is that the knowledge and resources necessary for innovation resides in the collective intelligence of employees, suppliers, customers, competitors, universities, etc. Thus, in order to accelerate innovation and leverage resources, ventures to need to create win-win partnerships and alliances with other organizations and entities.

The final reach of a new market potential created by a disruptive innovation is difficult to clearly foresee in advance. In order to succeed, individuals, teams and ventures need to identify new trends in the field innovation early enough to take advantage of opportunities and prepare for periods of change. Thus, another significant success factor in promoting and managing disruptive innovation is the ability to detect "weak signals" that herald new and previously unmet needs and interests. To accomplish this, a venture must create as large a network as possible of early adopters, pioneers, groundbreakers and trailblazers; i.e., "bats" who will be able to identify weak signals related to new opportunities, versus "frogs" who simply wait until the potential is obvious. By staying on the lookout for opportunities, teams and ventures can find opportunities that others fail to see.

It is natural for managers and leaders of existing businesses to fear that disruptive innovations might distract their venture from its current strategy and compete against cash-producing products and confuse existing customers. Thus, in the beginning, disruptive innovations are usually easiest to foster in a niche of early adopters who are not interested in buying the existing offerings of traditional product lines.

Stefan Crisan's development of the *Master in Management* (Cycle Supérieur en Management) degree program for the EDHEC Business School provides a good example of some of the dynamics involved in creating a successful disruptive innovation. Beginning in a niche within the business school for experienced, self-made middle managers who wanted to improve themselves, Stefan created a revolutionary, non-traditional program whose purpose was to transform the identity of the participants. To accomplish this, Stefan had to generatively collaborate with a virtual community of early adopters within is target group, pioneers within the business school and trailblazers within his network of potential partners who shared a similar vision and values. By creating synergies between these three groups, Stefan was able to put together a program that creates a high degree of transformation with concrete and practical results in a very short period of time. The success of the program within its initial niche has led to its expansion throughout France and internationally.

A major success factor for Stefan in fostering the generative collaboration necessary to support his disruptive innovation was the ability to "listen very deeply in order to understand the vision of others." This is what I have referred to as the ability to take "second position." Second Position is one of several key *Perceptual Positions* that are necessary to produce successful generative collaboration. A *Third Position*, or observer position, is necessary in order to view the collaboration from a more distant perspective to be sure that you are *Creating Win-Win Collaborations.*

When collaborations are win-lose or win-neutral they can have a degenerative effect on an entrepreneur's ability to reach his or her vision. The *SFM Collaborator Audit* is a tool that can help to find weaknesses in collaborations with others. Such collaborations may then be reevaluated, set aside or refreshed by applying other collaboration catalysts.

Fourth Position (the collective or "we" position) is necessary for establishing strong bonds with collaborators and forming a generative relational field. A collaboration catalyst that can be very useful to create a Fourth Position or virtual community is Identifying Resonance for Task Significance. In this process, group members present their projects or ventures to one another and register and track the level of "resonance" regarding task significance that they experience. This helps group members to "home in" on those with whom they share common purposes and interests and create opportunities for future partnerships and synergies.

Collective creativity catalysts promote generative interactions between collaborators and create greater fourth position and access to the "creative unconscious" on a group or organizational level by encouraging people to find and share ideas that they are passionate about and focus on "moving to where the puck is going to be" (i.e., next generation business). The purpose of collective creativity catalysts is to provide an environment and system of reinforcement that supports individuals to enhance their own creativity through group interactions and proactively contribute to "making the pie bigger."

References

- Misez sur les ruptures de marché ("Betting on Disruptive Innovations"), Benoit Sarazin
- *Alpha Leadership: Tools for Leaders Who Want More From Life*, Deering, A., Dilts, R. and Russell, J., John Wiley & Sons, London, England, 2002.
- *Success Factors of Disruptive Innovations*, Robert Dilts & Benoît Sarazin, 2008.
- *The Fellowship of the Ring*, J. R. R. Tolkien, Ballantine Books, New York, NY, 1965.
- The Lord of the Rings: The Fellowship of the Ring, Film by Peter Jackson, New Line Cinema, 2001.
- *Strategies of Genius Volume I*, Dilts, R., Meta Publications, Capitola, CA, 1994.

04

Making something from nothing

Creating a Generative Venture Community

It is the long history of humankind (and animal kind, too) that those who learned to collaborate and improvise most effectively have prevailed.
Charles Darwin

Individual commitment to a group effort—that is what makes a team work, a company work, a society work, a civilization work.
Vince Lombardi

ANTONIO MEZA

The Story of "Stone Soup"

Once upon a time, there was a village in a land suffering from years of war. The difficult conditions in which they lived had made the villagers become more and more pessimistic, untrusting and bitter. On top of that, there had been several years of meager harvests and people jealously hoarded whatever food they could find, hiding it even from their friends and neighbors.

One day, a wandering stranger came into a village and began asking questions as if he planned to stay for the night. "There is not a bite to eat in the whole province," he was told. "Better keep moving on."

"No problem, I have everything I need," he said. "In fact, because your tired fields have left you nothing to share, I will share something with you instead: the secret of how to make soup from a stone." The dubious villagers looked at one another, snickering and scoffing at the suggestion. The stranger proceeded to pull an iron cauldron from his wagon, fill it with water, and build a fire under it. Then, with great ceremony, he drew an ordinary-looking stone from a velvet bag and dropped it into the boiling water.

By now, hearing of the presence of a stranger and the rumor of food, most of the villagers had come to the square or watched suspiciously from their windows. As the stranger sniffed the "broth" and licked his lips in anticipation, hunger began to overcome their skepticism.

The story of "Stone Soup" is both an allegory and an illustration for how, through collaboration, we can create "something" from "nothing."

"Ahh," the stranger said to himself rather loudly, "I do like a tasty stone soup, and this is one of my best. I am sure you will all love it. Of course, stone soup with a little cabbage – that would be fantastic!"

Soon a villager approached hesitantly, holding a cabbage he'd retrieved from its hiding place, and added it to the pot. "Capital!" cried the stranger. "You know, I once had stone soup with cabbage and a bit of salt beef as well, and it was fit for a king."

The village butcher managed to find some salt beef . . . and so it went, through potatoes, onions, carrots, mushrooms, and so on, each villager contributing a small amount of something until there was indeed a delicious meal for all. The villagers ate and danced and sang well into the night for the first time in many years, refreshed by the feast and their new- found benefactor.

In the morning the stranger awoke to find the entire village standing before him. At his feet lay a satchel of the village's best breads and cheese. "You have given us the greatest of gifts: the secret of how to make soup from stones," said an elder, "and we shall never forget." The stranger turned to the crowd, and said: "The only reason it is a secret is because we so easily forget that it is only by sharing that we may make a feast."

And off he wandered, down the road . . .

The story of Stone Soup is an allegory about how "something can be made from nothing" with the contributions of small amounts of key resources from the members of a community.

Another one of the hallmarks of successful entrepreneurship is the ability to "make something from nothing." Clearly, the story of *Stone Soup* is an allegory about how this can be done. Beginning with nothing but a stone and boiling water, fabulous soup is made with the contributions of key resources from the members of the community. The lesson is that, by working together, with everyone contributing what they can, people can make something wonderful from what starts as nothing of obvious tangible value (a stone) and a vision of what could be.

The capacity to make something from nothing requires the awakening and activation of a "generative venture community" based upon a common sense of possibility, generosity, contribution, optimism, sharing and trust.

In terms of Success Factor Modeling, the stranger represents the "entrepreneurial spirit." The idea of "stone soup" is like the entrepreneur's vision. At first, it seems impossible to the villagers to make soup from a stone, and indeed, on his own, the stranger would not have succeeded. In a demonstration of effective persuasion, however, the stranger first addresses the villagers' egos (manifested through their jealous hoarding of their food) by offering them something new rather than threatening what little they have. His confidence in his vision, himself and the villagers allows him to create enough curiosity in the villagers that they are able to bypass and ultimately transform their scarcity mindset. Their collaboration reawakens their souls and the experience of possibility, generosity, contribution, optimism, sharing and trust. These are the characteristics of what we refer to in SFM as a "generative venture community."

The visions of entrepreneurs generally have no more substance initially than the stranger's stone. Whether it is stone soup, a personal computer, a hit Internet App or an electric car, the fact is that an entrepreneur's vision is an idea that only becomes a substantial reality through the participation and contribution of a larger community. This is expressed in Steve Jobs' image of the "inverse pyramid," described in *Success Factor Modeling Volume I* (pp. 275-276) in which he describes how the "tiny seed" of his idea for a personal computer grew into something that was benefiting the lives of many people through the successive contributions of people with diverse yet complementary skills.

Thus, in addition to the other skills and models that we have explored so far in this book, the capacity to make something from nothing requires the awakening and activation of a "generative venture community." Accomplishing this is perhaps the highest expression of next generation entrepreneurship and collective intelligence.

Community

Webster's Dictionary defines a *community* as "an interacting population of different individuals (or species)" who are "linked by common interests" or connected by the "awareness of some unifying trait." Thus, a community involves diversity at one level, but unity at another.

The people within a particular community often share a common geographical location, but sharing an environment is not a necessary factor for forming a community. Individuals in a community, such as the "medical community," for example, may be widely geographically disbursed. Other communities, such as the "Hispanic community," may be made up of a sub-population within a particular geographic area. This type of community would be formed by "a group of people marked by a common characteristic but living within a larger society that does not share that characteristic."

In an intentional community, there must be "conscious and purposive sharing . . . marked by a feeling of unity, but also individual participation which is completely willing and not forced or coerced, and without loss of individuality."

A further distinction may be made between "intentional" and "unintentional" communities. In an intentional community there must be "conscious and purposive sharing." According to Webster's, such a community involves "social activity marked by a feeling of unity, but also individual participation which is completely willing and not forced or coerced, and without loss of individuality." By this definition, the creation of "community" would require an ongoing context of sufficient safety for people to feel a sense of choice and the freedom to express their individuality. People in a community don't need to all "see the same picture" or vision, but should all be "looking in the same direction."

The value of community is that, by uniting individuals of different strengths and abilities in the service of a common interest, more can be accomplished than by individuals acting alone. A "learning community," for example, would consist of a group of diverse people, from diverse geographical areas and of differing professional backgrounds, but who share the common goal of learning and supporting one another's learning.

A community is a classic example of a "self-organizing" system. The members of such systems organize their own behavior in relation to certain focal points in their environment known as "attractors" (such as the stranger's stone in the story of *Stone Soup*). According to self-organization theory, order is formed around a "landscape" of "attractors" which help to create and hold stable patterns within the system. In human communities, the "attractor landscape" is created by unifying traits, shared goals, common interests and presuppositions, and the awareness of unity between community members.

Communities have different kinds of "attractors". In the story of Stone Soup, the attractor is the stone that inspires people to share their ingredients. In the same way, other communities form around symbols that represent their "purpose" or their common reason to collaborate together.

Community "attractors" can exist on a number of different levels of success factors: environment, behavior, capabilities, beliefs and values, identity, or spiritual experience. In some communities, for example, people are united simply because they share the same geographical location (e.g., a "mountain community" or "beach community"). Other communities are formed because people engage in similar actions or behaviors (e.g., a "mining community"). Still others emerge on the basis of shared capabilities (e.g., an "educational community"), beliefs and values (a "religious community" or "utopian community"), or identity (e.g., an "artists community" or "the gay community"). A "generative venture community" is one that forms around the "spirit" of entrepreneurship and the visions of its members.

Communities form around "attractors" – points of common interest, that may be on a number of different levels.

A "generative venture community" is one that forms around the "spirit" of entrepreneurship and the visions of its members.

Characteristics of a Generative Venture Community (GVC)

A *generative* community is one that expands and prospers through the individual visions, passions and contributions of its members. It is structured in such a way that there is a positive feedback loop between the growth of the individual and the growth of the community.

A key goal of the SFM process is to create a *Generative Venture Community* (GVC). The purpose of the GVC is to enable entrepreneurs, team members, stakeholders and partners to stay connected and to maintain their ongoing collaborations in order to increase the value and chances of success of each other's projects. The outcome for a GVC is for entrepreneurs and the members of their Circle of Success to continue to exchange resources, including introductions, coaching, professional services, investor leads, etc., and to directly benefit from those efforts. In addition, a GVC offers a means to share some level of ownership in one another's projects.

The purpose of a generative venture community is to enable entrepreneurs, team members, stakeholders and partners to stay connected and to maintain their ongoing collaborations in order to increase the chances of success of each other's projects.

Generative communities are formed from a culture that makes new developments possible because it promotes the possibility of resonance, synergy and emergence; thus, increasing the collective "luck factor." New and successful products frequently emerge from unplanned and unanticipated meetings and connections.

The story of the development of Post-it® Notes is a good example of how new and successful products frequently emerge from unplanned and unanticipated meetings and connections.

Consider, for instance, the case example of how Post-it® Notes were developed. A chemist named Spencer Silver was working in the 3M research laboratories in 1970 trying to find a strong adhesive. Silver developed a new adhesive, but it was even weaker than what 3M already manufactured. It stuck to objects, but could easily be lifted off. It was super weak instead of super strong. It was a "failed" attempt to make a stronger adhesive.

No one knew what to do with the stuff, but Silver didn't discard it (perhaps considering it to be "a solution to problem other than the one he was working on"). Then one Sunday four years later, another 3M scientist named Arthur Fry was singing in his church's choir. He used little paper markers to keep his place in the hymnal, but they kept falling out of the book. Remembering Silver's adhesive, Fry used some to coat his markers. With the weak adhesive, the markers stayed in place, yet lifted off without damaging the pages. This led to the idea of making small pads of note paper that had a strip of the weak adhesive on the back of them so they could be attached and removed from other pages easily. The idea of Post-it Notes as a product was a synergy or generative collaboration coming from Silver's weak adhesive and Fry's idea of using to temporarily affix his paper markers in his hymnal.

3M began distributing Post-it® Notes nationwide in 1980 — ten years after Silver developed the super weak adhesive. Today they are one of the most popular office products available. Had there not been interaction between the two scientists, the "lucky" link between the weak adhesive and the notepaper would have never happened. One purpose of a Generative Venture Community is to increase the chance that such unexpected synergies can emerge.

Swarm Intelligence

At the basis of a generative community is what is known as "Swarm Intelligence." Scientifically, *Swarm Intelligence* (SI) is defined as *"the property of a system whereby the collective behaviors of (unsophisticated) agents interacting locally with their environment cause coherent functional global patterns to emerge. SI provides a basis with which it is possible to explore collective (or distributed) problem solving without centralized control or the provision of a global model."*

A classic example of swarm intelligence is the fact that an ant colony can identify the closest and richest source of food without any individual member knowing it.

Generative communities frequently function using principles of "swarm intelligence" through which individual actions are able to produce collective decisions or solutions without the need for centralized control.

Ants leave a chemical pheromone trail as they depart from and reenter their colony. Each individual ant goes out in search for food and resources to bring back to the nest. As they do, they follow the strongest (freshest) pheromone trail. The strongest trails are the ones traveled most frequently by the most ants. When a food source runs out, rather than returning to the colony, the ants go in search again for nourishment. Thus, the trail to the depleted food source becomes weakened and the fresher trails lead to the new food source.

As a result, the largest majority of the ants will continue traveling to the nearest and most abundant food source, even though no individual ant in the colony knows where it is.

In a way, the pheromone trails of ants is analogous to the virtual "trails" left behind as a result of Success Factor Modeling and processes such as benchmarking and sharing best practices. The trails that lead most easily and quickly to the greatest success will be those followed most frequently by most individuals. Because this leads to the growth and success of the community as a whole, the community benefits as each individual succeeds in reaching his or her vision.

Success Factor Case Example
Randy Williams, The Keiretsu Forum
A Generative Venture Community

A culture of opportunities full of curious minds.

Randy Williams
Founder – Keiretsu Forum

Randy Williams founded the Keiretsu Forum, an "Angel Investor" group, in September of 2000 (http://www.keiretsuforum.com). A successful entrepreneur and investor himself, Williams wanted to create a community to discuss investment opportunities. His vision was simple: members talking to other members before they made an investment. "I started Keiretsu Forum because of my lack of discipline as an equity investor," quips Williams.

Having made money in real estate in the mid 1990s, Williams wanted to diversify his investments into technology. But, as he points out, "I had no business investing in ventures in which I did not have enough information or enough mind share to have a valid opinion about how to invest in that opportunity." William's basic goal was to create an effective atmosphere in which to decide whether or not to invest. "I wanted to create a community where no one had a vested interest, where we all enjoyed great thought leadership and great mind share—as I call it, 'swarm intelligence'—so we could make effective decisions."

The idea was a good one. The Keiretsu Forum grew and prospered during the early 2000s, a time when most "angel" investment money had dried up and many investors were losing their shirts in the "Dot.Com" crash. At the time of this writing, Keiretsu Forum is the world's largest angel investor network with over 2,500 accredited investors members throughout 46 chapters on three continents. Keiretsu Forum Members have invested over $400 million dollars in more than 485 companies to date in technology, consumer products, life sciences, real estate, and other high growth segments.

Williams started his first Keiretsu chapter with 50 of his friends, and eventually stopped when membership reached 150. "I wanted to keep it intimate," he says, adding, "There is a lot of intimacy and a lot of fellowship created through our community."

As a result of its success in the San Francisco area in Northern California, Keiretsu has expanded to open many other chapters around the world. Each chapter is limited to 150 investor members.

Randy Williams' vision is a world where angel investors can get together and enjoy great mindshare and great thought leadership, using "swarm intelligence" to support each other and make better decisions.

These chapters form a community whose stated purpose is to:

1. Support Keiretsu portfolio companies and presenting entrepreneurs with equity and resources in different capital markets.
2. Build additional quality deal flow for members in different geographical areas
3. Allow members to enjoy collaborative business and social relationships between chapters.

Randy Williams' ambition for Keiretsu Forum ambition has been to create the world's largest angel investors network, with over 2,500 accredited investor members throughout 46 chapters on three continents.

To select investments, each Keiretsu chapter holds a Screening meeting once a month. These meetings take place a week before the monthly Forum meeting in which investment decisions are made. Approximately 10 companies are invited to the Screening meeting out of about 25 or 30 candidates that are considered. The companies are brought in through the Keiretsu network and pre- screened by committees made up of Keiretsu members who have the appropriate industry knowledge and expertise.

About 25–30 Keiretsu members attend the Screening. "We want to keep it intimate," explains Williams. Entrepreneurs have 15 minutes in front of the group—7 minutes to present and 8 minutes for a question and answer period with the Keiretsu members in attendance. "After all the companies have presented, the presenters are excused and then we vote," says Williams. Before any voting takes place, however, there is a discussion about each company; and this is where the value of the collective expertise within the group is demonstrated. Attending members are encouraged to comment first on "positives" and then on "concerns" with respect to each company.

Harvesting Collective Mind Share

A rich array of expertise and experience is brought out by the discussions and each reflection by the group members offers the chance for all of the group to become more knowledgeable investors. Indeed, Keiretsu meetings are a fascinating opportunity to keep abreast of the latest innovations in technology and business models, and to learn from the knowledge and experience of successful and generous people. "Anyone can critique a company," explains Williams. "I wanted to set Keiretsu Forum up to talk graciously about companies."

Keiretsu meetings are a fascinating opportunity to keep abreast of the latest innovations in technology and business models, and to learn from the knowledge and experience of successful and generous people.

While Williams leads the discussion about the companies at the end of the meetings, he insists that he is not just a moderator. "I am excited about the feedback," he says. "So I am not moderating, I am bringing out the collective mind share in the group."

One of Randy Williams' unique contributions to the Keiretsu Forum is "bringing out the collective mind share in the group."

Following the discussion, Keiretsu members vote on which companies will be invited to attend the Forum meeting. "Each member has one vote: yes, no or 'bubble'," explains Williams, "'Bubble' means we don't really understand their proposition or technology enough and we need to send people out to help us understand their business or their offer."

If a company receives a "no" vote, a team is sent out to debrief them on why that decision was made and what they need to do if they want to make it to the next step. Williams points out that Venture Capitalists have a bad reputation about not getting back to people. "How can you grow if you have to guess and you are not debriefed?" he asks. "It is very important that we are gracious, because we care deeply about the entrepreneurial community," Williams points out. "We are getting companies we said 'no' to or the 'bubble', who have followed our recommendations and have come back and are now getting funding. And that's exciting."

As an example, Williams cites "a company came to us that is attempting to replace the cork in wine bottles. It is here, but acceptance and adoption has not yet been in the marketplace. We sent a team out to help them with their marketing plan. Now they are coming to the Forum."

Making Wise Decisions

The monthly Forum meeting is attended by 100 to 175 people. Four to five companies are chosen from those who have presented during the previous week's Screening meeting. At the Forum meeting, companies have 10 minutes to present and another 10 minutes for questions and answers with the attending members. Similar to the screening meetings, the presenters are excused at the end of the session and a discussion takes place about the positives and concerns relating to each company.

At the end of each company's presentation, a "gold" sheet is passed around. If a Keiretsu member is interested in discussing a possible investment in that company, he or she puts his or her name and contact information on the sheet. No one is required to invest and putting one's name on the sheet is simply a statement of interest in following up with the company to discuss the terms of investment and participate in the due diligence process.

Potential investors are encouraged to delete or add their names after the discussion has taken place at the conclusion of the meeting. Williams, however, encourages Keiretsu members to be decisive so that they don't waste the entrepreneur's time. "If you get to a 'no', tell them no now," he declares. "If you get to a 'maybe', take 30 days and then tell them."

The Keiretsu Forum process promotes the discretion and independence of both entrepreneurs and investors. Williams wants to be sure each deal is a win-win for both parties. "Keiretsu Forum members give entrepreneurs more than money," declares Williams. "They provide entrepreneurs the benefit of their experience as mentors and their networks."

Part of the Keiretsu Forum's success as an investment group is its selectivity. "We are funding only about 15 of 48 companies we see," declares Williams, "but that is better than any other Angel Forum in the world right now."

Even if a company is passed up by the Forum as a group, however, individual members are free to pursue investment in that company on their own if they wish. Keiretsu receives no percentage from any investments made. There is only a membership fee for those who qualify and are accepted as members and fee for companies chosen to present.

One characteristic success story is that of T.S. Pharma, a company that developed a product that effectively helps to treat diarrhea in AIDS patients. Seventeen Keiretsu members participated in a six week round. "It is great investing in things which truly do support and help humanity," claims Williams. "The lead on this came from three members. Because of the respect others had for them, and the fact there was no vested interest, these three mobilized seventeen members to support the company." As a result of the investment and support of those seventeen members, T.S. Pharma was able to move towards becoming acquired very quickly, which will helped to speed their product to the patients who needed it and produced profits for the investors.

The role of the Keiretsu Forum members goes beyond being an "investor". They also act as partners, giving entrepreneurs "more than money" and providing them "the benefit of their experience as mentors and their networks".

Even if a company is passed up by the Forum as a group, individual members are free to pursue investment in that company on their own if they wish.

Utilizing "Swarm Intelligence"

Clearly, a major key to the success of the Keiretsu Forum is a type of "swarm intelligence." This mode of intelligence comes from people with a variety of different domain expertise and experience focusing their attention on common goals and bringing together their collective knowledge. "My whole investment philosophy is to pick people who are smarter than me and who are fully focused on the task at hand," explains Williams. The group members form a "data base of great mind share," says Williams. "There is going to be expertise, whatever is brought forth."

The stated mission of the Keiretsu Forum is "Great association with quality deal flow." This is put into action by applying swarm intelligence to make good decisions and to support entrepreneurs. "Its all about good people being together and offering stimuli," says Randy Williams.

As an example, Williams sites an incident in which a reporter from a well-known French business magazine called him up and asked him to comment on data storage. Williams responded, "I know nothing about data storage, but I will put it out to our Keiretsu community." He sent out an e-mail to the Northern California Keiretsu members. Within 30 minutes he had 27 responses from people who had expertise in data storage, including 2 or 3 who had started companies in that area. The reporter was so impressed that she decided to change the focus of her article to the Keiretsu Forum.

According to Williams, such swarm intelligence reduces risk for investors, but also creates value because the members are able to contribute "intellectual capital" and other resources in addition to money. "Resources are more powerful than financial capital," claims Williams.

Williams is also emphatic that another key to Keiretsu's success is that Keiretsu members "share common beliefs about having fun and making good investments." In fact, the stated mission of the Keiretsu forum is, *Great association with quality deal flow.** "Its all about good people being together and offering stimuli," says Williams. "If you don't have the right membership, it won't work."

---

* *Deal Flow* involves the number and diversity of investment opportunities, in the form of new start-ups, that a potential investor gets to see. The quality of "deal flow" greatly influences the degree of success achieved by the investors.

Establishing Guiding Principles for Creating Community

Williams has built the Keiretsu community around four key values or "Guiding Principles":

1. Full collaboration

"We absolutely love collaboration and working with other Angel forums and investment groups wherever thtey may be," says Williams. The name Keiretsu, in fact, is symbolic of collaboration. *Keiretsu* is a Japanese term indicating "a group of affiliated corporations with broad power and reach."

Collaboration is essential for ensuring the success of Keiretsu Forum members and the entrepreneurs they support.

As Williams explains, "Angel investors are typically individuals who invest in something they know about and can help grow through their network." Thus, collaboration is an essential element for ensuring their success. According to Williams, the essence of successful collaboration is getting together and asking, "What can we do together that benefits *you?*"

2. Intelligent investments

The Keiretsu Forum members provide early stage capital in the range of $250k–$2 million, with individual members putting in $25k–$30k each. The Keiretsu Forum is not a fund and does not invest as a single entity. Members collaborate on "due diligence,"* but make individual investment decisions. The Keiretsu Forum considers a variety of opportunities including software, health care, telecommunications, media and entertainment, instrumentation and real estate or "brick and mortar." Investments are smaller and provide the opportunity for early monetization. "As Angel Investors, we like to see our investment lead to profitability or reach some type of return in 3–5 years," says Williams. "We are not looking at 8–10 year returns. Twenty-eight percent of our investments have been in real estate or other non-technology businesses."

Keiretsu Forum Members collaborate on examining and verifying key information necessary to accurately assess risks, but make individual investment decisions.

---

* *Due Diligence* is the process of investigation, performed by investors, into the details of a potential investment in order to accurately assess risks, such as an examination of operations and management and the verification of material facts.

3. The giving nature of members

Keiretsu members are themselves successful people who feel the desire to "give something back." When entering Keiretsu meetings, participants "check their egos at the door."

Williams claims that a core objective for Keiretsu is "teaching and encouraging other people to give." Every year, for instance, Keiretsu does a "warm coat drive." "Last year I went to a school and talked to one girl about it," recounts Williams. "She mobilized her whole school and collected 900 coats that Keiretsu gave away."

Keiretsu members are themselves successful people who feel the desire to "give something back." This comes out in what Williams describes as "the gracious and courageous sharing" that takes place between Keiretsu members and the people they support. When entering Keiretsu meetings, participants "check their egos at the door," Williams claims.

One of the foundational principles of Keiretsu is the notion of having "no vested interest." When discussing companies, for instance, it is important that the intention of the individuals involved stay clear and transparent. "Any time there is a discussion at Keiretsu," explains Williams, "people know they need to state if they are an advisor, a board member, investor or have a conflict of interest before they say anything, so we know how to gauge their remarks."

Guests to the Keiretsu Forum are advised that they cannot give someone else a business card unless they are offering something and not asking for something in return.

As a community, Keiretsu maintains a "no solicitation" policy. One example of this is that guests to the Keiretsu Forum are advised that they cannot give someone else a business card unless they are offering something and not asking for something back. "We care," claims Williams. "We want to be gracious."

Keiretsu has also established a strong, per chapter charitable foundation entitled the Keiretsu Forum Charitable Foundation. Williams reports with pride that one recent year, "We were fortunate enough to give away $250,000." This included a $50,000 contribution to a support group for battered women.

Williams maintains, "Our mantra is, 'the smarter the giving, the greater the gift'."

4. Having fun

In William's view, you can't build a community out of a bunch of hard-nosed people who are just in it for the money. "We get together and play together," explains Williams. "Fellowship is a direct consequence of trust." At Keiretsu, trust is fostered through relationship building events that focus on having fun together. "We have 3 to 5 major events every month," says Williams, "from ski trips and golf tournaments, to a flying club and dinner group."

Keiretsu has a Participation Committee set up to help people find ways to participate that are most in line with their areas of interest and passion.

According to Williams, "Participation is essential for creating community." Keiretsu has a committee system that offers many ways for people to participate. "Whatever you resonate with—whether it be real estate, telecommunications, charity, software, instrumentation, biotechnology—whatever floats your boat, get involved," says Williams emphatically. Keiretsu even has a Participation Committee set up to help people find ways to participate that are most in line with their areas of interest and passion. Williams points out, "Each chapter has a participation committee to show and share and guide each member to a place where he or she may want to interact."

These guiding principles show up strongly in the dynamics and interactions which take place during Keiretsu meetings. As one new member put it, "I've been to so many networking meetings, but this was a very different experience that had soul."

"The Keiretsu Forum is a culture of opportunities full of curious minds," Williams concludes. "Another sign of success is a peaceful mind," Williams points out, "and there are a lot of peaceful people at Keiretsu."

Randy Williams and the Keiretsu Forum Circle of Success

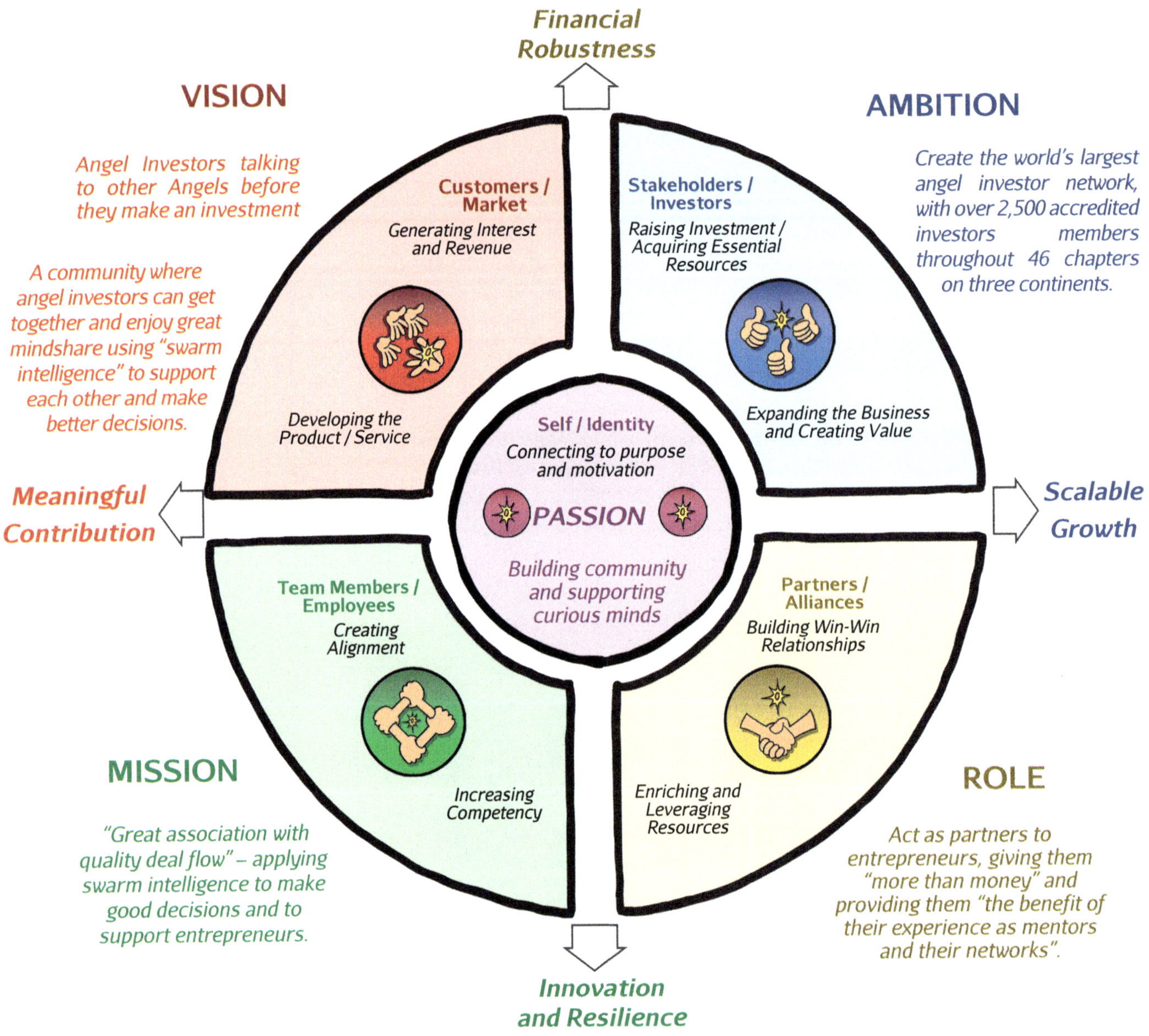

RANDY WILLIAMS AND THE KEIRETSU FORUM CIRCLE OF SUCCESS

VISION

* ANGEL INVESTORS TALKING TO OTHER ANGELS BEFORE THEY MAKE AN INVESTMENT

* A COMMUNITY WHERE INVESTORS CAN GET TOGETHER AND ENJOY GREAT MINDSHARE USING "SWARM INTELLIGENCE" TO SUPPORT EACH OTHER AND MAKE BETTER DECISIONS.

AMBITION

* CREATE THE WORLD'S LARGEST ANGEL INVESTOR NETWORK, WITH OVER 2,500 ACCREDITED INVESTORS MEMBERS THROUGHOUT 46 CHAPTERS ON THREE CONTINENTS.

MISSION

* "GREAT ASSOCIATION WITH QUALITY DEAL FLOW" – APPLYING SWARM INTELLIGENCE TO MAKE GOOD DECISIONS AND TO SUPPORT ENTREPRENEURS.

ROLE

* ACT AS PARTNERS TO ENTREPRENEURS, GIVING THEM "MORE THAN MONEY" AND PROVIDING THEM "THE BENEFIT OF THEIR EXPERIENCE AS MENTORS AND THEIR NETWORKS".

PASSION:

BUILDING COMMUNITY AND SUPPORTING CURIOUS MINDS

Randy Williams created the Keiretsu Forum as a result of his passion for building community and supporting curious minds.

A major success factor of the Keiretsu Forum is that it applies the collective intelligence processes of sharing and swarming to help both angel investors and entrepreneurs achieve enhanced performance, make wiser decisions and find creative solutions.

Conclusion: A Passion for Building Community and Supporting Curious Minds

So, what does it take to create a community like Keiretsu? "Passion," says Williams. "It takes a passion for building community. And you have to have the respect of the people you are bringing to the table. You also need to have a curious mind. I learn something new every day from Keiretsu members and entrepreneurs."

A major success factor of the Keiretsu Forum is that it applies the collective intelligence processes of *sharing* and *swarming* to help both angel investors and entrepreneurs (1) benchmark collective standards for making successful investments and (2) exchange best practices to support the implementation of successful strategies. This synergy leads to enhanced performance and wiser decisions for both investors and entrepreneurs. As Williams points out, this "intellectual capital" is far more powerful than financial capital alone in creating successful start ups.

Randy Williams' Keiretsu Forum is a powerful example of building a generative venture community. Williams' vision of creating a win-win framework for both investors and entrepreneurs has clearly attracted successful people from both the investment world and the world of entrepreneurs and created an opportunity for them to support each others' visions, missions and ambitions. The Keiretsu community is made up of people who share common beliefs and values that balance the needs and desires of both the ego and the soul. This is what I call a "winning culture."

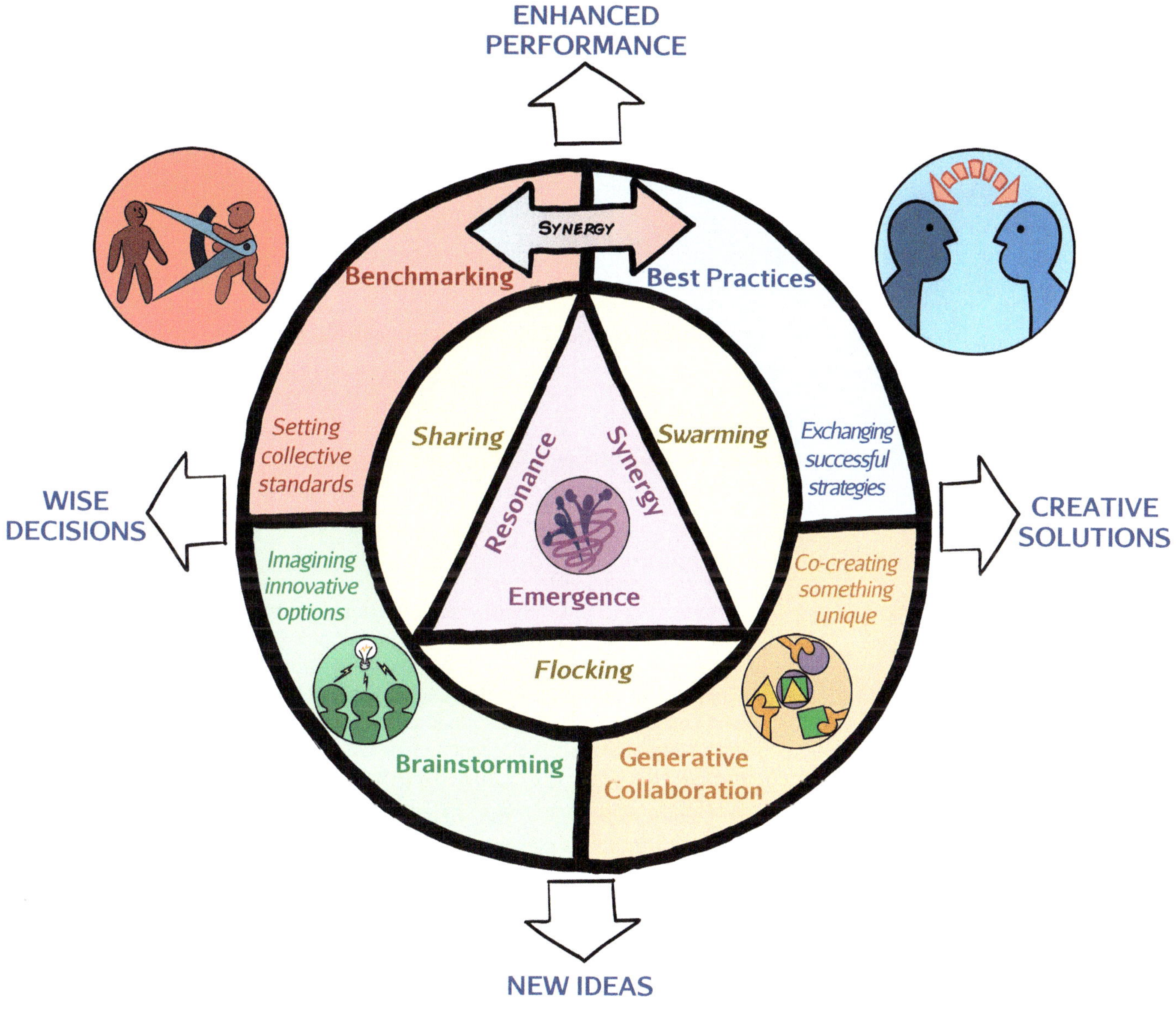

Randy Williams' Keiretsu Forum synergizes the actions of Benchmarking and Best Practices to create enhanced performance and wiser decisions for both investors and entrepreneurs.

Characteristics of a "Winning" Culture

Characteristics of a "Winning" Culture

The most general meaning of *winning* is "to succeed in arriving at a place or a state." The word win comes from the Old English *winnan* meaning "to struggle." Thus, the original implication of the term is "to reach or gain possession of by expenditure of effort" or "to obtain by work." The notion of "struggle" also implies the ability to "gain the victory in a contest." However, it is also important to note that *winnan* was also related to the noun *wynn*, which meant "joy, pleasure and delight."

Thus, a "winning culture" is one that is able to reach a desired state, mobilize the appropriate motivation for the effort and work required to achieve that state, successfully compete with others who are attempting to reach the same goal, and also take pleasure and delight in the accomplishment. In this view, winning cultures are "fit for the future." Thus, a winning culture is one that is able to support:

- An expectation of a positive future
- A feeling of capability and responsibility
- A sense of self-worth and belonging

Thus, a winning culture is one that is characterized by optimism, a focus on desired outcomes and the establishment of clear and consistent values that support the "soul" as much as the "ego." Winning cultures are able to maintain a balance of enthusiasm, innovation and creativity with skillfulness and pragmatism. They are also able to embrace and leverage diversity, such that the best characteristics of each individual involved is maximized; operating from the assumption that every member of the team or venture has something to contribute.

Culture is defined by the American Heritage dictionary as "the totality of socially transmitted behavior patterns, arts, beliefs, institutions and all other products of human work or thought." Merriam-Webster's Dictionary defines culture as "the customary beliefs, social forms, and material traits of a racial, religious, or social group" and "the set of shared attitudes, values, goals, and practices that characterizes a company or corporation." Thus the term can apply to a group as small as a family or as large as an entire nation.

The concept of culture was first explicitly defined in 1871 by the British anthropologist Edward B. Tylor. He used the term to refer to "that complex whole which includes knowledge, belief, art, morals, law, custom and any other capabilities and habits acquired by man as a member of society." These definitions of culture imply both the soft culture carried within individuals in the form of thinking styles, beliefs and assumptions about the world, and the hard culture which includes tangible expressions of values and behavior such as tools, art, pottery and other artifacts.

The totality or "essence" of a culture is the synthesis of its soft and hard elements. A culture is an integration of its environment, the patterns of behavior supported by that culture, the thinking style reflected by the culture, cultural beliefs and values, rituals, arts and the other outputs of the culture. Together these create a coherent whole, or what we have been referring to as a "field."

A culture is an integration of its environment, the patterns of behavior supported by that culture, the thinking style reflected by the culture, cultural beliefs and values, rituals, arts and the other outputs of the culture.

When this field is strong it has a self-organizing affect on the people acting within it. It becomes the water in which they swim. The culture of excellence Steve Jobs established at Pixar and Apple is a good example of the power of this type of field. As Jobs said, "If [people] are working in an environment where excellence is expected, then they will do excellent work without anything but self-motivation. I'm talking about an environment in which excellence is noticed and respected and is in the culture. If you have that, you don't have to tell people to do excellent work. They understand it from their surroundings."

Cultures exhert a strong self-organizing affect on the people interacting within them.

In fact, the source of the term culture is the Latin *cultura* which meant literally, "that which will be tended, guarded, cultivated."

From this perspective, the positive purpose of culture is to:

- Create cohesion — foster a sense of belonging and provide a framework of meaning for people's actions.
- Preserve what is good/effective — accumulate and transfer knowledge to succeeding generations.
- Preserve identity/roots — provide stability.
- Support and reward successful actions.
- Provide safety.
- Promote growth.

Half a dozen monkeys are held together in a large cage. A juicy bunch of bananas is hung from the top of a set of stairs.

When one monkey goes on the stairs to get the bananas, all of the monkeys get sprayed with cold water. Soon they learn to avoid going on the stairs.

Allegory of the Monkey Experiment

As the story of *Stone Soup* at the beginning of this chapter illustrates, however, not all cultures are winning cultures; even though the potential is always there. Adversity and scarcity can produce the opposite qualities from a winning culture by pushing people into survival strategies that can become unconsciously ingrained in the culture.

In a revealing experiment in creating unconscious cultural patterns, a half a dozen monkeys are held together in a large cage. A juicy bunch of bananas is hung from the top of a set of stairs. The cage is rigged so that as soon as one of the monkeys starts to climb the stairs, all the monkeys in the cage get soaked with high-pressure jets of cold water.

Very quickly the monkeys learn to avoid the stairs, and to prevent their fellow monkeys from getting too near the stairs. Interestingly, the avoidance behavior continues even when the experimenters turn the water off. The monkeys never realize that the water is off because they never get near the stairs for fear of what would happen based on their mutual negative expectation built from their experience of being soaked.

When one of the monkeys is replaced with a new one, the newcomer naturally thinks that the bananas are there for the taking, and begins to move towards the stairs. Fearing what would happen next according to their past experience, the rest of the group joins together to keep the newcomer away from the stairs. After several tries, the new monkey eventually learns the rule "these stairs are off limits," though it doesn't know why.

Next, another of the original six monkeys is removed and replaced with a new one. This second newcomer eventually sees the bananas and begins to go to the stairs to get them. Again, the rest of the group moves to prevent it, including the previous newcomer – who apparently is rather enthusiastic about joining in stopping the second new monkey. It no doubt figures, "If I can't go on the stairs, neither can you!"

A third original monkey is now replaced with a new one. This new group member is also prevented from approaching the stairs. Two of the five monkeys that move to stop it have no idea why they are not permitted to climb the stairs (they have never gotten wet and the water is still turned off). They have just learned from their interactions with the others that no one is allowed on the stairs.

Over time, all the monkeys that experienced the original negative consequences associated with mounting the stairs are removed one by one from the cage, and new monkeys substituted. The group teaches each new monkey "these stairs are off limits" and the taboo against climbing them to reach the bananas is perpetuated, even though none of the new monkeys in the cage was present when the water-jets were used on the original group of monkeys.

As a result, long after the water-jets have been turned off and all of the original monkeys who were sprayed by them have been replaced, the taboo against going on the stairs to get the bananas continues without question. This is because for the new group of monkeys "it has always been that way around here."

Though the experiment is most likely apocryphal, it provides a clear illustration of how what I call "thought viruses" are created. A *thought virus* is a limiting belief or "belief barrier" that has become dissociated from the experiences and expectations responsible for creating it. Thought viruses are especially difficult to change because they are no longer grounded in the experiences from which they were originally formed.

The only way to break the pattern in the case of the monkeys is to introduce into the cage a "rogue" monkey who flouts the convention, eludes the attempts to stop it, climbs the stairs and gets to eat the bananas. After watching in horror for a while, the group members begin to try out the stairs too. Soon, they are all using the stairs to get bananas and thus have all benefited from the actions of the rogue monkey.

If one of the first group of monkeys is replaced by a new one, the remaining members band together to prevent the new monkey from climbing the stairs to get the bananas for fear they will get wet. It soon learns the rule, "the stairs are off limits."

When another original monkey is replaced with a new one, the first replacement monkey joins the rest to prevent it from climbing the stairs because "that's how it is around here." Eventually all the original monkeys are replaced. The ones in the cage have never experienced getting wet. They continue to avoid the stairs without ever knowing exactly why.

Encouraging Entrepreneurial Attributes

Next generation entrepreneurs are a bit like the "rogue" monkey in the previous allegory. They are willing to bypass the belief barriers and the critics to achieve their goals and ambitions; and in doing so they frequently transform the cultural perception about what is possible and permissible.

The stranger in the story of *Stone Soup* at the beginning of this chapter is also an example of how entrepreneurs and an entrepreneurial attitude can awaken others and transform a culture that has become "infected" by a scarcity mindset.

The encouragement of entrepreneurial attitudes and attributes has played a key role in each of the Success Factor Case Examples presented so far in this book. Steve Fiehl and his partners' at CrossKnowledge made "entrepreneurship" one of their company's core values. Stefan Crisan's Masters in Management program for EDHEC was a product of his own entrepreneurial spirit. The program is infused with that attitude and participants are supported and encouraged to develop many entrepreneurial skills and attitudes. Randy Williams' success with Keiretsu Forum is clearly a demonstration of the power of creating a community based on fostering entrepreneurial attributes.

Next generation entrepreneurs have distinctive characteristics. They have discovered that they can make a difference, change things for the better, rebound from adversity and even do what others consider "impossible." They have creative ways of looking at problems and are able to keep finding different ways to overcome or transform obstacles.

As we have seen, next generation entrepreneurs have distinctive characteristics. They have a desire to live their dreams and are able to avoid becoming trapped by the "dogma" or "noise" of other people's opinions, as Steve Jobs pointed out. They have discovered that they can make a difference, change things for the better, rebound from adversity and even do what others consider "impossible." They have creative ways of looking at problems and are able to keep finding different ways to overcome or transform obstacles.\

In *Success Factor Modeling Volume I* (p. 192), I talked about Joseph Campbell's reference to the archetype of the "village." The *village* represents the "ego" and the life that has been mapped out for us by our traditional society and culture. It is founded upon the ego attributes of safety, control, self- benefit and fitting in. We succeed in the village by following the rules and, as Steve Jobs said, "not bashing into the walls too much, having a nice family life, having fun, saving a little money," etc. While life in the village gives us security and certainty, it can also be a "limited life." As illustrated in the story of *Stone Soup* and the monkey allegory, it can also impose constraints created by unconscious "thought viruses" and belief barriers.

Entrepreneurs, on the other hand, tend toward the archetype of the "journey." On the *journey,* we follow our hearts, vision and calling to find our own way and discover something new. This is the path of all great leaders, entrepreneurs and pioneers. Through the challenges and discoveries along the path we acquire courage, insight, wisdom, resiliency and greater awareness of ourselves and the world. Then, when we return to the village we are able to make our own unique contribution to others and become recognized and acknowledged for who we really are. As a result of our growth, we bring new ideas and new life to the village, making it possible for more to thrive there.

Life as a Villager provides security and certainty, but it can also be a "limited life."

While the "ego" and the "village" are necessary, the danger is that they can produce rigidity and unnecessary limitations if they are not balanced by the complementary attributes represented by the "soul," the "journey" and the entrepreneur.

The journey of the entrepreneur is about learning to live with your "channel open," in the words of modern dance pioneer Martha Graham. It is about discovering your vision and mission, living your dreams and making a better world. The following table contrasts some of the key attributes of entrepreneurs to those of "villagers."

Attribute	Entrepreneurs	Villagers
General approach	*Towards goals*	*Away from problems*
Locus of responsibiliy	*Proactive self-referenced*	*Reactive "other"-referenced*
Approach to tasks	*Options and choices*	*Following procedures*
Time frame	*Present to Future*	*Past*
Mode of comparison	*Differences*	*Sameness*
Chunk Size	*Big Picture-Vision*	*Details*

Comparison of Key Attributes of Entrepreneurs and "Villagers"

Life on the Journey involves following your heart, vision and calling to find your own way and discover something new.

Encouraging entrepreneurial attributes is important not only in small start-ups, but also in large organizations, which can so easily become bogged down in the "villager" attitude.

A winning culture is one that promotes entrepreneurial attributes by encouraging and rewarding individuals to:

- Think of what they want to go toward (as opposed to what they want to avoid).
- Be proactive and make more decisions on their own.
- Seek options and consider many possible choices.
- Focus on bringing the future present (rather than simply reproducing the past).
- Look for differences and try to find ways to make a difference.
- Think in terms of the big picture and the vision (rather than getting lost in details).

Encouraging these types of attributes is important not only in small start-ups, but also in large organizations, which can so easily become bogged down in the "villager" attitude. An entrepreneurial spirit is essential for innovation and progress. This type of cultural attitude is clear in Steve Jobs' comments that, "[Our culture] definitely rewards independent thought, and we often have constructive disagreements—at all levels . . . Our attitude is that we want the best. Don't get hung up on who owns the idea. Pick the best one, and let's go."

Creating a Winning Culture

Encouraging entrepreneurial attributes is at the root of creating what we have been calling a "winning culture" and is a cornerstone for building a generative venture community. As Randy Williams' success with the Keiretsu Forum illustrates, in order to build successful and generative ventures and communities, it is important for entrepreneurs and leaders to establish and foster a culture that can effectively support the accomplishment of the venture's vision, create value for stakeholders, promote the participation and development of the people who are involved in the venture, and provide quality products and services for customers and clients.

This type of culture creates a community in which members are:

- Aligned to a common vision and values
- Respectful of diversity
- Innovative
- Agile—quick to respond and adapt
- Flexible—responsive internally and externally
- Efficient—they seek to reduce waste and optimize resources

Attributes of a winning culture.

The SFM definition of success is based on the achievement of win-win results. It is obvious that a winning culture is also based on the assumption of "win-win" interactions, as opposed to "zero sum" interactions. As I defined in *Success Factor Modeling Volume I* (p. 130), a *zero sum interaction* is one in which one person or party in the interaction wins and the other loses—such as in a game, competition or conflict. The implication of the term is that winning (+1) and losing (-1) cancel each other out to make zero (0).

As the behavior of the villagers in the beginning of the Stone Soup story and the monkeys in the allegorical experiment demonstrate, zero sum interactions typically occur around situations in which there is a perceived or presupposed scarcity with respect to some vital resource, such that there is only enough for one party to succeed or survive. Zero sum interactions lead to dominance or power with respect to one of the parties in the interaction. *Win-win interactions*, on the other hand, presuppose that there is potentially enough of the needed resource to go around, or that everyone can benefit in some way, and typically create a positively self-reinforcing feedback loop that produces evolution and growth.

It is also possible to have "negative sum" or "lose-lose" interactions, in which neither party benefits from the interaction. This occurs when, out of spite or ignorance, one party drags the other down with him or her. While negative sum interactions are not rational, they occur more often than one might think. Frequently, this is because what appears to be a short-term win turns into a long-term loss (i.e., winning the battle but losing the war).

In contrast to zero or negative sum interactions, win-win interactions attempt to produce a mutual benefit for all of the parties involved in the situation. In a winning culture, for instance, people's actions aim to produce positive effects for as many elements of the system as possible. In the words of Abraham Lincoln, the aim of our actions should be to "do the greatest good for the greatest number of people."

A winning culture is both supportive and effective—it supports people and accomplishes quality results.

In summary, a winning culture is the foundation for a generative venture community. A winning culture is both supportive and effective—it supports people and accomplishes quality results. In a winning culture people change, grow and become more competent, and there is continual improvement in the processes with which tasks are achieved. It is effective because it is supportive, and it is supportive in order to be effective. A is clearly illustrated by Randy Williams' Keiretsu Forum, in a winning culture:

1. People work together smoothly and quickly—with "positive energy"
2. All members are involved and benefiting
3. All members contribute and are valued
4. People's interactions produce innovative results

The *Collaboration Catalysts* and *Collective Creativity Catalysts* that were presented in previous chapters, the *COACH Container* presented in Chapter 1 and the *Dynamic Teaming* development exercises presented in the next chapter are all powerful practices that help to create a winning culture.

SFM Collaboration Catalyst: Group Affirmation Exercise

In the winning culture of a generative venture community, people believe in one another and affirm each other's abilities to reach dreams and goals. The following is a collaboration catalyst that we often do in our Success Factor Modeling programs and coaching sessions with teams to create a "field" of support between team members or collaborators. It is one example of the application of what I have called "flocking."

This process is an application of *Finding Support and Sponsorship and Gathering Your Allies* presented in *Success Factor Modeling Volume I* (pp. 144-147). It is also a good follow-up and complement to the *Fostering a Field of Co-Sponsorship* process described in Chapter 1 of this book. *Sponsorship* involves creating a space in which others can act, grow and excel. Sponsors provide a context, contacts and resources (including, but certainly not limited to, financial resources) that allow the group or individual being sponsored to focus on, develop and use their own abilities and skills to the fullest. Sponsorship involves the commitment to promoting something that is already within a person or group, but is not being manifested to its fullest capacity. It involves seeking, supporting and safeguarding potentials within another person so that it can be fully expressed.

Sponsorship involves the commitment to promoting something that is already within a person or group, but is not being manifested to its fullest capacity. It involves seeking, supporting and safeguarding potentials within another person so that it can be fully expressed.

This is often done through the authentic and congruent communication of simple, yet empowering affirmations such as:

It is desirable and important for you to succeed.

It is possible for you to succeed.

You are capable to succeed.

You deserve to succeed.

The *Group Affirmation Exercise* is a way of deepening and enhancing a "field" of co- sponsorship in a group or team by applying these messages. It is usually done in a group of about 5 people. One group member is the entrepreneur/ presenter and the others are "sponsors." The sponsors are to stand around the presenter; one in front, one behind, one to the left, and one to the right. Each takes the role of expressing one of the affirmations listed above.

The congruent and supportive beliefs of others increase our level of confidence and motivation to accomplish the steps necessary to manifest our projects and ventures.

1. The group enters the COACH state and creates a COACH Container. The presenter then expresses the "elevator pitch" for his or her project or venture. Group members are to listen with a high quality of attention and experience the places where they feel resonance with the presenter's project or venture.

2. One at a time, each group member is to authentically and congruently say aloud the affirmation they have chosen to sponsor for the presenter. It is important for the "sponsors" to be sure that they can genuinely express the affirmation they have selected.

   As an option, when each sponsor has verbalized his or her affirmation, they may want to rotate (clock-wise) around the presenter and repeat each affirmation from another location. This can be done until the sponsor reaches his or her starting place.

   As another option, each sponsor can begin to repeat his or her affirmation three or four times at the same time the others are saying theirs, in any order and at any time they feel like it. When they have finished repeating the affirmations several times, the sponsors and presenter become silent. The group remains silent until the presenter nods his or her head, indicating that the messages have been received and internalized.

3. The presenter then shares with the group what has shifted or strengthened with respect to his or her sense of confidence and commitment to his or her project or venture.

4. Another group member then volunteers to be the presenter and the process is repeated, until all group members have been the presenter and in each of the affirmation positions.

A simple and touching example of the power of this type of group affirmation is illustrated in a short video* in which a very small boy is trying to vault over a stack of objects in a public children's gymnastics demonstration. After several failed attempts in which he does not even come close to jumping over the barrier — which is taller than he is — the child clearly becomes disheartened. He begins to wipe tears from his eyes as he gets ready to try again. Suddenly, his whole team comes out from their seats and gather in a circle around him; all simultaneously encouraging him and cheering him on. Buoyed by the confidence and energy of his teammates the boy easily clears the obstacle on his next try to the surprise and approval of the whole crowd.

---

*You can watch the video on Youtube under the title: *"Flocking" example Japan*

In a winning culture, collaborators' belief in one another creates a field of support for success.

Building Generative Relationships that Lead to Generative Collaboration

How to Go From Being "Nobody" to Becoming "Somebody"

The ability to make something out of nothing is deeply rooted in relationship building. Establishing supportive and productive relationships is the bedrock of a generative venture community; in particular, forming "generative relationships" that lead to generative collaboration. *Generative relationships* are those that create a result greater than the sum of the parts. They are an expressiont of the principle: 1+1=3. More than any of the other forms of synergy or collaboration we have explored thus far, generative relationships have the capacity to produce a major expansion of one's *identity*.

Generative relationships have the capacity to produce a major expansion of one's identity.

Frequently in our SFM programs and coaching sessions, we find that people limit themselves and their pursuit of their dreams and visions by making themselves "small." People say, "I have this great vision, but who am I? I am nobody. I am just 'little old me'. What difference can I make? If I was 'Steve Jobs' then I would be able to do something."

The fact is, most successful entrepreneurs and leaders start out as "nobody." Steve Jobs, for instance, was the illegitimate child of a college student, was raised in a working class family and dropped out of college in his first semester. How did he end up creating and becoming the CEO of the largest technology company in the world?

Successful people maintain contact with a broad network of friends and associates, which serves to create a network of luck – people who support them and inform them about new opportunities.

Of course, we have already acknowledged the importance of the "luck factor." It is easy to say that successful entrepreneurs like Steve Jobs just "got lucky." Building relationships, however, is a powerful way to "maximize your chances" of becoming lucky. As we have already pointed out, successful and "lucky" people maintain contact with a broad network of friends and associates, which serves to create a *network of luck* – people who can support you and let you know about new opportunities.

A major part of Steve Jobs' success, for example, resulted from his ability to build a critical path of key relationships that extended the influence of his vision and ideas into a larger and larger community of customers, team members, stakeholders and partners. It was establishing these relationships that led to the generative collaborations which formed what he described as the "inverse pyramid" that allowed him to grow the "tiny seed" of his idea for a personal computer into a global business. Generative relationships and generative collaborations open doors that make it possible to create something from nothing.

Jobs' comment (see *SFM Volume I,* p. 274) that he never found anybody that didn't want to help him if he asked for help is a powerful statement about how he increased his luck factor by building a "lucky network." Jobs' further comment that "when people ask me, I try to be as responsive to pay that debt of gratitude back" illustrates the type of attitude that is at the foundation of a winning culture and a generative venture community. Building relationships requires proactivity, however. As Jobs pointed out, "Most people never ask. And that's what separates the people who do things from the people who just dream about them."

Like our metaphor of hydrogen and oxygen combining to make water, generative relationships and generative collaborations transform us into something bigger than just an individual. Through his collaboration with Steve Wozniak that led to the design the first Apple computer, Steve Jobs, for example, was no longer just a college dropout; he became a "computer designer." After building relationships with other people who knew how to make computers, he became a "computer manufacturer." Then, by building relationships with people who had legal and financial knowhow, he became "CEO of a small company," and so on. As the spiral of relationships expanded, his own identity grew along with that of his ventures and projects.

A major part of Steve Jobs' success resulted from his ability to build key relationships.

The SFM Collaboration Spiral™

The effects of generative relationships can be represented as an ascending spiral where key collaborations lead to the creation of successive platforms, in the form of projects or ventures, which extend the entrepreneur's range of influence and move him or her along the trajectory of his or her mission towards the larger vision.

We have found this capacity to recognize the importance of building generative relationships, and the willingness to actively pursue them, to be one of the most important success factors for entrepreneurs and leaders in creating successful projects and ventures.

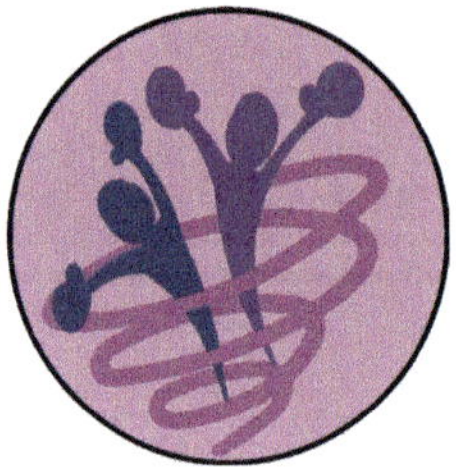

The effects of generative relationships can be represented as an ascending spiral, similar to Steve Jobs' "inverse pyramid," where key collaborations lead to the creation of successive platforms which extend your range of influence and move you along the trajectory of your mission towards your larger vision.

Most often, we begin our journeys as entrepreneurs on our own. Something awakens in us a vision of how the world could be different or better and we feel a sense of mission to make a contribution to that vision. When that combines with our ambition to leave our mark and our desire for growth and mastery, the "seed" of the project or the "stone" of the Stone Soup comes into being. In the beginning we are "nobody" with nothing but an idea, like the stranger and his stone for making soup. If we communicate our vision and mission to others with congruence and passion, however, we eventually find someone who "resonates" with them. If we are "lucky" this person introduces to others who also "resonate" and can provide key resources and support.

These relationships provide the foundation upon which to build a platform that extends our reach and supports our progress toward turning the vision into a reality. This platform emerges from the generative collaborations made possible by these relationships similar to water emerging form the interaction between hydrogen and oxygen atoms. As a result of our participation in the generative collaboration, especially in those in which we are fulfilling our mission in service of a larger vision, our identity expands into something more than we are as a single individual. As I pointed out in *SFM Volume I,* interacting with others in connection with a mission—such as a mother rat rescuing her babies or the captain of the jet in the Miracle on the Hudson—makes it possible for the actors to expand into an identity larger than just an individual rat or a man. Others no longer just see and respond to us as a lone individual, they see us and respond to us as an expression in this larger role and mission. And we perceive things and respond not just as a separate individual "ego," but from the larger identity and "holon."

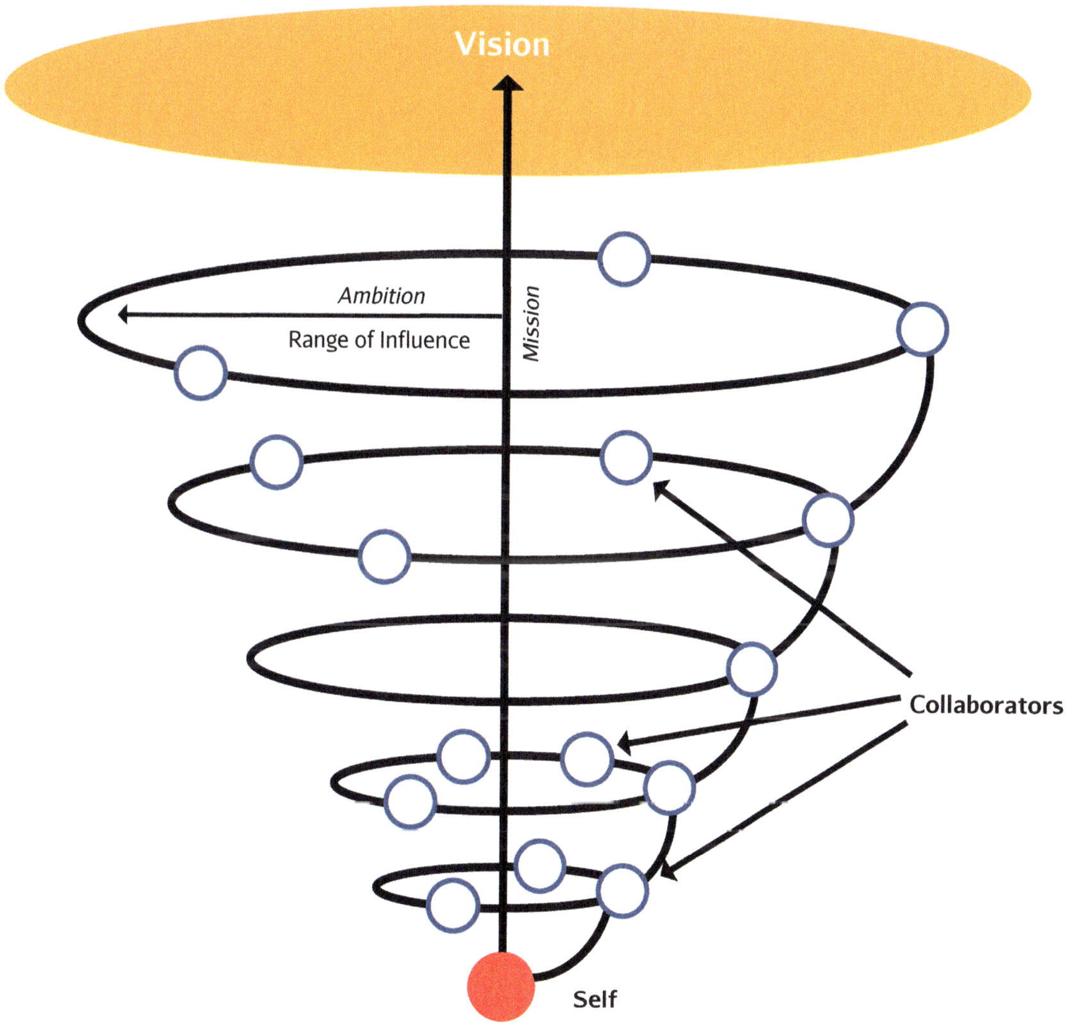

Collaborations Allow Us to Increase Our Range of Influence in Order to Achieve Our Missions and Reach Our Visions

As a simple example, participating in the production of a book such as this transforms the individual collaborators into the larger identities of "author," "editor," "publisher," "marketing director," etc. As another example, Mark Fizpatrick (profiled in *Success Factor Modeling Volume I*, pp. 156-161) started as just another "salesman" at a large company. His collaboration with a software engineer at the firm, however, transformed him from a "salesman" to a "software developer" and ultimately he spiraled to become the "chief executive" of a multi-million dollar company

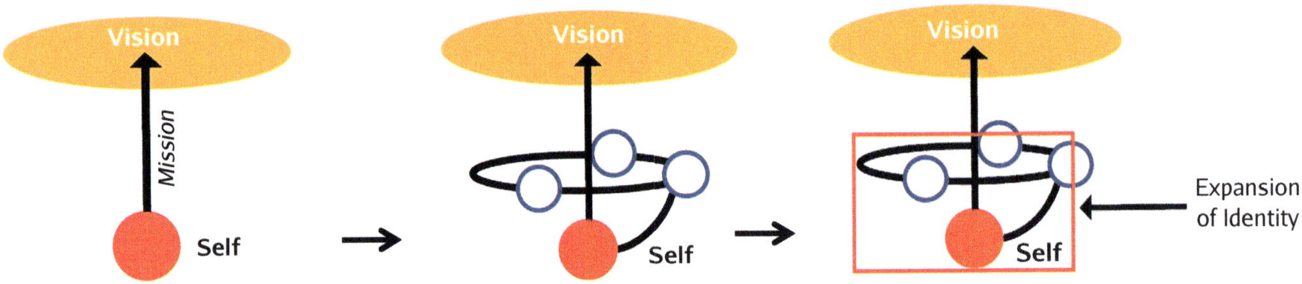

Generative Relationships Open Doorways to a Network of Collaboration and Support that Lead to an Expansion of Our Identity

It is not uncommon that, once we have completed a platform that allows us progress toward our vision and fulfill our mission and ambition, a new or expanded version of our vision emerges that is out of reach of the platform we have built. To achieve the bigger expression of the vision, the cycle of growth, mastery and relationship building must begin again. However, we generally do not "start from scratch" by regressing back to our individual identity as a separate "ego." Rather, we begin to build the new platform from the starting point of our previously expanded identity. In other words, if I am already an "author," I can begin building my next platform from that identity.

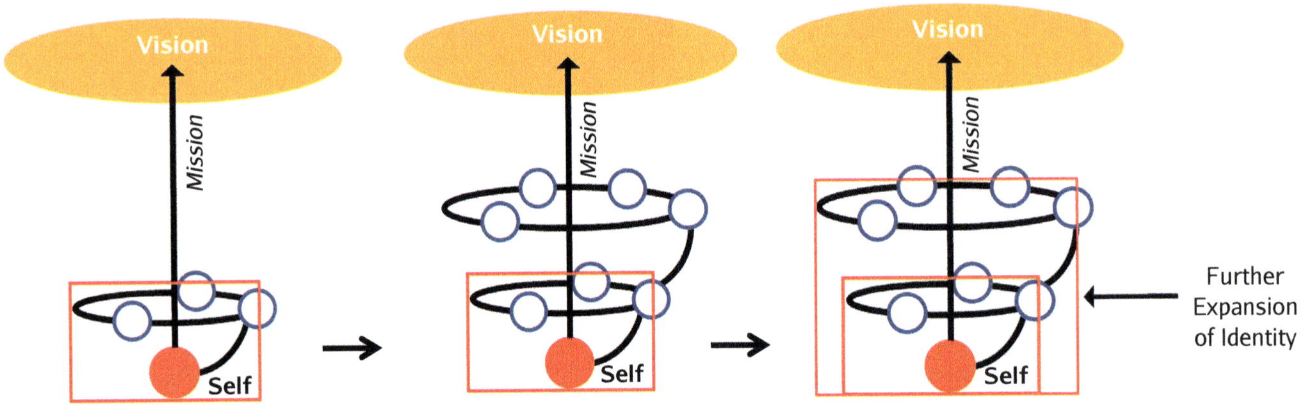

New Expressions of Our Vision Emerge When We Have Built a Platform Through Generative Collaboration, Leading Us to Create the Next Platform that Will Expand Our Reach and our Identity.

When you have a big vision, you need to work at building a number of successive platforms along the way, forming a type of expanding spiral. At the heart of the spiral is the entrepreneur's own sense of self and identity which continues to develop and expand as each platform is built in the individual's ongoing quest to reach his or her ultimate vision.

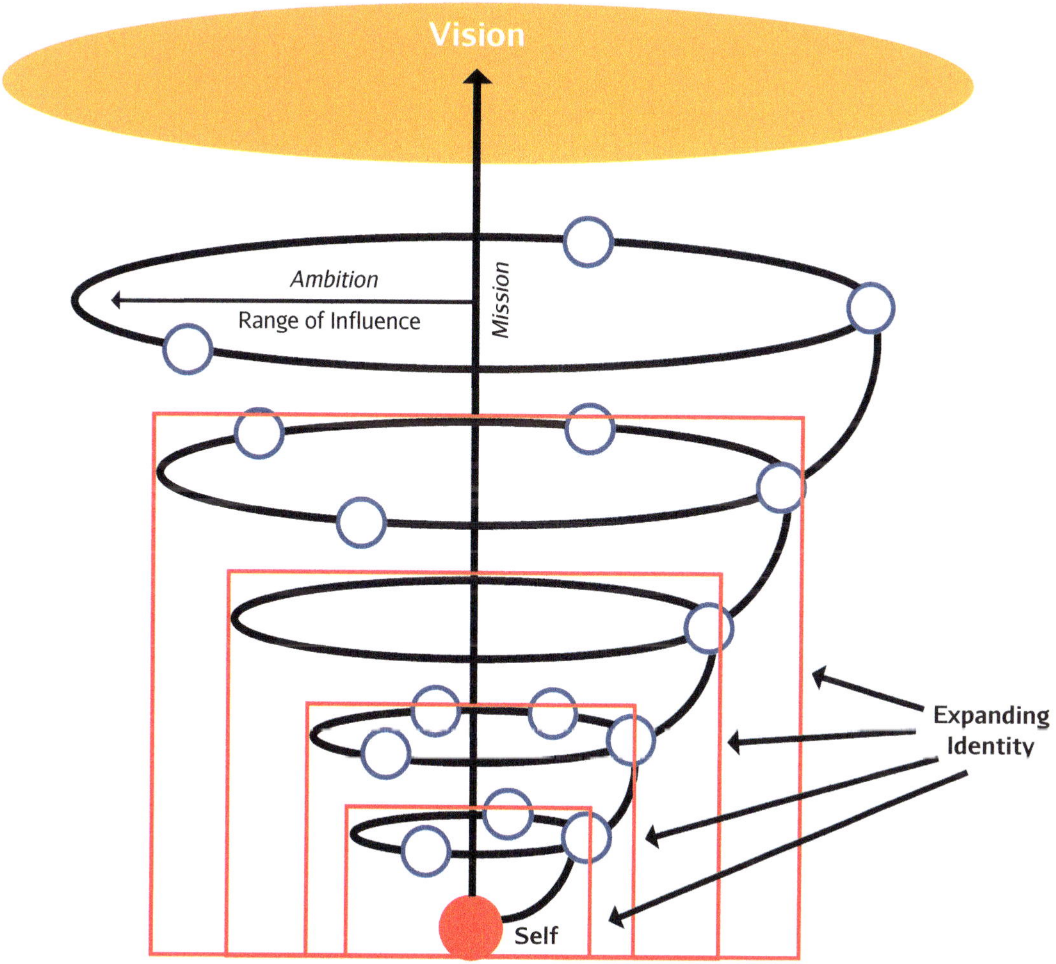

Each New Level of Collaboration and Influence Is Accompanied by a Corresponding Expansion of Identity

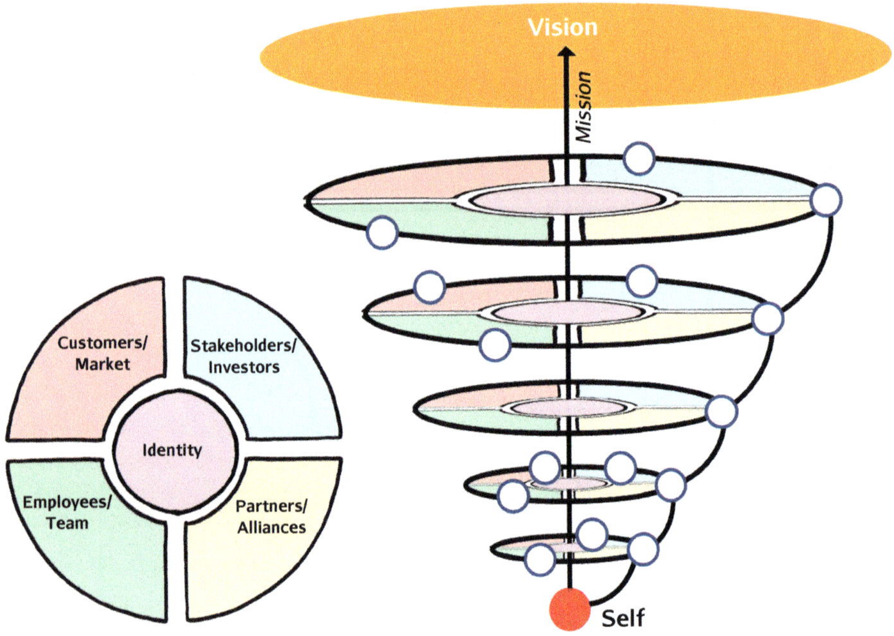

Successive platforms in your Collaboration Spiral are built by establishing relationships making up a new or expanded Circle of Success.

At each platform, the individual grows beyond the bounds of a perceived "box" of his or her current identity. If the entrepreneur becomes attached to or identified with this "box," it can often work to hold him or her back. Once the limits of each platform are reached and exceeded, an entrepreneur must continue to look upward toward new potential collaborations and broader platforms in order to achieve his or her vision, mission and ambition.

There is frequently a kind of tension with respect to interplay between the expanding levels of collaborative partnerships a person has developed and his or her perceived sense of identity. A person, for instance, may have the collaborative relationships in place that would allow him or her to jump to the next platform of influence, but is held back by the feeling that he or she does not have permission to take on the identity associated with that next level of influence.*

At other times, a person may desire to jump platforms at an identity level, but the necessary collaborative partners are not in place to provide the range of influence.

*This is where some of the processes described in *SFM Volume I* can be helpful, such as *Gathering Your Allies* (p. 147) and *The Identity Matrix* (pp. 180-186); or the *Dream Guardians* exercise at the end of this chapter (pp. 247-248).

Building New Platforms

In fact, to build a solid platform, the entrepreneur must establish key relationships relating to all of the various dimensions of the Circle of Success. Each new level of the spiral is generally embodied in the form of a project or venture and requires creating its own Circle of Success for which an entrepreneur must build sufficient relationships with new customers, team members, stakeholders and partners.

If the relationships which make up the Circle of Success are not strong enough at a particular platform, it may not be solid enough to support the creation of the next level of the spiral and can begin to crumble or come crashing down.

The strength of each platform will be largely determined by the entrepreneur's ability to engage in and facilitate collective intelligence with and between the various members of his or her Circle of Success. This requires constantly engaging in benchmarking, brainstorming, best practices and generative collaboration with customers, ream members, partners and stakeholders.

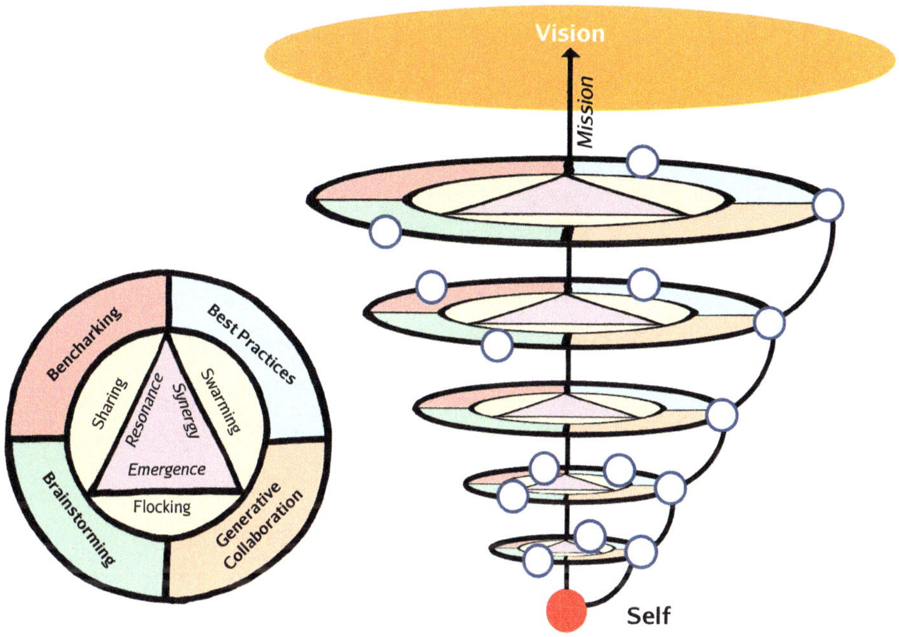

The strength and stability of a particular platform is a function of your ability to engage in and facilitate collective intelligence and generative collaboration.

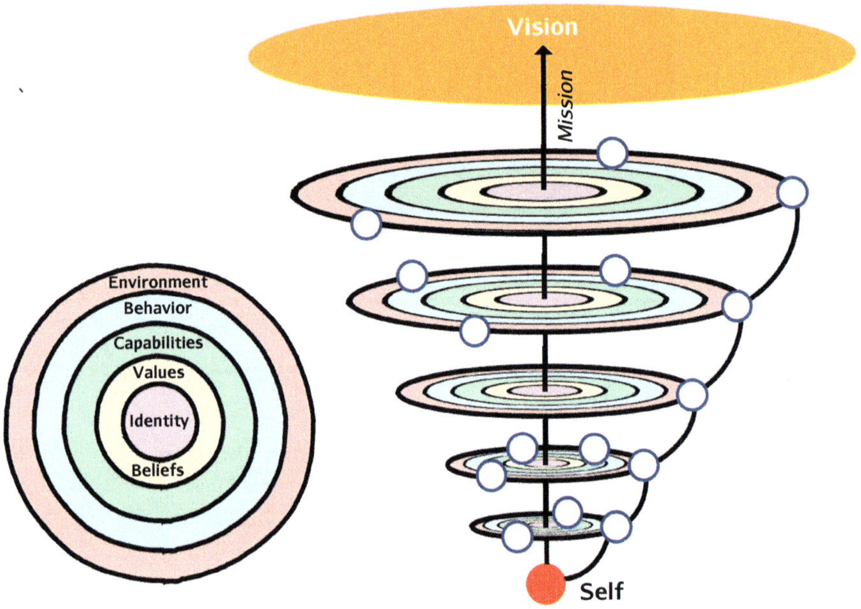

Each New Platform Requires Mastery and Alignment of All of the Levels of Success Factors Needed to Succeed Within that Environment and Scope of Influence.

Another factor determining the solidity of a particular platform is the entrepreneur's mastery and alignment of the different levels of success factors related to that platform (identity, beliefs and values, capabilities, behaviors and environment). From this perspective, we can also view each level of the Collaboration Spiral as founded on the entrepreneur's level of development and preparation with regard to his or her "inner game."

Each new platform will bring the entrepreneur into a new or more expanded environment that will require him or her to enlarge and diversify his or her repertoire of behaviors. This in turn requires the development of new capabilities and a corresponding deepening or strengthening of values and belief in him or herself, what he or she is doing, his or her team, etc. The enrichment and alignment of these success factors are necessary to support the expanded sense of identity associated with the new platform.

If our ambitions or our circumstances push us to try to jump to the next level of identity and influence before we are ready and able to ground in the beliefs, values, capabilities and behaviors required by that level of identity and influence, the consequences can be difficult and even disastrous.

Consider the example of child stars who are catapulted to fame and fortune before they are mature enough or ready to handle it. They are frequently not able to deal with the demands and stress of the situation which can lead to a significant break down or regression in their careers or their lives.

It is important to have a solid grounding in the beliefs, values, capabilities and behaviors required by one level of identity and influence before attempting to move to the next level.

This dynamic showed up in the career of Steve Jobs for instance. After a very rapid rise to success in a short period, he was forced to leave Apple because he lost the confidence of his stakeholders (Board of Directors and Stockholders) and was driven from the company he founded. It wasn't until he grew from building NeXT and Pixar that he had the maturity and mastery of all of the levels necessary to run Apple and take it to the next platform of its spiral. By more fully developing all the levels of success factors and solidifying his identity, he was able to come back to Apple and lead it to new levels of success.

This same dynamic of suffering from a too rapid an expansion without developing sufficient solidity and footing at all of the levels of success factors on a platform below can happen to an entire venture or organization as well as an individual.

In summary, the development, mastery and alignment of the various levels of success factors are the foundation of the center of our Circle of Success and are linked to the various dimensions of the Circle of Success through the entrepreneur's vision, mission, ambition and role. In fact, we can say that each platform in the Collaboration Spiral is built from three layers: (1) The entrepreneur's inner mastery and alignment of the different levels of success factors (identity, beliefs and values, capabilities, behaviors and environment); related to that platform and its range of influence; which become expressed in the form of (2) the entrepreneur's ability to engage in and facilitate collective intelligence and generative collaboration; which ultimately manifest through collaborations relating to (3) each dimension of the Circle of Success.

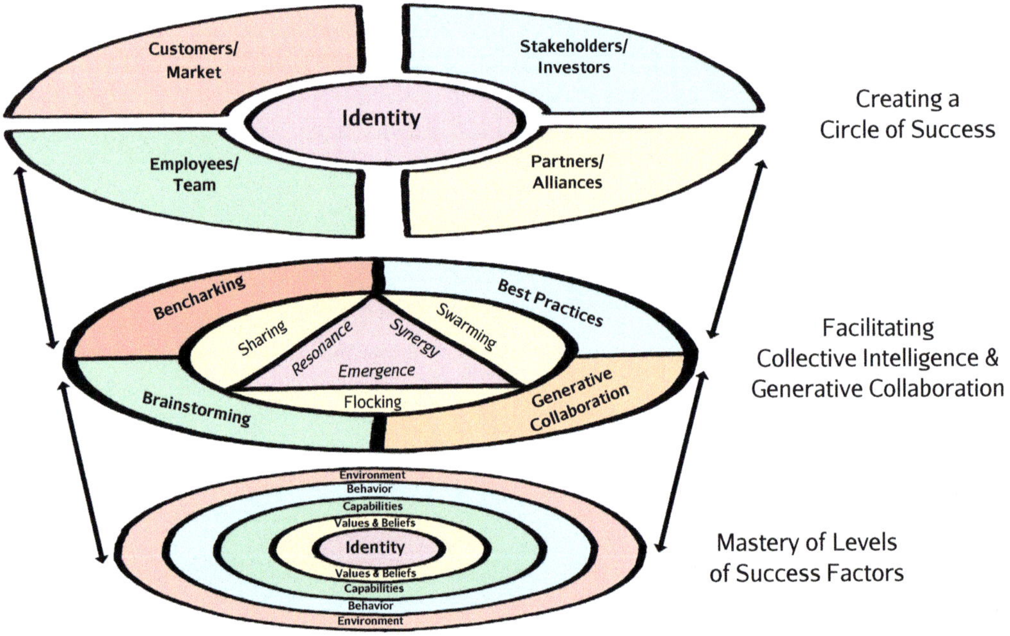

The Solidity of Each Platform in the Collaboration Spiral is a Function of:

(1) The Entrepreneur's Mastery of the Relevant Success Factors

(2) The Entrepreneur's Ability to Engage in and Facilitate Collective Intelligence and Generative Collaboration

(3) Building the Collaborative Relationships Necessary to Create a Robust Circle of Success

"Guardians" and "Gatekeepers"

Generative relationships are those that support all three of these layers required to build a solid platform. In addition to providing practical support in terms of customers, team members, stakeholders and partners, those with whom we enter a generative relationship provide guidance, coaching, teaching, mentoring and sponsorship. Each new platform represents a next milestone or "threshold" on our journey to our vision. It is a new heretofore unknown territory outside of our current comfort zone; a territory that forces us to grow and evolve, and requires us to find support and guidance. *Guardians* are our sponsors and mentors. They are the individuals with whom we develop key relationships that support us to build skills, believe in ourselves and stay focused on our objectives. Because the territory beyond the threshold is new for us, we cannot necessarily know what type of guardianship we will need ahead of time or who those guardians will be. Sometimes guardians will come from surprising places. Thus, we must stay open and available to receiving guidance and support at every step on our journey.

Guardians are our sponsors and mentors with whom we develop key relationships that support us to build skills, believe in ourselves and stay focused on our objectives.

One of the most important types of generative relationship in the terms of the Collaboration Spiral is with what could be called a "gatekeeper." *Gatekeepers* are those who "open the gate" to a whole new network of relationships at the level of influence that we seek or need in order progress with respect to our mission and vision. They have a position at the nexus of the next loop of the spiral we seek to enter. They are also frequently sponsors who see our potential and provide introductions that establish our credibility in the eyes of the people with whom we need to build relationships in order create and strengthen our next platform.

Gatekeepers are those who "open the gate" to a whole new network of relationships at the level of influence that we seek or need in order progress with respect to our mission and vision.

Finding such relationships and building a successful Collaboration Spiral is clearly one of the major purposes of Randy Williams' Keiretsu Forum. In my work with established companies, I also encourage large organizations to consider how to provide high potential managers with opportunities to develop their network of guardians and gatekeepers both inside and outside of the organization in order to support them in establishing solid collaboration spirals.

It is important to point out, however, that in some cases, given the extent of our vision, mission and ambition, we are ready to move to a next level in our own spiral and the gatekeeper at our current level may not be ready, able or willing to support us in that transition to move on. A little bit like a parent who does not want his or her child to leave home, the gatekeeper may even try to keep us from moving to the next level.

In some instances, gatekeepers at one level may attempt to hold us back from moving to the next level if they are unable to join us or support us.

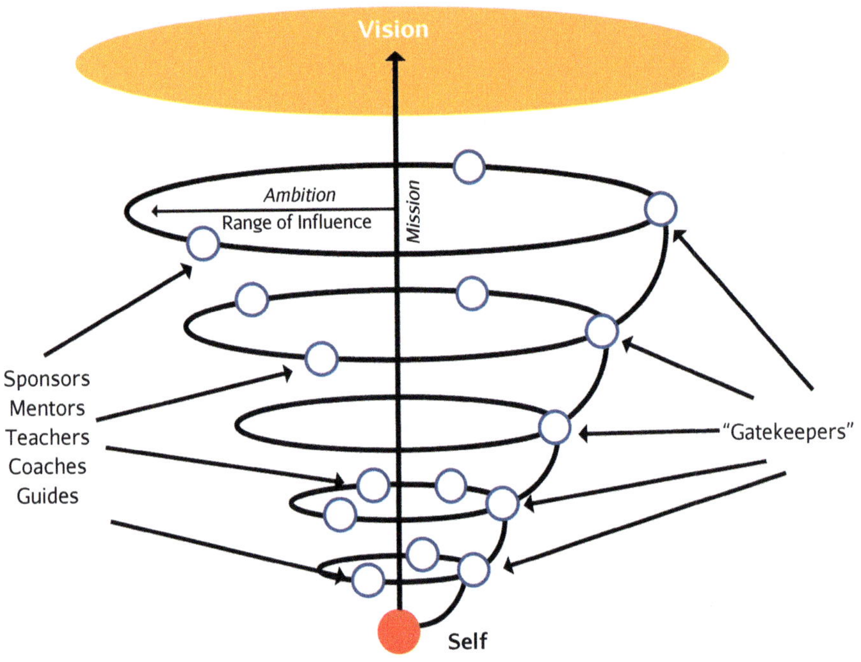

Relationships with "Gatekeepers" Form the Nexus for the Next Level of Influence and Accomplishment

As in the case of every other barrier, entrepreneurs must not allow potentially limiting relationships to hold them back. If a collaborative partner ceases to be supportive, that partner may need to be bypassed or left behind in favor of new positive relationships that support the entrepreneur's progress toward his or her vision. This can be one of the most difficult and painful episodes we can experience on our journey as an entrepreneur.

Steve Jobs' bitter and heartbreaking relationship with John Sculley is an iconic example of this. Jobs' brought Sculley into Apple thinking it would be a generative relationship. Instead, Sculley turned against him because of the differences in their visions, ambitions and roles.

Such dilemmas and transitions can also happen in our personal relationships as well as our business relationships.

It is important to keep in mind that such a decision to end a relationship in order to move ahead needs to be made from a place of deep connection and service to our vision and mission. In my coaching work and experience as an entrepreneur, I have seen time and again that trying to resolve such a situation on the basis of ambition alone will almost always lead to regret.

As I pointed out earlier, there are dangers in jumping ahead too quickly. It is crucial to build enough relationships to keep a platform in place, in case something happens to the other key relationships creating that platform. The third loop or platform in the spiral shown in the diagram on the opposite page, for example, has the "gatekeeper" as the only significant relationship. This puts too much onus on that one position to hold the whole platform in place. If something goes wrong with that relationship, the whole platform can collapse.

It is crucial to build enough relationships to keep a platform in place, in case something happens to the other key relationships creating that platform.

The top loop in the diagram illustrates that two key relationships have been established, but there is no gatekeeper yet to synergize it into a solid enough platform to allow for an expansion of identity. In the situation illustrated by this diagram, the entrepreneur would need to be looking carefully for such a gatekeeper on that level.

In the next section we will explore some ways to prepare yourself to be able to recognize and/or create generative relationships and successful collaborations.

SFM Collaboration Catalyst: Modeling Successful Collaboration

In many ways, finding generative relationships and building a successful Collaboration Spiral is largely a matter of luck. As we have already established, however, "luck" is the meeting of preparation and opportunity. We prepare for successful generative relationship building in two ways. First, we must do our own "homework." That is, we must develop the center of our Circle of Success through the discipline of self-mastery and continue our path of growth and mastery. As successful entrepreneur Mark Fizpatrick pointed out, it is important to "take steps to improve yourself." There is an old saying that "When the student is ready, the teacher appears."

The second area of preparation is to be clear what type of collaboration you are seeking and what makes a successful "generative relationship." A good starting place is to do some of your own success factor modeling.

Following are some questions and guidelines to help you reflect upon a successful collaboration that you have been involved in. Use these guidelines to define the characteristics of a successful generative relationship.

Who did you collaborate with? What was the background of your collaboration partner(s).

What was the context of your collaboration? What were the characteristics of the environment and the situation in which you collaborated.

What were some of the unique challenges that you faced that made the collaboration important or necessary?

What values and beliefs drove your collaboration?

What steps did you take to ensure a win-win interaction?

What were the key synergies between you and your collaboration partner(s)? What were the complementary capabilities, resources or know-how that you brought together through your collaboration.

Why was this a successful collaboration? What did you accomplish together that neither of you could have accomplished as individuals?

What is the evidence of your success? What were the results of the collaboration?

SFM Collaboration Catalyst: Preparing for a Generative Relationship

Applying the modeling you have done of a successful collaboration, use the following questions to clarify what type of collaboration you need or are looking for in order to move to the next step in your own collaboration spiral. You can use these questions to define the characteristics of a potential collaboration and collaborator that does not yet exist, or to reflect upon a collaboration that you are considering establishing.

Collaboration Spiral Questions for Yourself

1. What is my current platform and who am I currently?

Platform: ____

Identity: ____

2. What are some of the key relationships (gatekeepers and guardians) that I have now that support me in that identity?

3. What are my key resources with respect to this platform and identity?

4. What are my key attributes (behaviors, capabilities, beliefs, values, ambition, mission vision)?

____________________ ____________________

____________________ ____________________

____________________ ____________________

5. What is the next platform I need to establish in order to create the next expression of my vision? What will be my expanded identity?

Platform: ____

Identity: ____

6. What are my main needs in order to build that platform?

____________________ ____________________

____________________ ____________________

____________________ ____________________

7. What personal attributes will I need to develop, strengthen or expand in order to establish that platform (behaviors, capabilities, beliefs, values, ambition, mission)?

______________________ ______________________

______________________ ______________________

______________________ ______________________

8. What are some of the key relationships (gatekeepers and guardians) that I will need to support me to create my new platform and identity?

______________________ ______________________

______________________ ______________________

______________________ ______________________

Another question to explore with respect to your collaboration spiral is whether there are any relationships that are currently holding you back from expanding to your next platform or identity? If there are, how can you either transform them or move beyond them?

Collaboration Spiral Questions Regarding Your Potential Collaborator

1. Who is my potential collaborator currently? ______________________________

2. What are some of the key relationships that support my potential collaborator in that identity?

______________________ ______________________

______________________ ______________________

______________________ ______________________

Can any of these relationships help me to establish my next platform and identity?

3. What are my potential collaborator's resources? Which of these resources do I need?

______________________ ______________________

______________________ ______________________

______________________ ______________________

4. What are my potential collaborator's needs? Which of my resources could help address these needs?

______________________ ______________________

______________________ ______________________

______________________ ______________________

5. What are my potential collaborator's attributes (behaviors, capabilities, beliefs, values, ambition, mission vision)?

______________________ ______________________

______________________ ______________________

______________________ ______________________

6. Who could we be together if we partnered or collaborated?

____

7. What can we accomplish together that we could not accomplish individually?

____

Success Factor Case Example
John Dilts, Founder - Maverick Angels

Let your future pull you forward..

John Dilts
Founder – Maverick Angels

John Dilts rose from being just one of many staff members in a Silicon Valley law firm to becoming a special advisor to the Chinese government on how to develop entrepreneurism in their provinces in less than four years.

It is only fitting that the next Success Factor Case Example in this book be of John Dilts.

John was a co-creator of the Success Factor Modeling process and co-founder of Dilts Strategy Group. John's accomplishments, however, are much broader than that.

In 1999 at the age of 35, John was a relative "nobody"; just one of many people on the staff of a Silicon Valley law firm. Less than four years later, he was a special advisor to the Chinese government on how to develop entrepreneurism in their provinces, and a key part of a wave that would catapult China into its current position as a global economic power. John's rapid progress and transformation is a testament to the power of the Collaboration Spiral.

John's background was in law and finance. Like Mark Fizpatrick (see *SFM Volume I*, pp. 156- 162), John had originally followed in his father's footsteps (our father was a patent lawyer who moved to the Silicon Valley area in the late 1950s as an electronics expert). After earning a law degree from the University of San Francisco, John tried his hand in various law firms in the San Francisco Bay Area. John was never able to fully embrace law practice however. He was disillusioned with the win-lose nature of most legal proceedings. In law school he had excelled in negotiations. He and I frequently discussed the importance of collaboration and how to take second position with clients, as well as with their opposition and their representatives. John demonstrated a passion and a talent for negotiations that brought win-win solutions to both parties.

He eventually found business law most attractive because it was about building something rather than simply beating an adversary. The Silicon Valley law firm in which he was working represented venture backed start-up companies as well as handling mergers and acquisitions and initial public offerings. As a result, John gathered a lot of experience sitting on both sides of negotiations between entrepreneurs and potential investors, team members and partners. He began to notice that, after an unsuccessful meeting with an entrepreneur, a potential investor might say something like, "If they had only had addressed *X* or demonstrated *Y*, I would have been interested." John began to wonder, "Well, why didn't you tell them that so that they would have the opportunity to respond to the feedback and get a chance to make adjustments?"

During these meetings, John also became increasingly aware of the importance of the entrepreneur's ability to communicate his or her passion and vision in a way that inspired others, rather than just present their product or financial plan. He realized that investors rarely chose to invest in an idea, product or plan alone. They invested in the entrepreneur and his or her vision, mission, ambition, passion and commitment to make things happen. Investors didn't want to invest in a product or a particular plan, they wanted to invest in a business, which in a rapidly changing environment takes much more than a plan or product. The plan and product were important, but ultimately investors invested in people.

Given his natural talent and passion for win-win negotiations, John also witnessed how setting up the right partnership or alliance could immediately increase the perceived value of a struggling start-up, essentially "making something out of nothing."

As a result of participating in negotiations between entrepreneurs and investors, John realized that investors rarely chose to invest in an idea, product or plan alone. They invested in the entrepreneur and his or her vision, mission, ambition, passion and commitment to make things happen.

From Legal Assistant to Fund Manager and Venture Coach

These experiences began to seed in John the idea of a special type of "venture catalyst." A *venture catalyst* is an individual or collection of individuals (such as a fund) that puts both money and other resources into a start-up company in order to accelerate its growth and increatse its chances of success. John's idea was not only to put money into small start-ups with high potential and support them with legal and financial planning, but also coach the entrepreneurs in the behavioral and management skills they needed to grow their business. This idea would eventually grow into the vision of a generative venture community.

It all started with a box under the desk.

As a first step toward this vision, John began to dream of establishing his own venture fund, focused on investing in early stage technology companies. He liked to point out that this dream began to take shape in the form of a "box under the desk." The box held his files of ideas, contacts and plans. The box began to come to life when he found resonance with a colleague at the same law firm who handled the firm's investments. As their passion for the project increased, so did John's ambition and belief, and the box under the desk began to become the main focus of his attention. At a certain point, John realized it could no longer be a side project and would have to become the primary focus of his attention. This meant taking the risk of leaving the law firm.

John left his job at a Silicon Valley law firm to start his own early stage venture fund.

From Legal Assistant to Venture Coach

In addition to managing the fund and coaching the companies within its portfolio, John established Dilts Ventures and began coaching other entrepreneurs and leaders of start-up companies.

John and I began collaborating and founded Dilts Strategy Group, combining our two networks and significantly increasing John's range of influence and expanding his identity to International Trainer and Consultant.

He did, and he and his partner launched the IPF Fund, LLC, a private equity venture capital fund for which he served as Managing Director. John and his partner collected and invested $1 million in 14 start-up companies in the areas of Internet infrastructure and applications, enterprise software and telecommunications. Although the amount was not significant by Silicon Valley standards, the result of the collaboration was a shift in his identity from a "staff member" at a law firm to a "venture fund manager." This allowed him to begin to build a new platform leading closer to his vision. His identity of fund manager brought him in contact with many more people than he would ever meet through his law firm. In addition to managing the fund and coaching the companies within its portfolio, John established Dilts Ventures and began coaching other entrepreneurs and leaders of start-up companies. This expanded his identity further to include "venture coach." It also simultaneously expanded his network of relationships, leading to his serving on the boards of directors for numerous Silicon Valley technology companies addressing a variety of industries.

Expanding to International Trainer and Consultant

Given my background in NLP and modeling and my work with larger companies and organizations in the areas of leadership and innovation, John and I frequently found ourselves talking about what types of coaching, training and tools it took to make an effective venture catalyst. We also exchanged ideas about how to catalyze a greater entrepreneurial attitude in large organizations. This led to our development of the Success Factor Modeling process. John's new identity of fund manager and venture coach opened the possibility for us to collaborate on several projects. John excelled not only as a creative win-win negotiator but also as a public speaker. As a result of the success of our collaborations we founded Dilts Strategy Group. Combining our two networks created a significant shift in the range of influence we both had and expanded John's identity again to include "international trainer and consultant."

One of our projects was with the Fiat Group. The group had been growing rapidly throughout the 1990s and in the latter part of the decade acquired almost 1,000 companies in the space of two years. The group comprised more than 600 boards of directors. The leaders of the holding company felt they needed to establish a common culture and a shared leadership approach that would provide a shared sense of identity for the companies within the group. I had been working with a number of the top people at ISVOR Fiat, the human resource and organizational development branch of the conglomerate and their corporate university. They were fascinated by what had been happening in the Silicon Valley and realized that they needed to encourage a greater entrepreneurial spirit within their culture.

A collaboration between Dilts Strategy Group and Italian car maker Fiat applying Success Factor modeling to leadership development led to a joint venture in which John became CEO of an international training company.

Becoming CEO of an International Training Company

A collaboration between Dilts Strategy Group and ISVOR Fiat began in order to apply the Success Factor Modeling methodology to define the skills and characteristics of high performing leaders within the Fiat Group. This collaboration resulted in the development of the SFM Leadership Model (see *Success Factor Modeling Volume III*). A next step was to roll out the leadership model to the companies within the Fiat Group. A joint venture between the two companies, ISVOR Dilts Leadership Systems, was formed to facilitate this process. Given John's trajectory from legal assistant to fund manager, venture coach, international trainer and consultant, and co-developer of a unique behavioral modeling process, he was an obvious choice for chief executive officer of the new joint venture.

At this point, as result of developing his Collaboration Spiral, John had moved from being a relatively anonymous staff member at a law firm to the CEO of a high profile international leadership development organization in the space of a few short years. This new platform, however, did not yet bring John to fully achieve his bigger vision for a generative venture community.

From Venture Coach to International Trainer and to CEO of a global company

John formed a partnership with a colleagure from China to help bring Western managerial approaches to mainland China. This led to his selection as Dean of the Shool of Entrepreneurism at Jiatiai University and ultimately an advisor on entrepreneurism to the Chinese government.

John Dilts' identity eventually expanded from CEO to Dean of Entrepreneurship, to advisor to the Chinese Government, to founder of a Generative Venture Community.

Transitioning to International Venture Investment Consultant and Dean of Entrepreneurship

While head of ISVOR Dilts, John formed a partnership with a Chinese woman living in the United States who was helping to bring Western managerial approaches to mainland China. Together, they established GlobalAngels, an international consulting company whose purpose was to facilitate global business and venture investment between Asia and the United States. This expanded John's network even more, into a community thirsting for the expertise he had. During one of his visits to China, John's Chinese partner introduced him to the board of directors of Jiatai University, a prestigious new private business school located in Hangzhou, China. They were establishing a School of Entrepreneurism to serve young people entering the workforce as their country transitioned from Communism to Capitalism.

Given his background as a legal counsel to venture backed start-ups, a venture fund manager and venture coach, an experienced consultant and trainer, a CEO of an international leadership training organization, and a partner of a Chinese woman working with companies to integrate American management processes, John was asked to become Dean of the School of Entrepreneurism at the university, which he accepted.

Advising the Chinese Government

Shortly after that, when the Chinese government was looking for advice on how to "jump-start" entrepreneurship in their provinces, they naturally considered the "Dean of Entrepreneurship" at one of their newest and most prestigious business schools. John's journey along his Collaboration Spiral made him an ideal candidate for this role, and it was another platform for him from which to help encourage a generative venture community within the growing economic power.

Founding a Generative Venture Community

This was not the ultimate expression of John's vision, however. In early 2004, John met Randy Williams and discovered what he was doing with the Keiretsu Forum. John was impressed with the structure and immediately set up a Keiretsu chapter in Los Angeles. Given his background with Success Factor Modeling, however, John felt that much more could be done to provide tools, coaching and support to both entrepreneurs and business angels.

In 2006 John founded his own generative venture community called Maverick Angels, focusing on funding and mentoring early-stage companies. The structure of the Maverick Angels community was inspired by Randy William's ideas but added in all of the principles and tools of Success Factor Modeling to support the success of its members. Similar to the Keiretsu Forum, John created *Maverick Angels* as an angel investor network bringing together visionary entrepreneurs with great ideas and early stage investors. John created a structure in which entrepreneurs, who were carefully screened and coached, presented their vision and plan for their business to a group of qualified investors. The entrepreneurs were then supported with the types of tools, exercises and coaching that have been presented in this three-volume work on Success Factor Modeling.

In addition to establishing Maverick Angels Chapters in Southern California, Utah and in Europe, John leveraged his consulting and training background with large organizations to set up a corporate consulting division of Maverick Angels. Its purpose was to create competitive innovation acceleration strategies for larger companies based on Success Factor Modeling. The approach involved adapting the angel investment network process in large organizations by transferring strategies and catalysts modeled from both accomplished entrepreneurs and the entrepreneurial ecosystem in which they operate. John successfully applied this approach to help support sustainable innovation strategies inside global organizations such as Nestlé, Kraft, Amgen, Warner Bros., Sony, and Intesa Sanpaolo Bank.

MAVERICK ANGELS

In 2006 John founded his own generative venture community called Maverick Angels, focusing on funding and mentoring early-stage companies.

WILD
HORSE
LABS

Today, John's vision of a generative venture community lives on in Wild Horse Labs, an International Investment Accelerator which mentors start-ups to attract investments and build successful ventures, applying the principles of Success Factor Modeling.

At the time of his untimely and unexpected death in August 2010, John was working on television shows to promote entrepreneurism and principles of a generative venture community in several countries based on the format of *American Idol* or *Britain's Got Talent*. He envisioned a type of reality show format in which entrepreneurs would present their ideas to a panel of experienced investors and accomplished entrepreneurs who would comment on their presentations. The viewers would vote on which ventures would receive funding. These programs have now become realities in a number of countries.

John also expressed his passionate commitment to the creation of generative venture communities in his personal involvement with groups like El Nido Family Centers in Southern California. El Nido is an organization supporting disadvantaged and at-risk children, youth and families. John volunteered his time and was particularly dedicated to helping teenagers and young adults. Like the stranger in the stone soup story, John's goal was to inspire them with his vision of what was possible and his belief in what they could co-create if each person contributes something to the common cause. At John's funeral, the director of El Nido spoke in tears about how the enormous amount of time John had given to the young people had transformed their lives.

Today, John's vision of a generative venture community lives on in Wild Horse Labs, co- founded by John's wife Julie Davis Dilts (www.wildhorselabs.com). Wild Horse Labs evolved out of Maverick Angels and operates as an International Investment Accelerator which mentors start-ups to attract investments and build successful ventures, applying the principles of Success Factor Modeling.

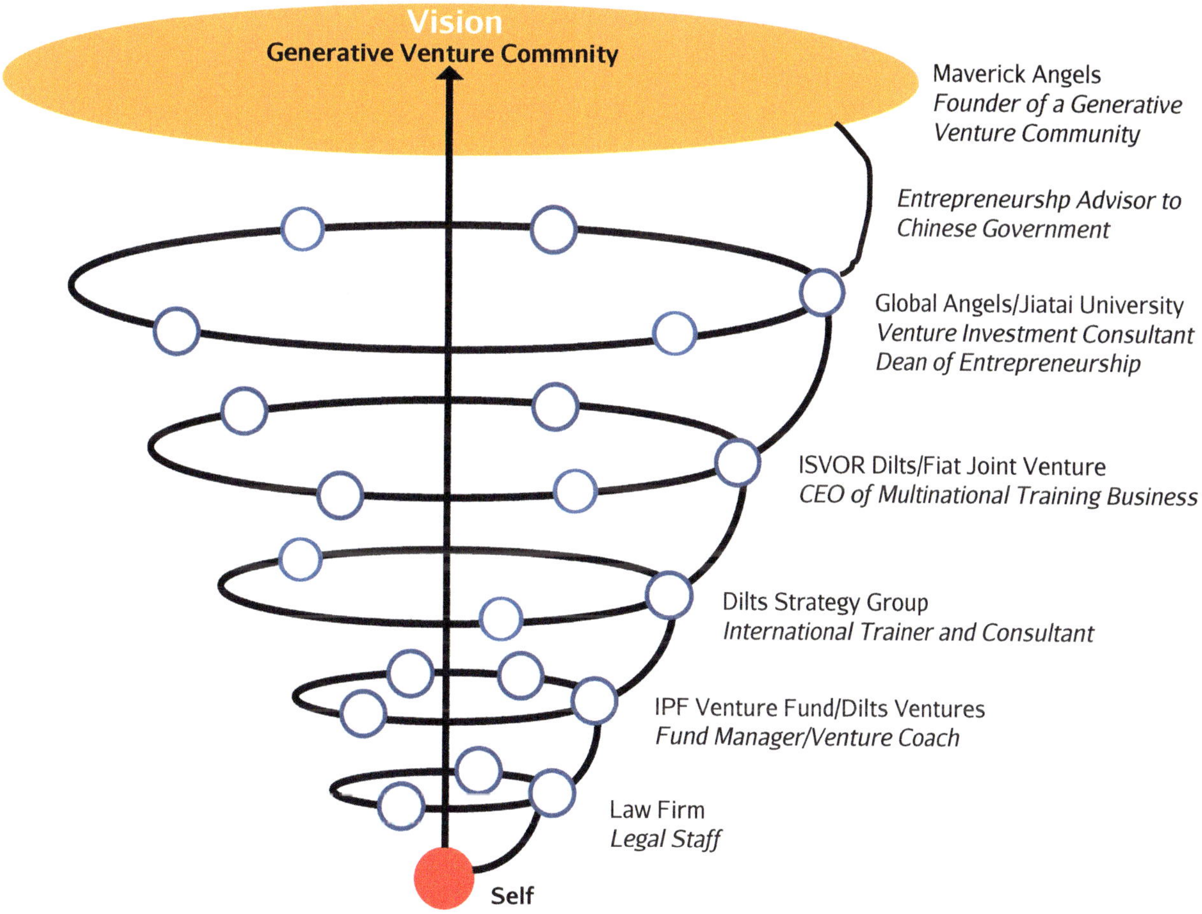

John Dilts' ability to create an effective Collaboration Spiral allowed him to expand from being a relatively unknown legal staff member in a Silicon Valley law firm to an advisor on entrepreneurship to the Chinese government and founder of an international venture community in less than five years.

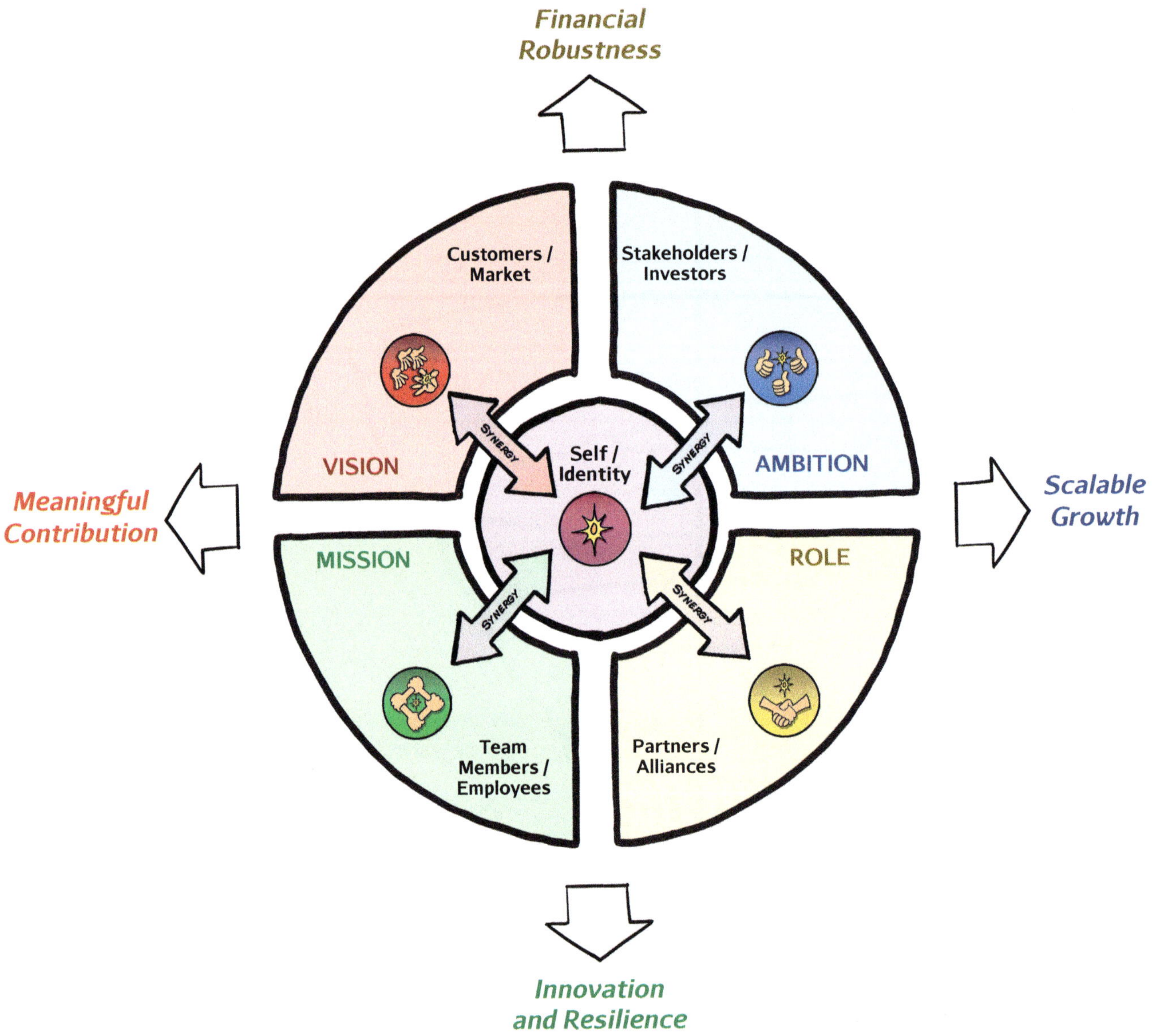

Similar to Randy Williams, John Dilts believed that strengthening the entrepreneur's center of the Circle of Success through strong relationships with stakeholders, such as angel investors, would enrich all of the other parts of their Circle of Success.

Summary: Key Success Factors for Creating a Generative Venture Community

Like Randy Williams, John Dilts placed a great deal of attention on strengthening the synergy between entrepreneurs and their stakeholders. In their vision of a "generative venture community," stakeholders serve as sponsors and guardians as well as investors; providing support and intellectual capital as much as financial capital. John, in particular, believed that by strengthening the center of the Circle of Success through strong relationships with stakeholders, such as angel investors, the synergy between the entrepreneur and all of the other parts of the Circle of Success would be strengthened as well.

John also believed that a strong sense of identity and passion on the part of entrepreneurs was essential to their success. The strength, clarity and creativity of the rest of a particular Circle of Success depended on the strength, clarity and creativity of its center – the entrepreneur and his or her passion and vision.

John Dilts understood that the strength, clarity and creativity of the rest of a particular Circle of Success depended on the strength, clarity and creativity of its center – the entrepreneur and his or her passion and vision.

According to the Circle of Success, the outcome of achieving *scalable growth* is predominantly achieved through the actions of *expanding the business and creating value* for stakeholders and investors and *building win-win relationships* with partners and allies.

As I mentioned earlier, John's genius was in thinking of win-win collaborations. He felt that partnerships were a particularly important area of collaboration that was frequently overlooked by entrepreneurs and organizations. He saw them as a powerful leverage, as demonstrated by Steve Jobs' partnership between Apple and Microsoft described in *SFM Volume I* (p. 268). Multiple times, I witnessed John increasing the valuation of start up by over $1 million by negotiating a simple partnership with a large or high profile organization for joint project that cost nothing to either party.

As his work through Maverick Angels and El Nido demonstrates, John was deeply committed to spreading the benefits of a generative venture community throughout the world. He fervently believed that creating a new generation of entrepreneurs who were living their dreams would contribute to creating a better world.

He fervently believed that creating a new generation of entrepreneurs who were living their dreams would contribute to creating a better world.

The following is John's philosophy and formula for entrepreneurs to create a winning culture and a generative venture community.

Reflections on the Power of a Generative Venture Community "Let Your Future Pull You Forward"

- *Begin to acknowledge your future assets. Identify them, and work your way toward them using the tools and models you have learned.*
- *Tap your personal generative power and the power and resources of the community to which you passionately give as well.*
- *Overcome limiting beliefs by acknowledging your belief in the power of your ideas and the very real catalyst that awaits them.*
- *Remain open to the positive and constructive ideas of others in the community and allow their sponsorship to support you in a win-win manner—they need and rely on your ideas.*
- *Don't judge yourself too harshly, and don't allow the limiting beliefs of others outside the community who lack your understanding, abilities and passion to hold you back.*
- *When you feel that happening, focus on the strength of your passion for following your own true self and recall the sponsorship and collaboration that you have received in this community. It is real; rely on it and don't waiver.*
- *This will enable you to fully realize the possibilities of your ideas, skills and the generative power of the community.*
- *You have a duty to share this unique power with the world—it is very special.*
- *When you give yourself over to the strength of your personal power and abilities and the passion that drives them in the community, there will be no stopping you.*
- *The potential for the future of this generative force that you have created together is absolutely limitless.*

Hopefully, you have discovered the truth about your limiting beliefs—they are inherently "limited" and inaccurate. Others in the room see much more in you, in your ideas, in your abilities and, in fact, they rely on them. Therefore, the needs and perceptions of the group toward you now become your reality, not the lies you create about yourself in your own personal "cave." This new reality is the launch pad for your future and the future of this powerful new community.

Let your future pull you forward.

SFM Collaboration Catalyst: Dream Guardians Exercise

A key resource for "making something from nothing" is to get support and encouragement from others who see your vision and believe in your ability to reach it. As John Dilts' comments above so eloquently state, this is one of the gifts and benefits of a generative venture community. In our Success Factor Modeling programs and coaching sessions with teams and new ventures, one of the key exercises we invite participants to complete is what we call the Dream Guardians exercise. *Dream Guardians* are those who help us to build a new platform on our Collaboration Spiral by supporting us to identify the resources we need to overcome obstacles and transform barriers to reaching our dreams. That is, they help us to have creative ways of looking at problems and search out different ways to overcome or transform obstacles.

This exercise is best done in a group of seven: A presenter/entrepreneur and six guardians. Guardians are to choose a level of success factors upon which to focus; i.e., environment, behavior, capabilities, beliefs and values, identity or spirit (vision and purpose).

In the Dream Guardians Exercise, the team explores potential obstacles and the needed resources at multiple levels: environment, behavior, capabilities, beliefs and values, identity and vision or purpose.

1. Beginning with the whole group in the COACH state, the presenter presents his or her "Impossible Dream" or BHAG ("Big Hairy Audacious Goal") to the group of "guardians." This is most easily done by presenting an "elevator pitch" such as that described in the Introduction to this voluem (pp. 26-29). It is also useful for the presenter to include a description of the next platform he or she is attempting to build in his or her Collaboration Spiral.

2. The presenter and the group then begin to explore what types of problems or obstacles could arise to block or interfere with the presenter's progress to creating the platform and progressing toward the dream. The team should explore potential obstacles or interferences at all levels: environment, behavior, capabilities, beliefs and values, identity and vision or purpose.

3. One-by-one, the guardians then ask about or suggest possible resources, on the level that is their chosen focus, which could address or get around the obstacle.

    - Are there resources in your *environment* that you have or need in order to get around or transform this obstacle?
    - What *behaviors or actions* could you or others take that would help to bypass or transform this obstacle?
    - What *skills or capabilities* do you or your team have or need in order to get around or transform this obstacle?
    - Which *beliefs and values* will support you and your collaborators to bypass or transform this obstacle?
    - In what way can clarifying or strengthening your connection to your *identity* (i.e., mission or role) support you and your collaborators to get around or transform this obstacle?
    - If you and your team are able to stay deeply connected to your *vision and purpose*, what possibilities emerge to bypass or transform this obstacle?

4. The process is repeated until all major obstacles to the presenter's dream have been identified and resources or solutions explored at all of the levels.

Chapter Summary

As the story of *Stone Soup* illustrates, by working together, with a vision of what could be and everyone contributing what they can, people can make something wonderful from what starts as nothing of obvious tangible value. This is the essence of what we refer to in SFM as a *generative venture community.*

A *generative* community is one that expands and prospers through the individual visions, passion and contributions of its members and is structured in such a way that there is a positive feedback loop between the growth of the individual and the growth of the community. Generative communities are formed from a culture that makes new developments possible because it promotes the possibility of resonance, synergy and emergence between individual members; thus, increasing the collective "luck factor" and "swarm intelligence."

As the Success Factor Case Example of *Randy Williams and The Keiretsu Forum* illustrates, these principles can be applied to create a "generative venture community" in which entrepreneurs and potential investors can mutually support one another to increase their chances of success. Such a community is built from creating a "winning culture" founded on win-win values promoting generosity, sharing and support.

Cultures create a type of field which becomes the "water" in which people within a community "swim." The expressed and unexpressed values of the culture both consciously and unconsciously shape and direct the thoughts and actions of people within the community. A *winning culture* is one that promotes an expectation of a positive future, a feeling of capability and responsibility within the community members and a sense of self-worth and belonging.

Not all cultures are winning cultures. Many are formed from survival strategies resulting from perceptions of scarcity and threat as illustrated in the Stone Soup story and the *allegory of the monkey experiment*. Patterns of behavior that restrict people's sense of possibility, freedom and permission can be formed and transmitted to community members without conscious intention or awareness. When they become disconnected from the conditions that established them in the first place they function like a *"thought virus"* that continues to produce limitations even after conditions have changed.

Encouraging Entrepreneurial Attributes such as being goal directed, proactive, oriented toward future possibilities and constantly looking for new choices that support progress toward a shared vision is a key strategy for establishing a winning culture and building a generative venture community that can make something from nothing.

Creating a Winning Culture involves emphasizing the importance of win-win interactions and collaborations and acting toward one another from the principle of positive intention. It is both supportive and effective. People support each other to change, grow and become more competent, and there is continual improvement in the processes with which tasks are achieved. In the winning culture of a generative venture community, people believe in one another and affirm each other's abilities to reach dreams and goals. Processes like the *Group Affirmation Exercise* can help to create an empowering "field" of support between team members or collaborators that increases each person's chances of success.

Building Generative Relationships that Lead to Generative Collaboration is a way to go from being "nobody" to becoming "somebody." Like the metaphor of hydrogen and oxygen combining to make water, generative relationships and generative collaborations transform their participants into something bigger than a group of independent individuals. *The SFM Collaboration Spiral™* is a model that illustrates how establishing key relationships and collaborations can create an ascending spiral of successive platforms, in the form of projects or ventures, which extend our range of influence and move us along the trajectory of our mission towards our ultimate vision.

Platforms are built through a network of generative collaborations that help us to build a Circle of Success and enrich or strengthen the various levels of success factors (environment, behaviors, capabilities, beliefs and values and identity) needed to be effective in the project or venture connected with that platform. The successful establishment of a new platform creates an expansion our identity and scope of influence beyond who we have been. The most significant relationships to establish in order to build an effective Collaboration Spiral are those with "*Guardians*" who serve as teachers, mentors and sponsors, and "*Gatekeepers*" who open the doorway to new networks of relationships. Not all relationships and collaborations are generative, and some can even shift from being supportive to holding us back, and will need to be bypassed or left behind.

Modeling Successful Collaboration involves exploring key questions and guidelines in order to reflect upon a successful collaboration that you have been involved in and become more clear about what type of collaboration you are seeking and what makes a successful "generative relationship." You can then increase your "luck factor" in creating and effective Collaboration Spiral by using some key *Collaboration Spiral Questions* to prepare yourself and your potential collaborator.

The *Success Factor Case Example* of SFM co-developer *John Dilts* demonstrates how he applied the Collaboration Spiral to move from being a relatively anonymous staff member in a Silicon Valley law firm, to a venture fund manager and venture coach, to an international consultant and CEO of a high profile international leadership development organization, to the dean of entrepreneurism for a prestigious university in China and advisor on stimulating entrepreneurism for the Chinese government in the space of a few short years. Each of these platforms represented successive expressions of his vision of a generative venture community. His creation of Maverick Angels was the final expression of that vision and of a deep desire to share his insights into harnessing the power of a generative venture community to make it possible for more people to, in his words, "Let your future pull you forward."

As an example of how a generative venture community functions, the *Dream Guardians* exercise helps us to build a new platform on our Collaboration Spiral and make something from nothing by supporting us to identify the resources we need to overcome obstacles and transform barriers to succeeding in our projects or ventures and reaching our dreams. Dream guardians and our generative venture community are like the "Sangha" of the "Zentrepreneur"—the group of supporters that help us to be the best of ourselves and stay on our path.

References

- *Stone Soup*, Marcia Brown, Simon & Schuster, New York, NY, 1979.
- History of Post-it® Notes, http://www.post-it.com/3M/en_US/post-it/contact-us/about-us/.
- Swarm Intelligence, http://en.wikipedia.org/wiki/Swarm_intelligence
- Keiretsu Forum, http://www.keiretsuforum.com/about/
- Edward B. Tylor, https://en.wikipedia.org/wiki/Edward_Burnett_Tylor
- *Stephenson, G. R. (1967). Cultural acquisition of a specific learned response among rhesus monkeys. In: Starek, D., Schneider, R., and Kuhn, H. J. (eds.), Progress in Primatology, Stuttgart: Fischer, pp. 279-288*
- *From Coach to Awakener*, Dilts, R., Meta Publications, Capitola, CA, 2003.

05
Dynamic Teaming

Teamwork is the ability to work together toward a common vision. The ability to direct individual accomplishments toward organizational objectives. It is the fuel that allows common people to attain uncommon results.
Andrew Carnegie

If you want to build a ship, don't herd people together to collect wood and don't assign them tasks and work, but rather teach them to long for the endless immensity of the sea.
Antoine de Saint-Exupery

If everyone is moving forward together, then success takes care of itself.
Henry Ford

ANTONIO MEZA

Dynamic Teaming

Creating and building a successful venture requires that we enlist the support and energy of others in reaching the dreams and visions upon which our venture is founded. Success in today's business environment requires more and more emphasis on effective "teamwork" based on the principles of generative collaboration. In this chapter we will explore some of the principles and processes necessary to support "dynamic teaming."

In an effective team, group members share the responsibility for results and work together to achieve more than is possible by the sum of the individual efforts.

A *team* is generally defined as "a number of persons associated together in work or activity." More specifically, a team can be considered "a small number of people with complementary skills, common purpose, mutual accountability and collective responsibility for results." The term comes from Old English and is derived from the word *teon* which meant "to draw or pull." One of the earliest uses of the word "team" was to describe "two or more draft animals harnessed to the same vehicle or implement." Thus, a team can be considered a group of individuals who "pull together" in the same direction. This produces a generative effect.

To be a successful next generation entrepreneur, it is important to be able to form teams quickly and effectively. *Dynamic teaming* involves integrating different competencies and personal traits in a way that each team member is clear about the purpose, roles and responsibilities and operating principles of the team. In an effective team, group members share the responsibility for results and work together to achieve more than is possible by the sum of the individual efforts. As my earlier example of the team of 20 people who outperformed the group of 1000 demonstrates, "a small number of people with complementary skills, common purpose, mutual accountability and collective responsibility for results" can achieve remarkable results.

Two mules pulling together can move at least 50% more weight than when they pull by themselves.

As a concrete example of the generative effects of teaming, consider the fact that single mule can pull roughly two times its weight. That is, if a mule weighs 1,000 pounds (450kg) it can pull about 2,000 pounds (900kg) by itself. So, two mules pulling separate carts can draw about 4,000 pounds (1,800kg).

However, if the same two mules are hitched to a single cart as a team, together they can pull at least 6,000 lbs. (2,700kg)! Meaning that when working together as a team, each mule is suddenly able to pull at least three times its own weight instead of only two times its weight, as it would if working by itself. This is a concrete illustration of the principle that "1 + 1 = 3" at a behavioral level. What is impossible for one mule to do by itself becomes possible when it collaborates with another mule.

In the days before tractors, trucks and trains, a 20-mule team could pull 73,200 pounds (33.2 tons) of cargo; almost twice their individual capacity!

While the example of a mule team shows the potential of a team to increase performance beyond the sum of individual efforts, it is not yet truly an example of "dynamic teaming." The mules are clearly being directed by the driver who harnesses them to the wagon to accomplish a goal for the driver. In dynamic teaming, all of the members share a common vision and cooperate together in a framework of meta leadership, sharing "common purpose, mutual accountability and collective responsibility for results."

A 20-mule team can pull almost twice the amount of weight than they can as individuals.

Lessons in Dynamic Teaming from Geese

Geese flying together in a "V" formation extend their flying range 71% further than if they flew alone.

One naturally occurring example and allegory for "dynamic teaming" is the migration of geese. The remarkable annual migration that some birds make between their breeding and wintering grounds is one of the wonders of our natural world. Most of the world's 29 or so species of geese migrate yearly, and some routinely accomplish amazing feats. In Asia, Bar-headed Geese, for instance, regularly migrate over the Himalayan Mountains, even over Mt. Everest at an altitude of 30,750 feet (9375 m) where the air is thin and the temperatures drop to minus 60 degrees F (-50 Celsius). Snow geese make an annual round trip journey of more than 5,000 miles (8,000 km), from the arctic areas of North America to Central America, at speeds of 50 mph (80 km per hour) or more.

It is these birds' capacity for dynamic teaming that makes these exceptional feats possible. Consider the following so-called "lessons from geese" which provide both a demonstration of and a metaphor for dynamic teaming.

Fact 1

As each goose flaps its wings, it creates an "uplift" for the birds that follow. When a goose is able to position itself in the right location behind the flock mate in front of it, it is able to ride on the energy produced by the one ahead, requiring less effort. By flying in a "V" formation, the whole flock adds 71% greater flying range than if each bird flew alone.

Lesson

People who share a common direction and sense of community can get where they are going more quickly and easily because they are traveling on one another's inspiration and energy.

As each goose flaps its wings, it creates an "uplift" for the birds that follow. When a goose is able to position itself in the right location behind the flock mate in front of it, it is able to ride on the energy produced by the one ahead.

Fact 2

When a goose falls out of formation, it suddenly feels the drag and resistance of flying alone. It quickly moves back into formation to take advantage of the lifting power of the bird immediately in front of it.

Lesson

If we have as much sense as a goose, we stay in formation with those headed where we want to go. We are willing to accept their help and give our help to others.

Fact 3

When the lead bird tires, it rotates back into the formation to take advantage of the lifting power of the bird immediately in front of it.

Lesson

It pays to take turns doing the hard tasks and sharing leadership. As with geese, people are interdependent on each others' skills, capabilities, and unique arrangements of gifts, talents, or resources.

The annual migrations of geese provide a good naturally occurring example and allegory for "dynamic teaming."

Fact 4

The geese flying in formation honk to encourage those up front to keep up their speed.

Lesson

We need to make sure our honking is encouraging. In groups where there is encouragement, the production is much greater. The power of encouragement (to stand by one's heart or core values and to encourage the heart and core values of others) is the quality of honking we seek.

Fact 5

When a goose gets sick, wounded, or shot down, two geese drop out of formation and follow it down to help and protect it. They stay with it until it dies or is able to fly again. Then, they launch out with another formation or catch up with the flock.

Lesson

If we have as much sense of geese, we will stand by each other in difficult times as well as when we're strong.

If a goose gets sick, wounded, or shot down, two geese drop out of formation and follow it down to help and protect it

The complex patterns produced by flocking birds are an example of a type of dynamic teaming.

Flocking and the Power of Process

Of course, geese are not the only birds that flock. Birds like starlings are known to flock in very sophisticated patterns, called "murmuration" (see http://www.huffingtonpost.com/2013/02/01/starling-murmuration-bird-ballet-video_n_2593001.html). Such flocking behavior is a fascinating example of dynamic teaming and collective intelligence.

While the movements of flocks of birds seems very complex, they can be reproduced to an impressive degree on a computer with a few simple process guidelines. Consider the following instructions for action:

- The motion of individual birds is generally random
- Birds are able to identify other birds (flockmates)
- Birds try to get close to other birds, but not too close
- Birds follow the general direction of the flock

These simple principles allow the individual birds to begin to act as an integrated "holon."

One of the first flocking simulations, called "Boids," was created by Craig Reynolds as a result of his research on coordinated animal movement. Each "boid" was guided by a few fundamental rules:

- Rule 1 – *Cohesion* (steer to move towards the average position of local flockmates)
- Rule 2 – *Separation* (steer to avoid crowding local flockmates)
- Rule 3 – *Alignment* (steer towards the average heading of local flockmates)

Each "boid" is designed as an autonomous unit, but each is guided by this common set of rules that allows them function as a coordinated group (see http://www.red3d.com/cwr/boids/applet/).

The GitHub flocking simulation (http://black-square.github.io/BirdFlock/) is a slightly more sophisticated 3D version of flocking phenomena. The simulation follows and enriches the model presented by Reynolds:

- Each bird is modeled individually and maintains its own state.
- Each bird has the same process guidelines, prioritized as follows:
    1. Avoid collisions with solid (non-bird) objects.
    2. Avoid collisions with other birds.
    3. Match velocity with nearby birds.
    4. Move toward the center of the flock.

When the flock meets an obstacle, each member individually applies the rules to its current circumstances. As a result, the flock successfully navigates its way around the obstacle as a cohesive group.

These simulations provide us with some powerful examples and principles for fostering collective intelligence and dynamic teaming. Interestingly, the rules guiding the birds' flocking behavior parallel the three focuses of attention I outlined in Chapter 2 (pp. 118-119) for a "generative performance state":

1. Connection to oneself as an individual and one's unique passion and motivations
2. Connection to a common intention (a shared direction with one's teammates)
3. Connection to the "field" of resources (the sense of cohesion with the larger holon of the team)

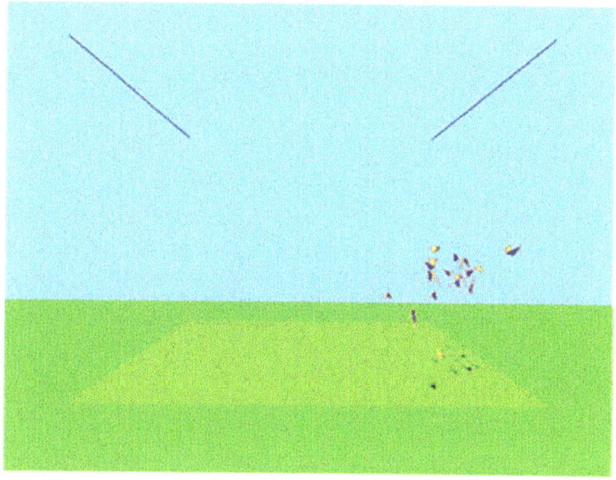

Following a few simple rules, Craig Reynolds "boids" are able to simulate aspects of the complex flocking behavior of real birds.

The GitHub Bird Flock Simulation

Lessons in Dynamic Teaming from the Battle of Midway

Flocking behavior is not only for the birds. It can be an extremely effective way of achieving some very serious goals. Consider the Battle of Midway, cited by my colleagues and I in our book *Alpha Leadership* (2003), which was a turning point in Pacific campaign during the Second World War.

In the Battle of Midway, which was a turning point in Pacific campaign during the Second World War, the Japanese armada outnumbered the American forces 18 to 1.

In early June 1942, US naval reconnaissance planes spotted a huge Japanese fleet of 185 ships, including nine battle-ships and four aircraft carriers, heading for the Midway Islands in the central Pacific. Under the command of Admiral Isoroku Yamamoto, commander-in-chief of the Japanese navy, and chief architect of the attack on Pearl Harbor, the armada's mission was to secure the islands as the launching base for an invasion of Hawaii.

The Japanese fleet vastly outnumbered the American forces defending the Midway Islands which consisted of only 10 ships (three aircraft carriers and seven heavy cruisers), and the warplanes stationed on the islands. On the morning of June 4, planes from the Japanese carriers attacked airfields on Midway. At the same time, the American planes from Midway and three US aircraft carriers of the Pacific Fleet, under the command of Admiral Chester W. Nimitz, attacked the Japanese fleet. The Japanese attacks inflicted damage on the Midway air bases, but the American dive-bombers were much more effective. In one five- minute attack they destroyed three Japanese carriers. In total, the Americans destroyed all four of Yamamoto's aircraft carriers, two Japanese cruisers and three of their destroyers. The Americans only lost two ships; the carrier Yorktown and one destroyer.

Though outnumbered by more than 18-to-1, the American forces won the battle due to their capacity for dynamic teaming. It is significant that, during the two-day battle, the two fleets never got close enough to exchange gunfire, let alone to see one another. Applying the metaphor we introduced in Chapter 4, we can say that the battle was fought and won by "bats" as opposed to "frogs."

As one significant success factor, Nimitz, an avid "weak signal" eavesdropper, was monitoring Japanese radio messages and, as a result, had early warning of the impending attack and was able to prepare for battle. Just as importantly, radio was used more effectively by the Americans than the Japanese during the battle itself. The remoteness of the two commanders from their airborne strike-forces made it very hard for them to orchestrate their forces directly. Japanese military tradition obliged Yamamoto to try to do so, but the pace at which air battles are fought meant that his radio instructions simply confused his pilots.

The US forces defeated the Japanese armada in The Battle of Midway as a result of dynamic teaming.

Nimitz and rear Admiral Raymond A. Spruance, commander of the US carrier task force, took a completely different approach. They made no attempt to direct the battle, but instead established simple rules of communication between their fighter pilots:

1. Keep all radio channels to other planes open.
2. Listen, but say nothing unless you are:
   a. coming under attack from enemy fighters, or
   b. in a position to attack an enemy ship.

These rules generated powerful, self-organizing dynamics among the American planes that allowed them to "flock" effectively, by gathering rapidly in critical areas of airspace. Although heavily outnumbered, the US pilots flew in overwhelming force to where they were most needed – a powerful example of "dynamic teaming."

The Battle of Midway was won not through the assembly of superior force, or by a brilliant commander, but rather by dynamic teaming driven by collective intelligence and sensitivity to weak signals.

Similar to my example at the beginning of Chapter 2 (p. 98) of the team of 20 people who outperformed the team of 1,000, the Battle of Midway was won not through the assembly of superior force, or by a brilliant commander, but rather by dynamic teaming driven by collective intelligence and sensitivity to weak signals. Recognizing the limitations of command in a fast-moving and constantly changing situation, Nimitz gave his team the means, the freedom and the trust to use their individual initiative while acting as a coordinated holon.

Dynamic Team Development

Dynamic team development involves engaging people in activities that both strengthen relationships and clarify tasks, and the competencies and actions necessary to collaboratively accomplish those tasks.

Teams form along the dimensions of both *relationship* ("persons associated together") and *task* (their "work or activity"). *Dynamic team development* involves facilitating both of these aspects of team development. That is, it engages people in activities that emphasize either (a) encouraging or strengthening relationships, or (b) defining and clarifying tasks, and the competencies and actions necessary to accomplish those tasks.

The collaboration catalysts that we have explored in previous chapters are an important foundation for dynamic team development. Processes like creating a COACH Container, for example, facilitate the strengthening of relationships between team members. Other collaboration catalysts like Exploring and Sharing Best Practices through Success Factor Modeling, Developing a Generative Performance State, Promoting Synergy Through Intervision, Making a "Second Position" Analysis and Creating Win-Win Collaborations Through Third Position are all very useful for promoting dynamic teaming.

Some other key factors for dynamic team development that we will be covering in this chapter include:

- Identify shared values and aligning different capabilities and actions in relation to a common vision and mission.
- Establishing a "communication infrastructure and creativity infrastructure" by defining the key success factors required for dynamic teaming and generative collaboration and instituting the practice of continuous reflection upon the presence of these success factors during team interactions.
- Encouraging the recognition of various team member's strengths and challenges, and helping team members to appreciate their differences and to use those differences in the service of their common mission and vision.

Thus, a key objective of this chapter is to provide tools and skills that can help you to create dynamic and generative teams that are capable of working effectively and creatively together in order to achieve a common mission.

As I mentioned in *SFM Volume I*, entrepreneurship and entrepreneurial success is not limited to small companies or Silicon Valley start-ups. Many of the success factors applied by new companies can also be applied to encourage effective entrepreneurship in established organizations. One of the goals of this book series is to show how principles and practices modeled from successful entrepreneurs can be applied to help larger, traditional companies stay innovative and better manage the challenges of change.

The purpose of dynamic team development is to create dynamic and generative teams that are capable of working effectively and creatively together in order to achieve a common mission.

The following Success Factor Case Example demonstrates how the principles of Success Factor Modeling and the application of some key Collaboration Catalysts can produce entrepreneurial success in the context of larger, more traditional organization.

Success Factor Case Example: Comau Pico Custom Products Team

In 2002, Chuck Dudek, Dave Redys, John Vance and Mike Mercer were presented with a formidable challenge. As members of Comau Pico's newly formed Custom Products Team they were essentially charged with reinventing their company.

The members of Comau Pico's Custom Products Team were essentially charged with reinventing their company.

Founded in 1973, Comau Pico (now the Comau Group) built a strong niche for itself, providing automated welding operations for the automotive industry. Comau Pico had grown into a tremendously successful business, primarily functioning as a boutique welding service for the so-called "big three" American automakers: General Motors, Ford and Chrysler. It had a captive market and high quality products.

Transitioning from Managers to "Intrapreneurs"

By the early 2000s, however, the world had changed quite a bit. There had been a paradigm shift in the Comau Pico customer base. The "big three," in fact, no longer existed; Chrysler was now Daimler-Chrysler (eventually to become Fiat Chrysler). The market was changing and the company was no longer bringing in the same revenue.

The company had to create new products and find new customers. Chuck, Dave, John and Mike had been given that responsibility. They had essentially been assigned the task of becoming internal entrepreneurs, or what can be called "intrapreneurs."

The team intuitively started at the center of the Circle of Success working to "identify and re-identify who we were" and exploring "What do we have now that we never had before?"

Intuitively, they started with the center of the Circle of Success. As Chuck pointed out, "We had to identify and re-identify who we were." They also intuitively understood that their success would depend on effective generative collaboration. So they got together and essentially began by doing their own form of intervision. They started with a "brain dump," asking questions such as, "What is success?" and "What do we have now that we never had before?"

Thinking Outside the Box

They knew they had to think "outside of the box." They could not succeed with their customers using traditional thinking. They would need to enrich their Circle of Success. "Because we were in an uncharted area, we took sales guys to help us," Dave comments. They found that they could repurpose a lot of their technology, know-how and other resources for new uses. They could provide project management consulting to companies that had complex projects in industries other than automotive production, for instance, but who did not have the internal competence to coordinate intricate and complicated combinations of equipment and procedures. They could also use their painting and welding resources to help smaller companies that had sophisticated fabrication problems but lacked or could not afford the tools to do them effectively or inexpensively.

At one point Chuck talked about getting into his car, driving around and "looking for anywhere there was a smoke stack." He would go in and ask what they were doing in order to get ideas.

As a result of this type of generative thinking, they formed a big list of market targets, created a document, and began to set up the process for reaching those new markets.

Their vision was to repurpose their technology, know-how and other resources for new uses. They began their search for new customers by "looking for anywhere there was a smoke stack."

Building the Team

They began to assemble the larger team that they would need to put it all together. Rather than hire new people, they did a kind of "internal" outsourcing. "Why start over?" they thought. They didn't want to reinvent the wheel, so they did "resource mining" within the company. "We had an advantage with selection," says Dave, "We could choose people with the same philosophy."

They started with their market strategy and developed a business plan (specifying "what" they were attempting to achieve and "why") for each unit. Each director established budgets, then an action plan detailing how, specifically, they would achieve their goals.

The team viewed their mission as "internal" outsourcing" and created a culture of "servant leadership"

The team shifted their role to "engineers who think like entrepreneurs" an focused on "managing contracts versus making tools."

To succeed, the Custom Products Team knew that they would need to make a transformation from "making tools" to "managing contracts." Up to this time, their basic business approach had been "do the job first and then settle the bill" (kind of like "keeping score at the end of the game"). The new approach required a shift from project management to contract management. This meant the ability to *compete* in addition to the ability to perform.

The company had to marry the technical and commercial sides of the business. "Engineers have to think like entrepreneurs," commented Mike Mercer. "Every single person has to understand his or her responsibility and look for opportunities to do it."

Setting up "Collaboration Catalysts"

They had a kick off meeting, described the vision and the plans and started getting buy-in. To build and support the team, they needed to use an open approach, "knocking down walls between engineering and manufacturing." This helped to widen the scope of their ability to collaborate generatively.

To accomplish their vision and mission, the team needed to use an open approach, "knocking down walls between engineering and manufacturing."

They also needed to set up ongoing "Collaboration Catalysts" to successfully support their transformation. So they set up weekly meetings, every Monday at 7:30 am. To facilitate the contract management process, they went over purchase orders with the team. They discussed the scope of the contract and went over relationship management issues.

In addition, they scheduled monthly internal staff meetings, in which they had a "guest speaker"— usually someone from one of the other teams who would present ideas and "best practices." A main goal of these meetings was to provide an overall picture with respect to where they were with sales, talk about the quarter and discuss key relationships and suppliers.

They also had a monthly executive review in which they went over jobs in detail with the project manager, director, financial manager, etc. The purpose of these meetings was to "work the plan," going over questions such as "what are your problems?" "where are you heading?" "what are you doing?" etc.

Creating a Culture of Servant Leadership

Their motto was, "Look at yourself not as a manager, but as an enabler." They built a culture based on principles of "servant leadership." *Servant leaders* are those whose job it is to "make other people's jobs easier." As John Vance described it, "It is an empowered way of doing business and an open relationship." "Make people feel good and they will work like crazy," he added.

The Comau Pico Custom Products Team's generative collaboration strategy was extremely effective in "making the pie bigger." Their efforts grew to account for half of Comau Pico's business. By the end of 2002 Comau Pico had more work on their shop floor than they had ever had before.

Their relationship with famed motorcycle maker Harley-Davidson is a good example of their success. They went from a cold call to $15 million in sales in 2 years.

The Comau Pico Custom Products team set an ambition to "compete in addition to perform." Within 2 years, the compny had more work on their shop floor than they had ever had before.

Reflections on the Comau Pico Custom Products Team Case

The Comau Pico Custom Products Team success story is another example of the effective management of the SFM Circle of Success. By reflecting upon and reexamining the center of the circle (i.e., reidentifying who they were), they were able to "re-vision" their role with respect to their customers and the rest of the company, enhance the competencies of the team, build internal partnerships and alliances with other groups and divisions with the company and create new value for their stakeholders (the parent company). Significantly, they were able to achieve a new level of *financial robustness* as a result of the actions of acquiring and leveraging existing essential resources from their company stakeholders and generating interest and revenue from new customers.

It is also clearly an example of generative collaboration and dynamic teaming. The members of the Custom Products Team had to work together to create something new and unprecedented by getting outside of the box of basic collaboration and seeing themselves, their tools and the way they worked together in a completely different light. They could not simply continue at the level of basic collaboration, doing their job to accomplish the task they were hired to do. They had to create a new "group mind" and find innovative ways of combining and applying their skills and resources.

The members of the Custom Products Team had to work together to create something new and unprecedented by getting outside of the box of basic collaboration and seeing themselves, their tools and the way they worked together in a completely different light.

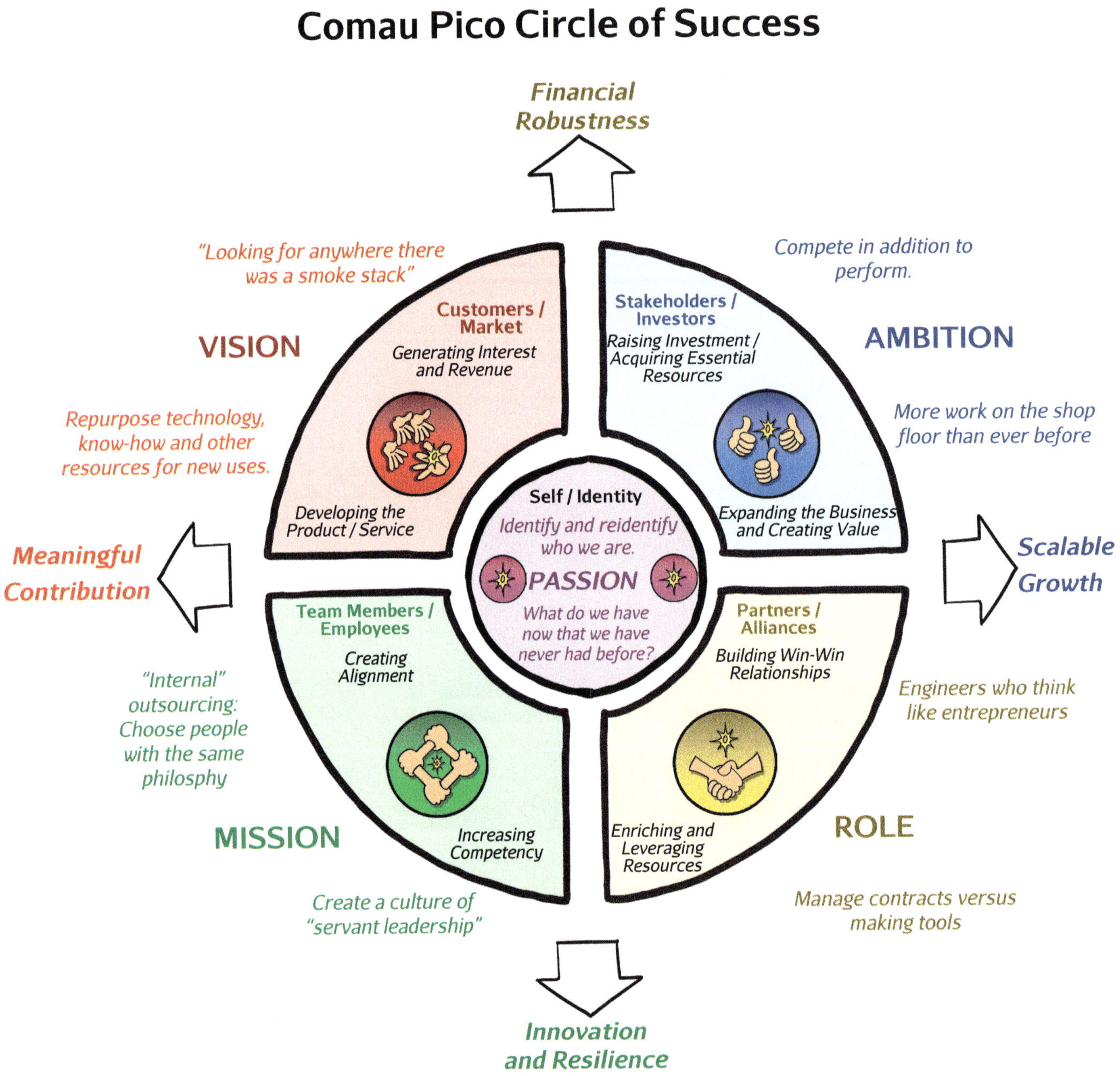
Comau Pico Circle of Success
Financial Robustness
"Looking for anywhere there was a smoke stack"
Compete in addition to perform.
VISION
Customers / Market
Generating Interest and Revenue
Developing the Product / Service
Stakeholders / Investors
Raising Investment / Acquiring Essential Resources
Expanding the Business and Creating Value
AMBITION
More work on the shop floor than ever before
Repurpose technology, know-how and other resources for new uses.
Self / Identity
Identify and reidentify who we are.
PASSION
What do we have now that we have never had before?
Meaningful Contribution
Scalable Growth
Team Members / Employees
Creating Alignment
Increasing Competency
Partners / Alliances
Building Win-Win Relationships
Enriching and Leveraging Resources
"Internal" outsourcing: Choose people with the same philosphy
Engineers who think like entrepreneurs
MISSION
ROLE
Create a culture of "servant leadership"
Manage contracts versus making tools
Innovation and Resilience

COMAU PICO CIRCLE OF SUCCESS

VISION
Customers / Market

* LOOKING FOR ANYWHERE THERE WAS A SMOKE STACK
* REPURPOSE TECHNOLOGY, KNOW-HOW AND OTHER RESOUCES FOR NEW USES

AMBITION
Stakeholders / Investors

* COMPETE IN ADDITION TO PERFORM
* MORE WORK ON THE SHOP FLOOR THAN EVER BEFORE

MISSION
Team Members / Employees

* INTERNAL OUTSOURCING: CHOOSE PEOPLE WITH THE SAME PHILOSOPHY.
* CREATE A CULTURE OF "SERVANT LEADERSHIP"

ROLE
Partners / Alliances

* ENGINEERS WHO THINK LIKE ENTREPRENEURS
* MANAGE CONTRACTS VERSUS MAKING TOOLS

PASSION:
WHAT DO WE HAVE NOW THAT WE HAVE NEVER HAD BEFORE?

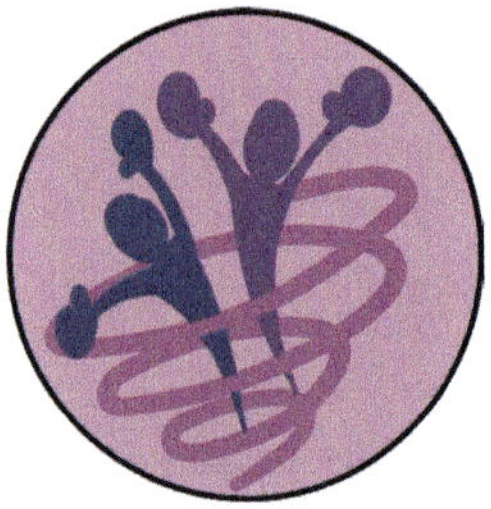

The Comau Pico Custom Products Team case provides a number of good examples of different types of "Collaboration Catalysts."

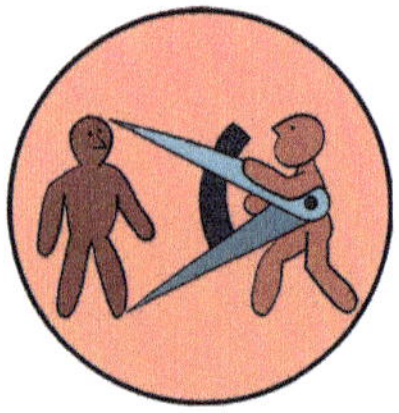

Benchmarking

Best Practices

Brainstorming

Generative Collaboration

The case also provides some good examples of types of "Collaboration Catalysts." The "brain dump" and brainstorming with the "sales guys" are natural forms of intervision. They also applied what we call *Resource Mining* both externally and internally by looking for matches between needs and resources with customers and with people from various divisions within the organization. This creates the possibility of effective "flocking" – working together to bring available resources where they are most needed. We will go into the process of Resource Mining in depth later in this chapter.

Some other Collaboration Catalysts the Comau Pico Custom Products Team developed or applied include:

- *Synergizing goals and resources* by "marrying the technical and commercial sides of the business."
- *Knocking down walls* by getting, engineering, manufacturing and marketing people interacting with one another.
- *Sharing criteria for collaboration* by identifying and working with others who had a common philosophy.
- *Establishing repetitive communication regarding key areas of the Circle of Success* by holding periodic meetings at different intervals in order to go over relationship management issues, share best practices between different teams and discuss key relationships and suppliers.
- *Promoting the attitude of partnering and "servant leadership"* by emphasizing the mind set that part of each person's job was to "make other people's jobs easier."

The Comau Pico Custom Products Team case gives several good illustrations how the different areas of the SFM Collective Intelligence Model combine to facilitate dynamic teaming. The members of the Custom Products Team applied *brainstorming* to define new markets by imagining innovative options. They engaged in *benchmarking* by asking "What is success?" and "What do we have now that we never had before?" And they continued setting collective standards in their monthly executive review. The Custom Products team members shared *best practices* in their monthly internal staff meetings with guest speakers, exchanging successful strategies with other teams. They also encouraged *generative collaboration* by "knocking down walls" between engineering and manufacturing in order to facilitate co-creating something unique.

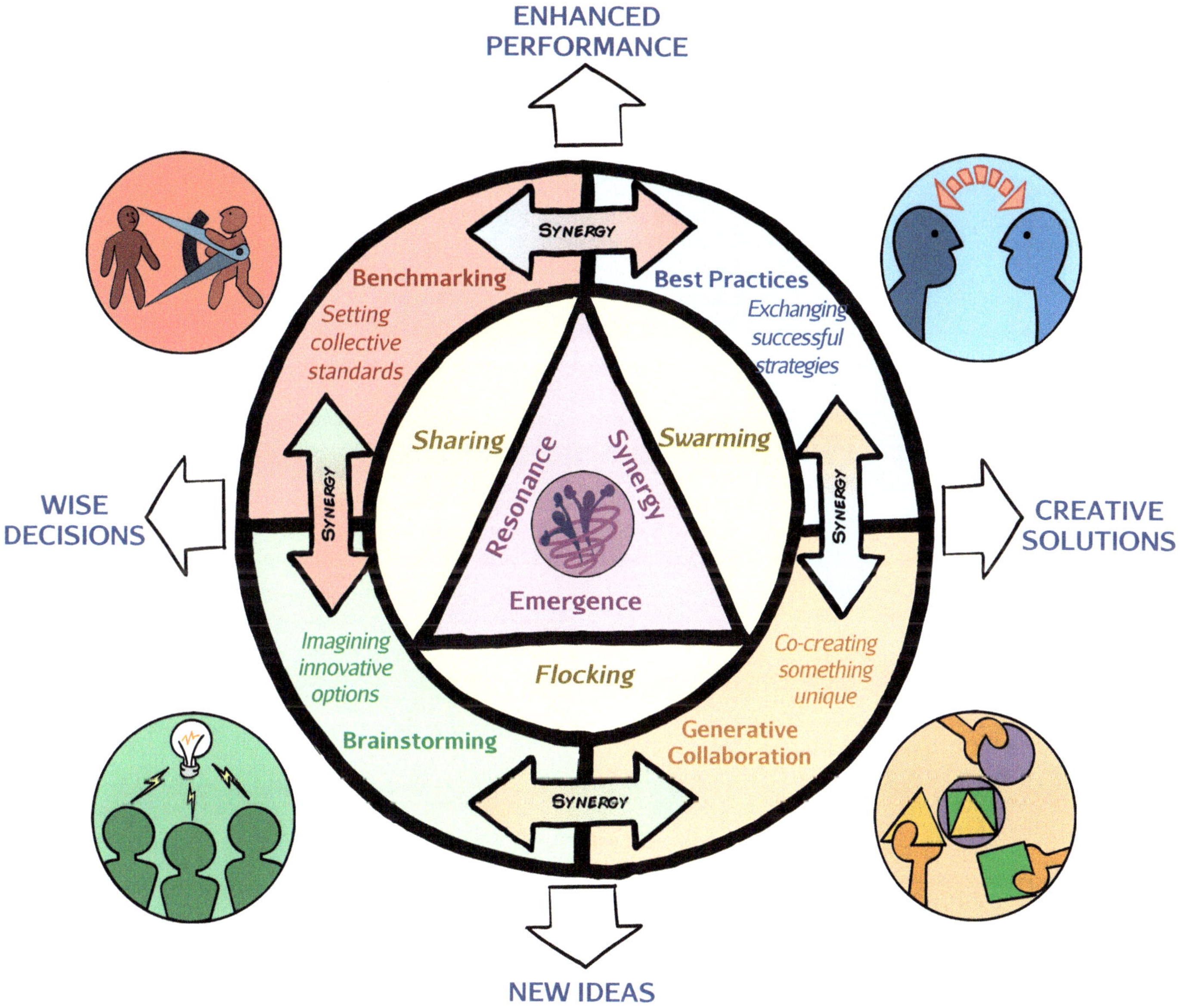

The Comau Pico Custom Products Team provides a good example of creating synergies between all of the processes related to collective intelligence as an application of dynamic teaming.

SFM Collaboration Catalyst: Dynamic Teaming Meeting Format

Meetings are one of the most common collaboration catalysts. Synergy and emergence in particular require some type of consistent interaction and feedback to be achieved and sustained.

The frequency and organization of meetings can be particularly important. I have been involved in many projects and ventures, frequently involving international and virtual teams. Depending upon the urgency, complexity and stage of the project or venture, meeting frequency can range from bi-monthly, monthly, weekly and even daily (or several times a day).

An effective meeting format must strike a balance between structure and open opportunites for sharing, synergy and emergence in order to produce "disciplined flow."

Of course, what is covered and how the meeting is structured will determine a lot about how much synergy, emergence, collective intelligence and generative collaboration occur. Meetings can be chaotic and inefficient if there is no structure. Too much structure can restrict interaction and prevent the opportunity for synergy and emergence. As we saw in our reflection on the flocking of birds, it is important to strike a balance between the two in order to produce a type of "disciplined flow." Consider the following description by Steve Jobs of how he managed his team in order to "orchestrate innovation":

> *What we do every Monday is we review the whole business. We look at what we sold the week before. We look at every single product under development, products we're having trouble with, products where the demand is larger than we can make. All the stuff in development, we review. And we do it every single week. I put out an agenda – 80% the same as it was the last week, and we just walk down it every single week. We don't have a lot of process at Apple, but that is one of the few things we do just to all stay on the same page.*

Jobs' account of his weekly team meetings outlines a type of "open structure," where there is enough process to keep everyone "on the same page" and yet is not so detailed that it prevents spontaneity and flexibility. Gabrielle Roth, founder of the transformational 5Rhythms® movement practice, pointed out that "It takes discipline to be a free spirit."

Similar to Jobs' account of his weekly meetings, we suggest the following simple meeting format for the entrepreneurs and leaders that we coach.

1. Make a brief description of a meeting you will be conducting and who will be (or needs to be) present.

2. *What are the goals or desired outcomes for this meeting?* – i.e., *What is the agenda?*

3. *What will you do to get to the goals* (address the agenda items)? *What are some specific steps and activities that you will use to achieve your goals during the meeting?* (e.g., discussions, presentations, show of hands, etc.) This, of course, is an area for various types of collaboration catalysts. We will be presenting more possibilities in this and the forthcoming chapters.

4. *What are some problem areas or difficulties that need to be addressed during the meeting? What specific activities or steps could you build into your meeting format to most effectively handle them?* This is also an area for some types of collaboration catalysts which we will be presenting throughout the rest of this chapter and this book.

5. *What will you use as feedback to know you are accomplishing these goals? What is your evidence that the goals (agenda items) have been accomplished or dealt with adequately?*

Whether you are meeting with team members, customers, stakeholders or partners, we have found going through these questions to be a useful exercise. Even if you don't formally announce or present an agenda, the format helps you to prepare to collaborate effectively.

Addressing some agenda items can be easily done through basic collaboration. Others will require a greater degree of collective intelligence and generative collaboration. In the next part of this chapter we will be going more deeply into the principles, steps and collaboration catalysts necessary to increase resonance, synergy and emergence in order to produce a dynamic and powerful level of generative collaboration.

SFM Collaboration Catalyst: Resource Mining

One of the success factors demonstrated by the Comau Pico Custom Products Team Success Factor Case Example is the promotion of open communication so that people can synergize goals and resources and establish shared criteria for collaboration. As Dave Redys pointed out, it is important to select people who have a common philosophy if you are going to establish effective generative collaboration.

It is also important to get outside of the box and look for ways in which different needs and resources can complement or combine with one another to enrich the possibilities for collaboration. We call this process *Resource Mining.*

The purpose of the Resource Mining process is to help groups find areas of overlap and synergy with potential collaborators with respect to needs, resources and criteria for collaborating.

1. To begin, write the title of your venture or project below.

   Project/Venture: ____

2. Make a *Needs and Resources Analysis.* The ability to supply needed resources for one another is the basis for effective collaborations of all types. As we have pointed out, the fundamental criteria for success on a personal level are the feelings of gratitude and generosity—*gratitude* for receiving opportunities and resources from others that contribute to your achievements, and *generosity* to share the resources you have with others. This is also the basis for creating effective win-win collaborations with others. Gratitude comes when others provide us with resources that we need. Generosity is our willingness to provide resources that satisfy the needs of others.

Project/Venture Needs Assessment Worksheet

In the spaces provided below, list the resources that you "need to have," "want to have" and would be "nice to have" in order to achieve the vision, mission and ambition of your project or venture.

Need to Have Essential to achieve your vision, mission and ambition.
Want to Have Important for achieving your vision, mission and ambition.
Nice to Have If possible, it would make your vision, mission and ambition better or easier.

Success Factor Checklist

Use the checklist below to be sure that you have covered all the levels of success factors that may be relevant to your project or venture. You can also use it to explore potential resources that you may be able to offer others.

I Need... **I Have...**

Environmental E.g., physical and social support, time, space, guidance.
Behavioral E.g., actions to be taken by you and others.
Capabilities E.g., know-how, technology, skills, teachers, etc.
Beliefs E.g., motivation, self-confidence, trust, mentoring, etc.
Identity E.g., sponsors, clarity about role, life direction, boundaries, etc.
Spiritual E.g., people, experiences, ideas, etc., that connect me to something bigger.

Resource Mining Worksheet

Now, in the columns below, summarize the key resources you need and then list any resources you have identified that you are able to offer to others.

NEEDS	RESOURCES

When you get together with prospective collaborators, you will be sharing your list of needs and resources and asking your potential collaborators about their needs and resources. This will help you to identify areas in which you can help or complement one another to be more successful.

Keep in mind that you may discover other needs that you have or resources that you can offer as you do this activity. Be sure to add them to your list.

3. Before beginning to check for areas of collaboration with potential collaborators, list your collaboration criteria. Why do you want to collaborate? What does the collaboration have to provide or embody in order for you to be interested and willing to be involved? (e.g., "increases resources," "is enjoyable," "is supportive," "shares common values," etc.)

   Collaboration Criteria:

   ______________________ ______________________

   ______________________ ______________________

   ______________________ ______________________

   ______________________ ______________________

4. Get together with a couple of potential collaborators. Start by sharing your criteria for collaboration. Be sure to express and identify your key collaboration criteria, especially the ones that you both share. These are the "bottom line" for your collaboration.

   At this stage, you don't know what ideas for collaboration might come up, but you know that whatever they are, they will have to satisfy these particular criteria. For instance, you and your potential collaborators may decide that your collaboration has to be "financially profitable" or "fun." Maybe it has to take advantage of certain resources. Maybe it has to occur within a particular time limit. In other words, what are the characteristics that your collaboration has to satisfy, even though you don't know yet what it will be.

5. Next, each person reads his or her list of needs and resources. When you are done, look for potential overlaps between the needs of one of the group members and the resources of the others.

   When you have finished, you should have been able to identify a number of potential areas of synergy and collaboration between all of the group members.

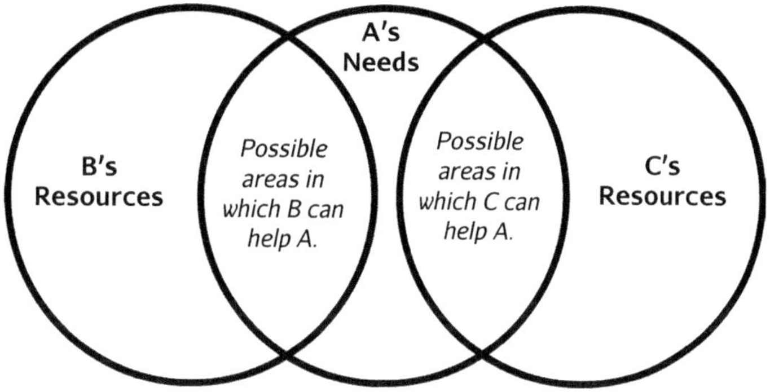

Finding Synergies Between Needs and Resources.

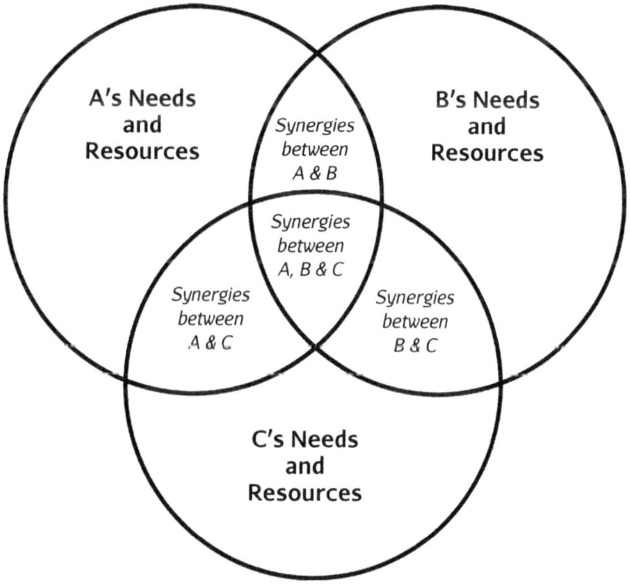

Resource Mining Involves Looking for Areas of Synergy Between the Needs and Resources of Potential Collaborators

6. The final step is making sure that the possible areas of collaboration fit your collaboration criteria. You may need to refine or fine tune the synergies so they fit the constraints imposed by the criteria that you expressed and identified at the beginning of the process.

   Specifically, as a group, you need to review each of the proposals that you've come up with during the Resource Mining phase, look at each of your criteria and find out if the potential collaboration satisfies that criterion. If it does, move on the next criterion. If it does not satisfy a particular criterion, do not immediately throw the idea out. Instead, try to figure out what you have to add or change about the idea to make it fit those criteria.

   Try to modify that initial proposal incrementally in order to make it fit with the criterion it did not satisfy. Keep checking each of the possible areas of synergy against your criteria until you've adjusted them all to satisfy each of the collaboration criteria.

Moving from Vision to Action

Creating a successful venture of any type requires the ability to form a vision and then establish and navigate the path connecting that vision to specific behaviors and actions. According to Success Factor Modeling, this path is made up of various levels of success factors which support the creation of the project or venture, including:

- The **Vision**: The image or dream which provides the "spirit" or highest level purpose for all the related resources and activities—the answer to the questions *for whom* and *for what* are our energies, skills and actions directed?
- The **Mission**: The sense of "identity," role, and calling people have with respect to the vision—the answer to the question *who* are we, or do we need to be, in relation to the manifestation of the vision?
- The **Inspiration**: The "values and beliefs" that are expressed by or encompassed by the vision and mission which provide the motivation to achieve it—the answer to the question *why* do we have this particular vision and mission?
- The **Strategy**: The "capabilities" and skills that are needed to manifest the vision and achieve the mission—the answer to the question *how* will we accomplish our mission?
- The **Structure** and **Plan**: The operational plan, or specific "behaviors" and "environment" which make up the particular project or plan that expresses the vision, mission and values— the answer to the questions *what*, specifically, will we do to accomplish our mission; and *when* and *where* (in what context) will we enact our project or plan?

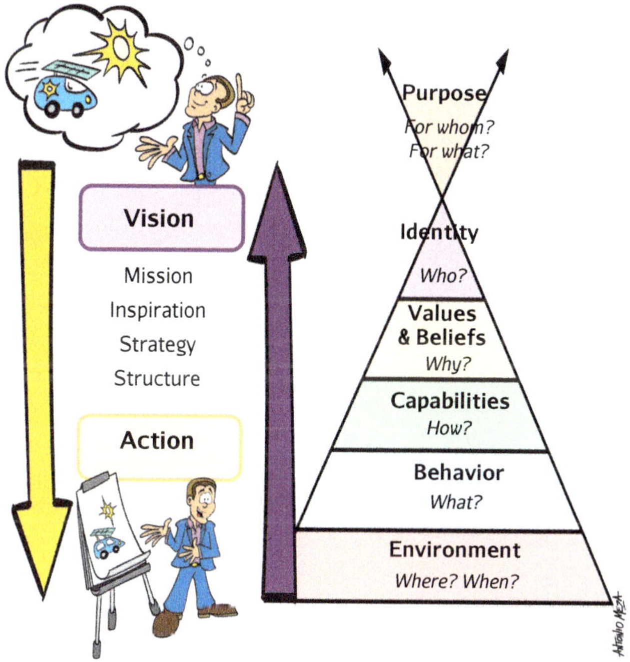

Different Levels of Success Factors Must be Established and Aligned In Order to Create the Path From Vision to Action

SFM Collaboration Catalyst: Aligning Roles Within a Common Vision

Aligning your team toward a common vision is one of the most important success factors for dynamic teaming and for creating an effective Circle of Success

The alignment of the entire team toward a common vision is one of the most important success factors for dynamic teaming and for creating an effective Circle of Success. The actions and goals of individuals within their specific environments must be congruent with the strategy and objectives of the venture. These objectives, in turn, need to be congruent with the venture's culture and mission with respect to its larger environment.

In a new venture, team members frequently "wear many hats." Like the birds in our flocking examples, each person is in a type of leadership position, often self-organizing his or her own role by interacting and coordinating with other team members. Usually there is no single "job description" to provide the ultimate guidance. Thus, a major success factor for dynamic teaming is helping people sort and align their activities with respect to one another.

The following worksheet can be used to accomplish this. The sheet is to be filled in by each member of the team. The process starts by having each team member identify his or her understanding of the vision and mission of the entire team. In order for the team to be aligned, it is important that these answers be congruent with the other members' understanding of the team vision and mission.

Each individual is then to define his or her understanding of his or her role, values and priorities, beliefs and assumptions, capabilities, tasks, and the contexts in which he or she will operate in order to support the team vision and mission. Each team member is then to read his or her answers to the other team members, who are to check the answers with their own understanding of the person's role and activities with respect to the shared vision and mission.

Team Alignment Worksheet

1. Our collective vision is:

____

2. Our collective mission is:

____

3. My role with respect to the collective vision and mission is:

____

4. Having that mission and being in that role, my values / priorities are:

____

5. Having that mission and being in that role, I believe / assume:

____

6. To participate in accomplishing the mission, I will use the following capabilities:

____

7. I will use those capabilities in order to carry out the tasks of:

____

8. I will carry out those tasks in the context(s) of:

____

Team members may wish to ask questions of one another in order to further specify answers that they think are unclear or imprecise. They should also check to make sure that the tasks and priorities of other team members, upon whose actions they depend, are defined and organized sufficiently to be able receive the support needed from that team member.

SFM Collaboration Catalyst: Modeling Dynamic Teaming Success Factors

Once the path from vision to action has been defined and the team members are aligned, it is important to create the conditions within which team members are able to travel the path and fully exploit current opportunities. This involves establishing a "communication infrastructure and creativity infrastructure" by defining the key success factors required for dynamic teaming and generative collaboration and then instituting the practice of continuous reflection upon the presence and degree of these success factors during team interactions.

To do this for your own venture, first identify a dynamic and "generative" team that you have had the opportunity to be a part of. Reflect upon the characteristics of this outstanding team and how it was led and consider your answers to the following questions.

What strikes you the most about the way the members of this team interacted, how the team was led and how it performed?

What were the key actions and qualities that typified this team and its leadership?

- *What did people do together?*
- *How did people treat one another?*
- *How did people communicate? Was there a communication infrastructure in place?*
- *How was creativity valued and promoted?*
- *What qualities (inner and outer) did the team, its members and its leadership possess that most influenced the level of relationship and performance of its members?*

Be sure to consider all of the levels of success factors that we have been exploring throughout this book: environment, behavior, capabilities, beliefs and values, identity/mission and vision/purpose.

Now, compare this team and the way it was led with your personal experience of being a part of (1) an average team and (2) an ineffective or "degenerative" team or group. Review the same questions with respect to these other teams and how they performed. [You can also do this exercise with respect to one particular team you have been involved with that performed in different ways or at different levels (generative, average, degenerative) over time.]

What are some of the "differences that make a difference"? Use the following worksheet to record your answers.

Modeling Dynamic Teaming Worksheet

	Generative	Average	Degenerative
Vision/Purpose			
Identity/Mission			
Values/Beliefs			
Capabilities			
Behaviors			
Environment			

What is present in the dynamic and generative team that is only partially there in the average team and missing or very nominal in the degenerative team?

What levels of factors are there *more of* or *less of* that seem to impact the strength of relationship and/or the performance of the task with respect to the (a) degenerative, (b) average and (c) generative teams?

See if you can summarize your reflections into five to nine essential success factors.

If you already have your team in place, it is very powerful to do this exercise together as a team, as a form of "collective intelligence." I generally do this by having team members first reflect on their answers individually, choose their top three or four, and then share them in a type of "benchmarking" intervision process. Team members are to look for resonance between their answers by not so much focusing on the words as on the deeper meaning and experience to which the language is pointing.

SFM Collaboration Catalyst:
Making a Dynamic Teaming Scorecard

Once you have identified and defined the key success factors for dynamic teaming and generative collaboration, it is useful to formalize them into a type of "infrastructure" for the team by making a "scorecard."

Consider the example scorecard below. The key success factors for dynamic teaming are listed down the left-hand side of the table. The level of expression of each success factor is indicated on a scale of 1 to 5 between a "low level" connected with poor performance (1 + 1 = -1) and "high level" associated with effective, generative performance (1 + 1 = 3).

Success Factor	**Low Level**	1+1=-1	1+1=0	1+1=1	1+1=2	1+1=3	**High Level**
1. Project Purpose	*ambiguous*	1	2	3	4	5	*clear*
2. Discussion	*guarded*	1	2	3	4	5	*open*
3. Interaction	*avoided*	1	2	3	4	5	*engaged*
4. Support	*self only*	1	2	3	4	5	*each to all*
5. Use of Skills	*poor*	1	2	3	4	5	*full*
6. Rapport	*low*	1	2	3	4	5	*high*
7. Pace	*slow*	1	2	3	4	5	*fast*

To use the scorecard, at various key points during the project or a team interaction, the team members are to pause and reflect on the presence and level of these success factors by considering their answers the following questions:

1. Project purpose
How clear are you about the objectives and priorities of the project?

2. Discussion
How open and honest are you in discussing the issues you are facing and in evaluating the strengths and areas for improvement of other team members?

3. Interaction
How frequently and fully do you interact and communicate with each other?

4. Support
Do you support others to succeed in their tasks or do you tend to focus mostly on your own individual tasks?

5. Use of Skills
How fully are you applying your skills to reach shared goals?

6. Rapport
What degree of rapport do you have with one another?

7. Pace
How do you perceive your pace in accomplishing shared goals and objectives?

Team members rate and compare their ratings with respect to these various questions and the corresponding success factors, reflecting on their strengths and in what areas they think they can most improve.

Creating Your Own Dynamic Teaming Scorecard

Given what you have modeled about generative groups and teams, what different or additional success factors might you add to the example scorecard above to create your own Dynamic Teaming Scorecard?

Use the table below to list the key success factors you have identified for dynamic teaming and generative collaboration and establish the low and high levels of expression for each factor.

Success Factor	**Low Level**	1+1=-1	1+1=0	1+1=1	1+1=2	1+1=3	**High Level**
1.		1	2	3	4	5	
2.		1	2	3	4	5	
3.		1	2	3	4	5	
4.		1	2	3	4	5	
5.		1	2	3	4	5	
6.		1	2	3	4	5	

Now, for each success factor, write a question that will help you and your team evaluate at which level you are operating collectively.

1. ______________________________ 4. ______________________________

2. ______________________________ 5. ______________________________

3. ______________________________ 6. ______________________________

Again, it is a powerful exercise in collective intelligence to have the team members create their own scorecard together as a group activity. When doing this, I frequently recommend that each team member choose a success factor that he or she most resonates with and become the "champion" for that success factor. For example, in a team of eight people, each team member would propose one success factor, present the key question and then define the high level and low level of its expression with the participation of the rest of the group.

Example Dynamic Teaming Scorecard

As an example, the following Dynamic Teaming Scorecard was created by the members of a team that I was coaching who were about to launch a major investment fund. This company launched its investment fund in 2004 starting with six people and about 50 million euros. Within four years they had grown to 60 people and were investing over 6 billion euros!

Success Factor	Low Level	1+1=-1	1+1=0	1+1=1	1+1=2	1+1=3	High Level
1. Openness to Change	*Passive / Reactive*	1	2	3	4	5	*Active*
2. Planning	*Disorganized*	1	2	3	4	5	*Organized*
3. Communication	*Ambiguous*	1	2	3	4	5	*Clear*
4. Interaction	*Haphazard*	1	2	3	4	5	*Synergic*
5. Skill Enhancement	*Complacent*	1	2	3	4	5	*Ambitious*
6. Ownership/Commitment	*Not involved*	1	2	3	4	5	*Involved*
7. Respect / Recognition	*Not much*	1	2	3	4	5	*High Degree*
8. Exchange / Generosity	*Occassional*	1	2	3	4	5	*Systematic*

1. Openness to Change/Flexibility
How proactive are team members with respect learning about new tools and updating their knowledge and perspectives of others?

2. Planning
How organized is the team about maintaining a focus on medium-term and long-term goals?

3. Communication
How clear is the communication between team members?

4. Interaction
How synergic and generative is the interaction between team members? How well is the team able to go beyond the superficial to a creative sharing of knowledge and ideas?

5. Skill Enhancement
How ambitious are team members about enhancing and integrating the use of their skills?

6. Ownership/Commitment
How involved are team members in actively reaching the team vision and being a team? Do team members follow through without having to be reminded? Do team members put time into being a team?

7. Respect/Recognition
How much respect and recognition do team members show each other during their interactions?

8. Exchange/Generosity
How willing are team members to pitch in and help each other, even if they don't have to? How systematically do team members invest time to be sure other team members develop?

Chapter Summary

Dynamic Teaming is a form of (frequently spontaneous) teamwork in which group members complement each other's competencies and personal traits, share the responsibility for results and work together to achieve more than is possible by the sum of the individual efforts. Dynamic teaming is an example of how collaboration can be generative (i.e., 1+1=3).

The flocking behavior of birds presents some good examples of and metaphors for dynamic teaming. Geese, for example must travel thousands of miles per year as part of their migratory patterns. By flying together, and taking advantage of the uplift provided by their flockmates ahead, geese can fly over 70% farther than they can by themselves.

The complex "murmuration" patterns of birds such as starlings is another example of flocking. By following simple rules of cohesion, separation and alignment, collections of individual birds are able to move and respond together and avoid obstacles, acting as an integrated holon.

A similar set of rules was used by United States fighter pilots to attain an important and improbable victory during the Battle of Midway; a turning point in the Pacific campaign in the Second World War. By following simple rules of communication and action, American planes were able to "flock" effectively, by gathering rapidly in critical areas of airspace. Although heavily outnumbered, the US pilots flew in overwhelming force to where they could make the biggest impact.

Dynamic Team Development involves creating the conditions in which teams engaged in entrepreneurial activities can "flock" together to produce the greatest impact in the service of a common mission and vision.

The Comau Pico Custom Products Team Success Factor Case Example illustrates a number of collaboration catalysts that can be used by any group engaging in an entrepreneurial activity to promote dynamic teaming. These include synergizing goals, knocking down walls and silos that separate people in different roles, sharing criteria for collaboration, establishing repetitive communication regarding key areas of the Circle of Success and promoting the attitude of partnering and "servant leadership."

The *Dynamic Team Meeting Format* outlines a simple process that can be used for organizing ongoing meetings with team members, customers, stakeholders or partners. It provides sufficient structure to plan and conduct meetings, but allows for enough flexibility and spontaneity to allow resonance, synergy and emergence to occur.

A powerful Collaboration Catalyst for dynamic teaming is that of *Resource Mining*, in which prospective collaborators identify and openly share their needs, resources and their collaboration criteria. This helps people find the areas of complementarity necessary to establish strong and beneficial collaborative relationships.

The processes of *Aligning Roles Within a Common Vision* and the *Team Alignment Worksheet* help team members identify shared values and align their capabilities and actions in relation to a common vision and mission.

The *Modeling Dynamic Teaming Success Factors* process helps to establish an effective "communication infrastructure and creativity infrastructure" by defining the key success factors required for dynamic teaming and generative collaboration and creating a *Dynamic Teaming Scorecard.* This can be used to institute the practice of continuous reflection upon the presence of these critical success factors during key phases of a project and team interactions.

References

- http://en.wikipedia.org/wiki/Team
- **"Lessons from Geese"**, Robert McNeish,, 1972;
- http://www.team-building-bonanza.com/inspirational-short-story.html
- http://www.suewidemark.com/lessonsgeese.htm
- http://en.wikipedia.org/wiki/Flock_%28birds%29 http://en.wikipedia.org/wiki/Flocking_(behavior)
- http://www.huffingtonpost.com/2013/02/01/starling-murmuration-bird-ballet- video_n_2593001.html
- **Murmuration**:https://vimeo.com/31158841
- **"Boids"**, Craig Reynolds, 1987; http://www.red3d.com/cwr/boids/applet/
- **GitHub flocking simulation** (http://black-square.github.io/BirdFlock/)
- **Alpha Leadership: Tools for Leaders Who Want More From Life**, Deering, A., Dilts, R. and Russell, J., John Wiley & Sons, London, England, 2002.
- **Steve at Work**, Romain Moisescot; allaboutstevejobs.com, 2012.
- **Visionary Leadership Skills**, Dilts, R., Meta Publications, Capitola, CA, 1996.

06 Activating the Wisdom of Crowds

Who is wise? He that learns from everyone.
Who is powerful? He that governs his passions.
Who is rich? He that is content.
Who is that? Nobody.
Benjamin Franklin

Some of the greatest advances happen when people are bold enough to speak their truth and listen to others speak theirs.
Kenneth H. Blanchard

[Wisdom comes from] sitting together and truthfully discussing our differences— without the intent to change them.
Gregory Bateson

ANTONIO MEZA

Balance self-interest and the common good

See the world in shades of grey, not black and white.

Reflect thoughtfully on the lessons gained from experience.

Developing Wisdom

Activating the Wisdom of Crowds

In addition to passion, vision, mission and ambition, another significant factor related to mindset that is needed to create a successful and sustainable venture is a certain degree of wisdom. *Wisdom* is defined in the dictionary as "the ability to think and act using knowledge, experience, understanding, common sense, and insight." These aspects of "mindset" are applied to attain "an optimum judgment as to what actions should be taken." Thus, wisdom is about having a broad and balanced perspective that allows a person or group to make better and more ecological choices and decisions.

Developing Wisdom

Developing wisdom involves an understanding of people, goals and situations, and how they interact in order to determine an optimal course of action. It also requires the constant seeking of knowledge to apply to a given circumstance.

In his November 2013 LinkedIn article *How to Think like a Wise Person*, author and Wharton professor Adam Grant (cited several times already in this volume) outlines the following steps to develop greater wisdom:

1. Reflect thoughtfully on the lessons gained from experience.
2. See the world in shades of grey, not black and white.
3. Balance self-interest and the common good.
4. Challenge the status quo.
5. Aim to understand, rather than judge.
6. Focus on purpose over pleasure.

Benjamin Franklin's comment, "Who is wise? He that learns from everyone," indicates that wisdom also involves the process of inviting and integrating multiple perspectives. This is echoed in system theorist Gregory Bateson's claim that wisdom comes from "sitting together and truthfully discussing our differences—without the intent to change them"

Combining the reflections of Grant, Franklin and Bateson, we can outline several principles and guidelines for developing wisdom:

- Wisdom emerges not from experience itself, but rather from reflecting thoughtfully on the lessons learned from experience, taking different points of view.
- Wisdom results from embracing nuance and multiple perspectives. As Grant points out, the aim of wisdom is to "understand rather than to judge."
- Wise people and groups are willing to question the rules. Instead of accepting things as they have always been, wisdom involves asking whether there is a better path.
- Wisdom is a function of the balance between what I have called "ego" and "soul"; i.e., aligning "self-interest with the common good." It comes from encouraging and supporting people to find ways to benefit others that also advance their own goals and ambitions.
- Wisdom results from a constant focus on a bigger picture and larger purpose. It requires a connection to what Gregory Bateson referred to as a "larger Mind" or field intelligence.

Clearly, wisdom is something that is significantly enhanced through collective intelligence. In fact, making *wiser decisions* is one of the fundamental outcomes of fostering and applying collective intelligence.

Developing Wisdom

The Wisdom of Crowds

In his book *The Wisdom of Crowds* (2005), James Surowiecki makes the bold claim that:

> *Under the right circumstances, groups are remarkably intelligent, and are often smarter than the smartest people in them. Groups do not need to be dominated by exceptionally intelligent people in order to be smart. Even if most of the people within a group are not especially well-informed or rational, it can still reach a collectively wise decision.*

Collective decisions are most likely to be good ones when they are made by people with diverse opinions reaching independent conclusions, relying primarily on their private information.

In fact, Surowiecki claims that groups made up of some "smart" agents and some "not so smart" agents always did better than groups of only "smart" agents. According to Surowiecki, collective decisions are most likely to be good ones when they are made by people with diverse opinions reaching independent conclusions, relying primarily on their private information.

Surowiecki points to natural examples of "the wisdom of crowds" in the intelligent behavior of flocking birds (see Chapter 5, pp. 256-259) and the ability of ant colonies to find the shortest path to food sources (see Chapter 4, p. 191). He also references the self-correcting nature of markets and the development of Open Source computer codes (like Linux) as manifestations of the wisdom of crowds. Another example he brings up is the discovery of the solution the SARS epidemic in 2003. The solution was the result of research done and data collected by many different hospitals and universities around the world, working with no single central coordinating organization. It emerged naturally out of some larger collective intelligence.

A simple, tangible demonstration of the wisdom of crowds is that of estimating quantities. The average group estimate is always one of the closest to the actual amount.

Another very tangible demonstration of the wisdom of crowds Surowiecki presents is that of estimating quantities. As an iconic example, Surowiecki cites an anecdote by scientist and pioneer psychologist Francis Galton. Galton was at a county fair where there was a prize given to the person who came closest to guessing the weight of a large ox. More than 900 people ventured guesses. Out of curiosity, Galton added up all of the guesses and took the average. To his surprise, he discovered that, even though the individual guesses varied widely, the group average was closer to the ox's actual weight than the estimates of almost all of the crowd members, and also closer than any of the separate estimates made by cattle experts.

Surowiecki claims that the same phenomenon happens when estimating quantities of any type. For example, take a jar full of candy and ask people to independently write their guesses on pieces of paper. When the estimates are collected and added up, the average is almost invariably one of the closest to the actual number of pieces of candy.

I do this experiment regularly in my collective intelligence training programs. It consistently produces impressive results. The average group guess is always one of the closest estimates.

The chart below is an actual example from one of my seminar groups. As you can see, the individual estimates are astonishingly varied. Of the 40 guesses, the lowest estimate is 150, while the highest is 5,000! This degree of disparity is a powerful testament to how different our individual perceptions and judgments can be. However, the average of all of the guesses (884) is extremely close to the actual number of pieces of candy (836). Only two other estimates are slightly closer.

This example also shows how important it is to include every group member's input. For instance, if you threw out the highest and/or lowest guesses, the average would be farther from the actual number in the jar. Everybody's contribution is necessary to get the full wisdom of the crowd.

INDIVIDUAL ESTIMATES

1000	1384	737	300
1515	522	623	1250
480	1253	150	603
2708	252	623	1205
600	500	800	480
1062	321	288	816
190	3257	540	325
850	400	1263	5000
280	1124	417	500
222	350	780	424

AVERAGE: 884.85

ACTUAL NUMBER OF CANDY PIECES: 836

One Example of the Wisdom of Crowds is Estimating Quantities.
The Average Group Estimate is Always One of the Closest to the Actual Number.

Conditions Needed to Produce Wise Crowds

Obviously, not all groups and crowds are wise. In fact, the very same group may or not act wisely, depending upon the conditions of their interaction. One of the major interferences to the wisdom of groups, for instance, is conformity or "group think." Instead of increasing the group's wisdom, conformity and consensus restrict the exploration of other possible alternatives or ideas. In order to "fit in" or gain approval or confirmation of their own opinions, people are often swayed by what others say and think.

One of the major interferences to the wisdom of groups is conformity or "group think."

In the candy guessing experiment, for example, it is important that people make their own independent guesses without knowing initially what any of the other estimates are. If you did the same experiment and people one after the other each verbalized their guess out loud so that others could hear it, the previous guesses would begin to influence those that followed. The variation in estimates would probably be much smaller, but the average might be farther away from the actual number. The guesses of influential members of the group may unconsciously sway the estimates of others.

In group contexts, people frequently stop paying attention to their own knowledge and ideas and start making decisions based on what they think other people in the group know, think or approve of. Group members may stop expressing what they really think, especially if it is likely to create a disturbance and "rock the boat." In fact, it is the pressure to conform and to think and act like the rest of the group that is at the basis of fads, mobs and facism.

In group contexts, people frequently stop paying attention to their own knowledge and ideas and start making decisions based on what they think other people in the group know, think or approve of.

Surowiecki points out that homogenous groups are great at doing what they do well, but they become progressively less able to investigate new alternatives; "They spend too much time exploiting and not enough time exploring." Diversity contributes, not just by adding different perspectives, but also by making it easier for individuals to say what they really think.

Surowiecki summarizes the four conditions that produce wise crowds as:

1. *Diversity of opinion* (people represent a wide range of perspectives)
2. *Independence* (people's opinions are not determined by the opinions of those around them)
3. *Decentralization* (people are able to specialize and draw upon local information)
4. *Aggregation* (some unbiased mechanism exists for turning individual conclusions into a collective decision)

James Surowiecki defines the four conditions that produce wise crowds as diveristy of opinion, independence, decentralization and an unbiased way of aggregating individual conclusions into a collective decision.

When these conditions are met, the wisdom of the group as a holon can emerge.

Surowiecki's view of how the wisdom of crowds functions is reminiscent of political economist Adam Smith's notion of an "invisible hand" guiding the behavior of people within a free market. According to Smith, when people act rationally in their own self-interest, they are "led by an *invisible hand* to promote an end which was no part of their intention" – i.e., without intending it, without knowing it, they advance the interest of society. Smith claimed that, by pursuing their own interest, people frequently promote that of the society more effectually than when they consciously intend to promote it.

Smith's notion of an "invisible hand" is an example of a "larger Mind" or field intelligence, which is promoted by some of the same patterns that produce wise individuals: reflecting thoughtfully on the lessons gained from experience; embracing nuance and multiple perspectives with the aim to understand rather than to judge; exploring alternatives and asking whether there is a better path; focusing on "purpose" and finding the balance of self-interest with the common good.

For this reason, I would add the importance of people having *a common vision or purpose* to Surowiecki's list as a key part of producing wise groups. This creates the possibility for group members to balance self-interest with the common good (i.e., "ego" and "soul") and find ways to benefit the group while simultaneously advancing their own goals and ambitions.

Having a common vision or purpose is also a key part of producing wise group as it creates the possibility for group members to balance self-interest with the common good and find ways to benefit the group while simultaneously advancing their own goals and ambitions.

Google's Quest for the Perfect Team

In a type of success factor modeling, Google spent five years and millions of dollars gathering data on the traits and behavior patterns of people within teams that exhibited different levels of performance in order to determine how to improve their teams' "collective I.Q.s"

Several of the key points that Surowiecki presents are echoed in the results of a five-year research study conducted by Google to try to find out how to create the perfect team. Like many of today's most successful firms, Google realized that analyzing and improving individual workers —known as ''employee performance optimization''—wasn't enough. As the activities of organizations become increasingly global and complex, the majority of what it takes to make a successful venture is more and more team-based. In fact, a recent study, published in The Harvard Business Review, found that ''the time spent by managers and employees in collaborative activities has ballooned by 50 percent or more'' over the last two decades and that, at many companies, more than three-quarters of an employee's day is spent communicating with colleagues.

As a result, Google became focused on trying to build the perfect team. They spent millions of dollars gathering data on the traits and behavior patterns of people within teams that exhibited different levels of performance. As Surowiecki might have predicted, it was almost impossible to find evidence that the composition of a team made any significant difference. ''We looked at 180 teams from all over the company,'' said Abeer Dubey, a manager in Google's People Analytics division. ''We had lots of data, but there was nothing showing that a mix of specific personality types or skills or backgrounds made any difference. The 'who' part of the equation didn't seem to matter.'' Two teams, for instance, might have nearly identical members, but display radically different levels of effectiveness.

Equality in distribution of conversational turn-taking is one important success factor to increasing "collective I.Q."

All of this led the researchers to formulate the notion of a "collective I. Q." that emerges within a team that is distinct from the intelligence or personality of any single member; what we have been calling a "group mind." We could say that this collective I.Q. would be a measure of the degree of "wisdom" of the group. The big question, of course, was "how does a group promote the development of a collective I.Q.?

As the Google researchers tracked various groups, they noticed two characteristics that all the good teams seemed to share. The first was a phenomenon the researchers referred to as ''equality in distribution of conversational turn-taking." On the good teams, members spoke in roughly the same proportion. That is, each person had equal opportunity to contribute. ''As long as everyone got a chance to talk, the team did well,'' concluded Anita Woolley, the study's lead author. ''But if only one person or a small group spoke all the time, the collective intelligence declined.''

Secondly, the members of good teams all had a high degree of ''social sensitivity,'' meaning that they were skilled at perceiving how others felt based on their tone of voice, facial expressions and other nonverbal cues. This capacity is an expression of empathy and "emotional intelligence." It also relates to what we have called "second position"; the ability to take on someone else's point of view.

The combination of traits like ''conversational turn-taking'' and ''social sensitivity'' produce what is known as "psychological safety." *Psychological safety* is ''a sense of confidence that the team will not embarrass, reject or punish someone for speaking up . . . It describes a team climate characterized by interpersonal trust and mutual respect in which people are comfortable being themselves.'' According to Google's data, psychological safety, more than anything else, was critical to making a team work.

Psychological safety is also promoted by authentic self-disclosure, where people are able to share what they genuinely think and feel, and are able to reveal intimate information about themselves. In my Mastermind group, for instance, we often will open a face-to-face session by going around the group and have each member fill in the statement: ''One of the things most people don't know about me is . . .'' As people share something intimate and meaningful about themselves, it gives others permission to do the same.

Not surprisingly, another factor that emerged from the Google study was the importance of perceived task significance. In effective teams, the group members knew how their work fit into Google's larger mission.

Given the principles we have covered thus far in this book, it seems obvious that the combination of psychological safety and task significance encourages and allows team members to be both individual separate wholes as well as act as part of the larger holon.

According to Google's data, psychological safety, more than anything else, was critical to making a team work.

Social sensitivity and the capacity for empathy and emotional intelligence are other important success factors for enhancing collective I.Q.

It was also important for group members to know how their work fit into Google's larger mission.

Six Steps for Activating the Wisdom of Crowds

Based upon principles of Success Factor Modeling, Dr. Stephen Gilligan and I have defined six steps for producing effective, wise and generative collaboration.

In my collective intelligence workshops and the work on generative change that I do with my colleague Dr. Stephen Gilligan, we outline a series of steps for producing effective, wise and generative collaboration. These steps incorporate both Surowiecki's criteria for bringing out the wisdom of crowds and Google's conclusions from their search for the perfect team. In essence, the steps involve:

1. Create a COACH container.
2. Identify a common intention/purpose.
3. Develop a generative performance state.
4. Focus attention on a goal or problem, gathering multiple perspectives.
5. Hold all perspectives from a state of respect and curiosity.
6. Allow new ideas and possibilities to emerge.

The first four steps are supported by collaboration catalysts that we have already explored in this book. Creating a COACH container (pp. 73-75) and identifying a collective intention (pp. 78-79) were covered in Chapter 1. Creating a generative performance state (pp. 118-119) and focusing attention on a goal or problem, gathering multiple perspectives (pp. 120-127) were addressed in Chapter 2.

Holding all perspectives from a state of respect and curiosity clearly requires the creation of what the Google researchers referred to as psychological safety. Wisdom often emerges from what initially seems to be paradox and contradiction. The following collaboration catalysts can be applied to help groups hold all perspectives from a state of respect and curiosity and allow new ideas and possibilities to emerge.

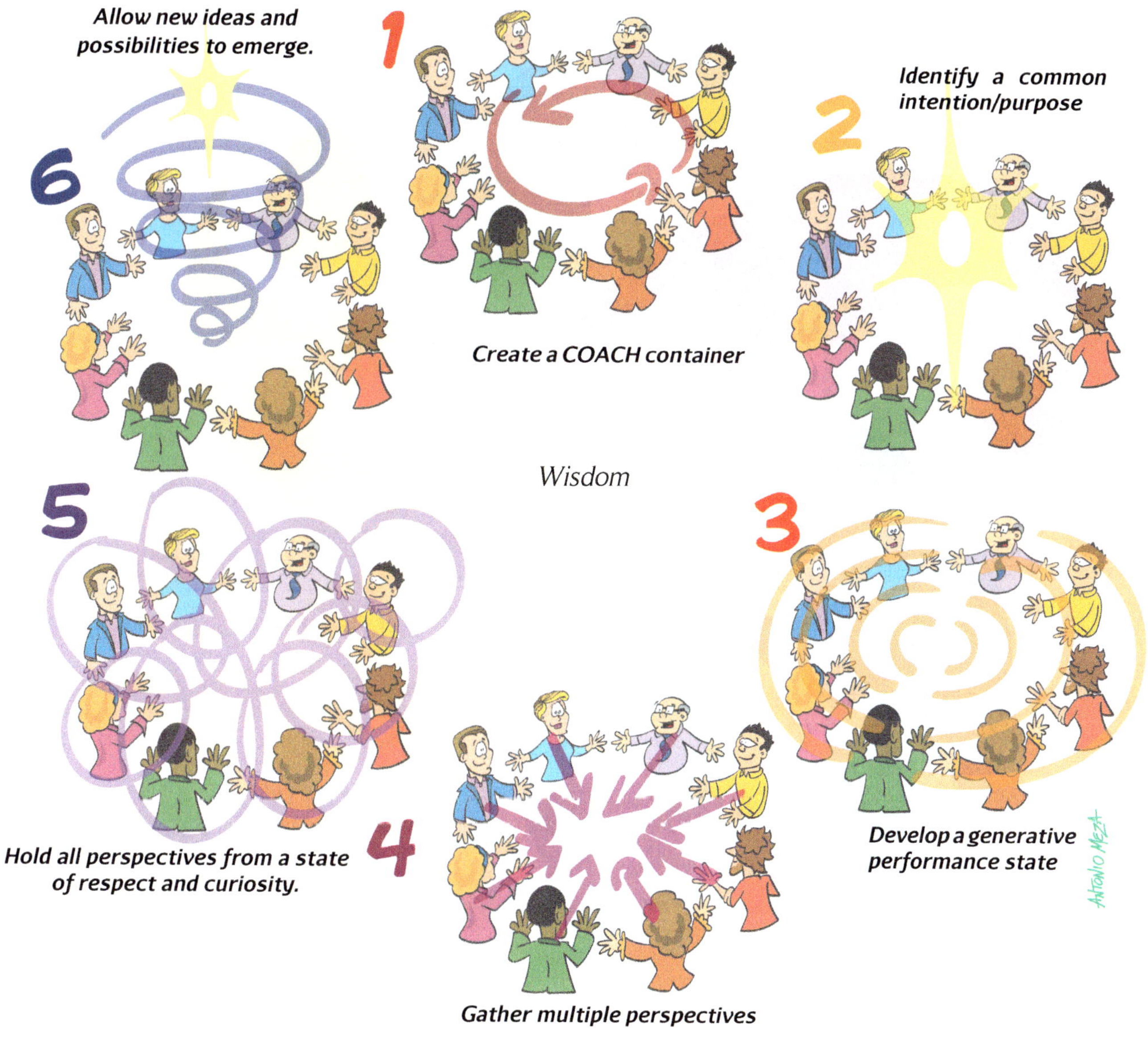

Six Steps for Activating the Wisdom of Crowds

SFM Collaboration Catalyst: Shifting from CRASH to COACH State

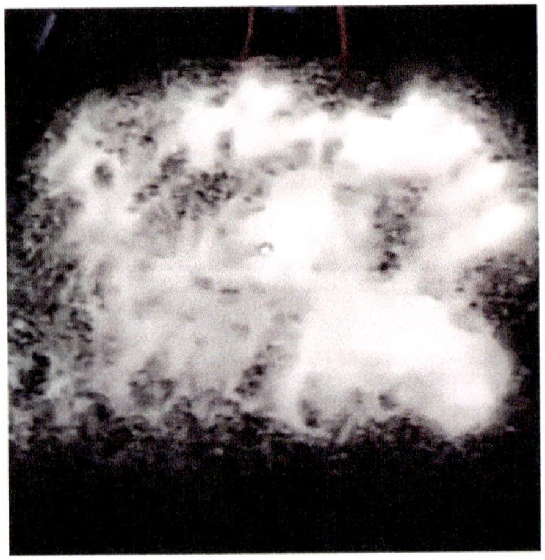

CRASH State

Versus

COACH State

In the vocabulary of this book, we can say that psychological safety is the product of a COACH container. When people are centered, open, aware, connected to themselves and each other and able to hold whatever is present with resourcefulness and curiosity, they feel safe to be who they are and to say what they authentically think. The opposite happens when people CRASH. Being contracted, reactive, overly analytical and feeling separated and hurt is destructive to collective intelligence and to activating the wisdom of crowds.

Making an analogy to the vibrating sand on the metal plate in Chapter 1 (pp. 50-51), we can say that the psychological and emotional state of the group creates a type of vibrational field. As the cymatics experiments show, it is the vibrational field that determines how the sand will ultimately be organized. In the context of a group or team, we can say that the sand is like the content of their discussion or their task. The plate is the context of their interaction. The level of vibration is the quality of their generative performance state. If the group enters a CRASH state, nothing creative or innovative is going to be produced. If the exact same group of people is discussing or working on the exact same content from a generative COACH state, it is much more likely that new ideas and possibilities will emerge.

When a group is in a "stuck" (CRASH) state, it is reflected in the nonverbal "music" of the interaction—conversation speeds up, breathing stops, rhythm is disjointed, people are no longer centered in themselves, and there is no "space" between people or words.

The following exercise supports group members to practice "social sensitivity" and to help each other back into a COACH state through some simple nonverbal "conductor signals."

1. The group identifies an area where they would like more creative collaboration (e.g., talking about the budget).
2. Group members select non-verbal signal for (1) slow down, (2) pause, (3) breathe, and (4) center. The purpose of these signals is to help the group return to or strengthen the quality of their COACH container and generative performance state.
3. The group creates a COACH container, sets a common intention to collaborate creatively regarding their chosen topic and begins to interact.
4. At any point that any group member becomes aware that he or she or any of the other group members is beginning to exhibit any of the CRASH behaviors (contraction, reactivity, overly analytical, etc.), the group member may give one of the non-verbal signals that he or she feels is most appropriate.
5. Group members collectively respond to the signal before continuing the interaction.
6. Every 10-20 minutes the group is to pause and reflect on the quality of their "field" and their interaction and to be sure that all members are having the chance to give input.

This type of "ritualized" practice is a powerful way of helping to bring dynamics such as "social sensitivity" and "conversational turn-taking" into group members' ongoing awareness. It puts the responsibility for the group's state into the hands of each group member. The ultimate purpose of such a collaboration catalyst is that these dynamics become incorporated into the natural and spontaneous interaction of the group. We have found that after a few rounds of intentional practice, groups will become much more sensitive to their degree of psychological safety.

Examples of Non-Verbal Signals for Helping to Maintain a COACH Container

Transforming Potential Conflicts through the Tetra Lemma

At the beginning of this chapter, I cited Gregory Bateson's claim that wisdom comes from "sitting together and truthfully discussing our differences—without the intent to change them." Holding multiple, contradictory perspectives frequently creates some of the biggest breakthroughs and most generative, "out of the box" solutions.

Holding multiple, contradictory perspectives frequently creates some of the biggest breakthroughs and most generative, "out of the box" solutions.

Groups, however, often CRASH when they encounter differing and/or seemingly contradictory perspectives among group members. Rather than reflect thoughtfully, see the world in shades of grey instead of black and white, and aim to understand rather than judge, group members begin to argue about who is right. They try to force agreement and seek consensus. Individuals may also begin to defend their own views and attack or criticize the opinions of others. Needless to say, this greatly diminishes the wisdom of the group and the creativity of the collaboration. The *Tetra Lemma* is a collaboration catalyst that helps groups to practice transforming such situations into opportunities for something new to emerge.

The Tetra Lemma Group Process is a collaboration catalyst that helps groups to practice transforming potentially conflictual situations into opportunities for something new to emerge.

Dilemmas within a group reflect conflict between different "truths" or perspectives. The Tetra Lemma is an approach for sensing the "positive value" of each conflicting position, thereby allowing an integrative "meta-truth" to emerge. "Tetra" is Greek for the number four. "Di" means two. "Lemma" is a Greek term that means a particular point or position that has been taken. Dilemma thus literally means "two positions." Tetra Lemma means "four positions." The four positions of the Tetra Lemma are:

1. X is True
2. The Contrary of X is True
3. Both X and the Contrary of X are True
4. Neither X Nor the Contrary of X are True

Obviously, a typical dilemma happens when a particular position or point of view encounters its contrary or opposite. If one group member claims, "We need more (support, time, resources, etc.)" and another maintains, "No, we have enough (support, time, resources, etc.)," the group has encountered a classical dilemma. Dilemmas are not always direct opposites statements like the previous ones. One group member could say, "It is important to take action and grow," while another states, "We need to work on becoming more stable with what we are already doing."

In either case, the Tetra Lemma process would give a place to each position; i.e., (1) "We need more X," (2) "We have enough X"; or (1) "It is important to grow," (2) We need more stabilitywhere we are." The truth and value of each perspective would be considered and respected. Each point of view would be considered to have value and a positive intention.

The first two positions of the Tetra Lemma typically create a type of dilemma.

The third position of the Tetra Lemma would be that, at some level, *both* positions are simultaneously true. "We need more X *AND* we have enough X." Or, "It is important to grow *AND* we need more stability where we are." This is typically known as a "meta position" in NLP. Meta position or third position is frequently known as a "wisdom" position because it creates the space for multiple perspectives. This third position is essential for practically any type of negotiation or conflict resolution.

The third position of the Tetra Lemma acknowledges the validity of both the first two positions.

The fourth position of the Tetra Lemma is the most intriguing and unusual. The fourth position involves taking on the mindset that neither position is ultimately "true." That is, "It is *neither* true that we need more X *NOR* that we have enough X." "It is *neither* true that it is important to grow *NOR* is it true that we need more stability where we are." This fourth position opens a space or field of possibilities that may not have been considered or even thought of. It is from this position that something truly novel or new can potentially emerge.

The fourth position of the Tetra Lemma, that neither of the first two are true, opens a space or field of possibilities that may not have been considered or even thought of.

In many ways, the Tetra Lemma reflects the four perceptual positions we explored in chapters 2 and 3. There are two perspectives that are equally and neutrally witnessed by a third. The fourth position is a "field" position. In the Tetra Lemma, that fourth position is a field of possibilities.

When Stephen Gilligan and I use this process with groups, we like to have the group members physically sort the positions into four different locations and rotate through each one, so that all group members have taken each mindset. We also add a fifth location in the center of the others for integrating COACH state; a position that holds all of the four simultaneously. This is essentially a position of choice. Any or all of the other perspectives may be considered without attachment to any of them.

SFM Collaboration Catalyst: Tetra Lemma Group Process

1. Identify a group dilemma created by conflicting or contradictory perspectives or opinions within the group that is producing some type of conflict or CRASH.
2. Physically lay out the positions of the Tetra Lemma in a type of diamond shape (as in the diagram) with the two positions of the dilemma across from one another and the third and fourth positions between and beyond them. Make place for an integrating COACH state in the middle of the four positions.
3. Group members step into each of the five locations so that all positions are occupied. Each member is to take on the mindset associated with his or her position.
4. Group members then rotate through the positions, until that each person has been in each location and experiences the mindset associate with each position.

   Note: If any of the members notices that he or she or other members of the group begin to CRASH, he or she can use one of the signals established in the previous exercise.
5. The group then discusses any new insights and possibilities that have emerged from the process.

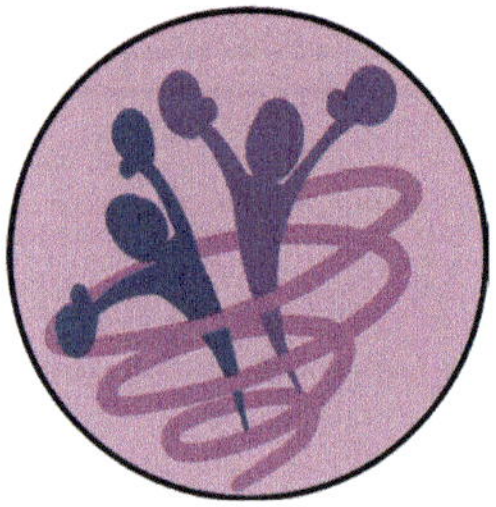

Repeatedly practicing the Tetra Lemma helps the process to become incorporated as an ongoing resource for addressing differing perspectives in a generative way.

Similar to the previous exercise, going through the Tetra Lemma as a group in such a structured way helps it to become incorporated as an ongoing resource for addressing differing perspectives in a generative way.

Of course, it is also possible and useful to practice the Tetra Lemma as an individual. Similar to the group process, you can lay out the four positions with a location for the COACH state in the center. Putting yourself in each location and the associated mindset can help you to gain a richer and wiser perspective with respect to multiple perspectives within a team or group with which you are involved.

The following Success Factor Case Study provides a good example of the importance of being able to wisely hold and integrate multiple positions and perspectives.

The Tetra Lemma Group Process involves the practice of integrating potentially conflictual perspectives.

Success Factor Case Example
Drew Dilts: United States Peace Corps
Benin Moringa Farm and Bee Keeping Project

Generative Empowerment.

Drew Dilts

Drew Dilts' defines his notion of generative empowerment as "empowering people with the skills and self-confidence to become leaders for societal improvement who then, in turn, empower those around them in the same generative way."

A Passion for Empowerment

Successful entrepreneurs begin their quest to create a new product or service because they see a problem that they want to solve or they dream of a better way of doing something. They have a "calling," or passion to create something new and different. The sense of calling and personal passion is what drives entrepreneurs to take risks and stay focused in the face of the many challenges they confront.

From an early age, Drew Dilts was conscious of a deep drive to improve the world. He also became aware of a fundamental personal desire for a type of immortality. He wanted to feel that a part of himself would live on pursuing his mission, regardless of his physical presence. This would allow him to have a more far-reaching influence not limited by what he personally could accomplish in one life.

The integration of these two drives — to improve the world and to have his mission live on beyond his physical presence — created in Drew a passion for what he calls *generative empowerment.* As Drew explains it, "By empowering people with the skills and self-confidence to become leaders for societal improvement who then, in turn, empower those around them in the same generative way, I can create a force of 'generative empowerment' that accomplishes more than anything I could do alone. This force is contagious, sustainable, and crucial to global advancement; by unleashing it, I can reflect on each day with the satisfaction that my mission continues, even if I am not there." According to Drew, a non-generative solution "dies when you die," or stops when you stop.

It was Drew's passion for generative empowerment that led him to volunteer for the United States Peace Corps in 2012 after getting undergraduate degrees in Business and International Relations from the University of San Diego. He was assigned to Benin in West Africa, among the poorest of the African countries, to help promote economic development. Here, his passion for generative empowerment took the shape of a vision of "communities that succeed in tackling their own serious societal problems in a collaborative, creative and empowering way."

Bringing a New Vision to Customers

Customers are the recipients and primary beneficiaries of the entrepreneur's calling and vision. It is through their relationship with their customers that entrepreneurs develop their products, services and ultimately their venture. To achieve sustainable success, entrepreneurs must generate enough interest and revenue to support their enterprise — establishing both sufficient "mind share" and market share.

Based in the town of Glazoue in central Benin, Drew's primary "customers" were the townspeople and the Beninese villagers living in small rural communities beyond the borders of the town. Many of the small villages are still fairly isolated and the villagers have seen very few "white people"– usually aid workers. The villagers still live much as people did hundreds of years ago, inhabiting mud huts with no electricity and only a single well as their water supply. Village families frequently get by on less than the equivalent of $4 per day. Drew also observed that many village children display the bloated belly associated with malnutrition. Even though the children generally have enough to eat, their food lacks sufficient protein and other nutrients.

This combination of relative poverty and malnutrition led Drew to form a vision of "a collaborative, empowering, sustainable income-generating project to combat malnutrition using natural resources in the local area."

As part of his orientation to the region, Drew had become aware of the moringa tree that grew naturally in the area. Sometimes called the "miracle tree," moringa leaves are packed full of vitamins and minerals and contain all 9 essential amino acids, making them one of the very rare plants that offer a complete source of protein. Gram for gram, powder made from dried moringa leaves contains four times more vitamin A than carrots, four times the calcium of milk, seven times the vitamin C of oranges, three times the potassium of bananas and more iron than spinach.

Drew's passion for generative empowerment led him to volunteer for the US Peaces Corps, where he was stationed in Benin, West Africa.

The combination of relative poverty and malnutrition in the area led Drew to form a vision of "a collaborative, empowering, sustainable income-generating project to combat malnutrition using natural resources in the local area" that integrated the moringa tree and beekeeping.

Drew's vision was of a community that could tackle their social problems, such as poverty and malnutrition, in a collaborative way.

Drew had to deal with a number of obstacles to launching his venture, however, including the local's lack of understanding of "nutrition" and their learned dependence on foreign aid.

Bringing together his vision with his knowledge of the local area, Drew formed the idea of a venture in the form of a moringa and beekeeping farm. The venture would integrate cultivating the moringa tree, which benefits from cross-pollination, and beekeeping, an operation whose honey yield doubles when conducted near to the almost-constantly-flowering moringa tree. The honey from the beekeeping operation also offered a better source of sweetener than the expensive and poor quality sugar used by the locals.

Beyond the nutritional benefits to village families, excess supplies of moringa powder and honey could be sold to nearby cities and even in neighboring countries to produce additional needed income for the villagers.

One of Drew's challenges in launching the venture, however, was that his "customers" didn't understand the concept of "nutrition." It is not in their cultural history nor traditional education to analyze the substance in what they eat. If Drew tried to explain, "vitamin C helps your immune system," they wouldn't understand. They would ask, "What are vitamins?" "What is an immune system?"

Moreover, the villagers thought it was normal and even desirable for their children to have bloated bellies because it meant they were "well fed." To get their "buy in," Drew had to show the villagers photographs of African babies with normal bellies and find a way to explain the concept of nutrition in a way that would be easily understood. He used the metaphor of a house (literally building one out of sticks), declaring, "the body is a house and food builds the house." The "foundation" of the house was what Drew called "constructors" – i.e., meat, protein, etc. The "walls" were built from "energizers" such as corn, rice, yams, etc. The "roof" was made of "protectors" – i.e., fruits and vegetables. After presenting the metaphor, Drew pointed out that every meal should be a "house" and asked, "Would you want your family to live in a house with no roof? Walls? Foundation?"

Another major challenge to the venture that Drew encountered was the locals' belief that "The answers lie in the hearts and minds of white people." As a result, they were always looking outside for guidance and solutions. Drew had observed that, in the interactions between foreign development workers and locals, often, the development workers were *not* helping locals to develop. Many locals simply viewed them as omniscient deliverers who held the only solutions to certain problems that the locals alone were incapable of solving.

In fact, it became evident to Drew that much of the Beninese economy depended on aid as their primary source of income. He noticed that the best and brightest of the local people would go to NGOs where money comes from the government or aid groups—a situation that is not sustainable—rather than to starting new businesses.

To offset this attitude, Drew enlisted the support of a Beninese woman employed by the Peace Corps, Marthe, who came from a village and spoke the local language. She was able to be a role model and mentor to the villagers because she had credibility and was not white. She was able to convincingly say to the villagers in their own language: "You can do better than that." "I know you can." "I am one of you."

The Challenges of Aligning and Motivating Team Members

Team members are the group of people who work most closely with the entrepreneur to fulfill the mission of the venture. To succeed, entrepreneurs must grow a team of competent individuals working cooperatively to achieve the mission of the venture.

Drew needed a team made up of the local villagers to construct and carry out the moringa farm and beekeeping operation.

Drew needed a team made up of the local villagers to construct and carry out the moringa farm and beekeeping operation. They had to clear the land to be used, build fences, plant the moringa seeds and start the beehives. The moringa farm team ended up consisting of 1 man and 16 women. The 10 beekeepers were all men. This division of labor reflects the substantial gender inequality that exists in Beninese culture that Drew had to contend with.

Drew discovered that, while village, tribal and family bonds are very strong between the locals, people didn't tend to work together very well as a group.

In addition to that, Drew discovered that, while village, tribal and family bonds are very strong between the locals, people didn't tend to work together very well as a group. Given their cultural relationship to time and dynamic and unexpected family commitments, team members do not all show up at the same time nor work the same amount of hours on any particular day. As a result, the work schedule of individual team members can be quite chaotic.

Because the profits of the venture were to be divided equally, Drew observed that the women, especially, would get on each other and "point fingers," criticizing the team members who they perceived as only working half as much. It also led some team members to take the attitude, "Why work harder if everyone makes the same amount no matter what I do?"

Drew at the Moringa Farm Site with a Fellow Peace Corps Volunteer and Two Villagers

Drew decided to allocate each team member his or her own parcel. This gave each person a type of autonomy within the collective and allowed them to see the direct results of their efforts

The mission of the venture was to align team members around community health and to foster the exchange or "best practices" and collective "benchmarking" amongst the parcel owners.

Drew's solution was to allocate each team member his or her own parcel. This gave each person a type of autonomy within the collective and allowed them to see the direct results of their efforts. It turned team members into partial stakeholder. They had a sense of pride and accountability for their own parcel and could not make "excuses" regarding other people's efforts. This move actually served to make them more of a true "holon" – being both separate individuals and also part of something bigger than themselves.

Interestingly, having their own individual parcels also stimulated people to develop more collective intelligence. It allowed them to make comparisons and provided a natural sharing of"best practices." It helped to spur people on and encouraged them to model one another. When they had their own parcels, team members could see who showed up, whose parcel was doing well and what "differences made a difference." If one person's parcel was producing more than the other parcels, the others realized, "I can do something different where maybe I don't have to work as hard."

Because profits were being shared, team members began to realize, "If we all work harder and smarter, we all make more money." Every slight increase anyone makes creates an exponentially positive difference for everyone. For example, imagine that one person develops an innovative and effective way of watering each of their trees. If there were no parcels and everyone worked simultaneously throughout the farm, the only trees that would benefit from this innovative watering technique would be the trees that the developer watered. However, with the parcel system, everyone could see the positive impact of the technique and *implement the best practice throughout their own respective parcel*, thereby magnifying the benefit of the best practice from one parcel's worth of trees to seventeen parcels' worth of trees.

In the case of the beekeepers, who necessarily attended their own hives, this same notion of autonomy within the collective effort was already built in.

Best Practices

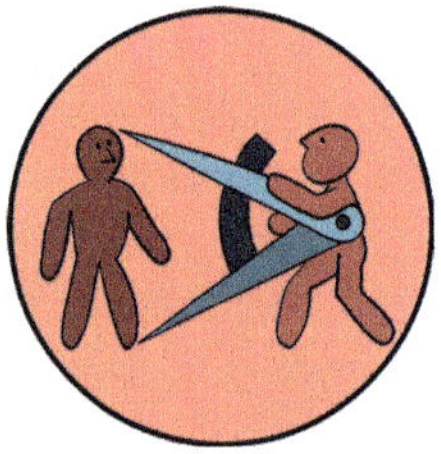

Benchmarking

Selecting and Satisfying Stakeholders

Stakeholders are any individual or group related to a project or venture who: affect decisions; are affected—positively or negatively—by the consequences of decisions and the intended results; can either hinder or facilitate reaching the expected results; or have resources or skills which can significantly affect the quality of results. Typically, stakeholders are individuals or groups who hold the key to essential resources (such as financial investment) that the venture needs in order to succeed.

In addition to giving team members a stake in their own success, choosing which external stakeholders to involve in his venture was a crucial decision for Drew. Given his vision of a generatively empowered community, Drew wanted to minimize the need for outside providers of key resources. Drew wanted to create a venture that did not take "a billionaire to donate thousands of dollars," did not "require a medical team" and where he would not have to take the funds out of his own account and "bankroll it personally."

Drew's ambition was to secure essential resouces primarily from within the community and to make the moringa farm project self-sustaining in the long-term. The key stakeholders in the venture were the local "patrons" and external aid organizations.

Ultimately, the supplying of resources came 60% from the community and 40% from Peace Corps and USAID Food Security Funds. The aid organizations provided funding to help secure the fencing materials and beekeeping equipment. Community resources, which covered the land, labor, seeds, and transportation of materials, were acquired with the support of local "patrons." In Beninese society, *patrons* are invariably men who have acquired status and power as a result of gaining a certain level of wealth and education. Patrons gain allegiance and respect from local community members by "giving back" to them in the form of actions or gifts that contribute to the welfare of the community.

Drew was able to secure 3 hectares for his venture with the help of a local patron, Lucien, who had sufficient status to lobby for the land. In the rural areas of Benin there are no official government land offices or real estate brokers. Rather, a local official, or Delegué, decides who has rights to which land. Lucien was able to convince the Delegué of the value of Drew's project and acquire land adjacent to the village to be used for the farm. In return, both Lucien and the Delegué became beekeepers, getting hives and the necessary gear.

A key role for Drew with respect to the Moringa Farm project was to become a "champion of empowered being" and partner with institutions such as the local Beekeeping Association, health center and seed bank in order to obtain key resources.

According to Drew Dilts, vision is the foundation of any entrepreneurial activity. "Entrepreneurship is creating something new. Nothing exists yet. All you are armed with is a vision."

Establishing Key Partners and Alliances

Partnerships and alliances are win-win relationships that allow an entrepreneur to expand or leverage resources or to increase visibility. The most successful partnerships are those in which the roles of potential partners complement each other, creating an effective synergy between their resources.

Establishing some key partnerships was crucial to the success of Drew's moringa farm and beekeeping venture. By collaborating with a Beekeeping Association in the area, Drew's team was able to get the necessary equipment for half price. Alliances with a local health center and local volunteer seed bank helped to acquire the seeds necessary to start the farm; without these alliances, it would have been too expensive to buy the necessary quantity of moringa seeds. Partnering with the seed bank allowed Drew and his team to work out an exchange. The bank provided seeds to launch the farm. These "borrowed" seeds were then replenished from the venture's crops when they produced seeds, enabling the seed bank to sustain itself.

The Power of Vision

Vision relates to people's view of the larger system of which they are a part. As we have established, a vision is "a mental image of what the future will or could be like." It provides the overall direction for the team and defines the purpose of their interactions; i.e., *for whom or for what* a particular venture or path has been created.

For Drew Dilts, vision is the foundation of any entrepreneurial activity. "It is crucial," he says. "It is everything." Drew goes on to explain, "Entrepreneurship is creating something new. Nothing exists yet. All you are armed with is a vision."

Drew claims the most powerful visions are those in which you "visualize a future state that is a paradigm shift." The challenge, as Drew points out, is then "to help people get on board with a completely new concept for them." In the case of the moringa tree and beekeeping venture, Drew's vision was "not just growing plants on a big farm; but rather, an integrated system of moringa trees and bees in which everyone has their own parcel. However, you don't sell individually but rather sell together."

The combination of autonomy and collectivity was critical. For the reasons described earlier, it was important that each woman involved in the venture to have her own parcel. Drew notes, however, that he would not have been able to get the land for individuals. It had to be the whole community. "One woman could not have done it," he concludes.

Furthermore, selling the moringa and honey as a whole group enabled the villagers to attract bigger and wealthier buyers who could pay more. Marketing as a group allowed them to make twice as much for their excess crops as they would get selling as individuals because they could get better prices. This underscores the power of being a holon.

Of course, it was important to balance selling to large, wealthy buyers with improving the nutrition of their own village by keeping sales to locals affordable.

The approach Drew was proposing was quite new and unfamiliar to the villagers, however, and it took a lot of creative effort on Drew's part to convince them to participate. To be successful as an entrepreneur, "you need to have a deep grasp of your vision and a connection with the people you are trying to involve," he claims. "You have got to know the people you are working with, emphasizing points that will appeal to them."

Material wealth, for instance, was not a big motivation for the villagers. They lived simple lives (many in small mud huts) without electricity or plumbing. Drew found his biggest motivator was pride in communal wellbeing. "Do you want your community to be known as a strong, healthy community?" he asked. "Who here wants to see your neighbor's child die?" (Unfortunately, this was not an uncommon occurrence.) "Who knows a child who has died because he was too weak? What if you could do something to help him and make money at the same time?" He then pointed out, "Without too much effort, you can use this tree to make your community stronger and healthier and make money. Isn't that awesome?"

As Drew explains, "I had to find a way to be give them a glimmer of my bigger vision, then be flexible and be strategic without compromising the vision (i.e., making money while doing good for the community)."

It took a lot of creative effort on Drew's part to convince the villagers to participate in the venture. "You need to have a deep grasp of your vision and a connection with the people you are trying to involve," he claims. "You have got to know the people you are working with, emphasizing points that will appeal to them."

Drew found that his biggest motivator was pride in communal wellbeing. He was able to create resonance around the vision of "a strong, healthy community."

Creating Transformation at an Identity Level

According to Drew Dilts, "vision reshapes people's identity.

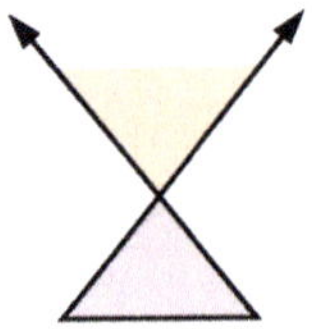

Identity relates to people's sense of their role or mission. These factors are a function of *who* a person or group perceives themselves to be, and who they are perceived as by others. The identity of a venture is related to the unique characteristics of its product, service or business and is what distinguishes a product or company from its competitors i.e., its branding.

As Drew maintains, "vision reshapes people's identity." In the case of his moringa/beekeeping venture, the consequence was to reshape the village into a "generatively empowered community." As an analogy for this shift in identity, Drew adds to the old adage that "If you give a man a fish, you feed him for a day; if you teach a man how to fish, you feed him for the rest of his life." Going one step further, he claims, "If you teach a person how to teach others to fish, you feed the community forever." In Drew's vision, the villagers would transform from "fishermen" into "problem solving community strengtheners."

As his vision and venture took shape, however, a number of identity issues emerged. Drew wanted his team to manage the farm as "businessmen and businesswomen," "sharing their story with other villages and trying to solve additional problems." In this way they would become "champions of empowered being" and would be able to authentically say, "We love solving problems" versus looking for handouts and quick answers.

In Drew's vision, the villagers would transform their identity into "problem solving community strengtheners."

One if his first challenges was how to get women to see themselves as businesswomen. Beninese village women, "don't see themselves as equal," Drew points out. The village women tend to be more followers. Women don't own property or even motorcycles (the primary form of transportation in the country). They can generally "only go as far as they can walk." They will say, "A patron is important because they have money and education. We are just poor women. We are nothing." Because they don't have individual pride, Drew had to leverage their tribal/community pride. When he explored the question, "Who do you see yourself as?" he realized that the village women saw their mission as "the health and well being of their children and community." That is they saw themselves primarily as contributors to the larger "holon." As mentioned earlier, Drew leveraged this as the foundation for creating a "business."

The village men had different identity issues. Drew realized that the men had more of an "ego" and a need for status. The men were more conscious of how others would view the project and their community. For example, it was important to the men that things looked "proper." Drew brought to their attention that one of their rival villages had begun beekeeping and were getting a reputation as excellent beekeepers. Given their rivalry, the men began to claim, "*Our* village should be the best beekeepers."

Learning and Living Core Values and Beliefs

Beliefs and values provide the reinforcement that supports or inhibits particular capabilities and actions. They relate to *why* a particular path is taken and the deeper motivations which drive people to act or persevere. Values, and related beliefs, determine how events and communications are interpreted and given meaning. Thus, they are the key to motivation and culture.

"Values and beliefs guide people to make individual decisions in line with the vision," says Drew.

Drew maintains, "Values and beliefs are clearly crucial, especially for the future." He asserts that "values and beliefs guide people to make individual decisions in line with the vision." For example, he knew that his team members had "got it" when they explained why they chose the other crops to grow along with the moringa trees. "These do not need pesticides," they explained. "We remembered that you said pesticides have bad chemicals, and the purpose of growing moringa is to improve health." Drew notes that "shared values and beliefs help the majority keep everyone else in line. If twelve of the sixteen voices say, 'no pesticides' it is easier for the remaining 4 to go along."

Drew knew that his team members had "got it" when they explained why they chose the other crops to grow along with the moringa trees. "These do not need pesticides," they explained. "We remembered that you said pesticides have bad chemicals, and the purpose of growing moringa is to improve health."

In addition to improving the health of the village community, the core values of the moringa farm venture were self-sufficiency and self-empowerment. Drew wanted the villagers to truly take on the belief "We can and should do it ourselves," and to constantly ask, "How can we creatively do something (e.g., plant the trees in a straight line) instead of ask for help?" One example of this was that, instead of going out and buying wood for the fences and stakes, the villagers collected it themselves for much less cost.

A major part of Drew's mission was to support the villagers to begin to live from the core belief that "For almost all problems out there, *we* can find a solution." He knew that, for the project to succeed, villagers would have to truly believe in what they are doing and that *they* could do it. As Drew put it, "The success of the future of the venture depends on the belief that they can grow it themselves. It is what transforms a temporary project into a sustainable enterprise."

A major part of Drew's mission was to support the villagers to begin to live from the core belief that "For almost all problems out there, we can find a solution."

It is at this stage, Drew explains, "They have been trained on nutrition and have methods and materials. Now they have to go out and do it themselves instead of just showing up and working hard." He adds, "Now is the true 'entrepreneurial' part. They can't just believe it themselves, they have to convince other villagers." It was in this area that the local woman Marthe, mentioned earlier, was indispensable as a model and mentor to instill a sense of responsibility and accountability.

Once people believed in themselves, "Even if disaster happened and destroyed the farm, they would find another solution."

In Drew's view, beliefs and values were ultimately even more important than the results of the particular venture. Once people believed in themselves, "Even if disaster happened and destroyed the farm, they would find another solution." If, as a consequence of the venture, people felt empowered and informed about an issue we are trying to tackle, Drew says, then "It was a smashing success." This is because: "People would be aware of nutrition and cooperation strategies. They would know what good/poor nutrition looks like and know that they can do something about it as a community." Drew went on to clarify, "Moringa is not the only answer nor a complete answer. With conscious awareness and reflection, a community of people who believe in themselves can find other and better solutions."

Expanding Key Capabilities

Capabilities relate to the mental maps, plans, strategies and skills that lead to success. They direct *how* actions are selected and monitored.

In the case of a new and challenging venture, *conflict resolution* is a critical capability for an entrepreneur according to Drew. "When you start something new," he says, "you don't have anything to fall back on. You have to confront conflict and resolve it quickly; especially between key stakeholders."

A crucial capability for launching a new venture is conflict resolution. "You have to confront conflict and resolve it quickly; especially between key stakeholders," says Drew. He had to sort out a potential dispute between the villagers and a nomadic family camped on the land to be used for the moringa farm.

As an example, in the case of the moringa/bee farm, Drew had secured 3 hectares for the project. When the team started clearing the land, however, they discovered a Fulani family was living on the land. The Fulani are a nomadic group that herds cattle across central Africa. They typically stay in one place for a year or two grazing their cattle before moving on to another area.

In Benin, there is frequently an ongoing, low intensity conflict between the nomadic Fulani and the Fon (the biggest ethnic group in the country). Because they are nomadic, the Fulani don't own land. Because their cattle trample parts of the crops of the land they cross, there is frequently tension between them and the Fon farmers.

Some villagers wanted to displace the family and tell them to move. Drew, however, felt that they were part of the extended community, even if they were a minority, and thus also a type of "stakeholder." Furthermore, it was a family, and the purpose of the venture was to support the wellbeing of the "whole community." Beyond that, Drew felt that displacing the family would incite friction (which had historically been there) and be a major distraction. He concluded that this was not how he wanted to start a new venture, creating bad energy and bad publicity. He believed, "we can find a way around it" and began exploring how to find a win-win solution, transforming the dilemma into a tetra lemma.

According to Drew, it was important to remember to keep asking, "What are we trying to do here?" This helped keep the connection to the larger vision and purpose of the venture. "It was clear," he says, "that we were not trying to drum up conflict between ethnic groups and tribes. And we don't want to uproot this family." Again the question was, "How can we deal with it without compromising the vision?"

Drew Surveys the Fulani Family Huts Discovered on the Moringa Farm Site

Drew convinced the villagers to start the farm on 1 1/2 hectares first. This would give an opportunity to establish the project and work out all of the challenges on a smaller scale, increasing its chances of success. It would simultaneously give the Fulani family time to move in their natural cycle.

This example points to another capability which is "sensitivity to feedback" from what could be called "field" indicators from the larger system in which one is operating. According to Drew, the Fulani incident was like a "sign from God" not to get too ambitious. When launching a transformational venture, Drew claims, "it is important to stay very aware of what works, what needs to change, what is ready and not ready." This is a subtle skill. It involves being aware of "energy" and your "instincts." Drew says it is not a matter of "blind trust" but rather using your instincts as a compass. It works best, he says, when this awareness of energy and instinct is combined with "research and due diligence."

Another key capability for entrepreneurs is that of social/ emotional intelligence. This means knowing customers', team members' and stakeholders' "worries and wants" and understanding how your project fits into that. "It is important to stay very aware of what works, what needs to change, what is ready and not ready," claims Drew.

A complementary capability for successful entrepreneurs, Drew maintains, is that of social/emotional intelligence. This involves being aware of what other people think about the venture and asking "What makes people motivated?" The earlier example of "money" versus "malnutrition" as a key community motivator is a good illustration of this. Drew asserts, "It is important to be in tune with what stakeholders and team members want." To accomplish this the entrepreneur must "Look into it. Be diligent. Know the culture that you are working with. Spend time with them. You cannot just 'survey a room'. You have to know the culture."

This means knowing stakeholders' "worries and wants" and understanding "how the project fits into that." Drew points out that it is important to "be strategic in executing the project in a way that gives them joy and satisfaction." Sometimes this means "meeting them half way."

As an example, the Beninese villagers did not understand the concept of "nutrition," but Drew had observed that Beninese people love potions and "cures" (the primary religion in the country is voodoo). He told them, "Take two spoons of this (moringa powder) every day and you will avoid a variety of illnesses." They responded with curiosity and enthusiasm. As Drew says, "Don't lie but frame it in a way they can understand it."

Another example was setting time frames for the work schedule on the farm. One of the more frustrating things about Beninese culture is that "people don't show up and they forget things." Trying to set deadlines in terms of a particular hour or even a specific time period each day would have been an impossible request. Instead, Drew used a week timeline. This created enough structure so that he and the team could be sure that things that needed get done were done on time, but gave the flexibility needed to match the cultural relationship to time.

Grounding Results in Behavioral Change

Behavioral factors are the specific action steps taken in order to reach success. They involve *what*, specifically, must be done or accomplished in order to succeed.

"The behavioral plan is an essential step," claims Drew. In the context of Drew's vision, success is measured in behavioral change. As he says, "The goal is ultimately to bring about behavioral change rather than a particular project result." "Other ventures may be more concerned with business results than behavioral change," he explains. "In this context, results matter but only to support your further goal which is behavioral change . . . I care for success at the level of the farms results because it will facilitate behavioral change."

According to Drew, to achieve generative empowerment, "success is measured in behavioral change." Drew found that "it was important to have written records or other evidence of participation" as a "silent, visible reminder and to bring attention to what people normally do but don't pay attention to."

Drew goes on to say, "Everyone's behavior is really important, more than words or even monetary results. If they start making money, it will facilitate behavioral change. Who cares if a specific project succeeds if people feel empowered and become empowered to start their own projects?"

As an entrepreneur, Drew believes "it is never OK to accept behavior that compromises the quality of the project with respect to the vision" (for example, using chemicals and pesticides when the whole purpose is to improve nutrition). On the other hand, Drew felt he had to be flexible with time schedules, as mentioned earlier, because of the culture, as long as it did not compromise the values and purpose of the project. It is not part of Beninese culture to think specifically about time or expectations.

In this regard, however, Drew found that "it was important to have written records or other evidence of participation – not for me but for them." According to Drew, "It was a silent, visible reminder and brings attention to what people normally do but don't pay attention to." It began to create a sense of accountability. Team members would begin to feel a sense of embarrassment when they realized their participation had been lagging, feeling "Oh gosh, I guess I haven't been doing very much this week." It also supported the egos of those who wanted to be able to say, "See. I was there!

Another key issue at the level of behavior for Drew involved his own actions. "How can I behave to get them to change their behavior?" he asked. "I am sure I could go out and make the project a success. I could dictate all of the steps of the project, with the villagers carrying it out. But that would defeat the purpose." On the other hand, he says, "It was important to be flexible with people's demands for my attendance. I didn't think it was necessary, but it turned out to be the best way to get everyone out there together; the best way for the motivated ones to get the other ones to work."

Another key issue at the level of behavior for Drew involved his own actions. "How can I behave to get them to change their behavior?"

A good example of how Drew adjusted his behavior to encourage initiative and "generative empowerment" was his strategy for dealing with village children. Drew explains that, in Benin, kids are always asking the "yovo" (white person) for money. Instead of giving money (which would just feed the belief that white people have all the money and all the answers) or ignoring the children as a "nuisance," Drew involved them in helping with the farming project.

Because Benin has a hot climate, people drink a lot of water. The water most often comes in small plastic bags. People drink the water and throw the bags along the side of the road, creating a sizeable amount of unsightly litter. Drew realized that, for the moringa project, they could use the bags to help grow the moringa seeds. "You cut off the top of the bag and punch holes in the bottom; fill the bag with soil and put in a single seed," Drew explains. "The bags allow you to line up the seeds more easily and make them easy to water. Moreover, to get started, you don't need land." Drew found that he could fit 900 bags in his small cement backyard.

Instead of just giving the kids money, Drew would pay them 50 Beninese francs (about 10 cents) for a hundred bags. This reduced the litter and supported the farming project at the same time. The kids got money, but with the sense that they "earned" it by doing something valuable.

According to Drew Dilts, environmental factors do not "dictate the vision" but they do determine how the vision will be expressed. "Vision transcends environmental factors, but environment influences the whole approach to the vision."

Adapting the Vision to the Environment

Environmental factors are the external circumstances and features that determine the concrete opportunities or constraints which individuals and organizations must recognize and to which they must react in order to succeed. Environmental factors relate to *where* and *when* actions must be taken.

Drew contends that ultimately, "environmental factors were the whole reason we did the thing." He goes on to clarify, "It did not dictate the vision (about nutrition, self-empowerment and collaboration), but determined how the vision was expressed." As Drew explains, he chose an agriculture project because the context was a rural environment. He chose moringa trees because malnutrition is a big issue in the local community. "We picked moringa because it was nutritious, durable and does not need special soil conditions. It can grow in sand. We knew what our constraints were for a number of other crops such as water requirements and soil quality." Beekeeping was chosen because they could get discounts and it synergized well with the moringa farms.

He chose a farm because they could get the land. Drew was aware that the Delegué was a supporter of moringa and believed he would be willing to give the villagers the land for such a project. He points out that if he hadn't been able to get the land, "maybe we would have just gone door to door and asked people to plant moringas in their yards."

The environment was a challenge for the farm. They had to clear the land and get started during the dry season. There was no rain and the villages have no irrigation. So the project was delayed 2 1/2 weeks because rains didn't come.

Drew concludes that "vision transcends environmental factors, but environment influences the whole approach to the vision."

Conclusion

Drew's case shows clearly how he created a significant "platform" in his Collaboration Spiral through the:

1. mastery of the relevant success factors
2. capacity to build the collaborative relationships necessary to create a robust Circle of Success
3. ability to engage in and facilitate collective intelligence and generative collaboration

Drew Dilts built his Circle of Success by applying many of the principles that we have been exploring in the first two volumes of this *Success Factor Modeling* series. He had a deep intuitive understanding of the various levels of success factors defined in *Success Factor Modeling Volume I* and summarized at the beginning of this book – Vision, Identity, Values and Beliefs, Capabilities, Behaviors and Environment. Drew was able to recognize, align, integrate and effectively address all of the levels of success factors necessary to bring his vision into action.

Drew also systematically worked on developing each quadrant of his Circle of Success: applying his vision to his customers to create a unique and beneficial project; aligning his team around the common mission of improving the health and well being of their community; leveraging the ambition of his stakeholders to acquire needed resources; and using his role to collaborate with partners in order to reduce costs and make win-win alliances.

Further, Drew intuitively applied many of the key concepts I have been presenting in this volume. Drew's passion for generative empowerment – his desire to improve the world and have his own mission live on beyond his life – is a good example of the *integration of ego and soul.* It shows an appreciation for oneself as a separate independent individual and also as a part that is in service of a larger whole.

Drew systematically worked on developing each quadrant of his Circle of Success: applying his vision to his customers to create a unique and beneficial project; aligning his team around the common mission of improving the health and well being of their community; leveraging the ambition of his stakeholders to acquire needed resources; and using his role to collaborate with partners in order to reduce costs and make win-win alliances.

Drew Dilts Moringa Farm's Circle of Success

DREW DILTS MORINGA FARM'S CIRCLE OF SUCCESS

VISION
Customers / Market

* GENERATIVELY EMPOWERED COMMUNITIES: COMMUNITIES THAT SUCCEED IN TACKLING THEIR OWN SERIOUS SOCIETAL PROBLEMS IN A COLLABORATIVE AND EMPOWERING WAY.

* A SUSTAINABLE INCOME-GENERATING PROJECT TO COMBAT MALNUTRITION USING NATURAL RESOURCES IN THE LOCAL AREA - AN INTEGRATED SYSTEM OF MORINGA TREES AND BEES IN WHICH COMMUNITY MEMBERS EACH HAVE THEIR OWN PARCEL.

AMBITION
Stakeholders / Investors

* SECURE RESOURCES FROM LOCAL COMMUNITY, PATRONS, THE US PEACE CORPS AND USAID FOOD SECURITY FUNDS.

* GAIN LOYALTY AND RESPECT FROM LOCAL COMMUNITY MEMBERS BY "GIVING BACK" TO THEM IN THE FORM OF ACTIONS OR GIFTS THAT CONTRIBUTE TO THE WELFARE OF THE COMMUNITY.

MISSION
Team Members / Employees

* THE HEALTH AND WELL BEING OF CHILDREN AND THE COMMUNITY

* ENCOURAGING THE RECOGNITION AND SHARING OF "BEST PRACTICES".

ROLE
Partners / Alliances

* CHAMPIONS OF EMPOWERED BEING

* KEY PARTNERSHIPS WITH LOCAL BEEKEEPING ASSOCIATION, LOCAL HEALTH CENTER AND SEED BANK.

PASSION:
GENERATIVE EMPOWERMENT

Drew's vision of a "generatively empowered community" is an excellent expression of the notions of "holon," "hologram" and "task significance." Each member contributes to the larger whole and also benefits individual from the success of the larger whole. Drew's idea for "a collaborative, empowering, sustainable income-generating project to combat malnutrition using natural resources in the local area" created multiple wins at multiple levels of holons; individual, family, village, community and ultimately country.

A large part of Drew's success resulted from his ability to create synergies between stakeholders, customers and team members. Drew's development of an integrated system of moringa trees and bees in which community members each have their own parcel is an expression of creating and leveraging different types of synergy. On an environmental level, it leveraged the synergy between moringa farming and beekeeping, keeping the trees cross-pollinated and doubling the honey output of the bees. This in turn created better community health, greater crop yields and extra income for villagers.

Drew was able to align his team members around the mission of improving the health and well being of children and the community, creating a strong perceived "task significance" for their actions. By allocating each team member her or his own parcel and creating autonomy within the collective, Drew was directly leveraging the dual nature of peoples' reality as holons. As separate individuals, it fostered a sense of pride and accountability. At the same time it nurtured collective intelligence on the community level through the setting of collective standards and exchange of best practices. Additionally, the excess moringa powder and honey that the villagers sold as a collective could yield a higher price from neighboring towns than they would get trying to sell the same items as individuals.

Drew's ability to persuade key external stakeholders, such as the local patron and Delegué who had succeeded as individuals in terms of material wealth and possessions, to contribute the land, funds for seeds, transportation of materials and other essential resources to the project was another major success factor. He was able to convince them that they would gain greater loyalty and respect from local community members by "giving back" to them in the form of actions that would contribute to the welfare of the community; thus reinforcing the win-win loop between individual success and community success.

By having those involved in his venture take on the role of "champions of empowered being," Drew was able to establish key partnerships with the regional beekeeping association, local health center and seed bank in order to substantially reduce costs and make the project viable.

In summary, Drew Dilts' Beninese moringa farm/beekeeping project provides a clear and powerful example of applying the success factor we have defined in the first two volumes of this work to create a successful and transformational venture. Even though the specific contents and contexts may vary, the process that Drew followed furnishes an explicit framework for bringing a transformational vision into reality.

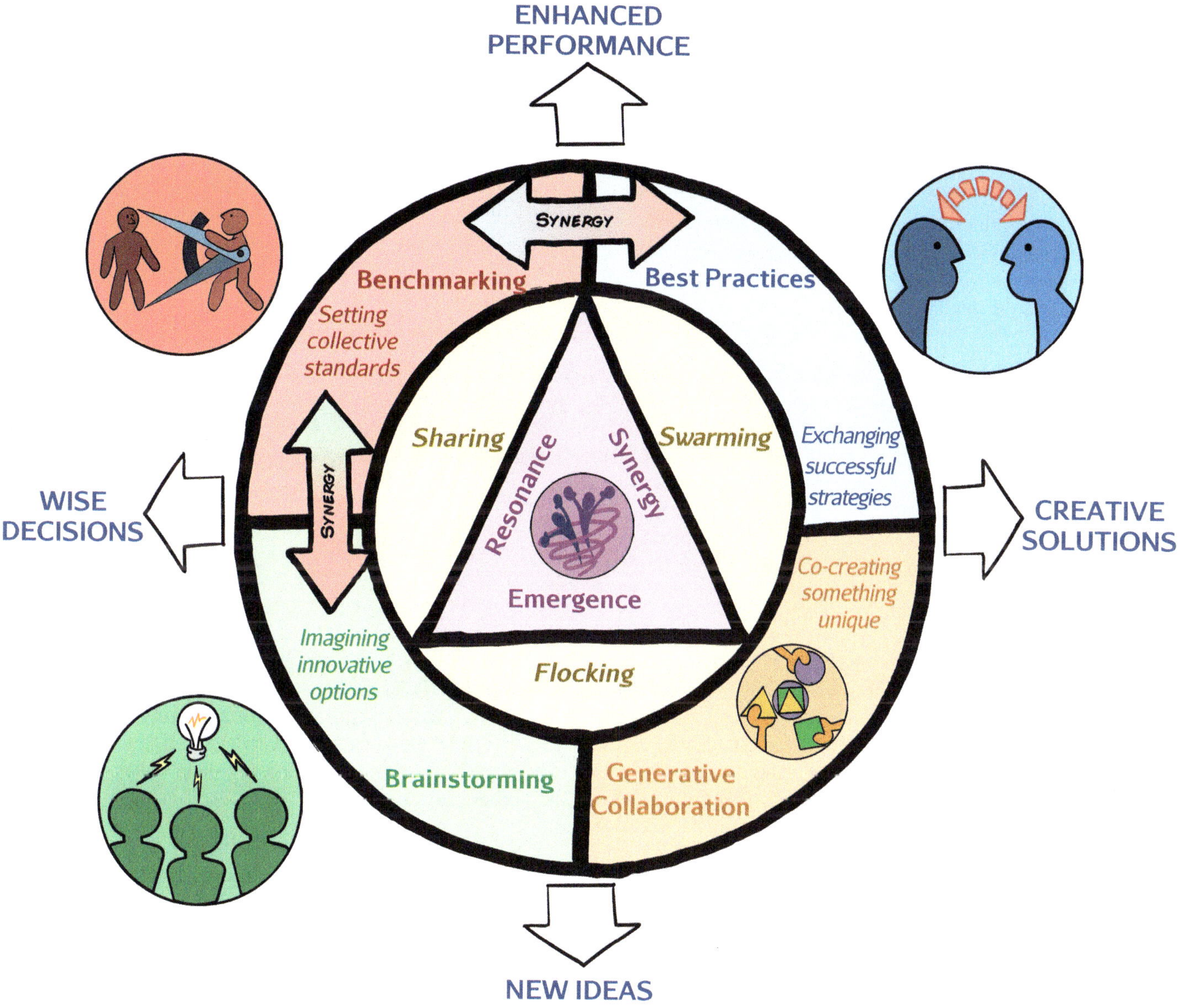

Much of Drew's success resulted from his ability to create synergies between stakeholders, customers and team members.

Chapter Summary

Wisdom is "the ability to think and act using knowledge, experience, understanding, common sense, and insight." It involves having a broad and balanced perspective that allows a person or group to make better and more ecological choices and decisions. Developing wisdom requires an understanding of people, goals and situations, and how they interact in order to determine an optimal course of action. This presupposes the ability to invite and integrate multiple perspectives. *Making wiser decisions* is one of the primary benefits and outcomes of fostering collective intelligence.

The *wisdom of crowds* refers to the phenomenon that, under the right circumstances, groups show remarkable wisdom and intelligence "and are often smarter than the smartest people in them." According to author James Surowiecki, collective decisions are most likely to be good ones when they are made by people with diverse opinions reaching independent conclusions, relying primarily on their private information. Under these conditions, a type of collective wisdom emerges, guiding the group, like an "invisible hand," to an optimal outcome.

The fact that the average group estimate, when guessing quantities (such as the number of pieces of candy in a jar), is generally much closer to the actual quantity than almost all of the individual estimates is a simple but compelling illustration of this. Other examples include the development of Open Source computer codes (like Linux) and the discovery of the solution the SARS epidemic in 2003, which resulted from research done and data collected by many different hospitals and universities around the world, working with no single central coordinating organization.

One of the major interferences to the wisdom of groups is conformity or "group think." Instead of increasing the group's wisdom, conformity and consensus restrict the exploration of other possible alternatives or ideas. In order to "fit in" or gain approval or confirmation of their own opinions, people are often swayed by what others say and think. Thus, it is important to have:

1. *Diversity of opinion* (people represent a wide range of perspectives)
2. *Independence* (people's opinions are not determined by the opinions of those around them)
3. *Decentralization* (people are able to specialize and draw upon local information)
4. *Aggregation* (some unbiased mechanism exists for turning individual conclusions into a collective decision)

In addition, it is important for a group to share a *common vision or purpose.* This creates the possibility for group members to balance self-interest with the common good (i.e., "ego" and "soul") and find ways to benefit the group while simultaneously advancing their own goals and ambitions.

The results of *Google's search for the perfect team* adds several other conditions that can increase the "collective I.Q." of a group. After spending millions of dollars and thousands of hours gathering data on the traits and behavior patterns of people within teams that exhibited different levels of performance, Google researchers concluded the composition of a team made little if any difference. Instead, they found certain key behavior patterns to be most important, such as *"equality in distribution of conversational turn-taking"* and *"social sensitivity"*; i.e., perceiving how how others feel based on their tone of voice, facial expressions and other nonverbal cues.

Google researchers concluded that these traits produce a sense of *"psychological safety"* and "a team climate characterized by interpersonal trust and mutual respect in which people are comfortable being themselves.'' According to Google's data, psychological safety, along with *perceived task significance* of how their actions fit in with Google's larger vision, were most crucial for making a team work effectively.

Creating the various conditions to bring out the wisdom of crowds and enhance a group's collective I.Q. can be summarized in the following six steps for activating the wisdom of crowds:

1. Create a COACH container.
2. Identify a common intention/purpose.
3. Create a generative performance state.
4. Focus attention on a goal or problem, gathering multiple perspectives.
5. Hold all perspectives from a state of respect and curiosity.
6. Allow new ideas and possibilities to emerge.

In addition to a number of other processes and exercises presented in this book, these steps are supported by two important collaboration catalysts. *Shifting from CRASH to COACH State* is a collaboration catalyst that involves group members establishing shared non-verbal signals whose purpose is to help keep the group in a COACH state and create a deeper sense of social sensitivity and psychological safety.

The *Tetra Lemma Group Process* is another collaboration catalyst that supports psychological safety by establishing a ritualized structure for transforming dilemmas created by differing and frequently contradictory perspectives into an opportunity for greater awareness and wisdom.

The Success Factor Case Study of *Drew Dilts' Benin Moringa Farm and Bee Keeping Project* for the United States Peace Corps provides a rich and clear example of how apply the various success factors that we have been exploring in the first to volumes of Success Factor Modeling to produce "generative empowerment." *Generative empowerment* is a form of collective intelligence that involves "empowering people with the skills and self-confidence to become leaders for societal improvement who then, in turn, empower those around them in the same generative way." Drew's vision for "a collaborative, empowering, sustainable income-generating project to combat malnutrition using natural resources in the local area" created multiple wins at multiple levels of holons; individual, family, village, community and ultimately country.

References:

- https://en.wikipedia.org/wiki/Wisdom
- http://www.dailygood.org/story/607/how-to-think-like-a-wise-person-adam-grant/
- The Wisdom of Crowds, James Surowiecki, Anchor Books, New York, NY, 2005.
- What Google Learned From Its Quest to Build the Perfect Team; Charles Duhigg, NYTimes.com, 2/28/2016 — http://www.nytimes.com/2016/02/28/magazine/what-google-learned-from-its-quest-to-build-the-perfect-team.html?emc=eta1&_r=0

Conclusion

A human being is a part of the whole called by us universe, a part limited in time and space. He experiences himself, his thoughts and feeling as something separated from the rest, a kind of optical delusion of his consciousness. This delusion is a kind of prison for us, restricting us to our personal desires and to affection for a few persons nearest to us. Our task must be to free ourselves from this prison by widening our circle of compassion to embrace all living creatures and the whole of nature in its beauty."

Albert Einstein

I get by with a little help from my friends.

John Lennon & Paul McCartney

I GET BY WITH A LITTLE HELP FROM MY FRIENDS
ANTONIO MEZA

Conclusion

Our world is changing rapidly. It is also becoming increasingly complex. The limitations of the intellect and energy of a single individual are more and more apparent as the new generation of entrepreneurs and leaders tries to tackle problems relating to our global economy, national security, planetary environment, communal health, collective identity, etc. If we are to accomplish anything of any significance, we must, in the words of the well-known Beatle's song, have "a little help from our friends." If we are to accomplish something of great significance, we will need a lot of help, including from those we have never met in person.

If we and our ventures are to survive and thrive in our modern world, we need to unleash the creative power of collective intelligence in order to foster generative collaboration, produce disruptive innovations, cultivate generative communities, promote dynamic teaming, release the wisdom of crowds and accelerate generative empowerment.

Throughout this book we have been exploring the various ways to apply the principles and practices that foster collective intelligence to solve problems, manage change and create new possibilities. Starting from the fundamental mindset that we are both separate, unique individuals and simultaneously also part of successively larger "holons," we have been examining ways to create *resonance*, *synergy* and *emergence* in groups and teams via basic processes such as *sharing*, *swarming* and *flocking*. Through the Success Factor Case Studies and SFM Collaboration Catalysts, we have seen how the actions of *benchmarking*, *best practices*, *brainstorming* and *generative collaboration* can be used in different combinations to achieve *enhanced performance*, make *wiser decisions*, come up with *new ideas* and generate *creative solutions*.

We have also seen how the actions and outcomes of collective intelligence can be strengthened and enriched through other key success factors such as *sharing a common vision and purpose*, having a clear perception of *task significance* and developing the capacity to take multiple *perceptual positions*.

When combined with the SFM Circle of Success, the principles and practices of collective intelligence greatly accelerate and increase our chances of creating a successful and scalable project or venture. Enhanced performance helps us to achieve *financial robustness*; wiser decisions support us to make *meaningful contributions*; new ideas are essential for generating *game changing innovations*; and creative solutions expedite our ability to produce *scalable growth*.

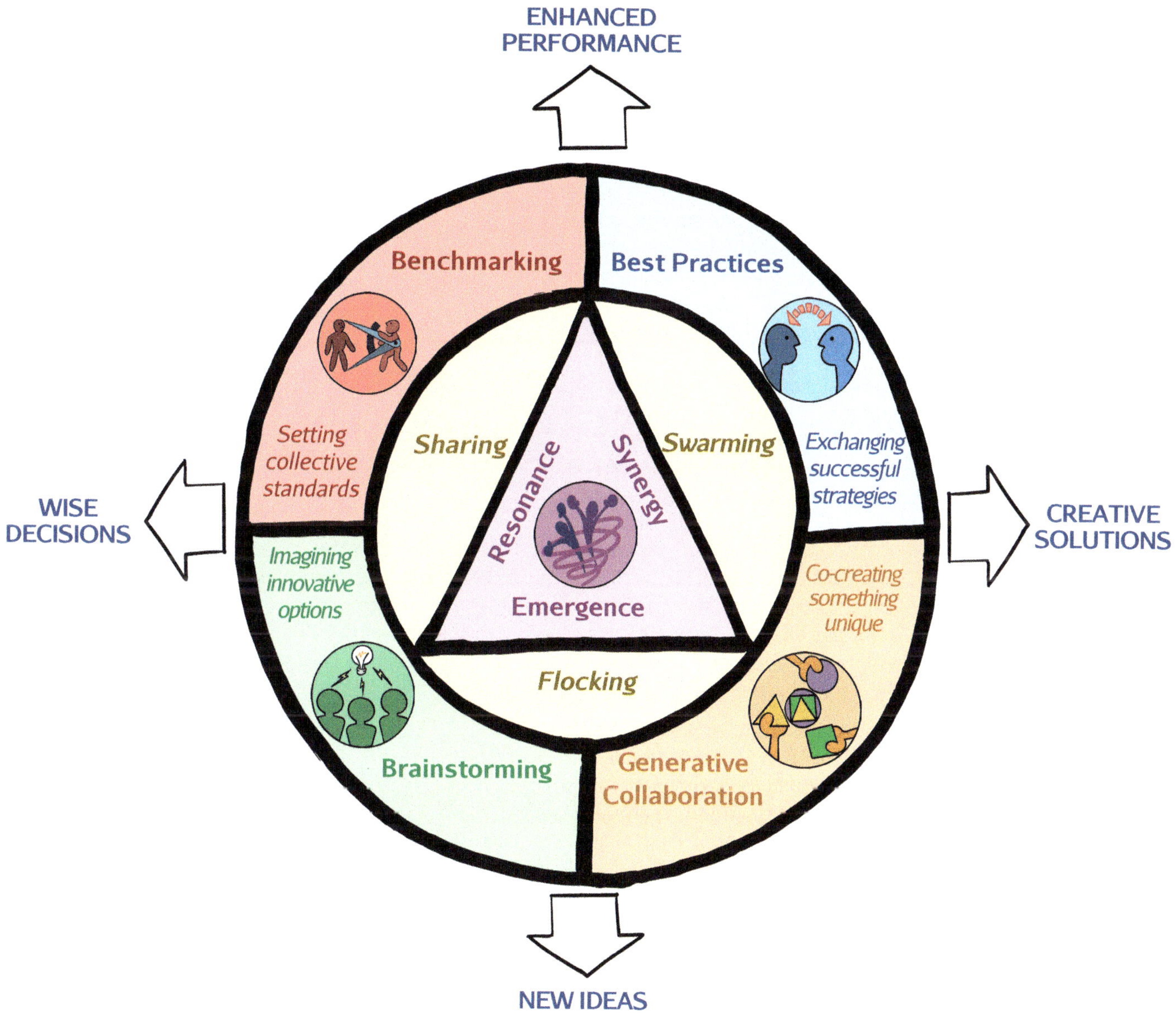

The SFM Collective Intelligence Model summarizes the fundamental features of mindset and the key actions and outcomes related to applying the principles of collective intelligence.

A Review of Key Themes

The purpose of this book has been to present, examine and explore a number of different ways that collective intelligence and generative collaboration can be supported and applied to increase the potential for success of groups, projects and ventures.

In Chapter 1 we established how collective intelligence can be applied in ventures and companies to share and leverage resources in order to expand business opportunities and create new markets— i.e., to make a "bigger pie" to share. I presented *Mastermind groups* as a powerful example of how collective intelligence can be applied to entrepreneurial endeavors by their offering a combination of brainstorming, education, peer accountability and support in a group setting in order to sharpen each member's business and personal skills. Facilitators of Mastermind groups assist the group to engage in various types of collaboration catalysts. *Collaboration catalysts* are processes that produce some degree of resonance, synergy and/or emergence between members of a group who are working together in some way. Creating a COACH Container, Fostering a "Field" of Co-Sponsorship and Exploring and Sharing Best Practices through Success Factor Modeling are examples of collaboration catalysts that create a foundation for collective intelligence.

In Chapter 2 we explored how the basic processes for collective intelligence could be expanded in order to produce generative collaboration. *Generative collaboration* emerges as a result of collective visioning in which people share and synergize their individual passions and visions; similar to bubbles joining together to create a larger whole, or two hydrogen atoms and an oxygen atom combining to form water. In generative collaboration, people stimulate each other to think "outside of the box" and support one another to achieve things that are new and unprecedented. Generative collaboration is enhanced through collaboration catalysts such as Creating a Generative Performance State, Intervision and Making a Second Position Analysis.

As we showed in Chapter 3, generative collaboration is essential for disruptive innovations. *Disruptive innovations* are those that create new markets and bring major changes for both customers and companies. Disruptive innovations emerge from synergies of values and identity between members of the different parts of the Circle of Success that create virtual communities whose vision goes beyond what currently exists. Disruptive innovations generally emerge from collaborations between early adopters among customers and pioneers within the venture. They also frequently require open innovation and generative collaboration between groundbreakers within a venture and partners who are trailblazers. These virtual communities can be likened to a colony of "bats" who are able to identify and act upon weak signals related to new opportunities and possibilities, versus "frogs" who simply wait until the potential is obvious.

Fourth Position (the collective or "we" position) is necessary for establishing strong bonds between collaborators within virtual communities and forming a generative *relational field*. Fourth position can be fostered through collaboration catalysts like *Identifying Resonance for Task Significance* and through *Collective Creativity Catalysts* that promote generative interactions between collaborators by encouraging people find and share ideas that they are passionate about and identify the weak signals related to future trends.

The theme of Chapter 4 was applying collective intelligence and generative collaboration to cultivate a generative venture community. A *generative venture community* is one in which members support one another to both grow personally as well as contribute to each other's ventures. Thus, there is a positive feedback loop between the growth of the individual and the growth of the community. Generative communities foster a *winning culture* that promotes an expectation of a positive

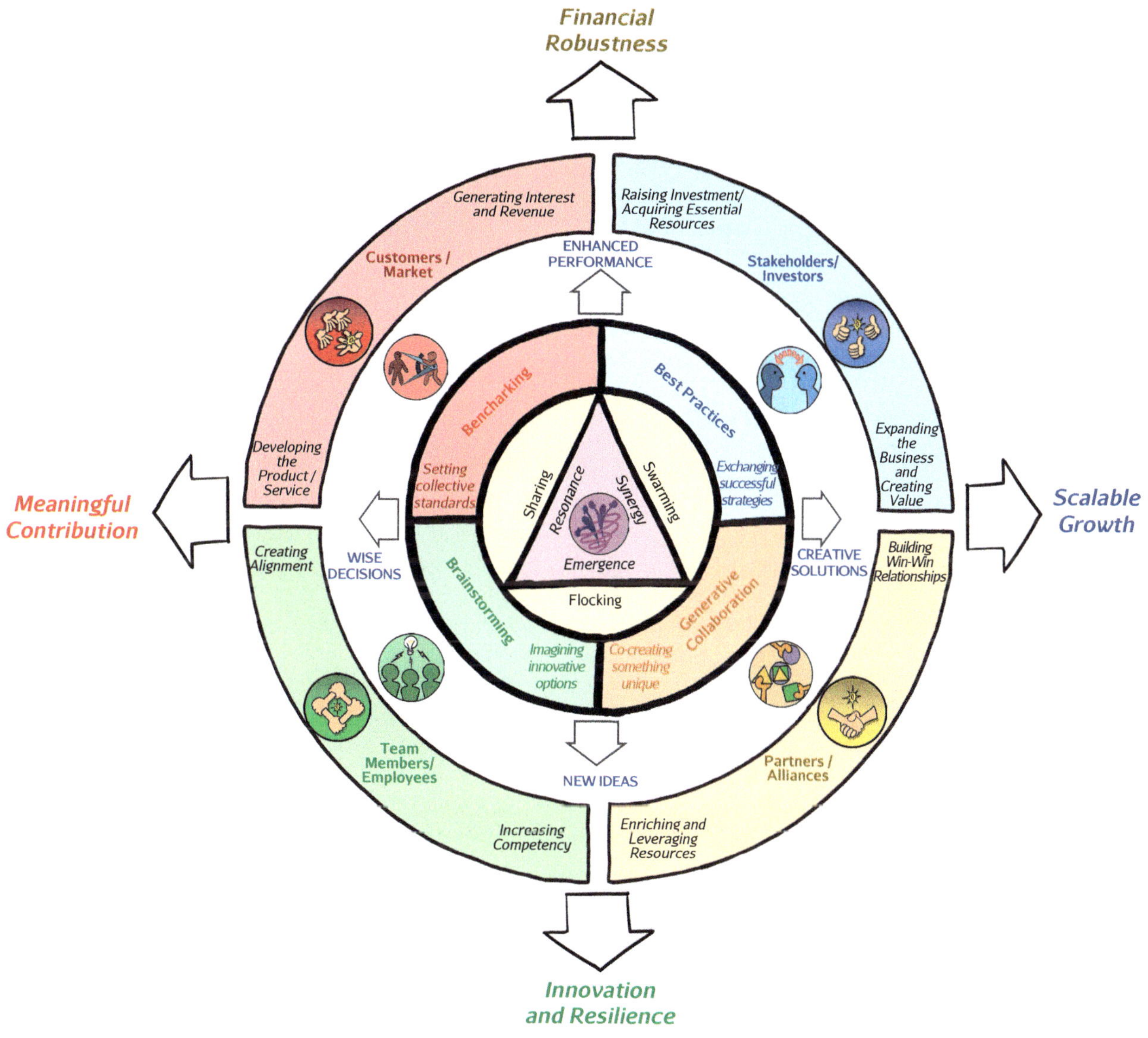

The principles and practices of collective intelligence greatly enhance our ability to build an effective Circle of Success.

future, a feeling of capability and responsibility within the community members and a sense of self-worth and belonging. In the winning culture of a generative venture community, people believe in one another and affirm each other's abilities to reach dreams and goals. Collaboration catalysts like the Group Affirmation and Dream Guardians exercises can help to create an empowering "field" of support between team members or collaborators that increases each person's chances of success.

The SFM Collaboration Spiral™ is a model that illustrates how establishing key relationships and collaborations can create an ascending spiral of successive platforms, in the form of projects or ventures, which extend our range of influence and move us along the trajectory of our mission towards our ultimate vision. Platforms are built through a network of generative collaborations that help us to establish a robust Circle of Success and enrich or strengthen the various levels of success factors (environment, behaviors, capabilities, beliefs and values and identity) needed to be effective in the project or venture connected with that platform. The successful establishment of a new platform creates an expansion our identity and scope of influence beyond who we have been.

The major theme of Chapter 5 was dynamic teaming. *Dynamic Teaming* is a form of teamwork in which group members complement each other's competencies and personal traits, share the responsibility for results and work together to achieve more than is possible by the sum of their individual efforts. *Dynamic Team Development* involves creating the conditions in which teams engaged in entrepreneurial activities can "flock" together to produce the greatest impact in the service of a common mission and vision. Collaboration catalysts like Resource Mining, Aligning Roles Within a Common Vision and Modeling Dynamic Teaming Success Factors help to establish an effective infrastructure for collaboration by defining and benchmarking the key success factors required for dynamic teaming and generative collaboration.

Chapter 6 examined the conditions necessary to activate the wisdom of crowds. *The wisdom of crowds* refers to the phenomenon that, under the right circumstances, groups show remarkable wisdom and intelligence "and are often smarter than the smartest people in them." Wise groups tend to be made up of people with diverse opinions reaching independent conclusions, relying primarily on their private information. In addition, it is important for the group members to share *a common vision or purpose*. The results of *Google's search for the perfect team* showed that the composition of a team made little if any difference. Instead, certain key behaviors amongst team members, such as *"equality in distribution of conversational turn-taking,"* and *"social sensitivity"* along with *perceived task significance* are most crucial for making a team work effectively.

The ability to invite and integrate multiple perspectives in the service of a common vision and mission creates the possibility for generative empowerment. *Generative empowerment* is a form of collective intelligence that involves "empowering people with the skills and self-confidence to become leaders for societal improvement who then, in turn, empower those around them in the same generative way."

A Concluding Example of the Power of Collective Intelligence

It seems clear that the fundamental actions of collective intelligence — *benchmarking, best practices, brainstorming* and *generative collaboration* — are the foundations for successful and scalable ventures. These actions can be facilitated by collaboration catalysts such as those presented in this book. It is important to remember, however, that the actions and collaboration catalysts that promote collective intelligence and the phenomena of generative collaboration flow naturally and spontaneously from a *mindset* that values collective intelligence and views individuals, teams and organizations as all part of the same larger holon.

A good example of this is the experience of my daughter Julia Dilts in her job with the online travel agency Expedia. Launched in 1996 as a small division of Microsoft when the Internet was still in its infancy, Expedia, Inc. has grown into the world's leading online travel company; with a portfolio including a number of the world's most notable travel brands such as Travelocity, Hotels.com and Orbitz.

Julia, then a recent graduate in Travel Industry Management from the University of Hawaii, started working for Expedia in November 2014 in their Honolulu office as a Market Associate. Expedia was in a period of rapid expansion and lodging is one of the most lucrative areas of their business. While the Hawaii Expedia group already had relationships with the big hotel chains in the region, they wanted to proactively seek new listings for smaller hotels and other types of accommodations. Julia was hired to facilitate this expansion.

Expedia's clients are essentially partners, and there are a number of steps necessary to bring a new listing on board. Julia's role was to have "frontline" contact with the new properties to be listed. She then had to coordinate with several other support functions in order to negotiate percentages, establish pricing, create the online listing, etc.

Because this was a relatively new activity within the company, and involved a significant number of new listings, Julia was trying to understand and organize the progress of her own work and how it coordinated with the other support functions and teams. Only a few months into her job, Julia was trying to clarify and keep track of where her properties were in the various stages of the process. She collaborated virtually with another team of individuals from the mainland (Seattle, where Expedia is headquartered), whom she had never met, and made a type of spreadsheet that tracked the progress of the various activities related to new property listings.

At the following weekly meeting of the Honolulu team, Julia's boss' boss, the Director of Market Management for Hawaii, Alejandro Moxey, asked about the status of several various new properties – as the team was trying to get them published online as quickly as possible. Julia responded, presenting the spreadsheet that she had created by collaborating with the Content Team in Seattle, and was able to show in a single view what the current state of each client was.

Alejandro recognized the value of the effort and said to Julia, "This is great. It is exactly what we had in mind when we hired you." He asked Julia to send him the basic bullet points outlining the process that she and her colleague had used to make the spreadsheet. Julia reflected on the process she had intuitively followed and generalized the steps so they could be applied by anyone else in her position, adding input from her colleague in Seattle. She then sent the summary of their key steps to Alejandro.

Alejandro proceeded to forward Julia's email to his own boss, the Vice President of Market Management for the entire region. The Vice President also saw the value in the process and decided to send out the summary to everyone in the entire North American region that were Senior Market Managers and above as information to help them to streamline their regions' practices for managing new listings.

The result was that the effective local efforts of a new hire were spread throughout the company, enhancing the efficiency and performance of others who never met Julia but were benefitting from her individual intelligence and contribution as well as her collective efforts with her colleagues.

There are a number of significant points in this example. Firstly, Julia's Director Alejandro could have easily discounted or belittled the input from a young new hire who had only been with the organization a few months. Secondly, if he believed the input was important and useful, Alejandro could have also taken credit for it himself and not forwarded Julia's message, but copied it as if it were his idea; as can frequently happen in many organizations.

Instead, Alejandro directly acknowledged Julia's and her colleagues' efforts and collaborative contribution. Similarly, the Vice President of the region did the same thing. Julia and her colleague benefitted by getting acknowledgement and exposure for their work. The company benefitted from the spread of an effective process that could be replicated by others in the company. Alejandro also benefitted by being the person who saw that Julia's individual contribution was valuable for the larger system of the organization.

Needless to say, Julia felt very validated and was highly motivated by this sequence of events to continue to do her best and contribute as much as possible to the company.

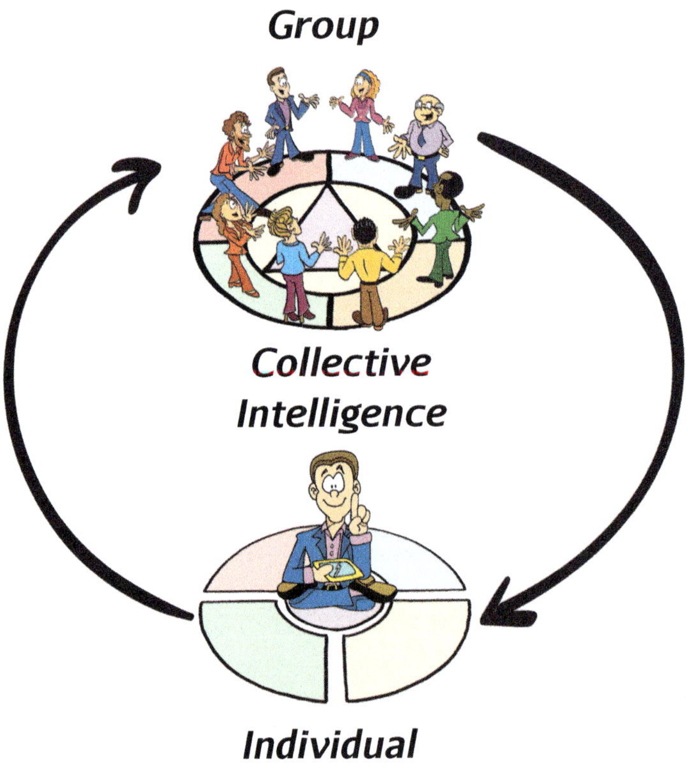

Closing Reflections

Julia's example with Expedia illustrates a fundamental principle that we have emphasized throughout this volume: that individual efforts and contributions benefit the effectiveness and performance of the larger system. When those contributions, in turn, create benefits for the individual, you have a "virtuous circle" that will produce an escalating pattern of collective success.

In this case, there were multiple examples of collaboration. Firstly was Julia's efforts at benchmarking and brainstorming with her colleagues in order to get a clearer sense of the business processes in which they were engaged. The next example of collaboration involved the sharing of best practices within Julia's team. A third instance of collective intelligence was Alejandro's dissemination of relevant best practices to his boss and ultimately the entire region.

It is clearly safe to say that companies like Expedia have grown and prospered by implementing a winning culture, establishing a collaborative mindset and encouraging generative empowerment.

From the perspective of Success Factor Modeling, a winning culture based upon collective intelligence emerges from the balance and integration of ourselves as both unique, independently thinking individuals and at the same time as part of a larger holon. The following quotation from Albert Einstein captures the relationship quite clearly:

> *The individual, if left alone from birth, would remain primitive and beast-like in his thoughts and feelings to a degree that we can hardly conceive. The individual is what he is and has the significance that he has not so much in virtue of his individuality, but rather as a member of a great human society, which directs his material and spiritual existence from the cradle to the grave.*
>
> *A man's value to the community depends primarily on how far his feelings, thoughts, and actions are directed towards promoting the good of his fellows. We call him good or bad according to how he stands in this matter. It looks at first sight as if our estimate of a man depended entirely on his social qualities.*
>
> *And yet such an attitude would be wrong. It is clear that all the valuable things, material, spiritual and moral, which we receive from society can be traced back through countless generations to certain creative individuals. The use of fire, the cultivation of edible plants, the steam engine – each was discovered by one person.*
>
> *Only the individual can think, and thereby create new values for society – nay, even set up new moral standards to which the life of the community conforms. Without creative, independently thinking and judging personalities the upward development of society is as unthinkable as the development of the individual personality without the nourishing soil of the community.*

As Einstein's comments imply, a healthy, creative and intelligent group, team or organization is one that expands and prospers through the individual vision, ideas and passion of its members. It is structured in such a way that there is a positive feedback loop between the growth of the individual and the growth of the group, team or community. Collective intelligence emerges as a result of creating this type of generatively reinforcing feedback loop between individual and group.

And, as we have seen in our Success Factor Case Examples, accomplishing this generatively reinforcing feedback loop in an organization requires a high degree of emotional intelligence and conscious leadership. These are the focus of next volume of this series on *Conscious Leadership and Resilience.*

Collective Intelligence

Collective intelligence Is not just a gathering.
It is a meeting of the souls,
Of the hearts and of the minds.
It takes a village to raise a child.
It takes water, sun, wind, stillness and a fertile soil for the seed to become a tree.
So ask yourself: "What part will I play in this collective?"
"How can I create the space to welcome your very unique contribution?"
Ask yourself: "With how much joy will you all jam your song like no one has heard before?"
"What is that merging dance of individual and group, of holon to holon, through holon?
I bring out the best in you.
You bring out the best in me, in us.
And together we are an incredible force, So much more than the sum of the parts.
Like the sand on the plate resonating with sound,
Ask yourself: "What is the vibration that allows us to vibrate together?"
And like the sand on the plate, notice how beautiful and meaningful this merging is!
Collective intelligence is the meeting of the best of me with the best of you for the best of us.
We are equal partners in this enterprise for we all value each other and have a vivid commitment to support the intention and the goal.
In this dance between structure and freedom, the power lies in the process that sustains inclusion, consent and transparency.
Anything is possible when we bring our super powers to the circle!
And I, for one, am really curious about what is possible when you and you and you and I are in resonance.

Dorothy Oger

Santa Cruz, California, August 20th, 2015

References:

- https://en.wikipedia.org/wiki/Expedia_(website)
- http://www.expediainc.com/about/history/
- *The World As I See It*, Einstein, A., Citadel Press, Secaucus, N.J., 1934.

Afterword

I hope you have enjoyed this exploration of Success Factor Modeling™ and the SFM Collective Intelligence Model™. If you are interested in learning about the principles and technology of Success Factor Modeling in more depth, other resources and tools exist to further develop and apply the distinctions, strategies and skills described within these pages.

Dilts Strategy Group

Dilts Strategy Group is an organization committed to providing the training, consulting and coaching in the applications of Success Factor modeling, including Next Generation Entrepreneurship, Collective Intelligence, Leadership and Innovation. Dilts Strategy Group also sponsors research projects promoting the development of new models and the identification of evolving success factors in the dynamic social and economic world in which we live. Dilts Strategy Group offers trainings and certification programs in Success Factor Modeling throughout the world.

For more information please contact:

Dilts Strategy Group
P.O. Box 67448
Scotts Valley CA 95067
USA
Phone: (831) 438-8314
E-Mail: info@diltstrategygorup.com
Homepage: http://www.diltstrategygroup.com

In addition to the training programs I offer through Dilts Strategy Group, I also travel extensively internationally, presenting seminars and workshops on a variety of topics related to personal and professional development.

For more information on scheduled programs, please consult my website: http://www.robertdilts.com or write for information to: rdilts@nlpu.com.

Journey to Genius

I have also written a number of other books and developed audio recordings based on the principles and distinctions of Success Factor Modeling and NLP. For example, I have produced several products based on my modeling of Strategies of Genius such as audio recordings describing the creative processes of geniuses such as Mozart, Walt Disney and Leonardo Da Vinci.

For more information on these and other products and resources, please contact:

Journey to Genius
P.O. Box 67448
Scotts Valley, CA 95067-7448
Phone (831) 438-8314
E-Mail: info@journeytogenius.com
Homepage: http://www.journeytogenius.com

NLP University

I am also a co-founder, director and trainer at *NLP University*, an organization committed to providing the highest quality trainings in basic and advanced NLP skills, and to promoting the development of new models and applications of NLP in the areas of health, business and organization, creativity and learning. Each summer, NLP University holds residential programs at the University of California at Santa Cruz, offering extended residential courses on the skills of NLP, including those related to business consulting and coaching.

For more information please contact Teresa Epstein at:

NLP University
P.O. Box 1112
Ben Lomond, California 95005
Phone: (831) 336-3457
Fax: (831) 336-5854
E-Mail: Teresanlp@aol.com
Homepage: http://www.nlpu.com

Success Factor Modeling illustrations and products

Antonio Meza and I have created this series of books with the intention of offering you something different, fun and visually rich. Through the pages of this book and the following volumes you will find many memorable illustrations and characters that will help you create a deeper connection with the content of the book.

We have created a special online store where you can find a variety of products like posters, t-shirts, mugs, etc that can help you to stay connected to the main concepts of Next Generation Entrepreneurship.

For more information on these and other products and resources, you can visit:

Success Factor Modeling website

Homepage: http://www.successfactormodeling.com

Success Factor Modeling product store

Homepage: http://society6.com/successfactormodeling

Antonio Meza illustrates books, articles, presentations and also performs as a graphic facilitator for conferences and seminars. He is also a business consultant, trainer and coach member of the Dilts Strategy Group.

If you are curious about Antonio's work as an illustrator, you can contact him at: t

Antoons

E-Mail: hola@antoons.net

Homepage: http://www.antoons.net

Conscious Leaders Mastermind

The Conscious Leaders Mastermind is an exclusive, accelerated growth program for successful entrepreneurs and business owners. Conscious Leaders integrates the seven core strategies shared by the world's most successful people with the practices of conscious leadership. This provides participants with a clear roadmap for sustainable success, accelerated growth, and positive impact (see Chapter 1, pp. 66-71). Current members include influential leaders from a variety of fields who have positively impacted the lives of hundreds of millions of people.

Conscious Leaders Mastermind was created by author Robert Dilts, Mitchell Stevko (a Silicon Valley growth expert who has helped over 150 entrepreneurs achieve their dreams, raising over $5 billion in capital) and Dr. Olga Stevko (a Russian MD and Belief Medicine expert who specializes working with high level professionals). The Conscious Leaders Mastermind program is available only by approved application and interview or member referral.

If you are ready to take your business and your abilities to an entirely new level of impact and influence, you can learn more and apply for membership at:

E-Mail: mitchell@consciousleadersmm.com

Homepage: http://www.consciousleadersmm.com

Logical Levels Inventory

Logical levels inventory (***lli***) is an innovative online leadership profiling tool based on the various levels of success factors that we have been exploring in this book. ***lli*** identifies the key qualities that leaders need to possess in order take advantage of opportunities and remain successful in times of uncertainty and crisis. Developed as a direct result of the first Success Factor Modeling certification program, ***lli*** takes you through a self-assessment process that helps you uncover the driving forces behind your actions and provides insight into what you can change to be a more successful leader in any area.

E-Mail: info@lld.uk.com

Homepage: http://www.logicallevels.co.uk

Appendix A: Ongoing Success Factor Modeling Projects

As I mentioned in the Preface to this book, as of the beginning of 2015 there are several ongoing projects applying Success Factor Modeling to study important trends for new and existing ventures. One on "collective intelligence in organizations" is sponsored by Gilles Roy, Formation Evolution et Synergie, and Vision 2021 in Avignon, France. Another on "next generation entrepreneurship" is being sponsored by Institut REPERE in Paris. The following overviews summarize two of these projects and their purpose.

Collective Intelligence Modeling Study

The purpose of this study is to identify current trends and ideas generated by teams and organizations to increase collective intelligence in order to address challenges and take advantage of opportunities in the current economic environment. Dilts Strategy Group members have contacted a number of teams and companies to participate in interviews and other activities ranging from one hour to several days. These teams and companies have been selected on the basis of their reputation as a strong leader in the area of collective intelligence among peers.

The following topics are being explored:

- What are the current challenges and opportunities the company or team is facing.
- How they view and value collective intelligence as a key means to succeed in today's business environment.
- How they modified their business strategy and management practices to encourage and increase collective intelligence.
- What specific steps they have implemented to support collective intelligence on a practical level.

Major trends will be documented in articles published in selected business magazines and on the Dilts Strategy Group website.

This study, under the title PERICEO, is being done in conjunction with Formation Evolution et Synergie and Vision 2021 in Avignon, France.

For more information, contact:

Formation Evolution et Synergie
Gilles Roy
3 Avenue de la Synagogue
84000 Avignon, France
+33 4 90 16 04 16
Gilles Roy <gilles.roy2@orange.fr>
www.intelligence-collective.net

VISION 2021

46 Boulevard Raspail
84000 Avignon, France
contact@vision-2021.com
www.vision2021.com

Next Generation Entrepreneurship Modeling Study

The purpose of the study is to identify the latest trends adopted by the emerging new generation of entrepreneurship with respect to how they address challenges and take advantage of opportunities in the current economic environment. The learning gathered during the study is intended to enhance the productivity, profitability and satisfaction of today's entrepreneurs and intrapreneurs.

Thus far, the project involved interviews with 18 selected "Next Generation Entrepreneurs." *Next Generation* Entrepreneur was defined as:

> *Someone who creates a sustainable business or project to live one's own dream, while delivering a product or a service that makes a positive difference in the world and personally growing through it.*

The four mandatory criteria of interviewee selection included:

- Living one's dream and passionate about something else than money
- Making a positive difference in the world
- Business is at least economically sustainable if not growing
- Delivering something new and innovative

Interviewees were selected to represent a wide scope of ventures including:

- Different Business Types

  Industry, Services, Technology, Environmental, NGO, etc.

- Different Business Sizes

  Small and middle sized companies, Intrapreneurs within large scale/ multinational companies, Social entrepreneurs, etc.

- Different Business Phases

  Start up, Growth, Expansion, Maturity

- Different Entrepreneur's Reputation and Notoriety

  Reputation amongst peers could be local, regional, national, international

Major trends will be documented in articles published in selected business magazines and on the Dilts Strategy Group website.

This study is being done in conjunction with Institut REPERE in Paris, France.

For more information, contact:

Institut REPERE
78 Avenue du Général Michel Bizot
75012 Paris, France
+33 1 43 46 89 41
commercial@institut-repere.com
http://www.institut-repere.com

In Physics, a Field Is Represented as 'Lines of Force' Extending Out into Space

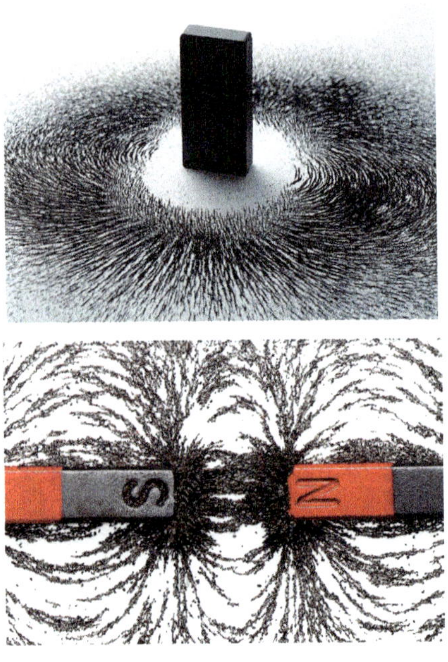

Iron filings reveal the "lines of force" produced by bar magnates.

Appendix B: Reflections on Collective Intelligence as a "Relational Field"

The notions of *relational field* and *generative field* are fundamental to the Success Factor Modeling view of collective intelligence and generative collaboration. A "field," from the SFM perspective, is essentially a type of energetic quality or "vibration" emerging from relationships and interactions within a system of individuals. Central to this view of field is the idea that relationship itself is a "third entity" generated between those involved; similar to the way that hydrogen and oxygen can combine to produce the third entity of water. The relationship becomes a type of container that is both produced by and exerts influence upon the thoughts, emotions and experiences of the individuals involved.

In physics, a *field* is defined as "a region of space characterized by a physical property, such as gravitational or electromagnetic force or fluid pressure, having a determinable value at every point in the region." A field, in physics, relates to the movement of energy through a widely disbursed area of space. An electromagnetic field, such as a radio signal for instance, is typically represented in terms of "lines of force," extending out in every direction from their source, which exert an influence on objects within their range. It is the density of these lines of force that determines the intensity, and thus the degree of influence, of the field.

This stands in contrast to the notion of a "particle," which is an object that exists only in a very limited and defined region of space. A field is less tangible than a particle, and is more about energy, movement and relationships than "things" or "objects." A field is both generated by relationships between "particles" – i.e., objects and individuals – and exerts an influence on the behavior or actions of objects and individuals.

A gravitational field, for instance, is a function of a fundamental attraction between all objects in space. The pull of gravity does not exist without the presence of the objects being drawn toward one another. The gravitational field generated between two objects (say, two planets) will also affect the behavior of other objects (a spaceship or meteor, for example) that enter the range of influence of that field.

The examples of forms emerging from water and cornstarch on an oscillating speaker and the cymatics experiment involving shifting patterns of sand on a vibrating metal plate presented in Chapter 1 (pp. 14-15) are other examples of the influence of fields. Such natural phenomena have important implications (both direct and metaphorical) for our understanding of collective intelligence and generative collaboration.

"Mind" and Intelligence are a Function of Fields that Emerge from Interactions

Social scientist and systems theorist Gregory Bateson pointed out:

> *[A]ny ongoing ensemble of events and objects which has the appropriate complexity of causal circuits and the appropriate energy relations will surely show mental characteristics. It will compare . . . it will "process information" and will inevitably be self-corrective either toward homeostatic optima or toward the maximization of certain variables.*

What Bateson is essentially saying is that with enough resonance and synergy, any system can produce a relational field that will enable it to reach a higher level of integration and show characteristics of intelligent self-organization. This is the principle applied by Peter Russell in his concept of *The Global Brain* (1983, 1995). Russell perceives evolution as the progressive collecting together of units into larger self-organizing systems – from elementary particles to atoms, to molecules, to cells, to tissues, and so forth up to self-conscious organisms and ultimately conscious communities.

Bateson's observation is also quite congruent with our reflections on the significance of resonance, synergy and emergence as success factors in producing collective intelligence in ensembles of people. The key is getting the *appropriate complexity* of interactions and the *appropriate energy relations* from which collective intelligence can emerge. When these conditions are met, separate individuals are transformed into a cohesive group, creating a team in which the whole is truly greater than the sum of its parts.

In fact, the impression of being a part of a larger system or field is a common subjective experience of almost every human being. We often speak of the feeling of "team spirit," for instance, which is a sense of being part of a group that includes us but is bigger than ourselves. Such experiences emerge from a felt sense of the interpersonal "relational field" arising from the interactions between ourselves and others; forming a type of larger physical and mental holon.

Characteristics of "Group Mind"

Our participation in such a field produces an influence on our thoughts and emotions, individually and collectively. Sufficiently strong relational fields can generate a type of group *mind* that has characteristics and qualities of intelligence that are quite different from the individual minds of the members of the group. According to the psychologist Le Bon (1895):

> *The most striking peculiarity presented by a psychological group is the following. Whoever be the individuals that compose it, however like or unlike be their mode of life, their occupations, their character, or their intelligence, the fact that they have been transformed into a group puts them in possession of a sort of collective mind which makes them feel, think, and act in a manner quite different from that in which each individual of them would feel, think, and act were he in a state of isolation. There are certain ideas and feelings which do not come into being, or do not transform themselves into acts except in the case of individuals forming a group.*
>
> *The psychological group is a provisional being formed of heterogeneous elements, which for a moment are combined, exactly as the cells which constitute a living body form by their reunion a new being which displays characteristics very different from those possessed by each of the cells singly.*

Le Bon's notion of a distinct "collective mind" is quite consistent with James Surowiecki's notion of the "wisdom of crowds" (pp. 296-299) and Google's discovery that the "collective I.Q." of their teams had little to do with the mix of specific personality types or skills or backgrounds of the individuals who comprised the teams (pp. 300-301). Le Bon's comment that "there are certain ideas and feelings which do not come into being, or do not transform themselves into acts except in the case of individuals forming a group" reveals one of the most powerful contributions of collective intelligence to creativity and innovation. A type of greater intelligence emerges as a consequence of the healthy relationship and interaction between people that does not manifest when individuals are isolated from one another. As Gregory Bateson claimed:

> *The individual mind is immanent but not only in the body. It is immanent in pathways and messages outside the body; and there is a larger mind of which the individual mind is only a sub-system.*

Bateson is saying that our individual minds emerge as a type of field, resulting from interactions taking place within our body and nervous system and from our interactions with the world around us. He is also suggesting that a "larger mind" emerges from and influences the interactions of our individual minds with other intelligences.

The "larger Mind" to which Bateson refers is perhaps what is meant by "intuition," the "creative unconscious" in the works of Milton H. Erickson, or the "collective unconscious" in Carl Jung's writings. Another phenomenon relating to what Bateson called the "larger Mind" is what Rupert Sheldrake termed morphic fields. Sheldrake proposed the idea of *morphic fields* to explain phenomena which involve action at a distance, from the development of embryos to healing through prayer and the "the hundredth monkey" phenomenon—i.e., situations in which change in a part of a population stimulates change in another member of the population, or the group as a whole, without any direct physical contact. It also reflects the notion of "hologram" presented in Chapter 1 that the whole is in some way contained in each part, and that the part can recreate the whole.

Essential to Sheldrake's model is the process of *morphic resonance*. This is a feedback mechanism between the field and the corresponding interaction of elements from which it emerges. The greater the degree of similarity of interaction between the individual elements, the greater the resonance, making the existence, strength or persistence of the particular form of thought or behavior contained in the larger field more likely.

Sheldrake proposes that the process of morphic resonance leads to stable morphic fields, which are significantly easier to *tune into*. He suggests, for instance, that this is the means by which simpler organic forms synergetically self-organize into more complex ones, and that this model allows a different explanation for the process of evolution itself, as an addition to the Darwin's evolutionary processes of selection and variation.

One implication of Bateson's notion of a "larger mind" and Sheldrake's idea of "morphic resonance" is the possibility that we can tap into networks of intelligence greater than our individual minds. In other words, types of latent ideas and insights will spontaneously emerge in individuals as a result of being part of a group that would never happen for the same individuals if they operated by themselves – regardless of how much time those individuals spent thinking about something on their own. A person could spend years thinking about something individually and never achieve certain results that would happen easily and instantaneously if that person were interacting with others under the proper conditions.

It is very important to remember, however, that, as Bateson points out, "the mental characteristics are inherent or immanent in the ensemble as a whole." When we separate ourselves or become disconnected from the larger system, we lose access to the intelligence that it holds. We must be connected with ourselves and with one another (i.e., in a COACH state) in order for the intelligence in the larger holon to emerge in us as individuals.

As an example, a child raised in isolation of interaction with other humans (such as so-called "feral children" raised by wolves or other animals) never learns a language. In fact, feral children typically have trouble learning to walk upright and display a complete lack of interest in the human activity around them. They often seem mentally impaired and have almost insurmountable trouble learning a human language if they are discovered after a certain age. Two or more children raised together, however, even in the absence of outside influence by adults, will spontaneously invent their own language, even if they have never been exposed to verbal interaction.

In other words, interaction, resonance and synergy with others awakens and releases intelligence, ideas and capabilities latent within the larger collective or holon. This is no doubt why so many successful organizations have arisen from generative collaborations, such Jobs and Wozniac (Apple Inc.), Hewlett and Packard (HP), etc. Success Factor Modeling itself, of course, also emerged as a co-creation of two people: John Dilts and Robert Dilts.

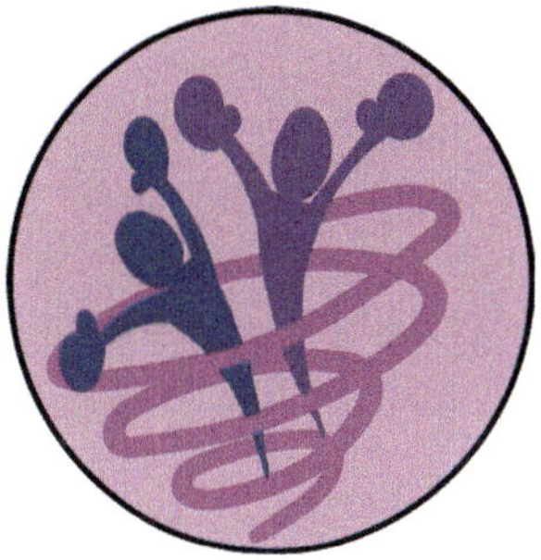

References:

Steps to an Ecology of Mind, Bateson, G., Ballantine Books, New York, New York, 1972.

The Global Brain Awakens, Russell, P., Global Brain, Inc., Palo Alto, CA, 1995.

The Crowd: A Study of the Popular Mind, Le Bon, G., Digireads.com Publising, 2008 (1895)

A New Science of Life: the hypothesis of formative causation, Sheldrake, R., J.P. Tarcher, Los Angeles, CA, 1981

NLP II: The Next Generation, Dilts, R. and DeLozier, J. with Bacon Dilts, D., Meta Publications, Capitola, CA, 2010

Photos

Page 50 - Image taken from the video "Non-Newtonian Fluid on a Speaker Cone" in YouTube

Page 51 - Images taken from the video "Cymatix Experiment" in YouTube

Page 56 – Adam Grant - https://www.linkedin.com/in/adammgrant

Page 101 – Steve Fiehl, Michaël Ohana, Pascal El Grably and Hervé Goudchaux
http://www.crossknowledge.com/group/management-team

Page 105 - Photo courtesy of Robert B. Dilts

Page 117 - Image taken from the DVD "Yanni at the Acropolis"

Page 154 – Stefan Crisan, photo courtesy of Stefan Crisan

Page 176 – Google and Pixar workspaces
http://www.home-designing.com/2008/10/seriously-cool-workplaces

Page 177 – Disney's Dreaming Room
Finch, C.; *The Art of Walt Disney* ; Harry N. Abrahms Inc., New York, New York, 1973.

Page 178 – Walt Disney
The Walt Disney Family Museum, San Francisco, CA

Page 178 – Walt Disney
Thomas, F. & Johnson, O.; *Disney Animation; The Illusion of Life* ; Abbeyville Press, New York, New York, 1981.

Page 192 – Randy Williams - https://www.linkedin.com/in/randy-williams-86b4581a

Page 236 – John Dilts photo courtesy of Robert B. Dilts

Page 258 - Images extracted from the video: A Bird Ballet by Neels Castillon

Page 259 - Images from:
http://www.red3d.com/cwr/boids/applet/
http://black-square.github.io/BirdFlock/

Page 261 – The Battle of Midway
http://superhypeblog.com/marketing/smart-data-business-lessons-from-the-battle-of-midway

Page 310 – Drew Dilts photo courtesy of Robert B. Dilts

Page 314 – Moringa farm site, Benin photo courtesy of Robert B. Dilts

Page 321 – Fulani family huts, Benin photo courtesy of Robert B. Dilts

Page 350 – Bar magnets
http://hypescience.com/o-que-e-magnetismo/
http://www.alamy.com/stock-photo-bar-magnets-with-iron-filings-showing-magnetic-repulsion-between-31266486.html

Bibliography

- *Success Factor Modeling, Volume I – Next Generation Entrepreneurs: Live Your Dream and Create a Better World through Your Business*, Dilts, R., Dilts Strategy Group, Santa Cruz, CA, 2015
- *From Coach to Awakener*, Dilts, R., Meta Publications, Capitola, CA, 2003.
- *Tools for Dreamers*, Dilts, R. B., Epstein, T. and Dilts, R. W., Meta Publications, Capitola, CA, 1991.
- *Strategies of Genius Vols I, II & III*, Dilts, R., Meta Publications, Capitola, CA,1994-1995.
- *Alpha Leadership: Tools for Leaders Who Want More From Life*, Deering, A., Dilts, R. and Russell, J., John Wiley & Sons, London, England, 2002.
- *Visionary Leadership Skills*, Dilts, R., Meta Publications, Capitola, CA, 1996.
- *Modeling with NLP*, Dilts, R., Meta Publications, Capitola, CA, 1998.
- *Encyclopedia of Systemic Neuro-Linguistic Programming and NLP New Coding*, Dilts, R. and DeLozier, J., NLP University Press, Santa Cruz, CA, 2000.
- *Effective Presentation Skills*, Dilts, R., Meta Publications, Capitola, CA, 1994.
- *Skills for the Future*, Dilts, R., Meta Publications, Capitola, CA, 1993.
- *NLP II: The Next Generation*, Dilts, R. and DeLozier, J. with Bacon Dilts, D., Meta Publications, Capitola, CA, 2010.
- *The Hero's Journey: A Voyage of Self-Discovery*, Gilligan, S. and Dilts, R., Crowne House Publishers, London, UK, 2009.
- *Innovations in NLP*, Hall, M. and Charvet, S., Editors; Crown House Publishers, London, 2011.

Success Factor Modeling Volume II – Generative Collaboration was created using:

- Aurulent Sans - by Stephen G. Hartke
- Roman Serif - by Mandred Klein
- COMIC GEEK – WWW.BLAMBOT.COM
- COMIC BOOK – WWW.PIXELSAGAS.COM
- BADABOOM BB - WWW.BLAMBOT.COM

Robert B. Dilts - Author

Robert Dilts – Author

Email: rdilts@nlpu.com
Homepage: http://www.robertdilts.com

Robert Dilts has had a global reputation as a leading coach, behavioral skills trainer and business consultant since the late 1970s. A major developer and expert in the field of Neuro-Linguistic Programming (NLP), Robert has provided coaching, consulting and training throughout the world to a wide variety of individuals and organizations.

Together with his brother John, Robert pioneered the principles and techniques of Success Factor Modeling™ and has authored numerous books and articles about how they may be applied to enhance leadership, creativity, communication and team development. His book *Visionary Leadership Skills* draws from Robert's extensive study of historical and corporate leaders to present the tools and skills necessary for "creating a world to which people want to belong." *Alpha Leadership: Tools for Business Leaders Who Want More From Life* (with Ann Deering and Julian Russell) captures and shares the latest practices of effective leadership, offering approaches to reduce stress and to promote satisfaction. *From Coach to Awakener* provides a road map and set of toolboxes for coaches to help clients reach goals on a number of different levels of learning and change. *The Hero's Journey: A Voyage of Self Discovery* (with Stephen Gilligan) is about how to reconnect you with your deepest calling, transform limiting beliefs and habits and improve self-image.

Past corporate clients and sponsors have included Apple Computer, Microsoft, Hewlett-Packard, IBM, Lucasfilms Ltd. and the State Railway of Italy. He has lectured extensively on coaching, leadership, innovation, collective intelligence, organizational learning and change management, making presentations and keynote addresses for The International Coaching Federation (ICF), HEC Paris, The United Nations, The World Health Organization, Harvard University and the International University of Monaco. In 1997 and 1998, Robert supervised the design of *Tools for Living*, the behavior management portion of the program used by Weight Watcher's International.

Robert was an associate professor at the ISVOR Fiat School of Management for more than fifteen years, helping to develop programs on leadership, innovation, values and systemic thinking. From 2001–2004 he served as chief scientist and Chairman of the Board for ISVOR DILTS Leadership Systems, a joint venture with ISVOR Fiat (the former corporate university of the Fiat Group) that delivered a wide range of innovative leadership development programs to large corporations on a global scale.

A co-founder of Dilts Strategy Group, Robert was also founder and CEO of Behavioral Engineering, a company that developed computer software and hardware applications emphasizing behavioral change. Robert has a degree in Behavioral Technology from the University of California at Santa Cruz.

Antonio Meza - Illustrator

Antonio Meza has been drawing cartoons ever since he can remember, but his professional cartoonist work started only recently in his life.

A native of Pachuca, Mexico, Antonio is a Master Practitioner and a Trainer of Neuro-Linguistic Programming (NLP). He has a degree in Communication Sciences from Fundación Universidad de las Américas Puebla, a Masters degree in Film Studies from Université de Paris 3 –Sorbonne Nouvelle, a diploma in Cinema Scriptwriting from the General Society of Writers in Mexico (SOGEM), and a diploma in Documentary Films from France's École Nationale des Métiers de l'Image et du Son (La Fémis).

He has recently certified as well in Generative Coaching with Robert Dilts and Stephen Gilligan at the Institut Repère of Paris; and in Success Factor Modeling with NLP University and the Dilts Strategy Group.

Antonio's career includes work in marketing research, advertising, branding, corporate image, film production, and scriptwriting. His professional photography work has been exhibited in Mexico, Belgium, and France.

He had participated in animated cartoons startups in Mexico before moving to France where he works as a consultant, coach, and trainer, specializing in creative thinking and collective intelligence. He offers his services under his brand: Akrobatas.

His NGO and Foundations clients include the European AIDS Treatment Group (EATG), OXFAM, the European HIV/AIDS Funders Group, the Open Society Foundations (OSF) and the European Public Health Alliance (EPHA). He has conducted training workshops for business schools such as the ESCP-Europe and international organizations such as the IABC (International Association of Business Communicators).

Antonio is also an experienced public speaker member of Toastmasters International. In 2015 he was awarded best speaker at the International Speech Contest of District 59, covering South-West Europe, and reached the semifinals at international level.

His cartoons and illustrations have been published by the Université Pantheon-Assas (Paris 2), he co-authored three books (as illustrator); two with Jean-Eric Branaa: "English Law Made Simple" and "American Government Made Simple" published by Ellipses in Paris and "Les Vrais Secrets de la Communication" with Beatrice Arnaud.

He also uses his skills as a cartoonist and trainer to collaborate in seminars, conferences and brainstorming sessions as a graphic facilitator.

He has several illustration projects including "Carl Jung - Explorer of the Mind" and the three volumes for the *Success Factor Modeling* series with Robert Dilts.

Antonio Meza – Illustrator

Email: hola@antoons.net
Homepage: http://www.antoons.net
Photo by: Susanne Kischnick

Lightning Source UK Ltd.
Milton Keynes UK
UKOW07f1616200716

278844UK00012B/57/P

9 780996 200424